Power at Sea

Power at Sea

VOLUME 3

A Violent Peace
1946–2006

Lisle A. Rose

UNIVERSITY OF MISSOURI PRESS

COLUMBIA AND LONDON

Copyright © 2007 by
The Curators of the University of Missouri
University of Missouri Press, Columbia, Missouri 65201
Printed and bound in the United States of America
All rights reserved

ISBN-13: 978-0-8262-1703-5
ISBN-10: 0-8262-1703-6

Designer: Kristie Lee
Typesetter: Phoenix Type, Inc.
Typefaces: Adobe Garamond, URW Antiqua, Arsis
Book Club Edition

For Harriet

CONTENTS

CONTENTS

MAPS

IN THE SIXTY-ONE YEARS since the end of World War II, American sea power has been both an irresistible force and a defining factor in world affairs. During this period of "violent peace" (a term coined twenty years ago by Chief of Naval Operations James Watkins), the United States Navy participated in four major wars and numerous lesser conflicts, confronted and eventually faced down an increasingly formidable Soviet fleet, transformed itself from an industrial to a nuclear armed force, and spearheaded a national social revolution by actively recruiting and promoting minority populations, all the while maintaining freedom of the seas for everyone.

Each of these achievements came at a heavy price. Combat in the waters off and skies above Korea and Vietnam was almost invariably frustrating and inconclusive; riverine warfare on the Mekong and its tributaries was worse. The two Gulf wars imposed their own particular strains and challenges, while the Soviet threat was always exhausting and often demoralizing. The incessant advances in ship, aircraft, ordnance, and communications technologies were destabilizing; the adjustments in race and gender relations intensified ancient animosities and created new ones. And over all, for forty-five years loomed the cold war with its daily possibilities that a single miscalculation, one false move, could bring about nuclear and thermonuclear Armageddon.

The sudden decline and fall of the Soviet Union brought little respite. The year 1991 proved a particularly frustrating one for America's sailors who were largely marginalized during the first, brief, victorious Gulf War, then humiliated shortly thereafter by scandal at an annual aviators' convention that revealed the ugly side of naval life. Yet through it all, the service continued to fill its many mission responsibilities as best it could. When 9/11 provided an overeager George W. Bush and his "neoconservative" followers with the pretext to proclaim a global imperium, the United States Navy stood ready to enforce it with an unmatched integrated sea-air-amphibious capability honed over many years.

The current quagmire in Iraq, recalling the earlier frustration in Southeast Asia, raises once again long-held questions about the pertinence and effectiveness of sea power. In an age of free-floating transnational terror as in earlier eras of international stress and tension, large, costly battle fleets, even those able to project power *from* the sea deep into adjacent landmasses, seem to many to possess far less enforcement capability than boots on the ground, or even long- and short-range ground-based aircraft. In fact, the long reach of naval power, when coupled with national intelligence capabilities and international police agencies, might well provide the solution to a problem that bedevils us all: how does one defeat the terrorist and terrorism without antagonizing everyone else?

Alert readers will note several rather glaring omissions in this volume, most notably the absence of any reference to either the *Liberty* or *Pueblo* incidents. I have concluded that while both are important and certainly highly controversial, their influence on the development and use of sea power is marginal. The same can be said about the loss of the submarines *Thresher* and *Scorpion* and about the terrible carrier accidents off Vietnam that illustrated the increasingly parlous state of the U.S. Navy as the Southeast Asian war lengthened. Such incidents do, however, form an integral part of the U.S. Navy's operating history in what may well turn out to be its age of greatest glory. I hope, therefore, to recount them elsewhere at an early time.

Finally, the general reader needs to know about my choice of Chinese names. The People's Republic of China adopted the "pinyin" system of romanization of Chinese characters, while on Taiwan (Formosa) the older Wade-Giles system is still preferred. In general, I have used pinyin for Chinese names and place names, but I have used Wade-Giles when discussing Taiwan. Thus, Mao-tse Tung (Wade-Giles) becomes Mao Zedong (pinyin), while Chiang Kai-shek (Jiang Jieshi in pinyin) is retained. I have striven in each instance where an individual or a territory is first mentioned to include the alternative term in parentheses.

It is only when one reaches the end of a long project such as this that the true scope of the support received becomes clear. George Thompson and Randall Jones at the Center for American Places in Harrisonburg, Virginia, were among the first to see some merit in the work during its early stages. The research staffs at the Suzzalo and Odegaard Libraries at the University of Washington, Seattle; the National Maritime Museum in Greenwich, England; the Nimitz Library at the United States Naval Academy at Annapolis, Maryland; the Naval Historical Center in Washington, D.C.; and the Naval Undersea Museum at Keyport, Washington, were unfailingly helpful in pointing me toward important sources. The direct access to stacks and materials at the Suzzalo and Nimitz Libraries made the work there especially pleasant and rewarding; the research staff at the National Maritime Museum was always willing to take long moments out to talk twentieth-century naval history and sources with a visitor from across the sea. Former chief of naval operations Admiral Thomas B. Hayward was kind enough to speak with me on several occasions, recounting the grim days of the late seventies when a declining U.S. Navy confronted the surging power of the Soviet fleet and what was done to reverse its fortunes. Edward J. Marolda, Robert Love, David Alan Rosenberg, Kenneth Kohlstedt, and John M. Rose placed in my hands critically important materials and information that I might otherwise have missed. Edwin Finney Jr., photographic curator at the Naval Historical Center, spent several hours with me by phone tracking down essential photographs, and Laura Weavers at the Naval Historical Foundation ensured that they got to me promptly so as to meet a tight production schedule. Robert Ferrell, Scott Truver, and several anonymous readers have gone through various iterations of the manuscript over the years with great care and insightful chapter-by-chapter advice that saved me from numerous sins of omission or commission. John M. Rose has made the maps that are so critical to a proper telling of any maritime story, while my wife, Harriet Dashiell Schwar, has again brought her skills as a professional historian to the volume, strengthening both story and wording at many points.

My debt to the University of Missouri Press is nearly boundless. The times are not propitious for publication of large-scale studies such as this. Costs alone give the publishing industry pause, and university presses feel a particular obligation to cater to the needs and interests of academe. Beverly Jarrett embraced the project enthusiastically, and Jane Lago, Clair Willcox, Karen Renner, and especially Annette Wenda have seen it through the publication process with professional skill. They are a great team to work with. Whatever errors of fact or interpretation that remain after such amazing support are, of course, solely my responsibility.

I would like to gratefully acknowledge the use of ESRI's data and map collection and its third-party vendor ArcWorld for providing the data used in the creation of the maps in this volume.

Norwegian and Arctic Seas

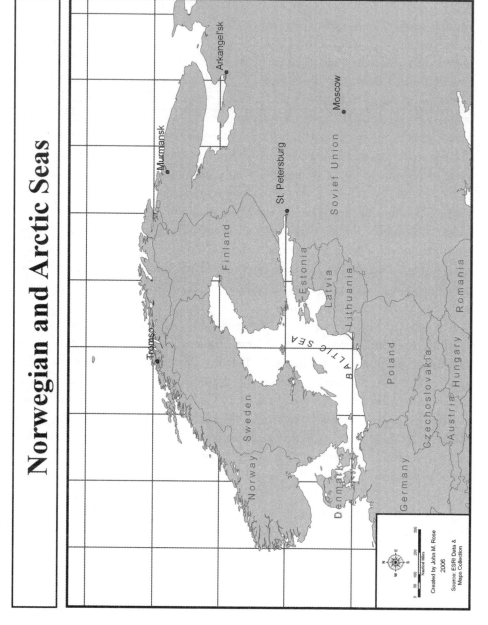

Created by John M. Rose
2006

Source: ESRI Data &
Maps Collection

The Eastern Mediterranean

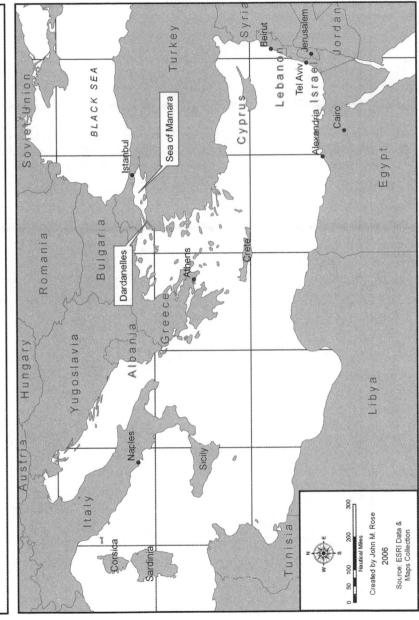

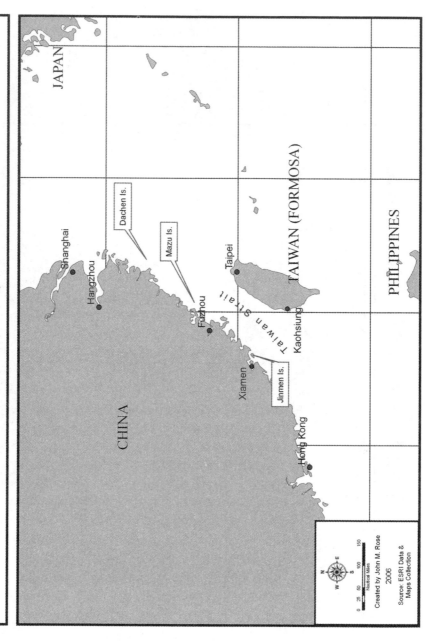

Taiwan Strait, 1950s

East Asia and Surrounding Waters

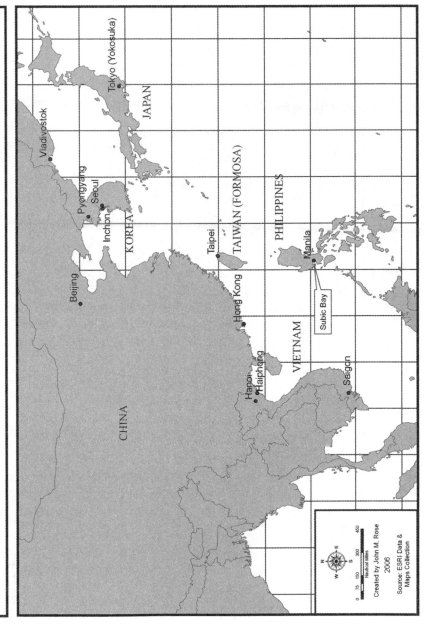

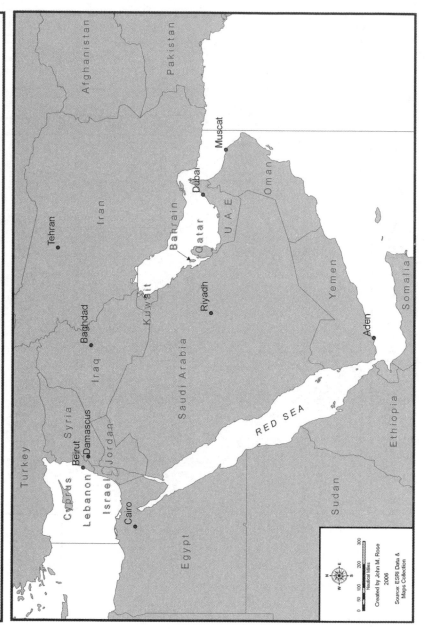

Power at Sea

Grand Strategy

AN APOCRYPHAL STORY has it that one frosty spring morning in 1943 on the North Atlantic, a division of frisky new American destroyers raced up to an embattled westbound convoy south of Iceland to take over escort duties from a squadron of British warships. Washington had just announced that the U.S. fleet was now the largest in the world, and the commander aboard the lead destroyer flashed to his English counterpart: "GOOD MORNING! HOW'S THE WORLD'S SECOND LARGEST NAVY?" Over the gray waters from His Majesty's proud line of storm-beaten ships came the reply: "FINE. HOW'S THE WORLD'S SECOND BEST?"

Two and a half years later, the United States Navy that came home from the Pacific was not only the world's largest sea service but incontestably the world's best—the most diverse and above all self-contained armed force in history. It wielded carrier-based airpower of enormous size (the U.S. naval air force was the second- or third-largest air force in the world), unprecedented mobility, and devastating striking power, which navy men were convinced had operated strategically as well as tactically to win the Pacific war. Its submarine arm had whittled the large Japanese merchant marine down to virtually nothing, then had savaged the Imperial Navy. Its Construction Battalions ("Seabees") and logistics services had built and filled the advanced airfields and bases required for continual fleet actions against the enemy. Finally, it possessed its own small army of highly trained and effective shock troops called marines, who man for man matched the very best soldiers that Hitler and the Japanese had put into the field. These sailor-soldiers, in turn, were supported by their own tactical air force, which had performed superbly all across the Pacific.

With their garlands of victory around them, the great carriers and battleships, the rugged cruisers and destroyers, and the nondescript but essential attack cargo and transport vessels steamed into a score of anchorages from Seattle to New Orleans to New York, the boast of the red, white, and blue. New York Harbor was especially festive on October 27, a crisp and bright Navy Day, as a line of warships stretched down the Hudson opposite 125th Street all the way to the Battery. The battleship *Missouri* was there, and hundreds of visitors trod its decks and saw where the Japanese surrender had taken place; so was *Enterprise,* the most combat weary and decorated carrier of the war, together with more than twenty other veterans of the Pacific and Atlantic conflicts. Harry Truman came up from Washington to review the fleet and lunch aboard its proudest battleship, which carried the name of his home state. Afterward, there was a huge parade of sailors down Broadway, and for nearly a week the city toasted its heroes. Never before and, perhaps, never again would the United States Navy stand so tall in public esteem.

The Second World War not only revolutionized international politico-military affairs but ushered in a new order of sea power as well. For centuries sea power had meant power *at* sea—in peacetime, control of a greater or lesser portion of the world ocean in order to secure seaborne commerce or lines of military, political, and economic communication between a mother country and its scattered oceanic or coastal colonies; in war, defense of a nation's own sea space and efforts to deny an enemy control over his. This was what the clash of battle lines had meant from the fight between Tromp and Blake off Dover Roads in 1652 through Trafalgar to Jutland. With the dramatic development of aviation and amphibious capabilities between 1939 and 1945, sea power expanded to include power *from* the sea, projected over ever wider and broader portions of the global landmasses as aviation and hotly anticipated guided missile technologies dictated. With such capabilities and technologies in hand, together with a sophisticated knowledge of how to employ them, the United States Navy in the autumn of 1945 found its exercise of sea power virtually limitless, unbounded. Beyond the three-mile territorial limit of the Soviet Union, its sailors could steam wherever they wished and do whatever they pleased.

There were a few signs that perhaps not all was well—or would be well—within the service. The citizen sailors who had projected American power across the Atlantic, the Rhine, the Pacific, and, indeed, most of the world were as proud of themselves, their country, and their navy as were the officers. But as the civilian sailors went on the town one last time in the autumn of 1945 before taking off their uniforms and heading home, many could not resist an opportunity to "exercise the inalienable American right to bitch and moan."[1] Their complaints all pointed in one direction: the gap between officers and men was unacceptable in a democracy. "In a lot of ways," said a machinist's mate from the destroyer *Aulick*, "it's still the American squadron of the Royal Navy." The young man was wrong, of course. Bottom to top, the United States Navy was less rigidly disciplined, more innovative, and more highly educated than any sea service in the world.[2] But navies are inherently aristocratic and conservative. So throughout the war officers on American warships came first, or so the sailors believed. Unlike fighting units in the U.S. Army or Marines where the needs of the men were paramount, naval ensigns, lieutenants, and commanders always got preferential treatment. The best food was theirs. So were the best clubs ashore and the most leave and liberty. They automatically went to the head of any line aboard ship. The men didn't enjoy being ordered to carry officers' gear and baggage like bellboys, didn't like the time and effort lavished on admirals' lawns and gardens when violent air and sea battles were raging not far away and every man could have been used in one capacity or another.

But "the enlisted men's comments bear the note of warning rather than angry resentment," wrote a perceptive journalist. If there was much folly in the relations between rank and rate in the wartime navy, little or no outright brutality could be tolerated in an atmosphere of perpetual crisis and emergency. In the crucible of battle there was no time (at least on the best ships) for that calculated condescension and power tripping that were universally known throughout the World War II American military establishment as "chickenshit."[3] Nonetheless, the ideas of the "Annapolis Club" were at variance with the judgment of the young Americans who manned the warships, and so, the young Americans said, the naval high command would simply have to change. "The men's advice to the Navy and to Congress is to bring a more democratic spirit into the Navy. If this advice is taken, say the veterans of this war, the Navy will be an even better combat force in another ten years."[4]

The high command, however, had other and possibly weightier matters to attend to, for the admirals of 1945–1946 were, if possible, even more pugnacious, suspicious, and antagonistic toward their supposed allies and the world in general than were their predecessors of 1919–1920. Not for another quarter century would the navy begin to heed the sensible advice of its temporary wartime sailors. And then it was almost too late.

America's only possible rival at sea was by now not only a firm ally but in a state of palpable and precipitate decline. For four centuries, British sea power had maintained a precarious European and global political balance. But between

1939 and 1945, the Royal Navy lost 1,525 warships, including 224 major surface ships of corvette size and larger. "More destroyers were lost (139) than were in service in May 1945 (108)." More than fifty thousand Tars had been killed, twenty thousand more than during the Great War of 1914–1918. As in 1919 Britain was once again practically bankrupt. Unlike 1919, however, its empire was clearly on its last legs, and there was no prospect of a favorable balance of world trade to revive it. Instead, the English "had become totally dependent on American aid to sustain" them, and when that aid was cut off near war's end, "only an American loan, negotiated on far from favorable terms, allowed Britain a short breathing space. This meant that any British government's vital and overriding priority was domestic reconstruction."[5]

Britain still seemed able to wield mighty fleets if the occasion demanded. Its naval forces east of Suez in the summer of 1945 numbered no fewer than 450 ships, including half a dozen or more battleships, a score of aircraft carriers of various sizes, and the necessary number of cruiser and destroyer escorts. But most of these vessels were obsolete and would be scrap two years later. When Lord Alanbrooke and the other British chiefs of staff at last inveigled their reluctant American allies to include a British naval task force in the final stages of the Pacific war, the Admiralty managed to scrape together only a comparative handful of fine, modern vessels: a single battleship, 3 fleet carriers (half the Royal Navy's entire arsenal), 6 cruisers, and 15 destroyers. This moderately powerful task group was dwarfed by an American invasion armada at Okinawa that comprised 1,205 vessels, including 10 battleships, 8 heavy cruisers, 4 light cruisers, 18 escort carriers, and 82 destroyers in addition to the transports, cargo vessels, and invasion craft. The invasion fleet was, of course, trumped by the mighty Fast Carrier Task Forces of the Third and Fifth Fleets (same ships but different fleet designations depending upon whether they were commanded by Admirals Bull Halsey or Raymond Spruance) that included 8 fast battleships, 16 fleet and light fleet carriers, 19 cruisers, and more than 60 destroyers. Not only were the British swamped by superior American numbers (and superior American ships), "what was worse, British aircraft carriers were mainly equipped with aircraft of American manufacture and the logistic support of the British fleet depended heavily upon American help," a "curious reversal of the situation in the First World War when the US Army had depended on Britain and France not merely for aircraft, but for artillery and tanks." By 1945 Britain had become, in the words of a recent history of the wartime Royal Navy, a "superfluous ally." Many a Tar painfully recalled palmier days just a quarter century before when American vice admiral William Sims arrived in London to be told that the Admiralty had no need of his newest battleships, though it and the Grand Fleet commander, David Beatty, were delighted to accept a squadron of slightly older American dreadnoughts.[6]

If Britain was no longer a force in American naval calculations, the Soviet Union most assuredly was. And for good reason. Strenuous wartime propaganda campaigns in Britain and the United States notwithstanding, the Grand Alliance among the "Big Three" that won the war was little more than a marriage of convenience between two mutually and eternally antagonistic power blocs, communism and capitalism. In the summer of 1945, Stalin summoned subordinates to one of his dachas, or country homes, near Moscow and, pinning a map to the wall, proclaimed that while he was generally satisfied with the new Soviet borders won with blood, he nonetheless harbored expansionist designs. Henceforth the chief aim of Soviet policy, as his foreign minister, Vyachelav Molotov, would later state, was "to extend the frontier of our Fatherland to the maximum." Molotov, if not Stalin himself, was filled with spite and malice toward his erstwhile Western allies, describing President Harry Truman as a "thin-lipped . . . hater, a bad man in any fight. Malicious and unforgiving and not above offering you his hand to yank you off balance and work you over with a chair leg, pool cue, or something out of his pocket"—an atomic bomb perhaps. There could only be "tense relations" . . . "cold war" between Russia and the West. "They were responsible," Molotov maintained, "perhaps because we were on the offensive. They were, of course, bitter about us, but we had to consolidate our conquests. Create our own socialist Germany out of part [of the country]" and do the same in Czechoslovakia, Poland, Hungary, and Yugoslavia. "We had to restore order everywhere. Squeeze out capitalist regimes. That's the 'cold war,'" Molotov maintained.[7]

America's military and naval leadership returned Soviet antipathy full bore. Franklin Roosevelt's longtime naval aide and wartime chairman of the Joint Chiefs of Staff, Admiral William D. Leahy, viewed Communism with revulsion and had actively resisted the president's efforts to forge a close wartime relationship, if not outright alliance, with Stalin. Leahy had "obstructed" Soviet efforts to have American shipyards build modern vessels for the Red fleet, including a sixty thousand–ton, thirty-five-knot battleship designed to mount eighteen-inch guns. Throughout the war, Navy secretary Frank Knox (who died in 1944) and his successor, James Forrestal, reacted "bitterly" to Stalin's unending demands for scarce American war materials, especially aluminum and machine tools. Forrestal was particularly incensed by those such as Vice President Henry Wallace who insisted that only a "close and trusting understanding between Russia and the United States" could prevent a third world war, and in 1944 Forrestal begged Truman to accept the vice presidential nomination if offered. That November, as Stalin's postwar demands began coming into focus, Forrestal wrote a friend in exasperation: "I find that whenever any American suggests that we act in accordance with the needs of our own security he is apt to be called a god-damned fascist or imperialist, while if Uncle Joe [Stalin] suggests that he needs the Baltic Provinces, half of Poland, all of Bessarabia and access to the Mediterranean, all hands agree that he is a fine, frank, candid and generally delightful fellow who is very easy to deal with because he is so explicit in what he wants." The secretary doubtless had in mind the matter of postwar Pacific-island bases currently being seized at great expense in blood and treasure. The War and Navy Departments were united in absolute insistence upon their retention. While the administration pursued its dream of postwar Allied harmony, navy planners, at Forrestal's direction, took the opposite tack. Just days before Roosevelt's death in April 1945, Chief of Naval Operations (CNO) Ernest J. King grumped in an informal luncheon meeting of high administration officials "about the speed with which we were reaching assumptions that permanent peace could be arrived at speedily."[8]

By the middle war years America's naval leadership had begun to glimpse the contours of the postwar world, and they reacted with instinctive conservatism. Both Knox and Forrestal wrote on the basis of assumptions that had pervaded the service at the close of the Great War a quarter century before: the Royal Navy would be responsible for European waters, whereas the U.S. fleet would control the western Atlantic and the Pacific. By the end of 1943 planners projected a postwar fleet manned by more than eight hundred thousand officers and men (including the Marine Corps), spearheaded by more than twenty aircraft carriers, and sustained by an annual budget of seven billion dollars, a staggering sum in those days.[9]

Just what purpose this fleet might fill began to come clear with a rush just days after Japan's formal surrender. In a memo to Forrestal, Marc Mitscher, former commander of the fast carrier forces in the Pacific and now deputy chief of naval operations for air, urged that the bulk of the fleet be kept in the Pacific, which would suggest little formal antipathy toward the Soviet Union. But on September 11, 1945, both Forrestal and King told a congressional hearing that the country had to retain a strong, powerful navy for possible use against now-friendly nations. Even as they spoke, the Pentagon's Joint Planning Staff without prompting sent to the Joint Chiefs of Staff (JCS) a paper titled "Strategic Concept and Plan for the Employment of United States Armed Forces" (JCS

1518) that focused on a "conflict with a major power over an issue vital to the interests of the United States, not capable of solution by the United Nations Organization." The document assumed such a war would pit the United States and Great Britain against the Soviet Union, most likely after the Kremlin had demonstrated an "intent to overrun Western Europe or China." The chief objective of any such conflict was to keep the enemy "at the maximum possible distance" while "project[ing] our own advance bases into areas well removed from the United States." Reviewing the draft paper, King argued that since no nation could effectively conduct war against the United States without an adequate navy and merchant marine, any "overall concept" of World War III should involve the "early destruction of [the enemy's] naval forces and shipping." Within Pentagon planning circles, at least, the navy had apparently won an important concession to the notion of a forward, rather than defensive, strategy.[10]

By February–March 1946 Soviet officials were complaining of "capitalist encirclement," while prominent Americans including the internationalist senator Arthur Vandenberg and Ambassador to Moscow-designate Walter Bedell Smith openly wondered, "What is Russia up to now?"[11] The Kremlin refused to withdraw its forces from the northern Iranian province of Azerbaijan while handing over captured Japanese weapons to Mao Zedong's Communist forces, hoping to occupy ever wider areas of Manchuria. Soviet officials became increasingly confrontational in the joint occupations of Germany, Austria, Korea, and Japan. A British diplomat was heard to mutter that the Kremlin was out to destroy his empire. Meanwhile, the Truman administration, and soon the American people, was made aware of shocking Soviet penetrations of wartime Allied programs and institutions. "Communist infiltration and disloyalty" all too soon became a staple of American thought and politics, driving Truman perhaps to take a more alarmed view of Soviet expansionism than he and his administration otherwise might have done. Reacting to mounting Soviet pressures, Forrestal and new chief of naval operations Chester Nimitz ordered that a "heavy striking force," soon designated the Eighth Fleet, be kept in *"constant readiness for offensive operations"* in the eastern Atlantic or Caribbean. Nimitz placed his old friend Mitscher in command. Mitscher later told his chief of staff, Arleigh Burke, that the fleet had been created as "a task force to go to the Mediterranean within three months, ready for combat."[12]

The rapidly deteriorating international situation prompted the Pentagon's Joint Planning Staff to develop a somber report on world affairs, which it sent to the Joint Chiefs of Staff in early March. Designated JCS 1641/1, the report concluded that increasing Soviet pressure in the eastern Mediterranean "posed such a threat to Britain's imperial position" that the rapidly declining empire "would be forced either to fight or surrender her station as a world power" unless the United States interposed its own much greater air, naval, and military strength into the scales. Britain's "defeat or disintegration," the planners warned, "would eliminate from Eurasia the last bulwark of resistance between the United States and Soviet expansion.... Militarily, our present position as a world power is of necessity closely interwoven with that of Great Britain." A month later— on April 11—the staff sent an expanded report (JCS 1641/5) for the Joint Chiefs' consideration. "Estimate Based on Assumptions of Occurrences of Major Hostilities" concluded that in a major war pitting the Soviets against the West, Russian forces would overrun most of Western Europe, European Turkey, Iran, Iraq, possibly the Suez Canal, Korea, Manchuria, and North China. Should such a scenario materialize, the planners assigned important, indeed critical, forward tasks to the navy. The first would involve rescue of American occupation forces around the periphery of the Eurasian landmass, that is, Europe, Iran, and East Asia. At the same time, the navy would also attempt to deny Soviet forces control of the Mediterranean, the Yellow Sea, and the Sea of Japan while securing the British Isles, Iceland, Greenland, the Aleutians, and Japan from attack. U.S. air forces would then begin a retaliatory strategic air offensive against the Soviet heartland from bases in Britain, the Middle East, and Japan. The planners also hoped that the army and navy could somehow retain a lodgment somewhere on the edge of Europe, Scandinavia perhaps, or Spain or Italy. Otherwise, the only land areas contiguous to the Soviet Union and its eastern European positions where resistance seemed worthwhile lay in the eastern Mediterranean and Middle East.[13]

As these reports were reaching the Joint Chiefs, Stalin began pressuring Turkey to allow joint Soviet-Turkish control of the Dardanelles with the added demand for Soviet naval bases in the Dodecanese. Deputy chief of naval operations Admiral Forrest P. Sherman, an emerging player in Pentagon politics and naval planning development, urged Forrestal to press on a receptive president the idea of dispatching a naval task force to Istanbul built around *Missouri*. Although the ostensible reason for the battleship's presence at the Porte was to return the ashes of Turkish ambassador Melmet Munir Ertegun, who had died suddenly in Washington during the late months of the war, it was also clearly meant as a signal to Stalin that his aggressive probes and truculent behavior had at last sent the West to general quarters. *Missouri* left New York City on March 22, just a week after headlines had screamed that "HEAVY RUSSIAN COLUMNS MOVE WEST

IN IRAN: TURKEY OR IRAQ MAY BE GOAL. STALIN SAYS CHURCHILL STIRS
WAR...MOSCOW DENIES TROOP REPORTS...U.S. SENDS NOTE."

The battleship received a boisterous reception at the Porte where the ambassador's ashes were transferred to Turkish authorities with all the pomp and circumstance the world's major naval power could muster. The ship and its handful of cruiser and destroyer escorts then sailed on to Greece where they enjoyed "an overwhelming welcome by a Greek government and people" embroiled in civil war with Communist forces and deeply fearful of Soviet encroachments into the nearby Balkans as well as Turkey. The small task force then steamed through the eastern and central Mediterranean for some weeks before heading home. At least one vessel, the cruiser *Providence,* visited Egypt where its crew took a tour of the Pyramids near Cairo.

Although the units accompanying the battleship were not as numerous as Forrestal would have liked, the *Missouri* mission had the desired effect. Soviet pressure on both Iran and Turkey eased. It now seemed clear to many in Washington, however, that Moscow had become a major antagonist, a regime possessed of power and appetites matching those of the recently vanquished Hitler gang. In a war-shattered world, only the United States could contest Soviet aspirations. The navy thus threw much of its increasingly slender force, including most of its newer ships, into the Mediterranean during the first postwar year. The presence of a powerful warship flying the flag of the world's mightiest navy riding at anchor a few hundred feet off a beleaguered southern European or Near Eastern port had an almost incalculable effect on the political situation. The brand-new light cruiser *Fargo* spent the pivotal period from June 1946 to March 1947 visiting "a variety of ports in Turkey, Lebanon, Greece, Italy, and France, as well as North Africa." At one point the ship "served as American representative" at Trieste during tense negotiations between Italian and Yugoslav officials at a time when Marshal Tito's allegiance to Moscow still seemed firm. One veteran recalled entering the harbor at general quarters following an alleged threat from Tito to "blow us out of the water."[14]

At the end of July 1946 the Joint Chiefs of Staff forwarded to the White House with their approval a paper titled "Presidential Request for Certain Facts and Information Regarding the Soviet Union," which baldly declared that Russia and the West "were locked in a deadly conflict," since "world domination was the Soviet objective." The Kremlin would do and was doing everything and anything to advance its objectives, from spying on Western nuclear-development programs to pressing for base rights in the Mediterranean and the Balkans. In closing, the Joint Chiefs recommended that for the foreseeable future "U.S. military policy be directed specifically against the Soviet Union." In an increasingly rare burst of agreement, the generals and admirals stated that although Stalin was too intelligent and "canny" to deliberately start World War III against the West, he could all too easily miscalculate and overreach himself, forcing his opponents into a deadly reaction. The following month the second brand-new *Midway*-class battle carrier *Franklin D. Roosevelt,* which had barely finished its shakedown cruise, was dispatched to Greece at the head of a task force designed "to bolster the government . . . during its successful fight against the Communists." When the JCS paper at last reached Truman's desk in September the president immediately ordered that all copies be impounded. "This is so hot," Truman complained, that "it could have an exceedingly unfortunate impact on our efforts to try to develop some relationship with the Soviet Union."[15]

As powerful U.S. naval forces began to converge on the Mediterranean in the spring and summer of 1946, Forrestal quietly directed the navy to steam "in any waters in any part of the globe" but quietly, "so as not to cause 'excitement or speculation' when crisis deployments were required." Few ports and countries in western and southern Europe failed to be visited by a U.S. Navy busily conducting midshipmen or reservist cruises.[16]

In September the Pentagon dispatched the carrier *Randolph* with supporting cruisers and destroyers to Italian waters and designated the small armada "the 6th Task Group." The following month Washington created a new command, U.S. Naval Forces Mediterranean, to help southern Europe's weakened nations resist what journalist Walter Millis characterized as "the seeping advance of Soviet power." On an inspection trip to Europe the previous summer, Admiral Sherman had been bluntly informed by Admiral Lord Andrew Cunningham, Britain's first sea lord, that the Royal Navy was simply incapable of any longer supporting British interests in the Mediterranean. Early in 1947 the U.S. Navy again returned to Greek waters and ports in a major display of naval might closely related to the administration's Greek-Turkish aid bill, and according to the informed military affairs correspondent, Walter Millis, the concentration of American fleet units in Italian ports and adjacent waters in 1948 "doubtless played" a "role in saving Italy from Communist engulfment." By this time the United States had established a permanent naval presence east of Gibraltar as the Sixth Task Group metamorphosed into the "Sixth Task Fleet," a name soon compressed to simply "the Sixth Fleet." Shortly after the establishment of the State of Israel, the cruiser *Manchester* was abruptly ordered to steam off Cyprus for several weeks "to help ensure the tranquillity" of the new nation. The ship left Naples so quickly that it missed its scheduled replenishment. Stopping at Suda Bay, Crete, the supply gang went ashore, "bought cattle [and] sheep on the hoof and had them slaughtered." By 1949 the Sixth Fleet had become a fixture on the sea-lanes and in the harbors stretching from Gibraltar to the Adriatic. During the following four decades, it would remain at a roughly stable force level of forty ships, including two aircraft-carrier task forces with escorting cruisers, destroyers, and a supporting service force, an amphibious task group with some eighteen hundred marines, and after the early sixties one or two strategic ballistic missile submarines. With establishment of the North Atlantic Treaty Organization (NATO) in April 1949, the newly formed fleet assumed formal responsibility for guarding NATO's southern flank. At the same time, the NATO commitment demanded an equally substantial U.S. naval force to help the drastically reduced British and French navies guard the Atlantic approaches to western Europe.[17]

In truth, save for Great Britain, Allied naval power in the late forties was nearly nonexistent. *Jane's Fighting Ships, 1949–50* listed only forty-three navies in existence, including such powers as Eire with a single coastal gunboat. France did maintain one splendid battleship, the modern, thirty-five thousand–ton, thirty-knot *Richelieu* with eight fifteen-inch guns. Completed early in the war, the vessel was gotten safely to an Allied port. The French arsenal also included a tired, thirteen thousand–ton light carrier purchased from Great Britain that could carry twenty-four aircraft and steam at twenty-five knots. A few supporting cruisers and destroyers completed the inventory. Italy was in even worse shape: two thirty-five-year-old battlewagons that could lumber across the seas at twenty-two knots, four light cruisers, and a cluster of destroyers. Out in the Pacific, Australia and New Zealand could each muster a light carrier task force built around ex-British ships. Even some Latin navies listed pre-1914 British-built battleships, but they seldom, if ever, left dockside. Returning from Antarctica early in 1957, I was taken aboard Chile's *Almirante Latorre* late one night by some Chilean sailors. No, we were told, we could not visit the engine room; the ship had not left pier side in more than a decade. Nor could we visit the bridge or any of the big gun turrets; everything was sealed shut. But we could visit the admiral's quarters, unoccupied, of course, for many years, but open for public inspection. I recall yards and yards of dark maroon drapery and the only gold-plated bathtub I have ever seen.[18]

America's sailors surrendered their image of the Pacific theater as the "Big Picture" with profound reluctance and no little anguish. The vast fleet of Chet

Nimitz, Bull Halsey, and Ray Spruance "had fought its way back from catas-trophe" all the way to the doorstep of Japan, and its glory had been closely witnessed by Leahy, Forrestal, and King. "The Navy's wartime relationship to Chiang Kai-shek's [Jiang Jieshi's] Chinese Nationalist government had been close and generally positive." Now the navy brass in both Washington and Asia watched as the essentially uninterested Truman government allowed Soviet forces at the end of the war to place Mao Zedong's Chinese Communist forces in the most favorable positions throughout Manchuria and North China to wage civil war against the Nationalists. In reaction, the U.S. Seventh Fleet trans-ported the Third Marine Amphibious Corps to North China in September and October 1945 "as a counter to feared Soviet advances" in the region. During several stormy meetings in November, Leahy and Forrestal demanded more mil-itary aid for Chiang and "a freer hand for the U.S. Marines occupying North China." When the diplomats in the State Department openly wondered what "a freer hand" might mean, Leahy and Forrestal dismissed them as "left wing boys" and "pinkies." Forrestal adamantly refused to withdraw the marines, fear-ing that Soviet troops would rush in to fill the void.[19]

By the spring of 1946 an unquenchable civil war between the Nationalists and Communists had broken out across Manchuria that General George C. Marshall was wholly unable to quell through on-the-spot mediation. The navy, especially Seventh Fleet commander Admiral Charles M. "Savvy" Cooke, threw itself (and its Marine Corps components) wholly onto Chiang's failing side, with occasionally fatal results. When an LST turned over to Chiang's sailors shelled Communist-held Manchurian ports, Communist forces promptly retaliated by ambushing a marine truck convoy, killing or wounding fifteen men. This was too much for Truman and his White House advisers, who ordered the marines out of Manchuria to concentrate at Beijing and several North China port towns.

The administration's growing inclination to devote the limited economic and military resources at hand to Europe and the eastern Mediterranean in order to confront Soviet probes drew the ire of leading sailor-bureaucrats. Leahy wrote in his diary in early 1947 that preservation of Chiang as a bulwark against Soviet expansionism in Asia was far more important "to the future safety of the United States than protection of the Greek and Turkish states." It was much too late, however, to reverse the "loss" of China. As Mao's forces cautiously moved into North China, the marines were removed from Beijing to concentrate at Qingdao (Tsingtao). By the spring of 1948 some thirty-six hundred marines guarded this "major fleet anchorage" used not only to support the cruisers, destroyers, and support ships of the Seventh Fleet but also as a Chinese naval training center "turn[ing] out thousands of Nationalist sailors."

It was all for naught; Chiang's armies were as inept as his government was corrupt. By January 1949 it was clear to all but the most fanatic Nationalist supporters—which included most of the Seventh Fleet and powerful elements at home in Congress and throughout the country—that "Nationalist China" was doomed. On the twenty-ninth, Washington formally abolished the Naval Advisory Group in China, and at the end of May the last U.S. naval forces steamed out of Qingdao, taking the marines with them. Within days Mao's troops occupied the deserted base, and on October 1 the "Great Leader" formally proclaimed the People's Republic of China (PRC) in Beijing's Tiananmen Square.[20]

As Chiang fled with the remnants of his forces to Taiwan (Formosa), chief of naval operations Admiral Louis Denfeld urged that the U.S. Navy go with them and establish a major base on the island. Admiral Oscar Badger, the new Seventh Fleet commander, lent force to Denfeld's suggestion by making port calls at Takao and Keelung in his flagship *El Dorado*. But the administration had had quite enough of Chiang by this time and entertained lingering hopes of coming to some sort of arrangement with Mao. Secretary of State Dean Acheson ordered the port calls ended, and he carried enough weight with the White House to make it stick.[21]

Throughout 1949, as the "fall of China" became ever more certain, the administration scrambled to formulate new basic security objectives in the Far East, eventually expressed in NSC 37/7 (August 22) and NSC 48/2 (December 30). The postwar occupation of Japan, the retention of base rights in the Philippines, and the acquisition of new ones in the Ryukyu Islands, together with the administration's loss of confidence in and quiet distaste for Chiang, largely defined policy. Since 1894–1895 China had never been a significant naval power, and the PRC air force in late 1949 was negligible. Sea and airpower, therefore, would contain any overt Communist thrust out of the mainland toward offshore Asia. The Hokkaidō-to-Mindanao island chain suddenly attained a strategic prominence it had never before possessed. The navy promptly established or upgraded major fleet support installations at Yokosuka in Tokyo Bay and Sasebo on the island of Kyūshū, on Okinawa, and even at relatively distant Guam in the Mariana Islands. The old naval base at Cavite in Manila Bay retained some importance, and Olongapo in Subic Bay awaited later development if and as needed.[22] From these bases after midcentury, the Seventh Fleet, including a peak strength four to six frontline carriers, prosecuted two major wars while maintaining freedom of the adjacent seas and establishing and protecting ocean supply routes across the thousands of miles from San Francisco, Long Beach, and Seattle to Tokyo and Manila Bays, Pusan and later Cam Ranh Bay.

The problem, of course, was Taiwan, still known to Americans as Formosa, sitting squarely in the middle of the Hokkaidō-Mindanao defense chain, its people suddenly and unwillingly occupied by a discredited army and leader who had utterly lost Washington's trust. In the scant months between the issuance of NSC 48/2 and the outbreak of the Korean War, the administration and the armed forces operated on the principle that although Taiwan was, of course, strategically important, that importance could not translate into military, naval, and air defense of the island "so long as the present disparity between our military strength and our global obligations exists." At a time when the Seventh Fleet was reduced to a single undermanned carrier task group and the Far East Air Force was little stronger, such a conclusion was unavoidable.[23]

Finally, Forrestal realized, as few did in the early cold war years, that America's booming economy and growing national security commitments were at last creating a demand for petroleum products that domestic resources and production could no longer satisfy. The United States would have to enter the scramble for Middle Eastern oil just at the moment that the creation of the State of Israel was threatening to destabilize the entire region. The secretary ordered establishment of a small but permanent naval force at Bahrain in the Persian Gulf.[24]

The navy's aggressive positioning around the Eurasian landmass during the first several postwar years should have convinced rival military chiefs and the Truman administration of the critical importance of modern, fast-moving, hard-hitting battle fleets to national security and global power projection in an emerging crisis environment involving the Soviet Union. Quite the opposite happened. Even as America's sailors and marines confronted new adversaries in the eastern Mediterranean and China, their service was being savaged by critics at home.

Throughout the early postwar months, the Pentagon was a seething hive of jealousies and animosities as commanders great and small, soldiers, airmen, and sailors alike, flashed their medals and service records at each other, knowing full well that, as in 1919, a war-weary nation had no interest in maintaining the huge military and naval establishments required to fight and win a world war. The navy had rather been Franklin Roosevelt's pet, and airmen, soldiers, and their civilian champions anguished over the fact. They convinced themselves that the sailors had achieved their ostensibly exalted postwar status not through superior capabilities but rather by luck and charm. One disgruntled flyer told Stuart Symington (assistant secretary of war for air, 1946–1947, and the first secretary of the U.S. Air Force, 1947–1950) that there were two governments in Washington: the U.S. government and the United States Navy. Symington himself recalled Royal Air Force (RAF) air chief marshal Sir John Slessor saying, "You know, Stuart, the Royal Navy has one power the Royal Air Force has never been able to equal, the 'dining out' power." Symington later told an interviewer that "in effect that was true" of the U.S. Navy in the early postwar years in Washington as well.[25]

Typical of the U.S. Army Air Force's public campaign against naval power was the talk given one evening in March 1946 by commanding general Carl "Tooey" Spaatz at the annual meeting of the American Aviation Writers Association. "Why should we have a navy at all?" Spaatz asked.

> The Russians have little or no navy; the Japanese navy has been sunk, the navies of the rest of the world are negligible; the Germans never did have much of a navy. The point I am getting at is who is the big [postwar] navy being planned to fight. There are no enemies for it to fight, except apparently the Army Air Force. In this day and age to talk of fighting the next war on oceans is a ridiculous assumption.

Ironically, it was Colonel Jimmy Doolittle's raid on Tokyo back in April 1942 with B-25 medium bombers launched from the flight deck of *Hornet* that demonstrated the aircraft carrier's potentiality as a prime strategic-weapon system. But Spaatz wasn't buying the argument.

> I see where some admiral on a carrier trip up around Greenland has announced that the voyage has proved that the larger carrier is essential to national defense in order to transport the atomic bomb. This is a false statement and assumption. There is only one airplane [the B-29], that can carry an atomic bomb; if they insist on an aircraft carrier, its flight deck will have to be 6,000 feet long.[26]

Doolittle himself was equally dismissive of the service and the weapon that had helped bring him so much renown scant years before. Testifying in November 1945 before the Senate Military Affairs Committee, the general stated bluntly:

> The Navy had the transport to make the invasion of Japan possible; the ground forces had the power to make it successful and the B-29 made it unnecessary. . . . If it (the next war) occurs in the next few years the weapons will be airplanes. . . . [T]he carrier has two attributes: One attribute is that it can move about, the other attribute is that it can be sunk. . . . I feel that it (the carrier) has reached its highest usefulness now and that it is going into obsolescence.

General Leslie Groves, who oversaw the Manhattan Project that created the atomic bomb, told a convention of businessmen in Detroit at the end of 1946 that "with the atomic bomb, the need for a navy has passed."[27] At the same moment, General Frank A. Armstrong, whose brilliant leadership in the violent skies over northwest Europe was supposedly the model for fictional General Frank Savage in the popular novel and film *Twelve O'Clock High,* warned an armed forces–businessman's dinner forum that its members

> had better understand that the Army Air Force is tired of being a subordinate outfit and is no longer going to be a subordinate outfit. It was a predominant force during the war and it is going to be a predominant force during the peace and you may as well make up your minds, whether you like it or not, and we do not care whether you like it or not, the Army Air Force is going to run the show. You (the Navy) are not going to have anything but a couple of carriers which are ineffective anyway, and they will probably be sunk in the first battle. Now as for the Marines, you know what the Marines are? They are a small bitched-up Army talking Navy lingo. We're going to put those Marines in the regular Army, and make efficient soldiers out of them. The Navy is going to end up by only supplying the requirements for Army Air and the ground forces too.[28]

Despite such hyperzealotry, there seemed much wisdom behind the attack of land-based aviation proponents upon sea power. The rapidly crystallizing Soviet threat was expressed overwhelmingly in military, not naval, terms. Stalin commanded the largest army and one of the largest air forces in the world. By 1947 Soviet military strength in Europe was estimated to be at least three times that of the Anglo-American and French forces combined. Belief was both widespread and increasingly well founded that as the West disarmed drastically in the months and years after World War II, the Red Army could probably overrun Europe west of the Rhine and seize the Low Country channel ports within a matter of a few weeks at most. Stalin's nation constituted one-sixth of the global landmass and dominated the Eurasian continent. The Soviet fleet was both small and obsolete; compared to the globe-spanning United States Navy of 1942–1945 it was no better than a coastal-defense force. During the recent "Great Patriotic War" it had provided modest seaborne support on the Red Army's northern and southern flanks and nothing more.[29] As Eurasia would obviously be the major theater of operations in World War III, the lessons and achievements of the recent Pacific conflict possessed no enduring relevance. Given the enemy, a third world war could only be an army and air force show. American strategic-planning formulations in the early postwar era were fixed on the Soviet land and air threat to Germany, France, the Low Countries, Scandinavia, and ultimately Britain as well as the Middle East. Of what use would a navy be against such an enemy, except as a support force?[30] On the other hand, atomic airpower deployed from Britain, Iceland, and perhaps Scandinavia and Japan might prove a decisive check on Soviet military pretensions and capabilities.

Moreover, World War II had clearly ended three centuries of world navalism defined by great fighting fleets of sail and steam spanning the globe to win and lose empires. Hundreds of shattered Axis and Allied hulls lined the floor of the world ocean, from South Pacific lagoons and North African harbors to the icy waters of the North Atlantic. Only two legitimate sea powers remained, and by the end of the first postwar year well over half of Britain's wartime battle fleet had been junked as woefully obsolete. When in early 1947 India and Pakistan insisted upon independence and the Attlee government notified the Truman administration that Britain could no longer sustain its responsibilities for Greek-Turkish security, it was clear that the sun was setting rapidly on the British Empire. Two years later Britain made one more effort to exert traditional rights and interests in China. As Mao's forces swept down the Yangtze in April 1949, Whitehall sent *Amethyst* upriver to Nanjing to resupply the embassy there and evacuate British nationals if deemed necessary. As the frigate neared Nanjing, it came under heavy fire from the north bank of the river and ran aground, with seventeen dead and twenty wounded. The destroyer *Consort* and then the cruiser *London* were sent to the rescue, and both ships were caught by heavy Communist fire. *London's* upper works were shot to pieces before its captain could turn it from harm's way. Days later, *Amethyst* managed to sneak back downriver in the dark, carrying with it the last tattered remnants of British "upriver" presence in China. The entire incident was, in the words of an eminent scholar, "an extraordinary gesture of anti-imperialist activism that the British were powerless to counter."[31]

The critics did not have to look far to find a weapon with which to beat the navy down. Back in the summer of 1944, a Missouri senator with a rising reputation as an enemy of wartime inefficiency and graft named Harry Truman argued that the war was being won despite a "scrambled professional military set up" that was "an open invitation to catastrophe." There was only one solution to America's often chaotic and wasteful planning for and prosecution of the war, Truman wrote: "a consolidation of the Army and the Navy that will put all of our defensive and offensive strength under one tent and one authoritative, responsible command. A complete integration that will consider the national security as a whole." Within days after Truman wrote those words—or had them written for him—he became vice president, and with Franklin Roosevelt's sudden death the following April, he was abruptly catapulted into a position where he could hope to transform words into reality.[32]

Reorganization of the national defense establishment had been a simmering issue since the turn of the century. Nearly sixty pieces of legislation had been introduced in Congress providing for "either a single national defense department or a separate Air Department." Elements within the navy itself led the charge. In 1941 the service's General Board had recommended unification of the War and Navy Departments. Two years later retired admiral Henry Yarnell wrote "a widely-circulated article recommending a single Department of War." In the spring of 1944, various congressional committees began hearings on the matter, and by the end of the following year no fewer than seven bills were in the House and Senate hoppers dealing either with the integration of the armed services as a whole or with the consolidation of the aviation and air defense activities of the army and navy.[33]

The immediate impetus behind all this activity was, of course, Pearl Harbor. Whoever was ultimately responsible for the disaster, no one could deny that coordination and cooperation between the military and naval commands in Hawaii in the weeks, days, and hours leading up to the disaster had been abominable if not nonexistent. The two commands, and particularly the intelligence offices, seldom if ever exchanged hard data, analyses, or plans. General Walter Short and Admiral Husband E. Kimmel pursued separate agendas and objectives, seldom consulting each other, though on occasion they golfed together.

Combined military, naval, and air operations in North Africa and Europe demonstrated the irresistible force of American arms. Since combined operations had generally been under the command of Dwight Eisenhower or some other ground-force commander, the army worked on the assumption that this pattern would continue as a matter of course in any future unified department of defense.

But if combined operations had served to inflate the influence of the army, the startling growth of airpower threatened to destroy it. By VJ day the prewar army air corps had expanded into a mighty army air force, and the airmen were unshakably convinced that the "strategic" bombings of Germany and Japan, culminating with the atomic blitz of Hiroshima and Nagasaki, had contributed more than any other endeavors to the winning of the war. All military and naval operations had been mere overtures to or in support of the bombing offensives. The aviators emphasized that for months and years, they and their bombers had been the only means of carrying the war directly to the enemy homeland while the armies and navies nibbled at the edges of enemy power. It seems to have never occurred to the flyers that their bases of operation in England, Italy, the Marianas, and Iwo Jima had been maintained or created through the exercise of Allied naval power. All that the airmen could see was that in the future, well-armed, high-altitude, nuclear- (and later thermonuclear-) carrying bombers with unlimited range (through in-air refueling) could and would enforce national policy anywhere on earth at a fraction of the cost of an aircraft carrier or an army division. Bombers were the instruments of America's future global missions. Compared to these frightening peace keepers, small, light, short-range carrier aircraft were of little account, whereas armies were chiefly useful to mop up and occupy nuclear-seared bombing targets. If postwar America truly wished to pare down its military establishment, it should concentrate what resources it was willing to expend on a strategic air force.

The soldiers soon realized that if they could make a deal with the obstreperous airmen, cutting them loose from army administration to form their own separate service, the flyers might well be induced to support a unified department of defense established along the lines of wartime combined operations, that is, with the army in practical charge. Moreover, if the airmen and soldiers united against the navy, the army might be able to wrest the marines away from naval jurisdiction, or at the very least (as the navy saw it) "restrict the use and size of the Marine Corps to police function and units not greater in power than a lightly armed regiment." It seemed to the navy that the army was willing not only to support a separate and independent air force but also to support the flyers in "remov[ing] from the Navy all land-based aircraft employed in anti-submarine warfare, long-range sea reconnaissance, protection of shipping, and air transport."[34] The aviators were delighted to help their colleagues in the infantry. With their own separate air force they could approach both Congress and the White House for funding to promote the holy cause of strategic airpower. The only loser in this complicated bureaucratic dance would be the navy.

To besieged sailors, talk of "integrating" or "merging" the armed forces sounded like an ill-disguised power grab on the part of an obviously jealous army and its restless and ambitious air force component. Between 1945 and 1949 the navy became locked in a deadly power struggle with its sister services and its commander in chief over the interrelated questions of defense organization and service responsibilities, roles, and missions. The sailors were divided among themselves as well, between those who in the early postwar era followed Arthur Radford, deputy chief of operations for air, in opposing a separate United States Air Force and those who agreed with Chester Nimitz, chief of naval operations from 1945 to late 1947, that the navy had no choice but to accept both unification and the creation of an independent air force or suffer a possibly fatal alienation from the administration.[35]

From the beginning, the air admirals felt themselves outmaneuvered, and they remained rigid in their determination to retain traditional roles and responsibilities. As Captain Arleigh Burke wrote in June 1947, "It is our firm belief that the Navy, to remain effective, must retain all of its components. Great opposition among Naval officers to the merger, is caused by this announced program of officers in high positions in the Army Air Forces to gradually absorb the functions of the Navy, and thereby render the Navy impotent." The future CNO added, "The caustic attacks and biting sarcasm against the Navy, that the Army Air Force personnel have resorted to, has intensified the Navy's feelings against the unification." True, Burke continued, representatives of the Navy Department had recently expressed support for unification, but these disheartened souls had been pressed into this position in the fatalistic belief that legislation pending in Congress was the best that could be hoped for.[36]

Despite the apprehensions of the soldiers and airmen, the sailors were poorly positioned to wage effective bureaucratic warfare in the early postwar era because of their own uncertainties as to the future direction of sea power. On the one hand, postwar planners continued to propound traditional doctrines and strategies of sea control and power projection "as the national policies dictated and facilities permit."[37] On the other, the war had raised new problems and issues. Who was the new queen of the fleet, the carrier or the submarine? How would the navy operate in a new age of steadily advancing military technologies that included very long-range bombers, atomic weaponry, and the first crude guided missiles? To what extent should it incorporate such weapon systems? To what extent would it be allowed to do so? Could battleships, cruisers, and even carriers be refurbished as missile platforms? Could submarines be designed as the ultimate in stealthy long-range power projection, surfacing suddenly and silently off enemy coasts to deliver shattering blows from on-deck missile launchers?

Did the United States have a credible enemy against whom the fleet should plan future operations, and if so who was it? Above all, would the fleet have the professional expertise and financial support to undertake all the many missions that might be assigned to or thrust upon it?

Early in 1948 Burke, then on the navy's General Board, drafted a lengthy appreciation of the latter problem that was suffused with gloom. Because the Truman administration, absorbed in foreign and domestic crises, had not yet developed guidelines for postwar national security policy, it was clear that the navy and its sister services were drifting dangerously. The problem was compounded, of course, by steadily declining defense budgets and force levels for all three services. Burke let his mind roam broadly over political, economic, and military factors and problems both at home and abroad, concluding that because of the looming Soviet threat coupled with steadily declining defense expenditures the service might be drowned with responsibilities, "that fulfillment of all demands may be beyond the capacity of the Navy in being." Burke's paper received wide dissemination, and historian David Alan Rosenberg has argued that it was instrumental in turning the admirals away from the "politically attractive but strategically and operationally extravagant plans to use carrier task forces as bases for strategic nuclear attacks against Soviet urban-industrial targets."[38]

Nonetheless, the navy countered air force pretensions and army initiatives, reminding anyone who would listen that no American fleet had ever fought so many diverse battles as the World War II navy, from carrier duels in the Pacific to antisubmarine warfare in the Atlantic to gunfire support on more than a score of beaches from Sicily to Okinawa.[39] Even in the realm of strategic airpower, sea-based striking forces were mobile, whereas land-based airpower was fixed.

This was the starting point for a series of strategy papers that Rear Admiral Forrest P. Sherman and his talented planning team had begun to draft and disseminate as early as 1946. Both a wartime commander (he had the carrier *Wasp* torpedoed out from under him off Guadalcanal and later served as one of Halsey's task-group commanders with the Third Fleet) and a staff man, Sherman possessed a sharp, if not brilliant, mind together with a clear vision of what the postwar navy should be like and what it should do. If the service was to survive as anything more than "a mere transport service," it would have to define its own important place in the postwar world. In the minds of Sherman and his colleagues, the most important and dramatic weapon system it could bring to the strategy table was the aircraft-carrier task force. Sherman and his people never quite succeeded in making their point during the feverish half decade between VJ day and the Korean War, but they made a heroic effort, "craft[ing] the naval component of the nation's new strategic concept" of power from the sea for the cold war era.

Sherman grounded his maritime strategy on the increasingly chilling premise of a "global protracted war." In such a conflict, the navy's task would be to boldly and persistently practice a *forward* maritime strategy in which it would conduct "offensive conventional operations" in support of mission and role responsibilities previously conceived by the Joint Planning Staff. The heart of the navy's offensive punch would be its fast fleet aircraft carriers. These vessels should not be squandered in peripheral operations in the Arctic, or in antisubmarine (that is, sea-control) operations. Rather, "the strategic counter to this sort of thing," Sherman wrote of a possible Soviet submarine menace, "is high emphasis on attack at the source of the trouble." Steaming in harm's way, navy carrier task forces would strike directly at the Soviet Union, concentrating on "destruction of [enemy] airfields, assembly depots, factories, shipyards, and submarine bases, and the seizure [by the marines] of critical ports, harbors, and base sites." Such operations, and only such operations, "offered the best method of protecting shipping from Soviet submarines and land based aircraft. Aerial bombardment and offensive mining by aircraft, submarines, and surface vessels would achieve these objectives," Sherman added. In other words, the navy would exercise *power projection offensively* over a wide area and deep into enemy territory in support of the historic *defensive* objective of *sea control*. "Carrier operations in the Mediterranean, the North Sea, ultimately the Barents Sea and the Sea of Japan would support the campaign in cooperation with the Air Force. Submarines would also play an offensive role by hunting down their Soviet counterparts."[40]

Naval Strategic Planning Study (NSPS) 3 of March 1947, an analysis of the offensive capabilities of U.S. aircraft carriers, fully stated the U.S. Navy's post–World War II cold war strategy. It called for Pacific Fleet carrier operations right up to the Soviet doorstep in the Sea of Okhotsk, the Yellow Sea, and the Sea of Japan. Atlantic Fleet carrier operations would be conducted in the Mediterranean. The Baltic was too dangerously confining; the Arctic was a possibility, should weather conditions and poor Soviet defensive capabilities permit. "The plan," Michael Palmer contends,

> included maps of the entire Soviet Union, showing the areas within range of carrier-based planes. Noticeably absent from NSPS 3 was a major Navy role in the strategic bombing campaign that planners of all three services

recognized would be central to war. The U.S. possessed few nuclear weapons in the late forties, and those it did have were comparatively crude and heavy. The Navy simply did not possess the heavy aircraft—or the long carrier flight decks necessary to launch and land them—that strategic nuclear warfare demanded. The planners thus concluded that the Air Force was best suited to conduct a strategic bombing campaign.

However, they did not rule out the importance of "surprise" in hitting the enemy where he was most vulnerable. In sum, "the planners saw carrier air power as assisting an Air Force strategic bombing campaign by engaging and destroying enemy fighter strength around the periphery of the Soviet Union."[41]

The U.S. Navy had now developed a doctrine of unprecedented forward-force projection to justify the role of sea power in the rapidly emerging cold war era. In January 1947 Sherman was able to place his ideas directly before the president and Congress. Should vast Soviet land and air forces erupt across the North German plain and through the Ardennes, while pushing north into Norway and south toward the Iberian and Italian peninsulas and the Middle East, "the United States and its allies would adopt the strategic defensive." But not the U.S. Navy, which would "assume the offensive immediately in order to secure our own sea communications, support our forces overseas, disrupt enemy operations, and force dissipation of enemy strength."

> Carrier task forces would strike targets, at sea and ashore, in the Soviet Far East and on the flanks of the Soviet advance in Norway, northwest Germany, and, most importantly to Sherman, in the Mediterranean. Submarines would conduct forward operations in the northeastern Pacific and in the White, Baltic, and Black Seas. Amphibious forces would reinforce threatened forward positions, seize new ones, and eventually open the Dardanelles.

Here was a cogently argued maritime strategy grounded firmly in a clear organizational structure. It was also, of course, firmly grounded, as most military and naval strategies are, in the experience of recent war and, at least to hypersensitive air force critics, too clever by half. In even suggesting a forward power projection role for its carriers, the navy was wedging open the door of strategic operations. When Nimitz stepped down as chief of naval operations late that year, he made explicit in his farewell remarks what Sherman and his planners had implicitly suggested. The bruising interservice fights of the past two years had roused his blood and focused his thinking. In his final report as chief of naval operations, made public in January 1948, Nimitz wrote that it was "improbable that bomber fleets will be capable, for several years to come, of making two-way trips between continents . . . with heavy loads of bombs. It is apparent then that in the event of war within this period, if we are to project our power against the vital areas of any enemy across the ocean before beachheads on enemy territory are captured, it must be by . . . aircraft launched from carriers."[42]

The navy's continued insistence on the pertinence of carrier airpower as a strategic weapon was part of a broader effort to create a fleet for the atomic age, one that would not only deliver nuclear blows but also withstand efforts to destroy it by nuclear weaponry. During the first year of the atomic era, the navy became obsessed with the question of survivability, an obsession that culminated at 9 A.M. local time on July 1, 1946, at a remote central Pacific atoll named Bikini Island. A B-29 named *Dave's Dream* began Operation Crossroads by dropping an atomic bomb on a fleet of old, damaged, and discarded vessels lying in the atoll's vast lagoon. The weather was perfect, "CAVU"—ceiling and visibility unlimited—and, as in Billy Mitchell's rigged tests against battleships off the Virginia coast a quarter century before, there were no enemy aircraft present to harass and distract the bomber's crew and possibly shoot them down. Although the navy readily admitted that the bomb "smashed" more ships than any similar weapon in history, blast damage lessened dramatically at more than one-half mile from the target vessel. Battleship *Nevada* survived the blast, as did its nearby sister, *Arkansas,* and lightly armored heavy cruiser *Pensacola.* All three vessels emerged with their propulsion systems and even topside turrets largely intact. "But their superstructures were badly wrecked," wrote the commander of Joint Task Force 1, Vice Admiral W. H. P. Blandy. However, *New York,* another old battleship from World War I lying several miles away, was "virtually undamaged," and the powerful German cruiser *Prinz Eugen* that "has been described as comparable to our latest heavy cruiser . . . escaped with superficial scars, a broken mainmast and a seared port side." Radioactivity was intense, but swabbing decks appeared an efficient way to wash it overboard before significant harm occurred to personnel.[43]

Although the air drop did severely damage some of the closely packed fleet, the real destruction occurred on "Baker Day," July 25, when a bomb slung beneath a landing craft in the middle of the lagoon was ignited. The underwater burst resulted in a "reverse Niagara Falls" of terrifying proportions. "Great ships were tossed about Bikini lagoon as if they were a child's toy boats," one observer wrote, "and the sea literally blew into the sky." *Arkansas,* which had survived the air burst with major damage only to its upper works, was torn to pieces and dropped instantly to the floor of the lagoon, followed hours later by the celebrated old carrier *Saratoga*. Millions of tons of highly radioactive water cascaded onto the decks of the entire fleet, followed in some instances by heavy waves that brought more radioactivity aboard. The navy believed it now had a firm understanding of the bomb, its potential, and its place in military arsenals as an antifleet weapon. Blandy ticked off the lessons learned. "Navies will not be obsolete"; design changes to hulls and superstructures were obviously needed; radioactivity was a serious problem. But all these matters could be solved by applying two new principles to naval warfare. The first was "disposition of forces," which meant dispersal. Fleets in the atomic era would have to be stretched out across scores of miles of oceans, not packed together as they were at Jutland or in the great carrier task forces of the recent Pacific war. Fortunately, the great strides in long-distance, secure, and hardened communications made such dispersal feasible. And second, naval vessels would have to be equipped with heavy sprinklers and wash-down systems to sweep radioactive materials from their decks. During an atomic attack, crews would remain inside hulls and superstructures until the blast occurred and the water protection systems went to work. Blandy did not dismiss the need for alterations in naval designs and hull structures, but he did not indulge in specifics, possibly for security reasons, though in fact U.S. Navy warships later in the century would display the same basic features as those of 1945–1946.[44]

The mantra of naval superiority through nimbleness found little support beyond naval circles. "The Navy said the atomic bomb wouldn't be used against ships," an exasperated David Lilienthal wrote one night in the summer of 1947 following a typically abrasive interagency meeting, "and if it were, there was little change in structure that would do much good." Nearly two years later, the director of the Atomic Energy Agency wrote once again "about the 'It's-just-another-weapon' argument which emanates principally from the Navy."[45]

The navy's argument was grounded in its fierce loyalty to sea-based aviation. Even as Operation Crossroads got under way in the Far Pacific, senior navy fliers began agitating for an aircraft carrier of unprecedented size and singular capability. The Doolittle raid had demonstrated to the navy's satisfaction the great strategic potential of aircraft carriers. Like bombers, carriers could be built large enough to fulfill a strategic mission, but unlike stationary bomber bases, carriers could stage such missions from all points of the compass while seeking and finding good weather. Even before the war was over, naval aviators were contemplating the huge ships and big aircraft that could keep the navy on the cutting edge of strategic warfare. The carriers would have to be big—more than a thousand feet long, though not the six thousand–foot monsters that U.S. Army Air Force Chief of Staff Carl Spaatz had facetiously proposed.

As is often the case with advanced technologies, the impetus for further carrier development came from some surprising sources.[46] The first appearance of Japanese kamikaze aircraft off the Philippines in late 1944 and the vulnerability of escort carriers off the Leyte invasion beaches to Japanese land-based plane attacks convinced Admiral Marc Mitscher that navy carriers needed larger and longer-range bomber aircraft to neutralize enemy airfields from afar. At the same time, the Atlantic Fleet had become "obsessed with ASW" (antisubmarine warfare) as a result of the imminent appearance of the German Type XXI U-boats, which seemed at the time capable of reversing the entire course of battle. "It followed that conventional ASW might require the assistance of deep strikes on enemy submarine bases" and above all against heavily reinforced submarine "pens." To the navy, its own carrier task forces were the obvious candidates for the job, but at the time carrier aircraft could lift, carry, and deliver general-purpose bombs no larger than two thousand pounds. Experts estimated that a missile six times as large would be required to penetrate a German U-boat pen. Analysis of strategic bombing on German towns by the army air force indicated that "lethal damage to many targets" also "required 12,000 lb bombs." For a variety of widely divergent reasons, the navy high command concluded by 1945 that future carrier aircraft, and thus aircraft carriers, would have to be much larger in order to deploy increasingly heavy ordnance. The navy's return to Japanese waters in February and again in July 1945 indicated that carrier aircraft sweeps over Tokyo and other Japanese cities were of minimal value compared to the massive firebomb raids unleashed by army air force B-29s.

Thus convinced that the carrier could be a major strategic weapon system if only it were made large enough to handle and deploy modern bomber aircraft, the navy at the end of the war laid plans both for a "super" 69,200–ton, twelve hundred–foot aircraft carrier and the long-range strike plane—initially designated ADR-42—that could deploy from its decks. The navy also rushed into design and production an interim carrier bomber aircraft, the AJ-1 Savage, designed to carry bombs of at least ten thousand pounds, which proved to be roughly the weight of the atomic weapons laid on Japan. A handful of Savages could be squeezed aboard each of the three brand-new "battle carriers" of the *Midway* class, clearly considered interim platforms between the much too small and wholly inadequate *Essexes* and the new supercarrier.

But navy defenders of the supercarrier and its bomber force were careful. After the first spasm of army and air force attacks and their own possibly exag-

gerated claims for the strategic value of carrier airpower, they backed off asserting the ultimate strategic role for carrier aircraft. Nuclear air strikes from sea
were *not* designed to interfere with the air force's strategic mission of destroying
the Soviet urban-industrial complex, but would be confined to "enemy targets
of naval interest, air power targets on the periphery of the Soviet and Satellite
territories, and retardation targets designed to slow Soviet advances into Western
Europe and the Middle East."[47] But, of course, the air force could be pardoned
if it interpreted such thinking as outright sophistry. In the midst or on the eve
of a desperate nuclear war, national leaders could be expected to reach for any
and every strategic weapon in their arsenal. Whether the navy would admit it
or not, nuclear bombers at sea were as much a strategic weapon as nuclear
bombers on land.

And many navy people remained more than willing to admit and assert
the carrier's primary strategic role. For every moderate like Chester Nimitz and
Arleigh Burke who sought to accommodate navy thinking to a strategic air
force, there were others, often far up the navy chain of command, who kept up
the drumbeat for the strategic equality, if not primacy, of the aircraft carrier.
Their champion was Arthur Radford, the deputy chief of naval operations for
air. One of the few sailors who relished Washington politics, Radford "fiercely
opposed nearly every unification scheme proposed by the Army and its allies."
Radford became so vociferous that Nimitz was forced to send him out of town
to command the Second Fleet in the Atlantic. But Nimitz's successor in early
1948, a hitherto obscure submariner named Louis Denfeld (one looks in vain
for his name among the prominent seamen of the war), wanted to curry favor
with the most powerful lobby in the naval establishment and promptly brought
Radford back. Denfeld's reward would be the rapid end of his own career. Truman wanted the obscure submariner as a compromise chief of naval operations
precisely because Denfeld was neither prominent nor an aviator. Once back in
town, however, Radford and his cadre swiftly dominated their superior. They
argued repeatedly that with the prospect of huge, fast floating airfields, each
capable of launching a score or more of nuclear-carrying bombers, together
with a powerful and experienced amphibious capability and missile-deploying
diesel submarines (the idea of a nuclear-powered strategic boat launching its missiles from a submerged position lay on the far horizon), the navy rather than
the air force could and should be the predominant postwar strategic service.[48]

In February 1948 the navy stepped up its offensive in favor of the carrier.
Captain Fitzhugh Lee of the public relations staff had asked Dr. Henry M. Dater
of the Aviation History Unit to prepare some half-dozen statistical studies of

the role of the aircraft carrier in modern warfare based on "six propositions
taken from the extreme advocates for [strategic land-based] aviation." Dater
found that in World War II, carriers had been clearly most vulnerable to enemy
navies and especially their submarines. Not only could carriers withstand heavy
enemy assaults by land-based aircraft, but American carrier aircraft and pilots
had clearly demonstrated their superiority to Japanese land-based planes.[49]

Carriers had not only proved more maneuverable and weather capable (because of their mobility) but also disproved those zealots who claimed that land-
based airpower alone could control the world ocean. The statistics Dater presented were mixed: shore-based aircraft had indeed played a major role in
winning the wars in both the Pacific and on the North Atlantic, but the combined force of submarines, surface ships, and land- and sea-based aircraft had
been the key to success.[50]

Shortly after Dater submitted his study, Captain James S. Thach, one of
the heroes of the carrier war in the Pacific, submitted a manuscript to higher
authorities in the Navy Department adding a further gloss to Dater's findings.
Even if the Soviet Union were to seize all of Western Europe, it would pose only
a limited threat to the continental United States, since no bombers in existence
could fly from the French or Dutch coasts, or even Britain, to the United States
and back. Soviet long-range bomber attacks must of necessity be suicidal—and
slow in speed in order to conserve fuel. Navy carriers with their deck loads of
efficient fighter aircraft would remain this country's first line of defense, inter-
cepting enemy bomber streams in midocean long before they reached the range
of land-based interceptors. "Not only can we break up these attacks before they
get started, but our mobile air bases gives us the means to launch a better offensive at an enemy than he could possibly throw at us." But what if Soviet nuclear
bombers went after American midocean carrier task forces in advance of a massive raid upon the U.S. homeland? Thach had a ready answer:

> Dispersion is the best defense against atomic bombs. Naval task forces
> cruise in a formation already dispersed. An enemy would have to send out a
> dozen perhaps two dozen bomb[er]s to insure a hit on one carrier, the others
> would be saved by distance. If we would persuade an enemy to expend his
> stockpile of atomic bombs expecting to knock out the fast carrier task force,
> it would be the best thing we could do for the war effort.[51]

The airmen derided the navy's claims, focusing on real and alleged weaknesses
of the long-range Savage carrier bomber. They falsely claimed that the plane
possessed a range of only seven hundred miles when prototypes demonstrated

that in fact it could fly more than two thousand miles, nuclear bomb an enemy target, and return to the carrier. But the Savage would not appear in the fleet until early 1950. Moreover, it could squeeze aboard only the three brand-new, forty-five thousand–ton *Midway*-class "battle carriers." The navy, desperate to get some sort of nuclear bomber to sea in order to head off air force demands for total control over strategic bombing, formed Composite Squadron 5 (VC-5) in September 1948 as a stopgap measure. For a year and a half, VC-5 flew the P2V-3C Neptune, normally a land-based patrol plane, now modified to fly from carriers with a nuclear bomb load, then to land either at air force bases ashore or ditch alongside the carrier fleet for crew recovery.[52]

The airmen and soldiers were, understandably, not impressed by such crude grandstanding. An unsigned memorandum titled "Imbalance within the Naval Establishment" written in the army Comptroller's Office stated that because the navy had maintained its attack-carrier aviation capabilities "since the War at a very high level," it had grossly neglected antisubmarine warfare at a time when Soviet undersea capabilities were advancing at an alarming rate due to capture of German U-boats, blueprints, engineers, and technicians. By the time VC-5 was formed, Truman had become disgusted with both services. "The air boys are for glamour," he noted sourly in May 1948, "and the navy as always is the greatest of propaganda machines."[53]

There was good reason for presidential disgust. Careful examination of the premises of airborne atomic warfare, no matter who conducted it, raised some disturbing questions about its efficacy. When military planners first approached the question of employing the atom bomb against Russia in the autumn of 1946, they reached some startling conclusions. There was no way to guarantee that an atomic blitz might prevent the Red Army from seizing Western Europe.

> The Russian transportation system, identified as "the most vital cog in the war machine of the U.S.S.R.," was too widespread to be vulnerable to attack. Bombing major industries such as steel, aircraft, and electric power would take too long to become effective. Only the Russian petroleum industry, vital to troop mobility, was considered possibly vulnerable to an air offensive, using either conventional or atomic weapons.[54]

Such a conclusion, of course, delighted the navy, which was fighting desperately to keep the army air force from subordinating all future military operations to strategic bombing.[55] Consistent cuts in the military budget, however, together with the persistent unwillingness of Congress and the country to support partial mobilization during the several European crises of late 1947 and early 1948, forced the Pentagon to consider the bomb as its first line of both offense and defense.

Yet there was no "bomb," or at least far too few to effectively prosecute a policy of nuclear intimidation against the Kremlin. At the end of June 1946 the national stockpile consisted of a total of nine weapons. Only four more were added in the following year. In December 1947 the Joint Chiefs of Staff asked for and obtained a sharply accelerated timetable of atomic production that would yield four hundred bombs by January 1, 1953, and within six months the weapons' makers had raised the nuclear inventory to half a hundred.[56] Joint Emergency War Plan "Halfmoon," approved in May 1948 (when the United States possessed only fifty unassembled atomic devices), called for the destruction of the Soviet will to resist by "a powerful air offensive designed to exploit the destructive and psychological power of atomic weapons against vital elements of the Soviet war making capacity."[57] Thereafter, Truman and the air force never revisited the issue.

Perhaps one reason they did not was the Berlin crisis. In March 1948 Soviet authorities abruptly blocked all ground access to the city through their East German occupation zone. They did so as a protest against the Anglo-American announcement of a common currency for the Western occupation zones, which the Soviets interpreted correctly as a de facto division of Germany into distinct political entities. Searching about for a suitable power response to Stalin's sudden move, Truman found the cupboard embarrassingly bare. Fifteen months earlier, when the president propounded the "doctrine" that the United States would support all "free peoples who are resisting attempted subjugation by armed minorities or by outside pressures," the U.S. military establishment was in no position to give it effective support. From a wartime-high ninety-plus divisions, the army had been reduced to ten understrength formations; if pressed, the marines could add two more to cover commitments that were literally worldwide. Truman was "playing with fire," his secretary of state, George Marshall, later remarked, "while we have nothing with which to put it out." The situation had deteriorated even further by the early summer of 1948 as the national defense budget steadily declined. The army was in no position to contest the blockade by sending troop-filled truck convoys through eastern Germany to the beleaguered city. The navy's handful of fleet carriers (perhaps four or five in the entire Atlantic and Mediterranean region) did not possess the heavy, long-range atomic-strike capabilities required to intimidate Stalin and the Kremlin. But the air force fancied that it did have the weapons, and Lucius D. Clay, the head of the U.S. military government in Germany, agreed. As the Berlin crisis intensified in the summer of 1948, Clay informed Army Chief of Staff Omar Bradley that the Soviets "are definitely afraid of our air might." Dispatching a squadron of B-29s to Germany and another to England, with their demonstrated capabilities to drop atomic bombs, would send a signal that Stalin could not miss. The planes were duly sent, and although the Soviet blockade persisted for another year until the unceasing allied airlift of supplies to the city at last wore the Kremlin down, Stalin made no effort to instigate further crises elsewhere.[58]

With the emphasis on ground-based airpower of all sorts, the Berlin crisis fortified air force assertiveness, and the flyers expressed increasing outrage at the navy's stubborn insistence on the advantages, indeed necessity, of a sea-based strategic strike force built around aircraft carriers. Between 1948 and 1950 the services engaged in an escalating public brawl that served the interests of neither and killed the one man who had the navy's interests firmly at heart. As navy secretary between 1944 and 1947, James Forrestal spent much of his time carefully crafting a tenable plan for a defense department that would substitute cooperation and coordination among the three services for unification and subordination. He stood his ground stubbornly against the army and army air corps, at one point telling his president flatly, "I am so opposed to the fundamental concept expressed in [a proposed presidential message to Congress on armed forces unification] that I do not believe there is any very helpful observation that I could make on the draft . . . referred to me." Because of his reputation as an effective and incorruptible civil servant, Forrestal was able to get his views widely heard, if not accepted. As early as November 1945 presidential aide George M. Elsey wrote Truman's most trusted adviser, Clark Clifford, of his own deep concern over the public assumption that "the President has become a partisan of the Army against the Navy, that he has developed prejudices against the Navy which cause him to disregard naval wishes, and that he will force the Navy into a single Department of Defense which will be dominated by the Army and Air Force."[59] Forrestal's widely acknowledged and admired integrity, if not his intense lobbying for the navy, was rewarded when he was appointed in 1947 the first secretary of defense. But the poor man was hoist by his own petard. Having battled successfully for an administrative arrangement that emphasized interservice cooperation and coordination over command authority, he now had to make it work and was torn to pieces by stubborn, seemingly irresolvable, interservice struggles over roles and missions that raged without interruption throughout 1947 and 1948.

Before he left office Forrestal hauled his fractious service chiefs outside Washington for two head-knocking sessions at Key West and Newport, Rhode

Island, in which he managed to broker several deals stipulating that the air force would cease "trying to kill off" the aircraft carrier, the Marine Corps would be saved from extinction or incorporation into the army at the cost of further reduction in size, and in exchange the navy would agree not to form its own strategic bomber force. The knotty question of which service would enjoy ultimate control over and distribution of atomic weaponry was never satisfactorily resolved. A supercarrier could be justified only as a base for a strategic bombing squadron, but the navy got an agreement from Forrestal and the air force that it could perform "collateral" bombing functions, including deep-strike penetration attacks on enemy airfields and land communications in the event of a Soviet attack on Western Europe. Truman reluctantly allowed the navy to move ahead with its supercarrier, whose design, slightly modified, resulted in a sixty-five thousand–ton, one thousand–foot-plus vessel to be named *United States,* carrying a more modestly capable nuclear bomber designated the ADR-45A. The air force, meanwhile, rushed into prototype production its first truly intercontinental bomber, the B-36, then bluntly warned Forrestal that its ever suspicious flyers had experienced a change of heart; they wanted the carrier fleet scrapped. Soon thereafter, Truman relieved his exhausted, stressed-out secretary of defense, and several weeks later Forrestal committed suicide by jumping from his sixteenth-floor room at the Bethesda Naval Hospital.[60]

Disaster for the navy struck when Truman picked Louis A. Johnson to replace Forrestal. A man of soaring ambition, the new defense secretary loved the air force and hated the navy. Having concluded that the best way to achieve his ultimate goal of the presidency was to outdo Truman in budget cutting, he suppressed a recent JCS report that again called into question the feasibility of wholesale atomic bombing. Denfeld responded by prudently downplaying the uniqueness of a super aircraft carrier. In a mid-1949 letter to Congressman Robert L. Coffey Jr., Denfeld wrote that the USS *United States,* whose keel was about to be laid at Newport News, was not a great leap beyond the existing *Midway* class; though it could launch the most modern long-range naval attack bombers, the ship was not intended to spearhead a strategic naval task force. Indeed, its cost-effectiveness lay in the fact that it would fit into existing task forces, albeit as a uniquely powerful component.[61] Of course, Denfeld was being too clever by half. The *only* justification for a supercarrier was its uniqueness as a strategic weapon system. By suddenly denying that uniqueness, Denfeld handed Johnson a sword to wield against the navy, and Johnson promptly used it. While the navy and air force engaged in a mad scramble for steadily diminishing funds, Johnson bluntly told Richard Conolly, "Admiral, the Navy is on its way out. . . .

There's no reason for having a Navy and Marine Corps. General Bradley tells me that amphibious operations are a thing of the past. We'll never have any more amphibious operations. That does away with the Marine Corps. And the Air Force can do anything the Navy can nowadays, so that does away with the Navy."[62] Scant days after its keel was laid, Johnson canceled the supercarrier, giving its construction funds to the air force.

After seething through the summer, a disgruntled group of senior naval aviators began a propaganda campaign in the autumn to undermine public confidence in the B-36. The plane, with its four big J-47 jet engines in underwing nacelles and six thirty-five hundred–horsepower piston engines on the rear of the wings, was a hybrid monstrosity and something of a lemon. Moreover, the plane's ostensibly heavy defensive armament failed to function properly in early tests. Excited navy propagandists and their allies within the federal bureaucracy circulated a notorious "Anonymous Document" asserting that the B-36 was a "billion dollar blunder" that the air force would not admit because Johnson and the secretary of the air force had a personal financial interest in the plane's construction and owed political and personal favors to its manufacturer, Floyd Odlum.[63]

Navy propagandists also developed compelling arguments that strategic bombers like the B-36 could not penetrate Soviet air defenses without prohibitive cost unless heavily escorted by effective fighter aircraft, which would drive the cost of strategic air operations far beyond that of similar naval activities. The navy readily acknowledged that airpower had had a measurable impact on the outcome of the European war, but argued that it was *tactical,* not strategic, in nature. The strategic Eighth and Fifteenth Air Forces had suffered crippling losses until finally escorted by long-range P-51 Mustang fighters. Major General Hoyt S. Vandenberg's Ninth Tactical Air Force, on the other hand, had paved the way for the successful Normandy invasion by sealing off the landing beaches from enemy counterattack through destruction of German airfields, railroad yards, bridges, coastal gun positions, and communication centers "stretching from the Netherlands to the Pyrenees."[64] Since the navy had practiced its own highly successful brand of tactical airpower in the Pacific, was it not reasonable to reassign that role to a fleet of ever larger and more efficient carriers?

In a reversal of the Billy Mitchell incident thirty years before, eager sailors also requested permission to test their brand-new carrier-based Banshee (F2H) or Panther (F9F) jet fighters against the B-36. The air force countered the move, arguing that its own tests had demonstrated quite convincingly that the B-36 could operate effectively day or night at forty thousand feet, an altitude that gave existing radar at best only a thirty-minute warning of impending attack.

Since the air force's own advanced fighter aircraft required at least twenty-six minutes to reach the bomber stream, it was clear to air force advocates that in most instances the B-36 could get through to do its job.[65]

Moreover, by early 1950 the air force had in the advanced development stage the stopgap, short-range jet-engined B-47. The splendid B-52, whose four huge jet engines could propel it to intercontinental distances, would soon follow. The admirals' "revolt" with its "Anonymous Document" was seen both in the White House and throughout the country for what they essentially were: an attack on the air force and its pretensions. By this time the naval establishment itself was torn to pieces by the carrier–air force bomber debate. There were those of flag rank such as Sherman, Robert B. ("Mick") Carney, and Burke (who had just been promoted to rear admiral) who argued that the navy must bend to the inevitable, accept unification, and fight for a carrier fleet within the existing defense structure. Johnson and Francis P. Matthews, his handpicked navy secretary, undercut them at every turn, and Burke's career was very nearly ended.

Matters came to a head in late September 1949 when Congress held its annual military appropriations hearings just as all work ceased on the supercarrier *United States*. Radford, now a four-star admiral and commander in chief of the Pacific Fleet, returned to town ready to testify vigorously against the B-36, while the navy launched a vigorous public relations campaign on behalf of the aircraft carrier. Denfeld invited Johnson and the other Joint Chiefs on a short demonstration cruise off the Virginia Capes aboard the big battle carrier *Franklin D. Roosevelt*. The highlight of the exercise was the JATO (jet-assisted takeoff) launch of two P2V Neptunes, one of which flew nonstop from the carrier's deck sixty miles out in the Atlantic down to the Panama Canal, before swinging north to the West Coast. Unimpressed, Johnson communicated his feelings to Navy Secretary Matthews, who ordered Radford and his colleagues not to bring up the B-36 issue. The admirals hotly replied that the air force was making claims that had to be challenged. Vice Chief of Naval Operations John Dale Price quietly leaked the matter to the *Washington Post,* which promptly charged Matthews with "muzzling" the navy. Matthews, now on a rampage, concluded that Arleigh Burke's shop was the source of the leak, and he determined to do something about it.

Burke had in fact become essential to the naval establishment. A pugnacious destroyer leader in the Solomon Islands during the early stages of the war, Burke had gone on to serve as Marc Mitscher's chief of staff in 1944–1945 as the legendary little admiral's vast carrier fleets scoured the Pacific. After serving on the navy's General Board and immersing himself in the unification debate, Burke

had returned to sea in command of a cruiser when on Christmas Day 1948 he
was abruptly summoned back to Washington to head a new office, OP-23, devoted to Organizational Research and Policy. Burke was just what the navy badly
needed. He possessed a brilliant, probing mind and a judicious temperament,
combined with clarity of thought and expression. He had run with the airmen
but was a surface sailor by training. He understood the need for a balanced naval
establishment. His colleagues found him invariably useful and stimulating.

Late on the afternoon of September 29, 1949, Commander Snowden Arthur,
attached to OP-23, burst into the office to tell Burke that the place was about
to be raided by the navy inspector general and his staff. Arthur did not know
why, but roaming the Pentagon halls he had picked up the rumor. Burke leaped
up, told everyone present there were files he did not want the inspectors to
"discover," and began opening drawers and cramming papers into a briefcase.
Soon the inspector general himself, Rear Admiral Allan R. McCann, appeared
at the door. "Arleigh, it's a raid," he said coldly. "I want to talk to you in the
hall." As the two men stood in the corridor, McCann's men began questioning
the OP-23 staff in "severe and intimidating" tones. It was like being in a police
station, one staffer recalled, as McCann's people grilled him and others about
office routine, contacts with the press, and so on. The grilling went on from
late afternoon to early the next morning, leaving everyone in a state of nervous
exhaustion. But the inspector general found nothing "incriminating." Burke
"had dodged the bullet."[66]

Soon after, following "stormy hearings" before the Senate Armed Services
Committee in which Radford did indeed raise the B-36 issue and Denfeld
stoutly backed his right to do so, Johnson had Matthews fire the chief of naval
operations and retired most of the ringleaders of the revolt. Radford and Burke
somehow escaped the ax.[67] The administration was supported by Joint Chiefs
of Staff chairman Omar Bradley, who in public testimony before Congress openly
derided the dissident admirals as crybabies and flatly suggested that Denfeld
was incompetent. The admirals fought back. Daniel V. Gallery charged that critics were out to "cripple the Navy," adding that those who sought to muzzle the
dissident sailors were engaged in a form of "thought control" that was wholly
antithetical to the kind of values America professed to defend in its cold war
struggle with Communist totalitarianism. Gallery, like "31 Knot Burke," had
become something of a wartime hero. Commander of an antisubmarine task
force built around the escort carrier *Guadalcanal,* Gallery had ordered his men
to capture U-505 after carrier planes and destroyers had blasted the hapless

enemy craft to the surface, then strafed and shot it up unmercifully. Seizure of the Nazi U-boat marked the first successful boarding and capture of an enemy ship since the War of 1812. But neither Gallery's earlier heroics nor his eloquent pen could save Denfeld and his colleagues who were cashiered. After a decent interval, Gallery followed them into retirement.[68]

By the end of 1949 the navy's leadership was exhausted and demoralized, tarred with the brush of insubordination, if not (in more feverish minds) outright treason. In early December the service reached its nadir when the symbol of its recent wartime greatness, the battleship *Missouri,* fetched up hard aground on Thimble Shoals in Chesapeake Bay off Norfolk after steaming wildly off course. A bemused nation watched for more than two weeks while the navy struggled to free the giant. The resulting court-martial revealed a chain of command aboard the ship that was at once poorly disciplined and fatally deferential to authority; the navigator simply called out bearings to a new and inexperienced commanding officer without informing him of what those bearings implied.

Indeed, the whole service seemed to have lost its bearings. The officer corps was filled with wartime reservists who, glancing at the uncertainties of postwar civilian life, opted to stay in. Experienced as they were, they carried with them wartime habits born of necessarily hasty training and relaxed discipline, in which victory was the only standard and professional traditions, customs, and courtesy were viewed with disdain as barriers to getting the job done. Young academy graduates entering the fleet quickly became disillusioned, and their resignation rate in the late forties reached century-high levels. So did absent-over-leave rates among the enlisted men. To veterans not only of the war but also of the astringent Depression years that preceded, the postwar sailors were the soft products of a suddenly booming wartime economy in which they "had romped through adolescence, danced to the music of the big bands, and learned to smoke and drink like the movie military heroes" while their fathers and older brothers had fought and bled and died. The enlistees shared the same "lassitude" as many of their officers and were far more assertive of their rights than aware of their responsibilities.[69]

But this bleak moment proved prologue to a drastic shift in national and naval affairs, as the cascade of world events at last forced the Truman administration to review, and ultimately to drastically revise, national security policy. In September 1949 it became clear that the Soviets had successfully tested an atomic device, fully three to four years before anticipated. Given the swiftness with which the Alamogordo tests in July 1945 had led to a workable bomb over Hiroshima, official Washington was forced to conclude that the Soviets not only had broken the American nuclear monopoly but might also reach parity in a frighteningly short period of time. As Dwight Eisenhower later remarked, "Americans realized that, as never before in their history, they must henceforth live under the specter of wholesale destruction."[70] The following month China officially fell to Mao Zedong's Communists, a gigantic blow both to American interests and to the national ego, which had long looked upon that vast, unhappy land as a favored arena of Christian and commercial endeavor. In January 1950 Mao went to Moscow for nearly a month of talks with Stalin. What mischief were the two leaders of "the international Communist conspiracy" plotting? The question gained added urgency when the two completed a "Sino-Soviet Treaty of Friendship" the following month. Only decades later would it be revealed that the frequently tense talks had been prologue to a growing and bitter rift between the "two Communist super-powers" (another favorite phrase of the day). As Mao and Stalin met in Moscow, the trial of American Communist Party leaders began in New York, and former State Department adviser Alger Hiss was convicted of perjury. A few weeks later yet another "atomic spy," Klaus Fuchs, was arrested in London for passing secrets to the Soviets.

These events threw the administration completely on the defensive. The containment of Communist expansion through the economic reconstruction of Western Europe and Japan, coupled with the threat of an atomic blitz from the air should all other measures against the Soviet Union prove insufficient, had clearly failed. In the words of a later secretary of state who did his own share of it, the time had come for an "agonizing reappraisal" of national policy. At the end of January 1950 Truman directed such an appraisal. The result, after months of occasionally outraged exchanges between the principals, and intense discussions, planning, and drafting by their State and Defense Department representatives, was National Security Council Report 68 (NSC 68). The first of many elaborations that would follow over the next year and more was sent to the president by Secretaries Johnson and Acheson (State) on April 7, 1950.

NSC 68 is difficult to summarize, since it was a *tour d'horizon* of the many issues, political, military, economic, social, ideological, cultural, and even moral, raised by the policy of Soviet containment. As George Kennan (who had a hand in the drafting) had emphasized back in early 1946, the Kremlin's cold war offensive was not only worldwide but comprehensive, ranging from local military action to economic aid and political infiltration and destabilization. The dominant theme of NSC 68 was clearly set forth at the outset: Stalin and

his Kremlin colleagues were driven by imperative "design" to rule the world
after first solidifying their hold over the Soviet and surrounding states.

> The design . . . calls for the complete subversion or forcible destruction of
> the machinery of government and structure of society in the countries of
> the non-Soviet world and their replacement by an apparatus and structure
> subservient to and controlled from the Kremlin. To that end Soviet efforts
> are now directed toward the domination of the Eurasian land mass. The
> United States, as the principal center of power in the non-Soviet world
> and the bulwark of opposition to Soviet expansion, is the principal enemy
> whose integrity and vitality must be subverted or destroyed by one means
> or another if the Kremlin is to achieve its fundamental design.

The forceful prose and the stark, confrontational ideas it expressed tended to
obscure an important assumption, namely, that all regimes that called themselves—or that Washington labeled—"Communist" must be, in the words of
NSC 68, "subservient to and controlled by the Kremlin." Although the danger
of Kremlin expansion across the Eurasian landmass by any and all means served
as a critical policy backdrop, the immediate concern expressed in NSC 68 was
military—the imminent threat of a surprise Soviet nuclear and even thermonuclear attack on the United States, "the bulwark of opposition to Soviet expansion." A nuclear or thermonuclear Pearl Harbor was a horrifying possibility
that had to be accepted. The recommended response to this unprecedented threat
to national security was an immediate and substantial upgrade of the national
military, air, and naval establishments.

> The United States now faces the contingency that within the next four or
> five years the Soviet Union will possess the military capability of delivering
> a surprise atomic attack of such weight that the United States must have
> substantially increased general air, ground, and sea strength, atomic capa-
> bilities, and air and civilian defenses to deter war and to provide reasonable
> assurances, in the event of war, that it could survive the initial blow and
> go on to the eventual attainment of its objectives.

In case anybody missed the point, Acheson and Johnson urged the president to
direct the National Security Council, which included General Bradley as chairman of the Joint Chiefs, "to coordinate and insure the implementation of the
Conclusions herein on an urgent and continuing basis for as long as necessary
to achieve our objectives." In other words, in a world where the enemy now
possessed the means of destroying a significant portion of the nation, puerile

turf battles among airmen, sailors, and soldiers were no longer acceptable. In his later account of the development of NSC 68, Acheson noted that the drafters shrewdly refused to discuss the financial costs of such a massive policy shift. "To have attempted one would have made impossible all those occurrences and prevented any recommendation to the President." This also applied to the bureaucratic implementation of the policy.[71]

Two months and thirteen days after Truman implicitly accepted NSC 68 by directing that further work be done to elaborate the policies contained therein, the North Korean People's Army invaded South Korea on a quiet, peaceful Sunday morning, abruptly ending nearly five years of uneasy international peace. To the administration and defense establishment it was evident beyond question that the Kremlin and its Chinese ally were behind this act of naked aggression designed to further by outright military force the Kremlin's long-term plan to control the Eurasian landmass and ultimately destroy the United States. Was it a matter of mere happenstance that Communist aggression in Korea occurred at a moment when Soviet nuclear weapon and delivery capabilities were advancing at a dramatic, indeed terrifying, rate? No one could be sure.

NSC 68 abruptly became frighteningly pertinent, a seemingly clear-eyed depiction of the cold war world that offered well-conceived responses to Soviet-directed international Communist expansion. Its ideas and assumptions would remain the centerpiece of the nation's cold war response down to the fall of the Soviet Union forty years later. NSC 68 reflected an eternal, driving fear at the core of mid- and late-twentieth-century American cold war policy: the Soviet appetite for world domination was insatiable, and the Kremlin would stop at nothing, including World War III, to achieve it. Eternal vigilance and hair-trigger response grounded in large, permanent, flexible, continually improving military, naval, and air establishments were the only sure guarantees of Western survival. Every cold war president from Truman to George H. W. Bush either accepted the premises of NSC 68, modified them, or played against them to a limited degree. But none could afford to ignore the document and the message it contained. The spirit if not the letter of NSC 68 justified stopping Communist aggression in Korea and became the foundation for Eisenhower's "New Look" military policy, which emphasized the need to combat possible nuclear and thermonuclear war through preponderant weapon stockpiles and superior delivery systems (of which the nuclear-powered strategic-ballistic-missile submarine came to be the chief symbol). The spirit if not letter of NSC 68 was behind Ike's "domino theory" in Vietnam, which both Kennedy and Johnson implicitly accepted, sending up to half a million troops to Vietnam in a feckless effort to re-

solve a civil war. And NSC 68 lay behind the "pactomania" that after the early
fifties tied the United States to Southeast Asia, the Middle East, Australia, and
New Zealand in addition to earlier commitments to Latin America and the Western European–North Atlantic area. NSC 68 perfectly articulated what might be
called reactive imperialism. It also provided the United States Navy with a framework within which to develop and pursue mission roles and responsibilities.

Despite more than four years of decline, the navy was far from powerless when
the Korean War broke out. It remained by far the world's largest sea service, the
only one capable of dramatic revival. Fortunately for both the service and the
American taxpayer, much of the huge fleet built between 1942 and 1947, ranging from aircraft carriers to replenishment vessels and LCIs (landing craft infantry), had been cocooned in "mothballs" by farsighted planners, their vital
guns and machinery protected from corrosion through a process of dehumidi-
fication followed by sealing in airtight plastic packages. Recommissioning took
minimum time, and the carriers, cruisers, and battlewagons that were hastily
brought back into service in 1950–1952 were large enough to accommodate
nearly all of the steadily advancing technologies that naval and civilian laboratories were providing the fleet,

Moreover, the navy fancied that it did have one unique and immediate mission responsibility in the pre-Korea cold war years. With more than three hundred submarines, the Soviets were assumed to have the capability of mounting
a significant challenge at sea. Though many Soviet boats were small and elderly,
fit only for coastal defense, many of Germany's leading naval architects and scientists had wound up in Russian hands in 1945, and the Kremlin thus enjoyed
access to such important advanced technologies as the Schnorkel and the acoustic
torpedo, which gave their larger boats both near-limitless underwater-cruising
capabilities and devastating firepower. In response, the United States steadily improved its sonar capabilities, developed throw-ahead depth charges that could
be fired in salvos, and began planning its elaborate SOSUS network of permanent and sophisticated detection devices to be sown across the Atlantic and
Pacific seabeds. In 1948 the New York Shipbuilding Yard at Camden, New Jersey, began construction of the world's first "hunter-killer" antisubmarine cruiser,
the fifty-six hundred–ton USS *Norfolk,* and a year later Congress approved funds
for three hunter-killer submarines and four advanced antisubmarine frigates of
the *Mitscher* class. At the same time, the first squadron of jet fighters completed
qualifications aboard the light carrier *Saipan* and in late 1949 prepared to
embark on its initial overseas deployment to the western Pacific aboard the fleet
carrier *Valley Forge.* Faced with ever more severe reductions in manpower (the

Valley Forge carried less than half its normal wartime complement when it became the only carrier available to respond to the North Korean attack), the
navy built up a large, organized reserve in the late forties, subject to immediate
recall in a national emergency. When mothballed carriers like *Princeton* and *Essex,*
together with supporting battleships, cruisers, destroyers, and fleet auxiliaries,
were hastily broken out and returned to duty in the late summer and autumn
of 1950, trained crews were there to man them and get them into action.[72]

Even strategic planning began moving the navy's way. When Forrest Sherman
became CNO late in 1949, he stressed his willingness both to fight for service
interests and to cooperate with the other members of the Joint Chiefs of Staff
in forging a grand national strategy. Early in 1950 the Joint Chiefs received
three sets of plans, which became the JCS 1844, 2143, and 1920 series. Each
of these plans envisaged an aggressive power-projecting role for naval carrier
aircraft against Soviet "shipping, naval and air forces, bases, and installations,"
together with blockade and mining operations by surface battle groups. The
1844 and 2143 series, developed around the turn of the year 1949–1950 when
overall American force levels were low, assumed such operations would be undertaken by the limited carrier forces currently in hand, that is, "the existing weak
force structure," together with just eight carriers mobilized from the mothball
fleet during the first two years of the projected conflict. Sherman and his colleagues rejected the plans as "not indicative of either naval thinking or naval capabilities." The 1920 series, a long-range strategic plan for war in 1957 called
"Dropshot," was more promising. Although never officially accepted as policy
by the Joint Chiefs, "it represented," according to the leading historian of the
subject, "the state of American strategic thinking." In case of war, Dropshot
advocated "an early offensive against Soviet submarines and aircraft and their
bases and supporting facilities." But it implied much more. According to an
accompanying map titled "Naval Air Target Coverage," U.S. fleet carriers operating from the North Pacific through the upper Arabian Sea, around to the eastern and central Mediterranean, and up to the Barents Sea would send air strikes
into the Soviet Union in a series of arcs 770, 1,220, and 1,500 miles in depth
to reach targets over nearly 80 percent of the entire Soviet landmass plus Western Europe, together with a substantial coastal strip of China. The objective of
these strikes would remain the same: destruction of enemy naval and merchant
shipping, submarine assembly and repair facilities, and naval bases and the air
defenses around them. Additionally, the navy would undertake a vigorous mining
of enemy sea approaches, hunter-killer operations against enemy submarines,
"and the destruction of enemy naval forces which get to sea." But the enormous

depth of operations, in which only Outer Mongolia and western Siberia would lie beyond the range of naval airpower, suggested that Sherman and his planners had won tacit approval from their army and air force colleagues to consider, indeed prepare for, critical tactical missions by carrier air over Western Europe against advancing Soviet ground forces, in southern Europe against key Soviet installations in the Crimea and beyond, and in the Far East as necessary. Since the heaviest and longest-range aircraft capable of operating from the three *Midway* battle carriers would soon carry nuclear weapons, and an even larger and more capable "supercarrier" was being talked about in the wake of the North Korean invasion, the navy might even serve as a complement or supplement to the air force's Strategic Air Command (SAC). Indeed, the navy's forward-positioned carriers might well be better placed to deliver the first heavy nuclear or conventional blows of World War III than the air force.[73]

By 1952, with the progressive miniaturization of nuclear weaponry (the "atomic" battlefield "cannon" was only three years in the future), most fleet carriers went on global deployments with atomic weapons in their bellies and were positioned, if not precisely where Dropshot proposed, then at least close enough so that twelve to thirty-six hours' hard steaming could place them there. The carrier navy was now on the periphery of the strategic-warfare game. Within just a few years, Dwight Eisenhower, pursuing his New Look strategy, would formally ratify the carrier's critical role, then take the navy's submarine force into the very center of strategic play.

CHAPTER 2

Going MAD

The Nuclearization of Sea Power

LESS THAN A DECADE after the "revolt of the admirals" the United States Navy had staged an astonishing revival, due in part to circumstance (Korea), in part to national policy commitments (continued elaboration and practical implementation of NSC 68), and in part to three men: Dwight Eisenhower, Secretary of the Navy Charles Thomas, and Chief of Naval Operations Arleigh Burke. Even as disgraced admirals went into retirement at midcentury, the outlines of yet another new navy were slowly taking shape in laboratories, factories, and testing facilities from one end of the country to the other. Ike, Thomas, and Burke brought it into being.

When the North Korean Army rushed over the thirty-eighth parallel that midcentury Sunday morning, *Valley Forge* swung rapidly toward the peninsula and its air group raced off the flight deck to attack the North Korean capital of Pyongyang before steaming south again to support American units rushed over from Japan to stop the enemy any way they could. Sister ships *Boxer* and *Philippine Sea,* the latter just transferred from the Atlantic, soon joined the fray, together with several escort carriers embarking Marine Corps close-support Corsair fighters. Roving over a constantly shifting, moving battlefield, striking oncoming enemy formations wherever they were found, navy and marine tactical aircraft proved invaluable in slowing a North Korean offensive strong in men and artillery but bereft of air cover. Within weeks Louis Johnson told Forrest Sherman, Denfeld's successor as chief of naval operations, "I will give you another carrier when you want it." Sherman successfully pressed for a revived (and revised) supercarrier design. The navy would name the lead ship of the class *Forrestal.* When the Korean War halted by truce in July 1953, the active carrier fleet had grown from seven to twelve attack vessels and from eight to fifteen light fleet and escort carriers, more than enough to maintain, indeed upgrade, the strength of the Sixth Fleet in the Mediterranean and the Seventh Fleet in the Far East.[1]

The introduction of jet aircraft onto comparatively small and above all straight carrier decks between 1949 and 1953 posed great technological and operational problems. "It is difficult for carrier pilots of later generations to appreciate the formidable emotional and physical tasks that faced pilots of the early 1950s, whether they were flying jets or props," wrote one veteran of that confused era of change and expansion. America's frontline naval aviators

> were often inadequately trained and, in jet squadrons, sometimes led by pilots who did not understand what jets could or could not do, and often, through ignorance or stubbornness, placed their pilots in situations from which there was no safe way out. It was difficult enough for the new pilot in his first fleet squadron, fresh from Pensacola and jet transitional training: he still had the physical reactions and invincibility of youth to get him through the rough times, if he was good enough or lucky enough.

Korea brought a flood of reservists back to the fleet. Many of them had been multiengine or seaplane pilots during World War II. Most were settled family men now with civilian careers, "suddenly thrust into flying situations that were totally foreign" to them, demanding "skills [they] did not possess." It made little difference whether a pilot was flying a Hellcat, Corsair, Banshee, or Panther. "The catastrophic accident rate of the [first] postwar decade was the worst in the history of peacetime aviation."[2]

Nonetheless, when Eisenhower came to power in 1953 he quickly grasped the value of aircraft carriers, telling congressional leaders the following year that "we must depend on our naval air arm through means of the big carrier. We need these carriers so that in time of emergency we can establish floating bases anyplace in the world from which we can hit the enemy. We must, therefore, put emphasis on air and naval air and," Ike added, obviously thinking of the potential of a future intercontinental ballistic undersea boat, "of course, submarines."[3]

The White House's newfound fondness for the aircraft carrier was part of the emerging "New Look" that Eisenhower himself pressed upon the various defense agencies and offices around and beyond Washington. Ironically, it was

Arthur Radford, newly appointed chairman of the Joint Chiefs of Staff, who coined the term during a talk at the National Press Club shortly before Christmas 1953. Essentially, Ike wanted to informally reorganize the Pentagon around strategic concepts rather than rigid service roles and, most important, to reallocate resources to serve and support those concepts. Ike maintained that modern combat forces could be classified under five basic categories: nuclear retaliatory or strike forces; forces deployed overseas; forces to keep the global sea-lanes open in times of crisis and emergency; forces to protect the United States from attack, primarily from the air; and, finally, reserve forces. The nuclear retaliatory or strike forces, of course, stood at the apex of the national defense establishment and national security apparatus, and here Eisenhower again warmed navy hearts. Although the Strategic Air Command's "heavy intercontinental bomber" remained the "backbone" of the nation's nuclear strike force, "the Navy, with its attack carriers," would also make "a contribution, particularly in the Far East." And, of course, only a war fleet could be guaranteed to keep the global sea-lanes open in peace and war. Although Eisenhower's defense budgets declined slightly after 1954, he maintained "a defense establishment in which all three of the services were to remain far larger, stronger, and more effective than ever previously in peacetime." The proposed budget for fiscal year 1954 "was three times that of 1950." The navy quickly fell into line, and CNO Mick Carney informed the president that "the Navy was tailoring its forces to follow these policies, increasing its early striking power and cutting back amphibious forces, not so necessary as formerly, in the early stages of hostilities."[4]

Assured of Eisenhower's support, the carrier boys promptly transformed their big ships with the addition of angled and strengthened flight decks, powerful steam catapults, and mirror landing systems, essential improvements for "the wholesale use of high-performance jet aircraft" at sea.[5] Enclosed "hurricane" bows were also adopted for greater watertight integrity and seaworthiness. All these design changes were the products of Britain's Royal Air Establishment that continued to flourish during the first postwar decade, even as Her Majesty's fleets declined steadily in size if not capability. The angled flight deck was particularly important, allowing simultaneous launch and landing of aircraft and a larger parking area that materially reduced launch times. *Forrestal,* the first of what would ultimately be seventeen "supercarriers," initially went to sea in the autumn of 1955, to be followed each year or year and a half through the late sixties by a sister ship or a carrier of even more advanced design. The four-and-a-half-acre reinforced flight decks of these superships permitted rapid and flexible operations by air groups composed of as many as ninety to ninety-five planes.

But what exactly did Eisenhower give his carrier sailors? In an age in which "massive retaliation," "balance of terror," and other phrases were in daily usage, it is easy to confuse nuclear strike capabilities with strategic capabilities. After 1953 Eisenhower assigned the carrier fleet the former but not the latter. In World War III the Strategic Air Command's B-52 heavy intercontinental bombers, not the small tactical bombers aboard Atlantic and Pacific Fleet supercarriers, would obliterate Moscow, Leningrad, and perhaps a score of other key enemy urban-industrial-communication centers. Within that firmly conceived framework, however, the carriers had a potentially decisive role to play. The Far East was important, but in World War III Europe was where the action would be. Sherman had articulated the navy's dream of bringing carrier-based conventional or tactical nuclear weaponry to bear from the Mediterranean and Norwegian Sea flanks onto Soviet columns and support forces crunching their way across Western Europe toward the Channel, while striking the "Soviet north" and southern Russia with "nuclear firepower." Carney sold it to the Eisenhower administration.

Not only did Carney run with the ball in Washington; he and his colleagues within NATO naval circles did just as well in Paris, getting NATO to agree on the formation of a multinational "Strike Fleet Atlantic." In the event of war the fleet would rapidly coalesce, then rush up into the Norwegian Sea to assault Soviet naval installations in the Murmansk–Archangel Oblast area, thus ending what even then was perceived as the rising threat of the Soviet Northern Fleet by "incinerating it at the source." The expected counterattack by Soviet submarines would be countered and destroyed by a strike fleet "far more heavily escorted than any convoy." NATO units in the Mediterranean, meanwhile, spearheaded by the Sixth Fleet, would strike at the Crimea and farther inland. These tactical nuclear missions "to be delivered against land targets" were "expected to be" the U.S. Navy carriers' "main contribution to a NATO war."[6]

The aircraft carrier thus resumed its place at the apex of American sea power. From the time that the first nuclear bomb components went to sea aboard the three *Midway*-class ships in the early fifties until a sufficient number of *George Washington*–class strategic-missile submarines became available a decade later, the biggest carriers were assigned a vital nuclear strike role as part of an emerging "triad" of national nuclear and thermonuclear capability. They also became prime targets of the slowly growing Soviet Navy.[7] The fifteen or so upgraded *Essex*-class ships provided invaluable tactical, defensive, and antisubmarine support.

But while the navy eventually won the battle over carriers (with substantial help from the North Koreans and Chinese), Eisenhower and his navy secretary, Charles S. Thomas, soon concluded that its leadership left something to be desired. When it became time to relieve Carney as chief of naval operations in the summer of 1955, Thomas discovered "a lot of things that he was dissatisfied with." Eisenhower's New Look was in full swing, but "the Navy was too slow in adopting a lot of new ideas, mostly in weapons systems." Moreover, Carney talked too much about the wrong things. When he told reporters in the spring of 1955 that the Communist regime in Beijing could take the Nationalist-held islands just offshore within a week or a month, Ike exploded in anger. "By God, this has got to stop. Those fellows like Carney" and U.S. Army Chief of Staff Matthew B. Ridgway, "don't yet realize their services have been integrated," he told his press secretary, James Hagerty, "and that they have in addition to myself, a boss in Admiral Radford who is Chairman of the Joint Chiefs of Staff. They are giving just their own service's viewpoint and presenting it as the entire Administration viewpoint." Ike added that he would speak to both Defense Secretary Charles Wilson and Radford about Carney's indiscretion.[8] The navy not only needed leadership that would ensure advances in weapon systems "reasonably and who would generate support for them" within a still badly fractured organization but also required someone who knew how to work with others, when to speak and when not. What the navy needed and wanted, in short, was a combination of John "Jacky" Fisher—the hard-driving sea dog who had transformed the British Admiralty and the Royal Navy in the early years of the century—and a Dean Rusk–type diplomat who understood administration policy and was comfortable in following it. Thomas thought he knew who that was; so did his immediate boss, Defense Secretary Charles Wilson, and so did Ike. They were all correct. Reaching far down the seniority list, Thomas summoned newly minted rear admiral Arleigh A. Burke to his office and told him, "You're it!"

Burke claimed uninterest. He didn't want it, "didn't want it at all, as a matter of fact—at that time." Too many exciting command experiences remained to be savored, including head of either the Atlantic or the Pacific Fleet, before he felt reasonably qualified to be CNO. "I wasn't very ambitious," he told an interviewer in 1972, "and I was very much concerned, the way I am concerned now, that the officials of the government felt that the Navy did not have good line officers who could become CNO." But orders were orders, and Burke was aware that the frustrating and prolonged bureaucratic struggles of the previous decade had obscured some dramatic advances within the navy in both weapons and ship design, advances that fitted right in with the nuclear-retaliatory or strike-force concept of the New Look.[9]

Robert Goddard, the father of American rocketry, had been launching crude, liquid-fueled missiles since the midthirties, and in the later war years far-seeing sailors and scientists, mindful of Nazi rocket developments, began to explore the possibilities of long-range, sea-based ballistic missiles but divided over whether they should be liquid or solid fueled and whether surface or subsurface vessels were the most feasible launch platforms. The navy and private enterprise teamed to develop a family of "Gorgon" ship-to-air pulse-jet missiles much like Germany's V-1 and a liquid-fueled ship-based surface-to-air missile with a solid fuel booster called "Lark," which served from 1946 to 1952 as an invaluable test vehicle. In 1945–1946 Operation Paper Clip brought several hundred former Nazi scientists, among them young rocket genius Wernher von Braun, to the United States, together with perhaps twice as many liquid-fueled V-1 and V-2 rockets. In September 1947 *Midway* became the first surface ship to successfully fire a long-range missile from its deck when it shot a captured German V-2 rocket into the Atlantic off Norfolk. "It was very spectacular but obviously not very practical," recalled Admiral William F. "Red" Raborn, father of the later Polaris program, "because of the size of the missile and because the ship moved around too much in the seaway."[10]

Engineers and submariners at Point Mugu, California, were already hard at work on a more feasible alternative. Several months before the *Midway* test, which received some public attention, the World War II fleet submarine *Cusk* launched a modified V-1 called "Loon." Radio controlled both by the submarine and a chase plane, the missile flew for several miles and dumped on target. "The *Cusk* had just made history." Indeed it had, for the test flight contained nearly every element needed to create an effective long-range, low-level attack "cruise" missile. Engineers had built and successfully tested a powerful "launch sled" configured to the short, narrow dimensions of the submarine's main deck (along with a two-missile hangar), together with a radio-control system employing *Cusk*'s own air-search radar modified to send codes. A year later the program almost came to a halt when an errant missile dove back on *Cusk* and exploded spectacularly in a burst of kerosene, convincing horrified onlookers that the submarine had been sunk. It wasn't even damaged, but the program was in decided jeopardy at a time when multiple communities within and beyond the service were fighting for every research and development penny they could find. Necessary modifications were made, and in 1949 *Cusk*'s sister, *Carbonero*, launched a Loon that found and flew over the fleet, despite radar detection, fighter-aircraft attacks, "and heavy anti-aircraft fire." From that moment on, the navy was determined to have some sort of missile capability. By 1951 Chance Vought Corporation had developed the "Regulus," which in a spectacular test was controlled in part by *Cusk* and in part by a chase plane near target, before diving supersonically and intact into the ground just a mile from its aiming point. "With a nuclear weapon on board," aviation writer and documentary filmmaker Nick T. Spark wrote half a century later with perhaps intended irony, "this would have been more than good enough." The navy promptly worked to improve its submarine onboard guidance system while converting four diesel-powered boats to guided-missile capabilities along with four heavy and six light cruisers. Early in 1956 the upgraded *Essex*-class carrier *Randolph* successfully launched a Regulus from its deck, and by the end of the year a number of carriers deployed to the Sixth and Seventh Fleets, either with missiles or with chase planes capable of guiding Regulus projectiles to target. From the midfifties to the early sixties, half a dozen Regulus-equipped submarines operated "as the Navy's front-line weapons in the Pacific." With their effective missile range confined to about three hundred miles, the Regulus boats had to cruise close to Russian shores. One of the boats found itself caught in the midst of a Soviet antisubmarine exercise, but managed to slip away before being detected. All boats were poised to deliver small, nuclear-tipped missiles to Soviet ports and submarine facilities. Several weapon tests were conducted in sub-Arctic waters, while at least one sub, *Barbero,* deployed with the Sixth Fleet in the Mediterranean during the Lebanon crisis of 1958. Regulus was such a powerful weapon system that deployment schedules were brutal. The notion of alternating crews did not occur to planners and schedulers prior to the appearance of the first nuclear-powered strategic-ballistic-missile boats in 1960. Some Regulus diesel boats deployed for up to sixty days before returning all too briefly to Pearl Harbor (the main staging base) for the hastiest of overhauls and crew rest and recreation before setting out again for the distant, dangerous coasts of Northeast Asia.

The navy carefully disguised Regulus capabilities and missions. Not until 1959, with the impending appearance of the first big nuclear-powered strategic-ballistic-missile submarines, did the Pentagon hint in a *National Geographic* caption beneath *Grayback* launching a Regulus missile that "today's nuclear weapons give the submarine far greater destructive power than a World War II aircraft carrier." "Latest guided missiles can be launched under water to pulverize cities a thousand miles away," the caption continued in a preview of the advanced Polaris design. With the hindsight of a half century, Regulus sailors realized that they had had in hand the world's first effective cruise missile and wondered why the navy had canceled supersonic Regulus II. Surely, such a low-level attack missile could have perfectly complemented the sub-launched long-range missiles from Polaris through Poseidon to Trident. A one-two missile punch from the sea could have overwhelmed the Soviet defensive system.

Unlike the submariners, the surface navy "blundered into the missile age," failing

> utterly to anticipate the risks and pitfalls of rushing quantities of unproved missile ships into the fleet. While components of the systems usually had been tested individually (computers, directors, fire-control radars, weapon direction systems, air-search radars, gyroscopes, switchboards, generators, telemetry, launching systems, and the missiles themselves), they had not been integrated and tested as an entity before being installed in the [four heavy cruisers].

Thus, "the gun ordnance world was unceremoniously dragged into the age of the digital computer and large, multidisciplinary combat systems that had tiny tolerances for error." One suspects this was also true of the submarine service, especially when it sought to marry its own complex technologies to that of the guided missile. Formidable and costly problems forced the realistic Arleigh Burke and his subordinates to acknowledge that even in the high cold war period that straddled the later Eisenhower and Kennedy years, there were insufficient funds to pursue every promising system or combination of systems.[11]

Burke's genius lay in grasping quickly and thoroughly both the necessity of the new technologies of war and their implications, then prioritizing them in terms of the navy's mission requirements. Fortunately, he was able to draw on the enthusiasm and talent of a remarkable corps of engineers and scientists to get what he wanted. Much of the development work came out of the U.S. Naval Air Warfare Center Weapons Division at China Lake, California, which in the mid and late fifties supplied the fleet with a whole array of first-generation, short-range air-to-air, air-to-surface, and even air- and surface-to-subsurface missiles including Terrier, Talos, and Tartar. Short-range rockets had been part of the navy—and air force—arsenals since World War II, but China Lake brought forth long-range, radar-controlled air-to-air and air-to-surface missiles including the effective Sparrows and Phoenix together with the far less capable Bullpups, Shrikes, and Condors. But one of China Lake's finest developments was the Sidewinder.

Around 1950 Dr. William McLean, head of China Lake's Ordnance Division, got the idea of building a "poor man's missile . . . in terms of cost." According to Admiral Thomas Moorer, a later chief of naval operations, McLean was apparently inspired when he walked past a toy store in Pasadena one day "and saw a little toy jet that uses as its motive power a slow burning propellant which generated gas and blasted out of the tail. . . . So he got the idea of using this slow burning propellant, which was about an inch long and about an inch in diameter to provide the power for the guidance and also run a generator for all the electrical devices in the Sidewinder." At this time, however, the cold war was heating up in Korea, and the armed forces were falling all over each other proposing development of thousands of different kinds of missiles. Fortunately, China Lake

> had some money left over from World War II from the VT [variable time or proximity] fuze development so we spent the money on the Sidewinder on the proposition this was a VT fuze because it had a[n infrared] seeker that focused on the target and as the rocket went past the target the seeker looked around at it. When it hit the stops it made an electrical contact and blew the thing up. So we said this is a fuze.

By 1958 the Philco-GE Ordnance surface-to-air missile was in the fleet as a cheap, workable, reliable system with limitations ("You can't fire it in heavy rain or in a cloud").[12]

None of these first-generation surface and air missiles were nuclear tipped; all were designed either for short-range support of ground offensives or for fleet defense against air and surface attacks. Not for another quarter century would the surface fleet be upgraded to a strategic role with the appearance of the Tomahawk land attack (T-Lam) missiles (developed in conjunction with the Harpoon sixty-nautical-mile short-range missile system). The navy also steadily upgraded its at-sea replenishment techniques and developed ever more elaborate electronic detection systems, not only for the SOSUS ocean-floor submarine identification and tracking system but also for command, communication, control, and intelligence.[13] The capstone of this surge of advanced technology was, of course, the nuclear-powered intercontinental ballistic-missile submarine. By 1956 the upper reaches of the naval establishment were satisfied that the service had regained the power, flexibility, and respect that it had enjoyed during the latter stages of World War II.[14]

No postwar weapon system was as costly, controversial, or overwhelming in its implications as the Polaris program, which married the new nuclear-powered submarine with the most advanced long-range-missile technology. For years, conventional wisdom had it that Polaris came about as a result of Eisenhower's express wish during the tense early years of his administration to counter the possibility of a Pearl Harbor–style Soviet air attack with A-bombs on the United States or its European and Japanese allies. "Not a damned bit" of truth to the story, Burke confidently told an interviewer in 1972, "not a damned bit." Polaris resulted from the ongoing "Air Force–Navy controversy over . . . strategic warfare, the delivery of nuclear weapons on an enemy territory." The airmen insisted that only their Strategic Air Command could do the job; nonetheless, the air force brass hedged their bets by working on development of an intermediate-range ballistic missile (IRBM) called Thor and then a follow-on intercontinental ballistic missile (ICBM) called Atlas. If successful, the programs would fall under SAC jurisdiction. The army was developing its own system called Jupiter. No one in the White House in 1955 was "getting hot" over the issue of ballistic missiles at sea, Burke added, because the research and development problems "were terrible"—and terribly costly.

In fact, the White House *was* "getting hot" about Soviet motives. In February 1955 Eisenhower's Technical Capabilities Panel, chaired by Dr. James R. Killian Jr., president of MIT, told the National Security Council that by the end of the decade, the United States would be extremely vulnerable to a multimegaton thermonuclear attack. The panel urged that the air force's missile program be given top priority, with a secondary initiative undertaken in sea-launched IRBMs. Burke, who had enjoyed frequent contact with the Johns Hopkins University Applied Physics Lab since his brief tenure on the navy's General Board in the late forties, seized the initiative that the Killian panel had provided and ran with it. He soon concluded that if an effective fuel could be developed, "sooner or later . . . reasonably-sized ballistic missiles were going to replace aircraft for the delivery of large quantities of nuclear weapons." Such missiles could not be land based, however, because they were "necessarily very vulnerable—three great big beasts sitting on a launching pad in those days were very vulnerable to very little shock."[15] The navy, however, had just been handed the perfect launch platform for long-range strategic missiles, not only mobile but stealthy to the point of invisibility.

Nautilus, the world's first nuclear-powered submarine, was put in commission in September 1954, six months before the Killian report and nearly a year before Burke became chief of naval operations. The vessel had been developed by a dedicated staff of zealots headed by one of the most complex, abrasive, forceful figures in modern American naval history, Hyman G. Rickover. Rickover eventually came to play Percy Scott, the dedicated early-twentieth-century Royal Navy technocrat, to Burke's Jacky Fisher, though by all accounts the

Briton's career was a model of easy ascent to flag rank compared to the American's tortured path. One might say of Rickover, as the entertainer Oscar Levant said of himself, that he was a very controversial figure whom people either disliked or hated, or, as Winston Churchill famously remarked of Charles de Gaulle, that he was a bull who carried his own china shop around with him. Many respected Rickover, few liked him, and even those who did admitted the man "exert[ed] an iron hold" on everything he touched or influenced. He drove his people to the breaking point, and occasionally beyond, in his relentless insistence on top-quality work and operations. Most found being around him "uncomfortable" and "very embarrassing," as he "browbeat" colleagues and subordinates alike. "I found he was just impossible," Vice Admiral Kent Lee recalled of a weekend cruise submerged with Rickover. "Insulting, never a decent word, 'those idiots from the shipyard and people like you' he'd say to the man." Future chief of naval operations Elmo Zumwalt found Rickover "distasteful to listen to, egotistical, critical, spoke down. I got nothing from the lecture that I recall." Many senior sailors were incensed by Rickover's unwillingness to wear the uniform once he reached the relative shelter of the admiral's star. Alfred Ward thought him "mean," "rough," "ruthless," claiming that his sour personality permanently alienated him from the secretaries of defense and of the navy as well as several chiefs of naval operations.[16]

Rickover's biting contempt for and patent distrust of people, their competence and their motives, was readily understandable. His background was that of the poverty-stricken, frequently despised Jewish immigrant child. Born in a small village north of Warsaw, he had come to America as a young boy, settling with his family on Maxwell Street in Chicago. He saw his driven father, a tailor, rise in the world by sheer grit and competence. Little wonder that as an adult, Hyman Rickover "preached and practiced the gospel of work." Winning one of the few Jewish appointments to Annapolis, the youngster watched as a Jewish classmate was isolated without a word spoken to him for every day of his four years because he dared to display a dash of academic excellence. The fleet Rickover entered, like the society it served, was implicitly, often more than occasionally explicitly, anti-Semitic. Brilliant as well as hardworking, Rickover never commanded a vessel larger than "an ancient minesweeper," the *Finch*, "pressed into use to move Marines to China" in the late thirties. At the outbreak of war, he was back in Washington at the navy's Bureau of Ships (BuShips), "one of the unsung engineers who planned and built the ships that others would sail to battle and glory." Stifled, ignored, marginalized, his career something of a humiliation, it is little wonder Rickover seethed with suppressed resentments and contempt that burst out irrepressibly when he at last found himself better positioned than anyone else in 1946 to design and build revolutionary new vessels.[17]

After World War II it was inevitable that the navy would go nuclear; the questions were how and in what ways. Some sailors believed that "primary efforts in atomic energy should go into weapons." Others, like Deputy Chief of Naval Operations Mick Carney wanted a global ban on nuclear warships, "fearing that if the United States had them at a future time so would its enemies." But one community was avid for nuclear power from the beginning. Submariners realized that harnessing this unique energy source would transform their weapon system from a surface ship with limited submergence capabilities into a virtually undetectable stealth system that spent the vast majority of its time far beneath the waves. The undersea community enjoyed the enthusiastic support of Chester Nimitz, hero of the Pacific war and himself a former submariner. Rickover swiftly aligned himself with these people, speaking out boldly for a nuclear-powered submarine and never letting obstacles or frustrations deter or defeat him. In 1946 he got himself assigned to the nuclear facilities at Oak Ridge, Tennessee, where he formed a small team of dedicated enthusiasts, and with the kind of ruthless cunning for playing bureaucratic politics he had first displayed during the war in BuShips, he eventually got to the right people (Edward Teller) and the right superiors (Nimitz and Navy Secretary John L. Sullivan) for concept support and eventual project approval. In July 1948, following months of maneuver and sweat, Rickover was at last given both the title and the practical authority over the navy's nuclear-power program. Six months later he was effectively "double hatted" as nuclear-propulsion czar by both the navy and the Atomic Energy Commission. He immediately proved to be as much an administrative genius as an able bureaucrat, blending the frequent administrative chaos of the New Deal with the costly crash research program of the Manhattan Project to build a shipboard atomic-power plant as rapidly as possible. "By the end of the year his organization involved two federal agencies (the Navy Department and the Atomic Energy Commission), two relatively autonomous groups within those agencies (the Bureau of Ships and the commission's division of reactor development), and three research organizations (Argonne National Laboratory, the Westinghouse Electric Corporation, and the General Electric Company)." Five years later facilities for building *Nautilus* and its later sisters stretched from Idaho (the National Reactor Testing Station) to Connecticut (the Electric Boat Company).[18]

Even those who came to dislike Rickover vigorously were forced to admire him. Unlike other chiefs of naval operations, Arleigh Burke exhibited "absolute warmest respect" for Rickover. The CNO was no fool. For the good of the navy

he would channel and control Rickover's insatiable thrusts for power and responsibility over the entire nuclear-submarine program. But within these limits Burke
treated Rickover decently, insisting that the apostle of nuclear power and his
wife be invited to all flag parties and urging those present "to make sure that
people talked with Admiral Rickover because he didn't want him to have any
feeling of being an outsider." Ward and others might willfully ignore some
understandable sources of Rickover's conduct, but they did understand that the
admiral's drive for perfection stemmed in part from a determination that the
American taxpayer obtain the most from very complex and costly programs.
They also appreciated his ability to handle Congress. Ward claimed in a 1972
interview that Rickover's skill derived from being Jewish "and therefore a minority race.... [A]nd the Congress was very careful not to alienate minorities." The
slur reflected more on Ward's attitude, which was regrettably widespread in the
service and the country even at that late date, than on Rickover's presenta-
tional capabilities. "More importantly," Ward added correctly, Rickover treated
congressmen and senators with extraordinary deftness, not only agreeing with
what they said but amplifying it in ways that suggested that Congressman X or
Senator Y was a genius. In short, Rickover was a more than able partisan for his
cause and an adept political lobbyist in the bargain.[19]

Rickover harbored a surprisingly sensitive side that few ever saw. One who
did was Captain Tom Weschler. For some while in the late fifties, Rickover
begged his CNO to come up to the Bettis factory in West Mifflin, Pennsylvania,
to familiarize himself with nuclear-power plants, their dimensions, what kind
of ships they could be used in, and so on. At last Burke made the journey, and
at the end of a long day he abruptly got in his limousine and was driven off to
an affair in Pittsburgh, leaving just Weschler and Rickover alone. When Rickover discovered that Weschler had to get to the distant Pittsburgh airport he
said, "I'll drive you." Speeding along, Weschler hesitantly began to query the
admiral about his work and methods and got some surprisingly candid replies.
Rickover explained his mania for safety: "I have a son. I love my son. I want
everything that I do to be so safe that I would be happy to have my son operating it. That's my fundamental rule." Weschler soon discovered that Rickover's
mania had a corollary: too many cooks spoiled any broth. "The second you get
a new project here in Washington, you're going to find out you have a million
helpers," Rickover told him. "Every one of them wants to help get your program
through because it's going to be a platform for their gadgets. I was building a
nuclear submarine, and that's what it was going to be, and I didn't need all those
other people who would have sunk my ship, or the project."[20]

Nautilus quickly demonstrated the astounding capabilities of the nuclear-powered submarine. On its shakedown cruise in 1955 (the same year the navy deployed its first conventionally powered supercarrier, *Forrestal*) the submarine traveled thirteen hundred miles totally submerged at an average speed of sixteen knots, remaining beneath the surface for eighty-four hours. Eventually, the vessel sailed more than sixty thousand miles (including under the North Pole), almost always submerged, on little more than eight pounds of uranium before its reactor core was pulled for replacement.[21] Carrier admirals were forced to take grudging notice of the possibility that such a vessel could sweep surface ships off the seas, especially after the fast, teardrop-shaped nuclear sub *Skipjack* later theoretically sank every aircraft carrier in the Sixth Fleet during maneuvers in the Mediterranean.[22]

Burke took note of nuclear-powered submarines for another reason. These comparatively large, roomy craft could be lengthened and widened even further to provide the prime launching pad for an effective sea-based ballistic-missile system. Burke went first to the air force, then to the army, saying that he wanted "about a foot in your missile to put in the equipment that's going to be needed for a Navy missile." He would pay a reasonable cost. The air force said no; its Thor and Atlas programs were too complex and too far along in development to make room for navy needs and requirements. The Army said yes, and the navy piggybacked its research and development on Jupiter for as long as necessary before splitting off to finish development of its own unique missile.

Burke's first task was "get the concepts" of a sea-based ballistic-missile system "moving. So I wanted to find somebody to run it." He wanted a man who "could get other people to do a hell of a lot of work and had an idea of organizing his work and who could get things done without creating a fight and without going around and demanding things. We've had enough of—like Rickover, for example," who was fine for research and development work but not for the critical follow-on where "willing participation" was essential. After an exhaustive search Burke settled on Captain William F. "Red" Raborn, called him in, and told him two things: First, he could have the pick of any top forty people in the service and no more, because forty was the optimum number that "one man can handle by himself." Second, "If this thing works, you're going to be one of the greatest people that ever walked down the pike. . . . If it fails, I'll have your throat."[23]

Burke first made sure that Rickover was "cut out" of the fleet ballistic-missile decision and the initial research work. Putting a complex missile system aboard a submarine was adding the kind of elaborate bells and whistles to an already successful program that sent Rickover into a rage. It was a wise decision, but even so, "Rick" would all too soon prove to be a major impediment to effective advanced submarine design. Simply put, his obsession with nuclear propulsion was not matched by a mastery of its problems. Some in the defense community harbored a suspicion that loss of the fast, deep-diving nuclear sub *Thresher* in the spring of 1963 was due to fatal flaws in Rickover's nuclear reactor, though others dismissed the idea out of hand.[24] Nonetheless, the doomed vessel and her sisters were already deemed too large and noisy for their hunter-killer role against Soviet U-boats. In January 1968 *Enterprise* tried to outrun a trailing Soviet submarine between the West Coast and Pearl Harbor only to discover that the Russian sub could easily match the nuclear carrier's top speed of thirty-one knots. Rickover's only solution to this startling advance in Soviet underwater capabilities was a reactor so big as to make the boats that carried it at once overlarge, too slow, and incapable of operation at sufficient depth to be effective against Russian counterparts. Rickover was still able to ram his solution through the Pentagon brass. According to one U.S. submarine admiral, American hunter-killer boats suffered from crippling disabilities in speed and operating depth right down to the end of the cold war. It was fortunate, I. J. Galantin maintained, that even the numerous boats of the advanced *Los Angeles* class never had to test their effectiveness in combat against Soviet counterparts. Rickover nonetheless continued to dominate the navy's nuclear-power program into the early seventies, with often disruptive effects on the navy's personnel system.[25] Powerful congressional supporters frustrated every White House and Pentagon effort to get rid of him.

Having nonetheless managed to brush Rickover aside from the ballistic-missile program, Burke then overrode those who had absorbed too well the lesson derived from the battle over the supercarrier *United States:* that naval power must never be designed for use against prime strategic targets like Soviet urban-industrial centers and complexes. The CNO established a Special Projects Office under now rear admiral Raborn's direction, then left the man and his team alone. Raborn and his men worked with physicist Edward Teller to develop both the solid-fuel propellant and the six hundred–pound nuclear warhead needed to create an effective subsurface-launched strategic missile that would ultimately come close to matching the air force's ICBMs in range, payload, and sophistication. Rickover was then given the specifications for the kind of submarine necessary to carry such weapons, and the sixteen-tube *George Washington* class was born by cutting open a nuclear-powered attack submarine already on the builder's ways and inserting a missile compartment amidships. Sixteen

*George Washington*s were eventually built (the last fifteen from the keel up), followed by the *Ethan Allen* class and several subsequent generations of ever more
advanced and elaborate boats. One of Burke's biographers has rightly emphasized that the admiral's bold decision to develop a fleet ballistic missile on a priority basis reflected not only his commitment to enhancing the navy's capabilities but also "his desire to integrate the service into the broader context of
national defense."[26] The CNO of 1955–1961 displayed the same strong team-
player spirit he had exhibited during the unification fight of the late forties.

Creating a submarine-based long-range ballistic-missile system posed a series
of brutally difficult interlocking challenges in advanced technology. Raborn later
emphasized that the program involved not just another rocket but "a wholly
new concept of weaponry, the dispatching of this 'bird' from beneath the surface
of the sea." Though Polaris could carry a thermonuclear warhead and possessed
the same fifteen hundred–mile range as army (Jupiter) and air force (Thor)
strategic missiles, it had to be built substantially smaller to fit into a sufficient
number of launch tubes (sixteen in all) in the narrow confines of a submarine.
Of even greater importance was the decision to use solid- rather than liquid-fuel
propellants. "There was just no practical way," Raborn said, "to store or handle
liquid fuels effectively or safely on board a submerged submarine." The Soviets
would never develop an effective solid fuel, and their liquid-fueled ballistic missiles—and torpedoes—were always an immediate danger to crew health and
safety. Another challenge confronting Raborn and his engineers involved "the
wholly naval problem" of designing ships to carry a long-range missile and the
equipment to launch it "from below the surface . . . in fact, from quite deep below
the surface." Raborn's job was to "design stowage, handling, launching, and fire
control equipment which would allow submarines to be used as the launching
platforms for the missile." A host of problems had to be overcome, and Raborn
identified three particularly difficult challenges. "One was to develop equipment which would fire such a missile from below the surface and get it up into
the air where its rocket engines could ignite and take over the job." A second
problem involved navigation. Physicists and engineers had to develop "new and
far more exact methods of determining a ship's position than anything needed
for normal navigation," and they had to do so long before satellite-based global
positioning systems were available. "Quite a few people" had no idea that "one
of the absolute 'musts' in firing a missile at a target fifteen hundred miles away
is to know where *you* are, and very exactly, at the instant of firing. Otherwise, you
can make an awfully costly error in your aim." A final and interrelated problem
involved the creation of a guidance system sufficiently accurate so that the mis-

siles "would actually go where they were directed to go." Every problem was solved, and by 1958 Raborn could—and did—boast that the United States had developed either the ultimate deterrent to war or its most fearsome expression: a combination of "the almost limitless cruising range of the nuclear powered submarine and the vast potential for concealment offered by the ocean depths with the longest range, highest speed and most lethal weapon system ever developed, the H-bomb Armed Ballistic Missile." Raborn, his people, and his superiors had no illusions about what they had achieved. Both sides of the world in 1958 were on hair-trigger alert. They remained so in late 1960 when *George Washington* first went to sea and on into the sixties, seventies, and early eighties when follow-on programs to Polaris—Poseidon and Trident—came into the fleet. Such weapons were not part of any space race or "scientific competition to solve the secrets" of the universe, the admiral said. They represented "a grimly realistic race to meet and cancel out weapons development beyond the Iron Curtain," to assure Soviet "potential aggressors" that no surprise attack, no matter how "thoroughly developed," could wipe out at a stroke all sources of nuclear retaliation.[27]

The strategic-ballistic-missile submarines (SSBNs), soon known as "boomers," were designed—along with the Strategic Air Command's B-52 bombers and a cluster of army and air force land-based intercontinental ballistic missiles—to constitute a "triad" of weapon systems designed for "massive retaliation" in response to any nuclear first strike against the United States. Such power would, at least theoretically, make the United States invulnerable to either thermonuclear blackmail or thermonuclear ambush. Some analysts have emphasized that Eisenhower's acceptance of the SSBN program reflected his desire to rein in the air force, which by 1957 had gone completely overboard, "indulging in" a policy of "gross overkill," to the extent that planned wartime nuclear attacks around the Soviet periphery would kill as many allied civilians as Russians.[28] In fact, if Admiral Robert L. Dennison is to be believed, the question of who would control the boomers remained a hot question up to the moment when the *George Washington* went to sea.

Dennison was commander of the Atlantic Fleet in mid-1960 when he encountered Thomas Gates, now Eisenhower's defense secretary, at a General Motors picnic in Quantico, Virginia. The affair was meant to bring defense contractors and key military people together for "consultations and briefings," food, and a few drinks. That evening Dennison and Gates found themselves closing the party down. The two men had known each other since Gates's tenure as secretary of the navy, and Gates unburdened himself of a problem. The ballistic-missile subs were certainly strategic weapons. The air force's Strategic Air Command "claimed to have exclusive rights over these weapons," though Gates, as an old navy partisan, instinctively thought sailors should have control of their own ships. Still, Gates had been out to SAC Headquarters at Omaha and had seen its superb command-and-control arrangements. Moreover, Tommy Powers, the air force chief of staff, had assured Gates that there were no command layers between the White House, SAC Headquarters, and the B-52 squadron commanders. Surely, the navy couldn't match that!

Dennison assured Gates that as Atlantic Fleet commander he certainly could. "If you assign these Polaris submarines in the Atlantic to me as a unified commander, I will guarantee you that I'll put in a better command and control system than SAC has over his bombers. I will command them personally, not through a whole echelon of division commanders and squadron commanders and so on." That wasn't what the navy had told him, Gates replied. "I'm told the Navy has such a great command organization that they'll control Polaris through the normal chain of command." "Well, I don't know who'd tell you that," Dennison said, "but that isn't what you're going to hear. I just told you what I will do and I'll guarantee it. I'd like to do it." A decision had to be made soon "because time was pressing." Gates "couldn't leave this issue hanging." The secretary pondered Dennison's offer, then made his decision. Within days the word was out. The navy would command and control the ballistic-missile subs.[29]

The ships, aircraft, and missiles of the U.S. fleet were now at the apex of the nation's retaliatory power. Brand-new or substantially upgraded aircraft carriers with atomic weapons in their bellies, a new generation of advanced aircraft on their flight decks, and guided-missile cruisers riding escort stocked the Sixth and Seventh Fleets that patrolled the Mediterranean and western Pacific flanks of what was widely assumed (erroneously) to be a united Sino-Soviet Communist bloc. Soon the first "boomers" would set out for their own undetected patrol areas in the vast seas ringing Russia and China.

The conversion of the U.S. Navy to atomic power, jet aircraft, and guided missiles had been an exhausting effort, and at least one acute naval critic, British writer James Cable, observed years later that one of the casualties had been substantial. "The impetuous pace of technology has not merely left history far behind," he wrote in 1983, "it has out-distanced strategic thought. Such concepts of naval operations as emerge from the Soviet Union or the United States seldom carry entire conviction in their efforts to assign to war at sea its necessary and appropriate place in a wider conflict." Constantly preoccupied with "the increasing intricacies of their matériel," American (and Soviet) admirals were forced to devote what little spare time they had to justifying expenses, rather than considering the most creative means of weapons employment. This emphasis upon technique at the expense of strategy would bedevil the U.S. Navy down to the end of the century and beyond. The post-2000 "network centric battlefield" clearly bewitched policy makers far more than whether, and when, it should be imposed.[30]

Others were bemused and not a little disheartened by the revolutionary changes. When the distinguished military analyst of the *New York Times,* Hanson W. Baldwin, visited the Sixth Fleet in the autumn of 1957, he found a navy dramatically transformed, and not always to his liking. The old commands of 1938 and 1944—"Up late hammocks" and "Sweepers man your brooms"— were superseded by shrill warnings on the loudspeaker of imminent atomic-, biological-, and chemical-warfare attacks demanding immediate removal of all flammable materials from exposed areas and orders to "prepare to rig washdown gear. All exposed personnel take shelter. Man gas masks and protective clothing." The navy, he concluded, had become "a strange blend of tradition and modernism" and filled with "startling contrasts." Gone forever were the familiar silhouettes of the war years. The thousand-odd warships and aircraft that now dominated the world ocean were the products of an ongoing technological revolution at sea "more sweeping than the transition from sail to steam." The new vessels and planes "look like some futuristic doodlings of a naval designer gone mad." Masts and carrier island structures were festooned with "the dark excrescences" of radar antennae of every shape and description, disk shaped, convex, vertical, and horizontal, ceaselessly twisting, revolving, and scanning sea and sky. The new carriers with their canted decks were lopsided and grotesquely misshapen. "Bow-on they seem to advance crablike, sideways," even though each one could make at least thirty-three knots. But the "awful power of the modern navy" lay in its nuclear arsenal. "The A bomb is now a standard part of the armory of all United States front-line carriers," and the captain, exec, and special weapons officer were custodians of "The Things" by virtue of a letter from the Atomic Energy Commission.

The service had changed as dramatically as its weapon systems, and not for the best. Echoing midcentury complaints at the time of the *Missouri* grounding, Baldwin stated that prewar professionalism had disappeared. Sailors were "the weak point in today's Navy." Leadership and experience levels were far too low, and most of the "kids" who ran the monstrous machines "have not really mastered the new technology, have not learned to handle with true professional skill the missiles, the ships, the planes, the electronic devices that make up the

modern fleet." The vast majority were determined short-termers, single-"hitch"
enlistees and their officers who came largely from reserve officer training corps
on the nation's civilian campuses and harbored no real interest in a naval career
at any level. Like the citizen sailors of the recent war, "they have personal pride
and intelligence—most of them—and they are knit together by a small hard-
core—too small, indeed—of professionals," devoted officers, chief and petty
officers "whose life is the Navy." But pride and intelligence were fatally weakened by indifference, Baldwin suggested, and the United States Navy of the late
1950s was something of a hollow shell.[31]

Navy men obviously did not see matters that way. "Nuclear power, supersonic speed, ballistic and guided missiles have set the stage for the golden age of
sea power," Gates enthused in 1956. "The Navy is the service of the future."[32]
Five years later John F. Kennedy discovered just how frightening that future
had become.

Very early in his brief presidency, Kennedy went down to Norfolk with Vice
President Lyndon Johnson, Defense Secretary Robert McNamara, and a gaggle
of congressmen and senators to go to sea with the Atlantic Fleet. Before he did
so, Admiral Dennison decided to put on a show. His sprawling, multistory command center was "built like an auditorium," with a "tremendous screen" that
contained a multitude of track charts, tabulations, information "on anything."
Seating the president at his own command chair close to "communications
outlets, telephones, and computer display screens . . . where he could see everything," Dennison then mounted a briefing platform "to explain what was going
to happen." Kennedy was told that there would be a mock exercise in which
several of the nation's brand-new nuclear-powered submarines would be ordered
to launch some or all of their sixteen nuclear-tipped Polaris intercontinental
ballistic missiles from submerged positions somewhere out in the North Atlantic.
Dennison warned Kennedy that things would happen "so fast that unless you
knew what you were watching you wouldn't realize what had happened. Just a
lot of bang, bang, bang, and then it's all over." Dennison ordered the exercise to
commence. "Well, of course, all hell broke loose. Bells and buzzers and everything else started going." Tapes of official-sounding telephone conversations,
"presumably from the President, the Chairman of the Joint Chiefs of Staff, and
so on, getting the necessary" targeting instructions "and giving the order to
shoot," were played over loudspeaker phones. All the telephones and telephone
keys necessary to order the submarines to launch their missiles were manned
and ready. "People would come in with keys and boxes under their arms and all
the rest of it. Then after the Polaris messages went out, we started sending the

fleet war messages." At that moment, Dennison stopped the exercise; he had made his point. Did Kennedy have any questions? "There was quite an appreciable pause." Finally, the young president asked quietly: "Can these missiles be stopped?" "No, Sir. The submarines are reeling in their underwater antennae, the count-down has started, and there's no way." JFK said nothing more, but he and everyone in that room knew that the United States Navy now possessed the world's ultimate weapon—the submarine-based intercontinental ballistic missile, limitlessly destructive in its capability to blast, burn, and vaporize tens if not hundreds of millions of people. The power of follow-on missiles—the longer-range, ever more precisely accurate Poseidon and Trident—was immeasurably enhanced when in the 1970s they were "MIRVed," that is, equipped with "multiple independently targeted reentry vehicles." The Soviets followed as best they could. In 1988, near the end of the cold war, the United States deployed 5,632 sea-based nuclear warheads, the vast majority aboard submarines. The Soviets possessed around 3,600, about half aboard their "boomers." So far as is publicly known, no patrolling U.S. ballistic-missile submarine has ever been detected.[33]

CHAPTER 3

"Grey Diplomats"

The Sixth and Seventh Fleets in the 1950s

AS THE NEW-LOOK United States Navy moved into the nuclear era, the Sixth and Seventh Fleets, absent significant naval challenge from China or the Soviets, maintained a powerful presence on the flanks of Europe and in the waters off East Asia. The ships and aircraft of these fleets protected key allies like Japan, maintained the "Chinese Nationalist" presence on Taiwan, and bolstered NATO's southern flank while showing the flag in Near Eastern waters.

The progressive whittling down of the Atlantic and Pacific Fleets in the late forties meant that there were few major fleet units available for duty in European waters and then not always on a continuing basis. The operating histories of the comparative handful of fleet carriers, cruisers, and destroyers during these years suggest that from late 1947 on, one of the three *Midway* "battle carriers" (the other two were *Coral Sea* and *Franklin D. Roosevelt*) was usually in the Mediterranean for part of a year, occasionally relieved or joined by one of the smaller *Essex* class. Often, however, the fleet carriers were either undergoing upkeep and overhaul or remained in home waters, the Caribbean, or the Arctic, training crews and engaging in mock air and antisubmarine warfare exercises. Washington did, however, maintain a full-time cruiser-destroyer force east of Gibraltar.[1] The enormous fleet expansion of the early Korean War years dramatically transformed this situation, and by the autumn of 1951 the newly designated Sixth Fleet in the Mediterranean was widely considered "the most powerful force under General Eisenhower's [NATO] command."

Prior to that time, the U.S. Navy had been "a polite but powerful visitor to many Mediterranean ports." That month, fleet commander Admiral Carney at last established a permanent headquarters ashore at Naples, a hot, smelly, dirty, noisy southern Italian city that no one liked but that was more or less centrally located for Mediterranean operations. Years later the fleet would move to Gaeta, farther up the coast toward Rome. As the tense second year of the Korean War began, the Sixth Fleet, a third of a world away, was almost at double strength, "pack[ing] the punch of four score combat ships plus supply and service craft." According to one contemporary report, "Its training was at peak. Every ship, from the mammoth *Coral Sea* to the LST's and LSD's of the landing divisions, was combat ready and combat loaded." Two months earlier the fleet had partici-pated in combined NATO exercises off Malta with units of the still substantial Royal Navy, together with the warships from the French and Italian navies. Carney alternated command with his NATO counterparts, even though their unit contributions were much smaller, even in the aggregate. "Carney believes in training admirals as well as crews; he wants flag officers among his allies who will know his ways and who will be able to operate intelligently and instinctively in the absence of communications or explicit instructions."[2]

At midcentury Britain still struggled to maintain an image of global power at a time when the national economic base was steadily eroding. Its Far Eastern "Fleet" comprised three cruisers, five destroyers, five frigates, and a survey ship. Whitehall maintained another two cruisers and five frigates in adjacent Southeast Asian waters; a cruiser and two frigates carried the flag on the South Atlantic Station, and two cruisers and four frigates remained in American and West In-dian waters. The Home Fleet in 1949 was composed of forty-five vessels, including three battleships, two fleet carriers, two light fleet carriers, five cruis-ers, a fast minelayer, and sixteen destroyers, while another battleship, two light fleet carriers, four cruisers, seventeen destroyers, and a dozen submarines cruised the Mediterranean, together with twenty-two support ships. Finally, a fleet car-rier, a light fleet carrier, two cruisers, eighteen destroyers, nineteen frigates, and twenty-two submarines, together with a mass of motor torpedo boats, were based in ports in the Channel and Irish Sea.[3]

But America's admirals knew the score. In a mid-1949 interview, Richard L. Conolly, then commander in chief of U.S. Naval Forces Eastern Atlantic and Mediterranean, stated flatly that the Royal Navy now relied on its Yankee cousins for assistance in controlling those portions of the world sea-lanes, especially the eastern Atlantic and Mediterranean, that the Pentagon had assumed just three short years before would be guarded by the British Fleet. The other allies in the emerging NATO structure were much weaker still, and, just four years after the end of a devastating European war, Conolly believed that the Sixth Fleet and other U.S. forces in adjacent waters could exercise naval dominance "more economically than European countries can in most cases." But not in all. The small postwar French, Italian, and Dutch cruiser-destroyer forces were better positioned to engage in minesweeping activities (never an American strong suit) and in local escort and coastal-defense than was the constantly roaming and free-wheeling Sixth Fleet. There would be no single NATO fleet, Conolly continued. "It is much more feasible, much more practicable to allocate the tasks to be performed to each one of the allies than it would be to try to merge them into one big navy, and then split them up" into specific task forces.[4]

When not on exercises, the Sixth Fleet rode "in high majesty" off the coasts of southern France and Italy, its war-making potential "breathtaking" to the peoples of southern Europe and North Africa.[5] Although the three big *Midways* were the center of attention, occasionally supplemented by *Missouri* or one of its three sisters prior to retirement, the fleet's amphibious-assault capabilities were of equal importance to military strategists. War-ravaged Europe could not rearm until Marshall Plan aid, begun in 1948, took sufficient hold to generate substantial economic growth. The United States Army had practically withdrawn from the Continent after World War II; only a few skeleton units remained near the Iron Curtain and in Berlin to serve as trip wires to a possible Soviet assault across the North German plain or into Austria. NATO commitments, together with the Korean emergency, stimulated a major debate within the administration and Congress that led to a decision early in 1951 to send four divisions to the Continent, but they were far from capable of stemming the expected massive Soviet advance. As Carney's ships and amphibious-assault personnel conducted their exercises that summer, the Central Intelligence Agency (CIA) estimated that "the armed forces of the USSR have the capability of overrunning continental Europe and the Near and Middle East (except India and Pakistan) within a relatively short period." A week later the National Security Council ratified the CIA appreciation. The council added that the Kremlin had enhanced its military power and capabilities to such a degree since the immediate pre-Korea period that it posed an even greater risk to U.S. and Western security, despite the beginnings of an impressive Western build-up. Moreover, estimates of Soviet atomic capabilities had been revised sharply upward. "It is now estimated that the USSR will have in mid-1953 the atomic stockpile formerly estimated for mid-1954. The date when a surprise attack on the United States might yield decisive results is correspondingly advanced." Evidence of a sharply intensified and "systematic campaign to prepare the Russian people psychologically for war with the United States," together with similar campaigns throughout the Soviet East European bloc and China, led to the inescapable conclusion that the danger to U.S. security was greater than it had been on the eve of the Korean conflict a scant fourteen months before.[6]

Should the Soviets overrun Europe, thus initiating a prolonged conflict in which atomic bombs might not be decisive,[7] the Iberian Peninsula, hemmed off from the rest of the Continent by the Pyrenees, seemed the only place that inferior Western forces could stabilize and hold while rebuilding their forces for a counterattack. Many apprehensive denizens of northwestern Europe thought this was Washington's goal from the beginning. As proof that their American allies were prepared to write them off, they pointed to strenuous efforts by the Truman administration after the outbreak of war in Korea to bring Franco's Spain into NATO and to secure air- and naval-base rights in Spain.[8] Whether, in a worst-case scenario, Washington was indeed prepared to abandon most of Europe to Russian occupation or not, an American fleet steaming on the southern flank of a Sovietized continent and possessed of both substantial airpower and some amphibious-assault capabilities could provide significant support to a Western toehold in Iberia while threatening Soviet bases and installations far inland.

Some who remembered the pounding that the Royal Navy took in 1940–1941 off Crete and Malta and the severe damage that American warships—and especially carriers—received off Okinawa openly wondered whether the United States could successfully operate a carrier task force or two in the narrow Mediterranean. U.S. fleet commanders harbored no such qualms. "I wouldn't call the Mediterranean narrow waters," one protested to a press panel in 1949. "The English Channel and the Adriatic are narrow waters" and so, admittedly, were certain straits "here and there" in the waters between Gibraltar and Suez. "But there is an awful lot of water over there," and with enough flight decks to provide decent aerial defense, "we proved pretty conclusively in the Pacific [that] we can operate [aircraft carriers] anywhere." By the end of 1954 more than a dozen original or modernized *Essex*-class fleet carriers were on duty together with the three *Midways*, while the first two ships of the even bigger *Forrestal* class were poised to join the fleet. Moreover, the naval build-up had been balanced. Each carrier task force contained sufficient escort and antisubmarine units to ensure, so the navy insisted, its own protection. Meanwhile, the coming of the hydrogen bomb and the prospect of intercontinental missiles had at last convinced the air force that its fixed bases, no matter how widely dispersed, were now fearfully vulnerable to preemptive Soviet attack. Maintaining much of the Strategic Air Command aloft on hair-trigger alert near Soviet borders was one solution. Another, the land-based airmen grudgingly admitted, was "mobile, seagoing air power capable of delivering," as the *Midways* and *Forrestals* could, "atomic attack from unexpected directions." The navy's assistant secretary for air, James H. Smith, boasted that a future fast carrier strike force of perhaps three flattops, seven cruisers, and two high-speed supply ships would spread out over an ocean area the size of Maine. "It will be so widely dispersed that no single weapon of any size we can now visualize can seriously damage more than one ship." This force could deliver atomic ordnance "under all weather conditions" to enemy installations "1,500 miles or more distant," while "advanced forces of nuclear-powered submarines" could launch "atomic missiles against targets at relatively short ranges." These powerful, "fully self-sustaining," yet widely dispersed fleets could operate under wartime conditions for up to thirty days, exerting "tight and exclusive control over an area of 60,000 square miles"— equivalent to the six New England states or a very large portion of the Mediterranean.[9] The inclusion of the new *Forrestal* supercarriers in the navy arsenal allowed strategists to expand the U.S. sea presence to include not only the southern but also the northern flank of any future Soviet war front and occupation zone in central and Western Europe. After 1955 the possibility of carrier-launched atomic air strikes directly at key Soviet targets—including Moscow—from off the coast of Norway (or even from within Norwegian fjords) became feasible.

Throughout the early and midfifties the Sixth Fleet, its carrier task forces incessantly steaming from one end of the "Med" to the other, more than proved its worth as a major cold war deterrent. But cold war imperatives and terrors at once stimulated and obscured another phenomenon that was beginning to convulse the postwar international order—the emergence of an incoherent but unmistakable and always turbulent "Third World" movement that shook and shaped non-Western societies from the Atlantic shores of Morocco across North Africa and the Middle East to India and Indonesia. Western sea power in the form of greatly diminished British and French fleets, together with the United States Navy, would find themselves in conflict with this movement on a number of occasions and at several points from Suez in 1956 and Lebanon two years later through the second Gulf War of 2003.

As early as 1950 Harry Truman, his secretary of state, Dean Acheson, and their Anglo-French colleagues were aware that Soviet expansionism together with the birth of Israel had made the Middle East a potential cauldron of both East-West and Arab-Zionist tensions. Although Washington had recognized the new state of Israel only minutes after it declared its independence in May 1948, both Truman and Eisenhower sought to maintain an evenhanded approach toward Israel and its Arab antagonists. In May 1950 Acheson and his British and French colleagues issued a declaration pledging to limit arms sales to both sides in the Middle East and to oppose any attempt to alter existing armistice frontiers or armistice lines by force. This represented an expansion of U.S. involvement in the region that, by implication, stretched the Sixth Fleet's area of responsibility geographically to the eastern shores of the Mediterranean, while expanding it operationally to include not only resistance to Soviet encroachments but also destabilization of the region by forces from within.[10]

But the area remained stubbornly unstable. Beneath the seemingly glacial surface of the cold war, seismic shifts were beginning to occur in the fragile global political system. The Arab world seethed with anti-Westernism, an explosive mix of resentment of Western colonial rule, and a desire to acquire Western weapons and technology, combined with fear that adoption of Western techniques and ideas would destroy traditional ways of life and a passionate desire for national independence and Arab revival. This was compounded by the creation of Israel, widely regarded as the latest form of Western imperialism. Years later anti-Westernism in the area would take the form of Islamic radicalism. In the 1950s, however, the author of militant Arab nationalism was Egypt's dynamic young ruler, Colonel Gamal Abdel Nasser. Nasser had been part of the cabal that had exploited decades of Egyptian resentment over British rule to topple London's client King Farouk in 1952. Two years later Nasser shouldered the cabal's leader aside and arrogated to himself the role of redeemer of the Arab world. Like so many revolutionaries, Nasser—emotional, intuitive, and opportunistic—kindled and swept up into his person and movement dreams and aspirations of which he was at first scarcely aware. Within months of his accession to power, he had transformed Egypt from the pathetic British client state it had been under King Farouk to a major player in regional and world affairs. Nasser shared with Nehru of India and Tito of Yugoslavia the vision of a great middle or nonaligned way between East and West in global politics. Either united or individually, members of this "Third World" could play each of the superpowers off one another, leveraging concessions and consent from both Washington and Moscow. The game would require great finesse and good luck, but Nasser believed he possessed both. Nasser was a prominent figure at the great Bandung Conference of nonaligned nations early in 1955 but then blundered badly in Western eyes as he steered Egypt "sharply leftward—toward Moscow."[11]

That September Nasser astounded everyone by announcing that he had reached an agreement with the Kremlin to barter the Egyptian cotton crop each year for substantial Soviet military aid, including trucks, armored vehicles, jet aircraft, tanks, and a handful of submarines and small naval craft. Even as Nasser asserted the virtues and value of nonalignment, Soviet-bloc technicians and agents flowed into Cairo together, with arms in abundance. In Washington's eyes, Nasser compounded his felonies by recognizing China's Communist government, which promptly made him persona non grata. With White House acquiescence, Congress blocked funds for a U.S. loan to build the Aswan Dam on the Upper Nile. President Eisenhower concluded that the mercurial Egyptian was no friend to the United States, commenting later: "If he was not a Communist, he certainly succeeded in making us very suspicious of him."[12]

Nasser replied in July 1956 with the dramatic announcement that he was nationalizing the Suez Canal, seizing control from the Paris-based, internationally backed company that had operated it for years, and that he would use the revenues to build the Aswan Dam. This action, along with a rising tide of Arab nationalism, shocked and frightened the declining European imperial powers and Israel, which was already feeling the effect of Nasser's support of Palestinian commandos. Washington heartily disapproved of the nationalization of the canal, but with a presidential election in the offing, Eisenhower and Dulles were not prepared to take any action beyond playing for time with a diplomatic initiative. Britain and France, however, felt as hard-pressed by Nasser as did the Israelis, and at the end of September the three countries cut a secret deal to recapture the canal. Israel would strike across the Sinai toward Suez, while French and British forces landed at Alexandria and marched toward the canal. The three armies would join at the waterway that would be taken from Nasser in the name of international freedom of transit and the rule of law. The twin blows of invasion and seizure would presumably bring down the obstreperous Egyptian leader. The scheme almost worked, and in the process inadvertently enmeshed the Sixth Fleet.

The Anglo-French operation against Suez began well enough. The Royal Navy had managed to scrape together a formidable force centered around carrier *Eagle* and two light carriers from the Mediterranean Fleet. Two commando carriers directly supported the amphibious assault, together with a supporting force of cruisers and destroyers. Britain successfully masked its intentions until the last moment by gathering its forces for an ostensible training exercise labeled Operation Boathook. Years later one of the British LST captains remembered that before leaving Malta, "we were led to believe that we were going to Suez to separate the Israeli and Egyptian armies, but when we opened our operational orders we discovered that the aim of the operation was for 'the RAF to bomb Cairo and break the will to resist of the Egyptian people.'" Commander John S. Pallot added that "the full story of that year will never be written since at least one of the records was fudged on orders from higher up."[13]

The Israelis pulled off a masterful coup of their own. Jerusalem convinced the world that Israeli forces were about to strike Jordan. At the end of October, Western embassies were busily evacuating their nationals from Amman as well as Cairo, Damascus, and Jerusalem in anticipation of war. Suddenly, on the twenty-ninth, Israeli paratroopers dropped into the Sinai just forty miles from Suez and waited for their armor to race to them. British and French fleets soon appeared off Alexandria and, together with RAF bombers from Cyprus, began a leisurely sea and aerial bombardment of the city and its environs. Unfortunately, these operations were conducted too slowly and methodically to serve Anglo-French diplomatic and political interests. Time was of the essence if Cairo and the canal were to be seized before world opinion could be mobilized against the attack. But planners in London and Paris had agreed on carefully mounted gunfire and bombing assaults to minimize civilian casualties (and save national reputations) before the decisive and comparatively small parachute and amphibious assaults were launched. As the bombardment-and-strafing phase continued "like a nagging toothache," world opinion began to crystallize. The UN General Assembly met in emergency session. The Soviets, who were about to brutally crush a rebellion in Hungary, were of course happy to join the general outcry against the British, French, and Israelis. The amphibious operation and complementary parachute drop that were meant to finish the business were carried out with polish, but by then the situation was diplomatically irretrievable. Not only did London and Paris run afoul of non-Western and Soviet opinion, but they had failed to secure the blessing of the free world's greatest power. Washington was incensed at not having been notified of the attacks in advance and at British and French duplicity in concealing the scheme from their closest ally. Eisenhower sent Secretary of State John Foster Dulles to New York with a draft resolution that the General Assembly promptly passed, urging an immediate cease-fire. A Kremlin proposal that Moscow and Washington dispatch a joint force to Suez to quell the fighting and maintain order was understandably rejected as preposterous.

Muddle was quickly added to embarrassment within the Western camp. In Egypt and Israel nearly two thousand Americans were trapped in the war zone when all the airfields were bombed. The Sixth Fleet had to bring them out, and

as the destroyers went in to the beaches of Gaza "they watched . . . Egyptian soldiers blow up their guns and smash their small arms or throw them into the
sea" as Israeli forces neared. "At Alexandria they found themselves in the middle
of a shooting war. Four miles inland, anti-aircraft guns were firing on the airfield.
To seaward, and beside them in the harbor, Egyptian destroyers banged away
furiously" at attacking British aircraft. As darkness came on, the British task
force commander, Admiral Durford-Slater, asked the Americans to move. The
Sixth Fleet commander, Vice Admiral Charles "Cat" Brown, refused to suspend
his evacuation efforts and plaintively cabled Washington to ask on whose side
he was supposed to be. Since the Sixth Fleet in Alexandria Harbor and at sea
operated with lights ablaze, the Royal Navy carrier task force off the port city
illuminated as well, so that any Egyptian bombers in the area might as easily hit
Sixth Fleet as British warships. It was not a high point in postwar Anglo-
American relations.

Luckily, no bombs struck American decks, and sailors "tensed for battle found
themselves busy helping terrified old ladies aboard, sterilizing bottles and nipples,
mixing formulas, spooning strained vegetables into fat babies and fashioning
diapers out of dishrags." Brown was furious, however. His mission was to protect
American interests, and by God he was going to do it. "If somebody had shot
at us we would have shot back. If the road to Cairo had been closed we would
have put the marines ashore to open it and keep it open. If it had been necessary
to put planes over the area, we would have done that, too." With their military
and diplomatic strategies in shreds, Paris and London were soon forced to surrender to U.S. and international pressure whatever gains their sailors, soldiers,
and airmen were about to win.[14]

Suez marked a great transition in Middle Eastern affairs. Nasser with inestimable help from the entire world, nonaligned, Western, and Communist alike,
had humiliated the last two great imperial powers. The Eisenhower administration, well aware that Suez had practically destroyed British influence in the Middle
East, decided to use a congressional resolution as the vehicle for a policy statement on the Middle East, which was intended to provide support to nations in
the area against pressure from Nasser and the Soviets. Early in January 1957
Eisenhower sent Congress a proposal for a resolution not only offering U.S. economic and military assistance to countries in the Middle East but also declaring
that the United States would use armed forces to assist any nation in the region
requesting support against armed aggression from any country controlled by
international Communism. The "Eisenhower Doctrine," as it soon became
known, was adopted by Congress in March.[15]

It framed the Sixth Fleet's mission responsibilities in the eastern Mediterranean from that time on to the end of the cold war. Cat Brown, who had been ready to send his sailors, flyers, and marines anywhere necessary at Suez, reveled in the fact that "tomorrow could be my Pearl Harbor," with Suez "and Soviet interference" creating "a dangerously explosive state." The fifty-six-year-old Alabamian and naval aviation pioneer insisted, "This is the best job in the whole U.S. Navy." He told a visiting reporter, "I've got in my own hot hands a large chunk of naval force," and in an age before satellite links allowed near-instant communications between the presidential bedroom and the bridge of a single warship, "the people back in Washington can sweat all they want—but I can muff it all by myself." The admiral was clearly not about to let that happen. His staff aboard the ultramodern cruiser *Salem* was "a good staff—lean, pared down and afloat. But if I took them ashore, they'd begin to write letters to each other and soon they'd begin to worry about getting home to cocktails on time."[16]

Brown believed that a naval battle for control of the Mediterranean "would change the lives of men for generations. It would decide whether the brutal slavery of Communism or the principles in which free men believe should have dominion in Africa and western Asia [and] along the shores of Southern Europe." The Sixth Fleet needed only forty-eight hours of survival to do its job, and those forty-eight hours were virtually guaranteed. The fifty-ship armada, far smaller than the vast war fleet that roamed the western Pacific in 1944–1945, was nimble and speedy; it anchored at ports around the Mediterranean far less than half the time, and never on weekends so as not to upset local holidays—or give Communist agents a hint of scheduling intentions. Most of the time it was at sea, replenishing and refueling as needed. Its "knockout punch" was now encapsulated in *Forrestal*, the first of the great supercarriers, which did have atomic weapons in its hold and twin-jet Skywarrior aircraft on its flight deck that could deliver nuclear holocaust to Moscow and even Leningrad, fourteen hundred miles away. Two modernized *Essex*-class carriers, *Randolph* and *Lake Champlain*, together with a cluster of cruisers and destroyers, supplemented their giant sister's power.

Observers aboard for a short exercise and accustomed to the tight fleet formations of 1944–1945 and even Korea were shocked upon awakening one morning to find the sea empty of ships. "Destroyers, cruisers, flattops, all are gone." Bikini had taught the navy that dispersal was the secret of defeating atomic warfare. Secure, effective command, communications, control, and intelligence (C3I) had become a prerequisite of efficient and coordinated power projection from the sea. Noisy, incessantly active aircraft carriers were not the most promising platforms for C3I. Moreover, there were too few of them, crowded with too much equipment and too many men. Cruisers were the answer. With their elaborate combat-information capabilities, these modern, elegant-looking ships broadened the air-detection and -control capabilities of an entire task force.

For three days in early December 1956, the Sixth Fleet cruised in dispersed formation, testing its defenses. "Land planes, flying from Italy, Greece and Malta roam through the skies, groping for target ships," while radars constantly searched for them and combat-information centers aboard the cruisers vectored carrier fighters "to targets far beyond the range of guns" and the new surface-to-air missiles. At the same time, submarines "dart in, trying to bring the flattops into torpedo range before the scurrying destroyers can spot them on their sounding gear." When the "tin cans" did detect a submarine, they dropped yellow-dye markers to indicate position, and referees determined if a kill had been made. In the midst of all this activity Skywarriors whipped and screamed down the flight decks of the three carriers and raced aloft against targets "at the ultimate limit of their range. The targets are on friendly shores, but they lie the same distance away as similar targets in Russia or her satellites." Neither the United States Navy nor the American media were reticent about the nation's readiness to "go toe to toe in nuclear combat with the Russkies." All it would take to make it real, a "weary" pilot told reporter Harold Marten aboard one of the carriers, "would be to hang the big bomb on and swing the compass needle over a little."[17]

When the fleet did go ashore, its sailors generally behaved well. Each ship had aboard numerous copies of a volume titled *Mediterranean Directory,* a combined shopping guide and etiquette manual compiled from the observations of thousands of sailors who had visited southern European ports in the decade following World War II. Ships' crews were expected to be generally conversant with local traditions and customs. They were warned never to discuss Egyptian-Israeli relations and strongly advised to avoid all political discussions. Otherwise, the navy and the host authorities allowed the sailors and marines to behave as sailors and marines historically had, so long as no real outrages were committed. At anchor, the carriers launched helicopters to patrol the harbors, checking to ensure that no ship sullied the waters with garbage; it was also a good way to enhance security. "When working on jet engines, the carriers put to sea, so that the scream of the jets will not disturb any citizens who may be taking a siesta."[18]

This was the formidable force that Eisenhower had on immediate call when,

in mid-1958, a crisis suddenly broke out in Lebanon. In February Nasser realized the first part of his pan-Arab dream with the formation of the United
Arab Republic (UAR) linking Egypt and Syria in such a way that Cairo would
control much of Damascus's internal and all of its external policies and institutions. Formation of the UAR was closely followed by street rioting in Amman
and to significant infiltration of Syrian agents and arms into Lebanon to foment
trouble and strife. Nasser's dream of a pan-Arab state seemed ever closer to reality,
and while Jordan's young King Hussein boldly faced down his opposition,
Lebanese president Camille Chamoun and his foreign minister, Dr. Charles
Malik, turned to Washington for support. Eisenhower shared their fears. "It
seemed likely," he later wrote, "that Lebanon occupied a place on Colonel
Nasser's timetable as a nation to be brought under his influence."[19]

Although Lebanon's population was largely Arab and Muslim, the country
contained a significant Christian element, enjoyed a reputation for broad religious
and political tolerance, and was, under Chamoun and Malik, firmly aligned
with the West. Indeed, Chamoun and Eisenhower had become personal friends
through official contact. Beirut, a beautiful city on low bluffs lapped by the
warm, blue waters of the Mediterranean, was known as "the Paris of the East"
for its charm and sophistication. But in a time of political turbulence, any miscalculation could upset the delicate political, religious, and social balance.
Chamoun had already incurred Nasser's wrath by refusing to break relations with
London and Paris over Suez and embracing the Eisenhower Doctrine. Now he
refused to deny rumors that he would support efforts to amend the national
constitution in order to seek an unprecedented second six-year term. He would
do so, Malik told a meeting of the French, British, and American ambassadors
in mid-April, for the sake of personal honor. Potential opposition from within his
own party left him "light hearted"; it was Nasser and the UAR that he feared.
The forthcoming Lebanese elections had become a contest in which "massive
outside forces" were engaged. U.S. ambassador Robert McClintock cabled
home that although Chamoun's "portrayal of himself as a lonely white knight
fighting a battle against international powers of darkness is more Wagnerian
than situation warrants," he was interpreting the situation correctly. Muslim
dissidents, doubtless encouraged if not supported by Damascus and Cairo, began taking to the streets in reaction to rumors of Chamoun's intent. Government army and police forces reacted with a distressing lack of enthusiasm.[20]

In early May Chamoun publicly confirmed his intention to revise the constitution in order to seek a second term, and fighting flared into what Washington

feared would become a full-scale civil war. Eisenhower met with his defense and foreign policy teams on the thirteenth to decide how to respond to a request from Chamoun asking what the Americans might do if he requested formal military intervention. The situation seemed extremely dangerous. "Although temporarily pursuing a 'soft' propaganda line," Ike later wrote, "the Soviets were pushing everywhere, stirring up trouble in Venezuela, Indonesia, and Burma. . . . Radio Cairo . . . was blasting forth its encouragement of the Lebanese rebels." After some discussion, he told the meeting that he thought they should "let the Lebanese know that we would help them in case it should become necessary" and that "the military should immediately issue a warning order to our forces to put them on the alert." He agreed that the marines of the Sixth Fleet should "start moving eastward."[21] The president and his advisers formulated a reply to Chamoun containing not only terms and conditions for intervention but also a firm exit strategy. American troops would enter Lebanon only with the public support of at least one Arab government, solely to protect American interests and the legitimate government, and with the proviso that Chamoun abandon any plans to seek a second term. Chamoun replied that he thought his forces could contain the burgeoning civil war, but late in the month he requested an emergency meeting of the UN Security Council, complaining that Egypt and Syria were behind the Muslim outbreak. The council voted to dispatch a UN observation team to Lebanon.

The situation continued to deteriorate, and in mid-June Arleigh Burke informed Admiral James Holloway, commander in chief of U.S. Naval Forces Eastern Atlantic and Mediterranean, that Chamoun had formally requested assistance. While the White House pondered its moves, Burke continued, the Sixth Fleet was to "keep 2 DD within 25 miles but over horizon and out of sight from Beirut." The destroyers should be prepared to enter Beirut Harbor and land a small force to evacuate American citizens "or furnish assistance when requested by American Ambassador by radio direct to destroyers." This minimal show of force enabled Chamoun to master the situation for the time being, and by early July, despite continued fighting throughout the country, it appeared that his people had the upper hand. Western intervention seemed unnecessary.[22]

On July 14, however, the whole Middle East went critical. King Faisal II of Iraq was murdered in a nationalist coup. Eisenhower was told that the CIA believed it was the work of pro-Nasser elements in the Iraqi army and a "mob" that now filled the streets of Baghdad. A "Republican" government had been formed there under Brigadier General Abdul Karim Kassem. It included many known pro-Nasser individuals, though it was not clear whether Nasser himself had been behind the coup. Young Hussein in neighboring Jordan was also the target of a coup, but he survived.[23]

Washington's attention immediately refocused on Chamoun. The domino effect that Nasser had set in train with the UAR and now, apparently, Iraq could not be allowed to topple Lebanon—or Jordan as well. Where were the nearest American forces? Joint Chiefs chairman Nathan Twining told the president of the three marine battalions immediately available aboard Sixth Fleet amphibious ships in the eastern Mediterranean. Ike decided they should go in to protect Chamoun and, if necessary, restore order throughout the country. Such a move would also strengthen Hussein. At 5:23 on the afternoon of July 14, Burke ordered Holloway to "Land Marines at 1500 Bravo [3 P.M. local] time, 15 July." Lebanese officials were not to be told before noon, but Holloway could notify all U.S. naval posts, commands, and units if he wished. Then Burke added: "Join your flagship now. Sail all Sixth Fleet eastward."[24]

Early the next afternoon, "the 'grey diplomats' of the U.S. Sixth Fleet" suddenly appeared off the bluffs and beaches of Beirut. Only four minutes past the landing time ordered by Burke sixteen hours before, "the first Marine leaped from a landing craft to the sun-bright sands of Ouzai beach" adjacent to Beirut's Qei Airport. Serious business quickly degenerated into farce. As the green-clad, sweat-stained troops in their camouflaged helmets tumbled out of their landing craft, they waded ashore past smiling, bikini-clad society girls and "goggle-eyed" sightseers. "Small boys cheered as the guns and equipment clanked down from LCVP's and LCM's. Ice cream vendors appeared with motorized wagons, one of which played nickelodeon music." As jet fighters from *Essex* and *Saratoga* (the second brand-new *Forrestal*-class supercarrier) "screamed overhead . . . Lebanese youths screamed back in delight."

McClintock had already seen Chamoun, who asked the ambassador to contact Lebanese army chief General Fuad Chehab and secure his complete cooperation. Chamoun also agreed to shut down the airport an hour before the expected landings. A major amphibious exercise seemed ready to go off like clockwork, when the advanced elements of the marine amphibious force secured Qei Airport in less than forty minutes. Shortly thereafter, Admiral Holloway arrived to take personal command of the invasion force. The buildup of ninety-two hundred troops, including thirty-one hundred army airborne units flown in from Germany, was well under way. At the same time, several thousand British troops landed in Jordan to, in Prime Minister Harold Macmillan's words, "help the . . .

government fight off a coup" whose source was obvious.[25] The first day ended quietly. The following morning, reality set in.

Chehab, "with an air of infinite sadness," had told McClintock the previous day that the only thing that had saved Lebanon during recent months was its army and that with the arrival of U.S. forces, he gravely feared it would disintegrate on religious lines: Lebanon would either survive as a "Christian Israel" or be "inundated in a sea of Islam." Turning from philosophy to practicality, Chehab "urgently" requested that the marines be kept aboard their ships in Beirut Harbor, though he stated that he and his troops would have no objection to a token force coming ashore to secure the American embassy grounds. McClintock took Chehab seriously and passed his recommendations on to the American military attachés, but, alas, by the time word reached Cat Brown and the fleet, the first marines were already ashore, with the rest pouring in behind.[26]

Neither the marines nor Admiral Holloway were aware of Chehab's opposition as the Americans prepared the following morning to march from the airport into the city. Beirut was now divided into Christian and Muslim enclaves. The Muslims ("Nasser rebels," according to Western journalists) controlled the Bastra area and had "sealed" it off with "deep tank traps, banked with sandbags, defended by carefully sited automatic rifles." The invading force would at the very least have to blockade the enclave; the Sixth Fleet marine force was prepared to do just that. But around eleven, as the leathernecks assembled under a "broiling" sun, fourteen Lebanese army tanks clanked into position on the road leading out of the airport toward the city and trained their guns on the marines. Chehab had not been kidding. Marine Brigadier General Sidney Wade immediately phoned McClintock, who promptly called Chamoun, who in turn summoned his fractious general, while the restless marines wondered what was going on. Learning of the potential crisis, Washington dispatched veteran diplomat Robert Murphy to Beirut. Chamoun wisely called an emergency meeting at his home between McClintock and Chehab who professed ignorance of what his troops had done. Exploiting Chamoun's presence, McClintock suggested that he and Chehab go to the Lebanese positions "in order [to] personally make arrangements for [the] safe passage of [the] marine battalion." The two men immediately drove out toward the airport, "where we met [the] entire [Marine] column stopped by Lebanese military who had meanwhile lined up every available tank and recoilless rifle in Beirut with guns trained on [the] US column." Fortunately, McClintock discovered Admiral Holloway at the head of the column, and together the three men went to a nearby command school where, after repeated calls and excited conversations, Chehab got his people to agree to allow the marines to proceed toward the city gradually, "by small detachments."[27]

Holloway, McClintock, and Chehab then led the marines by the seaside road into Beirut. The big Patton tanks began to "chew up asphalt on swank waterfront boulevards and wrecked the narrow streets in town" with their treads. The crowds were quiet, with only a few cheers and friendly waves. "Outside the U.S. Embassy, a Marine guard tossed an ice-cold beer can down to some thirsty buddies aboard a troop carrier, but there were many in the crowd who looked on glumly at the display of military hardware. On one vehicle, a local citizen had written with his finger on the dusty side: 'Down with Chamoun, Traitor of the People.'"[28]

Nasser and Soviet premier Nikita S. Khrushchev were meeting when they received word of American marines in Lebanon and the Sixth Fleet offshore. Western reports at the time indicated that Khrushchev counseled restraint. Without Soviet support, Nasser was in no position to do battle with the Sixth Fleet. Instead, he flew from Moscow to Damascus, where he gave a fiery speech to his Syrian lieutenants and a cheering crowd of ten thousand that was broadcast throughout the Arab world. "We shall all carry arms to defend the torch of freedom lit in Iraq," he cried, vowing to fight "to the last drop of our blood." The Arab-Muslim world did not "fear fleets of atom bombs," and "the flag of liberation will be raised in Beirut, Amman, Algeria. . . . No power in the world can destroy this Arab nationalism" that had "brothers" in Libya, the Sudan, and Yemen. In other words, the Arab world would not try to joust with the West on Western terms; rather, each Arab nationalist would become a soldier in the cause.

The American media responded with no little apprehension. "HOW FAR Will Nasser—and Reds—Go? HOW FAR Must We and the West Go?" "What's Up K's Sleeve?" In fact, there was nothing "up" Khrushchev's sleeve. Lebanon had been an act of U.S. naval power projection, and as the international community well knew, the Soviet Navy had no power to project in response. According to *Jane's Fighting Ships,* the dramatic strides in Soviet sea power since the end of World War II had been confined to subsurface warfare, and then only in terms of numbers, not advanced technology. The 1958–1959 volume reported an apparent increase in Russian submarine activity in the Atlantic and along the U.S. East Coast during the preceding year. Soviet leaders had forecast "an early appearance of guided missile cruisers and destroyers" to supplement their modest submarine-missile launch capabilities that roughly matched the American

Regulus program, and there was "evidence that Russian marine engineering and shipbuilding resources are being concentrated on nuclear-powered vessels." But all this constituted at best well-informed speculation about future capabilities. The Soviet surface fleet of 1958 possessed no aircraft carriers, no battleships, no heavy cruisers, and no missile vessels (the United States had just sent its first guided-missile heavy cruisers to sea). Above all, the Russians possessed no amphibious-warfare capabilities. Whereas the U.S. section of *Jane's* that year took up 103 pages, editor Raymond Blackman required only 25 to cover the Soviet Navy. The Kremlin possessed 35 conventionally armed and propelled light cruisers, 146 destroyers, 88 frigates, and about 500 conventionally armed and powered submarines. This was at best a fleet of promise.[29]

Khrushchev contemplated sending Eisenhower a letter likening the U.S. intervention to Hitler's invasion of Poland, but Deputy Premier Anastas Mikoyan and Minister for Light Industry Aleksey Kosygin (a key Khrushchev supporter) argued that Ike would be "infuriated" by such a missive, and Khrushchev backed down. Instead, as the marine columns moved piecemeal into Beirut, acting Soviet foreign minister Vasily Kuznestov summoned Ambassador "Tommy" Thompson and handed him a six-page declaration calling upon the United States to "cease its armed intervention in the internal affairs of the Arab states and to immediately withdraw its forces from Lebanon." The Kremlin huffed that it could not "remain passive toward events creating a serious threat in an area bordering on its frontiers" and promised to "take the necessary measures dictated by the interests of preserving peace and security." Thompson and Washington knew what this meant. The Soviets might take the issue to the UN but otherwise would do nothing. The only Soviet action was a "hastily conducted" naval exercise in the Black Sea area beginning July 19 and ending August 7. Khrushchev made no attempt to make a show of force in the Mediterranean and reportedly told Nasser the whole thing was a "bluff." Two days later, the UN General Assembly unanimously adopted a resolution sponsored by ten Arab states instructing Secretary-General Dag Hammarskjöld to "consult with the governments involved" about "practical arrangements" to uphold "the purposes and principles of the Charter in relation to Lebanon and Jordan." Hammarskjöld went to the Middle East in early September and quickly reached an agreement with British and American officials on a UN presence in the area to monitor events.[30]

By the second week the American incursion had settled into a calm routine. On the beach north of Beirut, "neatly spaced amid the welter of bulldozers, cranes, and sweating U.S. marines . . . stood five green and white umbrellas boldly emblazoned SEVEN-UP" with a friendly vendor beneath each one. The umbrellas were spaced with such orderly precision by the marine beach master, who had concluded that the vendors needed as much organization as the unloading operations. By early August withdrawal of at least part of the force was being seriously considered in Washington, and by the end of the month it was generally agreed that the last marine and trooper would be gone by the middle of October, which they were. Because the Americans entered with a well-thought-out plan (no second term for Chamoun; the support of at least one major Arab power— in fact ten proposed the milk-and-water UN resolution; and the achievement of relative political tranquillity throughout Lebanon), they enjoyed significant leverage from the start. Just hours after the Patton tanks rolled into Beirut, the leader of the rebel forces in Beirut, Saeb Salem, told *Newsweek* that if the marines withdrew, he would "guarantee personally that there would be a peaceful solution to the internal Lebanese crisis." Salem added that although he regarded Chamoun as an out-and-out traitor for calling in the Americans, he would sit down with the embattled president, McClintock, and Eisenhower's special envoy, Robert Murphy. As the weeks wore on, Chehab applied pressure from the opposite end of the spectrum, warning opposition leaders that "US forces would not be withdrawn until [the] security situation in Lebanon had been restored to normal." With everyone's interest converging on getting the Americans out, the situation stabilized, as Washington had hoped.[31]

Suez and Lebanon together marked a decisive shift in the history of the modern Middle East. Despite their successful intervention in Jordan, the British were supplanted as outside arbiters by the United States. The Sixth Fleet with its limited but strong amphibious force and fifteen hundred–mile-range Skywarrior attack aircraft was now and would remain the chief instrument of American power that could be projected throughout a region that stretched from Gibraltar to Baghdad and Suez to Istanbul. Whether that power was applied wisely in the case of Lebanon or whether sea power was an effective instrument for the Lebanon situation is another matter. In the short term, the Sixth Fleet intervention was effective. But along with Suez it represented the first of several humiliating setbacks for Nasser and Arab nationalism that would be neither forgotten nor forgiven in the Arab street.[32]

For all its strength and influence, the Sixth Fleet never fought a war throughout the nearly half century of tension and conflict between the Communist world and the West. The Seventh Fleet in the western Pacific fought two, and in between projected as powerful a presence as its sister fleet on the far side of the Eurasian landmass.

Mao Zedong's conquest of China in 1949 defined the dimensions and dynamics of Far Eastern politics, diplomacy, and military-naval policy for the next three decades. His defeated opponent, Chiang Kai-shek (Jiang Jieshi), was able to flee with a considerable army across the strait to impose himself on the hapless people of Taiwan (Formosa). Chiang also seeded the string of tiny islands and island groups immediately off the mainland with his own troops. These formerly nondescript bits of rock and sand that were home to only a handful of local fishermen and their families included the Dachens (Tachens), the Mazus (Matsus), and the Jinmens (Quemoys). The Mazus, in fact, lay only about fifteen miles east of the Chinese port of Fuzhou (Foochow), while the Jinmens (which, ironically, translates into "Golden Gate" in English) lay at the very mouth of Xiamen (Amoy) Harbor. The garrison on the Dachens was the most remote and vulnerable. The island cluster lay only about 20 miles off the Chinese mainland, but was some 210 miles north and west of Taiwan. Once Chiang and his followers were securely ensconced on Taiwan, they passed every day dreaming of regaining control of the mainland, while in Beijing Mao Zedong and his fellow Communists dreamed no less intensely of seizing the enemy fortress and its outlying island garrisons, in part to complete their reign over historic Chinese territory and in part to eliminate Nationalist claims that they remained the legitimate government of China. Tensions were compounded by Chiang's vociferous supporters across the length and breadth of the United States and in Congress who interpreted the "fall" of China to Godless Communism as one of the great and enduring catastrophes in all history. China became an instant partisan political issue in the United States where the exaggerated belief was taking hold that if one gave a Communist an inch, (s)he would seize the world. In the high cold war years of the 1950s and early '60s, the "Formosa Strait" between the two bitter Chinese antagonists was a recurrent source of tension and potential war between the Communist world and the West. Like a magnet, it drew certain elements of the United States Seventh Fleet into its waters.

In the months after he came to power, Mao may have contemplated either an amphibious or airborne assault against Taiwan. But one of President Truman's first acts after the outbreak of the Korean War was to direct the Seventh Fleet to prevent an invasion across the strait in either direction. The president thus "leashed" Chiang while putting paid to any idea that Mao with his minuscule navy might try a dramatic invasion of Taiwan. On that island Chiang and his perpetually restless circle read for a time reports that perhaps half a million loyal guerrillas on the mainland continued to wage increasingly forlorn warfare against the Communist regime. By 1951, however, nothing more was heard of them. As war raged in nearby Korea and Beijing suddenly intervened on a massive scale, people in Taipei and Washington wondered if perhaps guerrilla warfare staged against mainland towns and cities from Chiang's offshore islands, especially the Dachens, Mazus, and Jinmens, might well distract and even weaken the Beijing regime to the point that it would withdraw from the peninsula and perhaps eventually collapse. Soon a small, motley band of CIA operatives, some of whom called themselves the "Quemoy partisans," moved into the offshore islands and actively assisted Chiang's people in staging perilous raids and intelligence-gathering forays onto the China coast.[33]

Beijing was infuriated but not wounded, and soon after the Korean armistice was signed on July 27, 1953, Mao began increasing air and naval patrols around the offshore islands. With Washington's connivance, Chiang obligingly upped the ante. The U.S. Navy had been dispatching air patrols over the strait for years, and they routinely passed information on all ship sightings—including Communist-bloc vessels—to Nationalist authorities on Taiwan. As Dulles later explained to Eisenhower, Chiang's people treated this notification as "acquiescence, or invitation to action," and on two occasions after the Korean armistice Nationalist sailors seized Polish vessels, the tanker *Praca* and the new cargo ship *President Gottwald,* and brought them into the port of Kaohsiung.

Truman had instituted Seventh Fleet patrols in the strait back in 1950 as much to restrain as protect the obstreperous Chiang and his cohorts. The president's many and growing number of enemies had labeled him "soft on Communism" for this and other alleged acts of "appeasement." When the Republicans came to power in 1953 they took an ostentatiously hard line toward "international communism" in general and the Chinese Communists—fighting and killing American boys in Korea—in particular. In his first State of the Union message Eisenhower argued that "it was illogical for American naval power to 'shield Communist China'" so long as Beijing consistently refused to consider a Korean armistice. Although Washington harbored no overtly aggressive intentions toward Beijing, it was time "to lift the barrier against Nationalist offensive operations across the Taiwan Straits." But when in mid-June 1954 Dulles sent a memo to the Oval Office regarding "Soviet Tankers en route to Communist China," Eisenhower picked up the phone and called his secretary of state who "further explained" matters. Clearly, Chiang was now prepared to capture a Soviet ship, and Dulles was "rather disposed to let them [the Nationalists] go ahead on these boats. Our own hand won't be shown. Don't think it critical, one way or another. As to our moral position, & whether we're acting in good faith," Dulles "said it isn't the kind of thing we'd do openly. We're not sending American boat[s] or plane[s] to round up & stop this traffic. We do encourage the Chinese Nationalists who are theoretically in a state of civil war. They do it in exercise of their own belligerent rights, & [to] prevent their enemy from getting necessary materials. They take off cargo & let ships go." But this was not just any ship, it was a Soviet ship, and Dulles guardedly suggested that he, at least, had been and continued to encourage Chiang to go after the Russians. "There was [an] earlier ship we spotted last October," Dulles told Ike. "We were about to give information on it to the [Nationalist] Chinese so they could pick it up. Later information indicated that it might have been a decoy, so [we] let it go on by. But if it looks like real stuff this time, perhaps they can catch it."

"It" proved to be the *Tuapse* steaming off southern Taiwan, and Chiang's sailors did indeed "catch" the "big modern" Soviet tanker, bringing it into Kaohsiung, where it languished alongside the Polish vessels for months. Dulles had warned his president of the potentially serious consequences of such a seizure. Washington would have to insist that it had no part in the seizure itself, and "as a matter of habit, we gave this information to the Chinese." Aerial reconnaissance could not be considered an act of war in and of itself. Moreover, Moscow—and Beijing—knew full well that "our naval & air forces are under instructions to defend Formosa, & this is part of our whole scheme of affairs." Despite his secretary's casuistry—or perhaps because of it—Eisenhower "gave permission to give" Chiang's people "the information" about *Tuapse*. When the ship appeared in the Taiwanese port, Moscow promptly accused the United States Navy of piracy (surely no Chinese sailor could conceivably board a Soviet ship successfully) and dispatched warplanes and a few units of its still quite modest navy to escort other Soviet merchant vessels in the area. Nationalist officials stoutly maintained that *Tuapse*, like the two Polish vessels, was carrying war matériel to Communist China in the form of either jet fuel or electrical machinery. Soon thereafter, Chinese Communist planes shot down a British commercial airliner near the island of Hainan. U.S. search planes looking for survivors were attacked by two Communist fighters, but the fighters themselves were shot down by aircraft from two U.S. carriers that had steamed to the area to provide support.[34]

Dulles was not the only one inclined to dismiss complaints about Chiang's audacity. So was Admiral Felix B. Stump, commander in chief of the Pacific Fleet. The reassertion of American military power following 9/11 has led at least one prominent journalist to emphasize the supposedly overweening power that regional military commanders have assumed. These "Sinks, Proconsuls to the Empire," as Dana Priest has characterized them, have supposedly seized and exercised unprecedented political and diplomatic powers formerly in the possession of the White House and State Department.[35] In fact, contemporary "sinks" are acting within a long tradition of regional-command autonomy. Half a century ago, when both communications and travel were comparatively slow and crude, ambitious commanders in chief like Stump in the Pacific and the Sixth Fleet's Cat Brown enjoyed what would be considered in 2006 a remarkable independence of command. Moreover, as Brown demonstrated, they assiduously courted strongly conservative media sources like Henry Luce's *Life,* the *Saturday Evening Post, Colliers,* and *U.S. News and World Report* and used them as pulpits to make their views known and emphasize their own independent decision-making powers.

Unlike Brown's staff on *Salem,* Stump's subordinates in Honolulu did get home for cocktails, if not always on time. But their commander was as firm if marginally more discreet in his pronouncements as his colleague half a world away. When the Taiwan Strait became an arena of cold war tension in the summer of 1954 Stump granted an interview to *U.S. News.* Was there "anything" to the Communist Chinese charge that U.S. aircraft were "spotting" vessels heading for Shanghai and other Chinese ports for the Nationalists on Taiwan? "We conduct patrols over seas of the ocean in which we have an interest," the admiral shot back. Well, what about charges that Chiang's force had imposed a partial air and naval blockade on Shanghai? No aerial blockade was taking place. "However, the free Chinese do harass Communist Chinese coastal trade in this area by the use of naval craft. This results in increased costs to the Communists and reluctance of some [neutral] shipping firms to engage in Chinese mainland trade." Farther south, Stump added, Nationalist naval forces "maintain and protect the free Chinese islands near the mainland," namely, the Jinmens and Mazus.

Stump added that the Seventh Fleet was increasingly concerned about the growing Soviet submarine force and its capabilities. In its early postwar rape of the eastern half of Germany, the Red Army had seized naval units and technicians indiscriminately. Their haul had netted them most of the advanced German U-boat technologies, and Stalin had possessed both the wit and the desire to exploit this windfall, which at a stroke gave his formerly impuissant navy some significant muscle on the world ocean. By 1954, as the result of a forced-draft postwar submarine-construction program, Moscow had deployed about one hundred boats to the Pacific. Moreover, press reports from the mainland suggested that Beijing, too, was developing a significant underwater-warfare ability. But "there is no limit to our [maritime] rights," Stump said in response to a direct question. The United States had "traditionally upheld" such rights and fought to protect them from the time of the Barbary pirates 150 years before. "However," the admiral added prudently, "we do not ostentatiously do so simply to stir up trouble where our interests are not involved." Nonetheless, the United States Navy had a right to sail wherever it wished in Far Eastern waters "if it stays outside the three mile limit," the area traditionally defined as international waters. Stump was undoubtedly heartened by a recent presidential press conference comment that "any invasion of Formosa would have to run over the Seventh Fleet."[36] Eisenhower also authorized visits to the Dachens by Seventh Fleet destroyers, while calls arose in Congress and the Republican press (echoed, not surprisingly, in the Taiwanese capital of Taipei) for a mutual-defense treaty with Taiwan.

In September Mao abruptly escalated tensions. Coastal artillery in and around Xiamen shelled the Jinmens. On November 1, Chinese bombers began sporadically striking the Dachens. As the attacks continued, tensions mounted in Washington. Dulles signed a "U.S.-China Mutual Defense Treaty," which Chiang had long desired. Beijing replied with a pledge "to free Taiwan from the 'Chiang Kai-shek gang of traitors,'" together with a rather remarkable codicil stating that Taiwan's fall would be followed by an "armed occupation of the United States."[37] By the end of the year, Ike and others came to see the off-shore islands as a nuisance and an irritant. At one point the president moaned that he wished the offending pieces of rock and sand would just sink. Seventh Fleet aircraft carriers were never far from the Taiwan Strait during these anxious weeks. Nor was international attention, for that body of water was and remains a major world sea-lane. Daily, freighters carrying bulk cargoes from as far away as Europe and tankers laden with oil from the Middle East and Indonesia sailed the broad channel toward Shanghai, Vladivostok, and Tokyo Bay. In addition, the strait was at the time of the crisis a rich fishing ground, attracting Chinese from both sides; in short, the place was as strategically important, crowded, and even smaller and more constricted than the Persian Gulf thirty to fifty years later. "There are four navies of varying strength in this Strait," according to an October news report: "American, British, Nationalist Chinese and Communist Chinese." Nationalist warships "flit back and forth" between Taiwan and the mainland, "raiding Communist coastal shipping and bombarding shore targets."

Close to the mainland, warships of the Royal Navy's slowly declining Far Eastern Squadron escorted British merchant ships from Hong Kong to Shanghai,
Fuzhou, and other Communist ports. "Many American and all Chinese Nationalist officers" condemned such action as "decidedly 'unfriendly.'" But in 1949 His
Majesty's government had concluded that China itself remained too big, commercially attractive, and potentially powerful to ignore simply because its government had gone Communist. Britain had been one of the first non-Communist
nations to recognize the Mao regime and maintained its embassy in Beijing,
even as British soldiers fought beside their American cousins and other UN
forces in Korea.

   Above the strait, air activity was intense. From time to time, Chiang's people
made daring night penetrations of Communist airspace to parachute agents
onto the mainland. None were ever heard of again. Seventh Fleet carriers operating in waters north or south of Taiwan sent combat air patrols in periodic
dawn-to-dusk sweeps over the strait, while navy Mariner and Neptune patrol
planes "cruise lazily above the coast, watching for Communist ship or troop
concentrations." Although the fleet went "out of its way to be defensive and
precautionary," its patrol planes probed Communist defenses and electronic
capabilities aggressively. On two occasions in early 1953 and the summer of
1956, careless or unlucky aircraft strayed too close or learned too much, and
Chinese Communist gunners or pilots shot them down. For the most part,
however, Beijing remained defensive and cautious, keeping its "powerful air
forces based around Shanghai" firmly leashed. Taipei sporadically reported sight-
ing Soviet submarines in the strait, but the United States Navy was never able
to verify their presence. All in all, however, the Taiwan Strait in the 1950s was a
busy, stressful, and dangerous place.[38]

   For that reason alone, the Seventh's big ships and their escorts stayed away,
except for times of immediate crisis. Throughout the 1950s and early sixties, the
fleet was based primarily in Japan—at Yokosuka, roughly thirty miles down
the bay from Tokyo, and in the broad harbor of Sasebo on the southern island
of Kyūshū. Secondary bases were available: Cavite in Manila Bay and, by the
end of the period, Subic Bay, fifty miles to the north. Built around carrier Task
Force 77, the fleet, following the Korean War, maneuvered either in the open
waters immediately south and east of the Ryukyus or just south of the strait,
steaming in a broad triangle formed by the southern tip of Taiwan, Hong Kong
(a frequent port of call), and Luzon. Increasingly numerous and capable antisubmarine forces frequently "exercised" nearby. Task Force 77 was perpetually on

call, ready to "surge" into the strait at a moment's notice. With Pearl Harbor an always vivid memory, its sailors and airmen never completely relaxed. In 1958 fleet commander Frederick Kivette told a reporter that even in port, "we always tie up our carriers with the bows seaward. With our catapults, it is possible to launch a strike even while the carrier is in drydock."[39]

Eisenhower did not want a war in the strait, and he believed, correctly, that Mao felt the same. But both men displayed a disturbing willingness to try each other's—and the world's—patience by pushing the edge of the envelope. Fortunately, when one pushed, the other gave enough to avoid a fatal showdown. When Beijing launched a heavy air raid against the Dachens in January 1955, followed immediately by substantial shelling, then swift capture, of the nearby island of Yijiangshan, it represented a dramatic escalation in Communist Chinese amphibious-warfare capabilities. Eisenhower and Dulles realized what might be coming. Ike first ordered Task Force 77, which routinely maneuvered near the Dachens, to "avoid the area like poison," according to the disappointed Nationalist foreign minister, George Yeh.[40] With the Seventh Fleet suddenly nowhere in sight, Eisenhower and Dulles were able to convince a bitterly disappointed and reluctant Chiang that evacuation of the entire clearly indefensible island group was the only feasible course. In exchange, Chiang would be rewarded with a more specific pledge of American support. On February 7 the Seventh Fleet—the world's first "A-Bomb Navy," according to press reports—moved its five carriers (including the mighty *Midway* that had just transferred from the Atlantic), six cruisers, and fifty destroyers back toward the Dachens to cover the evacuation of Chiang's fifteen hundred–man garrison and those indigenous fishing families who wished to leave.

The Dachens were out of range of airfields on Taiwan but within easy distance for fighters and bombers on the mainland. Beijing could have readily established and maintained control of the skies over the embarkation beaches were it not for Seventh Fleet aircraft. Several hundred Cougars, Banshees, and propeller-driven Skyraiders raced aloft from their five flight decks to patrol the skies above the Dachens and to practice bombing and strafing in nearby waters. But the task force stayed well away from the mainland. The carrier *Yorktown* came closest when it steamed to within sixty miles of the China coast, well out of provocative range. Beijing radio reported that between January 24 and February 4, Seventh Fleet aircraft flew 2,200 sorties in 496 groups around the Dachens area. The Chinese should have known; their excellent radar could easily track the planes. Yet not a single fighter or bomber rose to challenge the American fliers.[41]

The Dachens were evacuated by the twenty-fifth, and the following day, with the surrounding seas empty of American warships, Chinese Communist troops moved in. Down in Hong Kong and later in Japan, rumors circulated that Chinese MiGs had made "dry" strafing runs on some of the navy transports and destroyers. Such tales were clearly false, though they summoned up the blood of one young sailor who foolishly wished he had been there. My shipmates, most of whom had served in Korea and some in World War II, quickly changed my mind.

At Eisenhower's request Congress passed the so-called Formosa Resolution, authorizing U.S. military action to protect Taiwan and such related positions and territories as the president deemed necessary. The language was meant to permit, but not guarantee, defense of the offshore islands of Jinmen and the Mazus. Eisenhower secretly promised Chiang help in defending the islands in case of an attack "at this time" but made no public comment. Further statements out of Washington hinting at the use of tactical nuclear weapons in case of war in the strait emboldened Chiang to ask U.S. approval for Nationalist air strikes against mainland air bases. Eisenhower, alarmed at the drift toward war, refused. Instead, he sent Admiral Radford, now chairman of the Joint Chiefs, and a high-ranking State Department official to Taipei to inform Chiang that the American pledge to defend the Mazus and Jinmens was now off the table. However, Radford was empowered to offer Chiang an even bigger prize: Seventh Fleet blockade of the sea-lanes along the China coast. Fortunately, the "generalissimo" angrily rejected the offer, declaring that he would defend the near offshore islands alone if he had to.

That proved to be unnecessary, as Beijing, too, was tiring of the game. At the Bandung Conference of Non-aligned Nations in April, Mao's deputy, Zhou Enlai, stated that his government was willing to enter into discussions with the United States on a variety of topics of mutual concern. The talks duly took place at the ambassadorial level, but dragged on for two years with little result.[42] The crisis eased, the Seventh Fleet continued its endless patrols of Asian waters, and the strait was left to its usual complement of freighters, cargo ships, tankers, fishing vessels, Chinese gunboats—and the squadron of American destroyers that had become a fixture in those waters since their first appearance shortly after the outbreak of the Korean War.

When Truman ordered the navy into the strait in the summer of 1950, he and his civil and naval commanders understood the practical and political limits of the gesture. The fleet's writ of responsibility ran from Singapore to the waters off Vladivostok, and the Korean conflict demanded the constant presence of carrier Task Force 77. Save in times of immediate crisis, a handful of destroyers would be sufficient to warn of a possible invasion build-up on either side of the strait while demonstrating American presence and resolve. So it was in 1951 and 1955, and so it would be until the recognition of China more than twenty years later rendered a permanent presence unnecessary. According to one well-informed reporter, one or two destroyers "prowl up and down the mainland coast and close to offshore islands. Their sensitive radar constantly scans the jagged inlets and rivers, and their crews carefully observe each of the hundreds of junks that put out daily from Communist ports and fishing villages." The ships were careful always to remain outside Communist China's declared twelve-mile territorial limit.[43]

Patrolling the Taiwan Strait was a dull, boring job punctuated by occasional moments of sudden high drama and excitement. In summer, "blistering heat . . . turns ships into ovens." In the spring and autumn monsoon winds turned the seas choppy, then raging, with enough force to spring a destroyer's frame. At other times horizons and waters were draped in fog. And always there were the junks, "which appear incongruous in the jet-powered twentieth century." The small, ungainly looking, wooden-hulled sailing vessels had been around for centuries, though many had recently become engine driven. They were prime weapons of invasion because, short of a direct hit, they were virtually unsinkable. When the Communists successfully invaded Hainan Island, south of Hong Kong, the three hundred–junk invasion force "carried bits of canvas and wooden pegs to plug holes resulting from Nationalist shore fire."[44]

A month after the Dachen crisis, with tensions in the strait still high, reporter William L. Worden rode the destroyer *Tingey* on a routine thirty-day patrol.[45] The ship and its sisters operated out of Kaohsiung, a city of half a million people in southwestern Taiwan. Typically, two destroyers of a squadron would sail the strait, while a third was on "R & R" in Hong Kong, and the fourth served as a communication vessel in harbor. Each month the vessels would exchange roles, and the entire squadron would be relieved every three to four months. Kaohsiung (which the Japanese occupiers of Taiwan between 1890 and 1945 had called Takao) "was one of the principal . . . invasion bases against the Philippines in 1942. Some of its better paving was done by American prisoners of war, held there for years." It was a typical Asian port of the time, its harbor "a still pond in a circle of hills tiered with tile-roofed houses and honeycombed by old Japanese caves and pillboxes." Rust-streaked Nationalist freighters clung to a double line of buoys, while *Tuapse* "still sits, steam up but going nowhere." At the piers a freighter flying the no-longer-frightening Rising Sun of Japan lay next to a line of Nationalist landing craft. "Junks, small trawlers, tugs and skiffs crisscross the bay like scores of waterbugs. Skiffs cluster at ships' gangways, ready to haul liberty-bound sailors toward the willing and adaptable young women waiting on shore." Out beyond most of the traffic lay a U.S. Navy oiler, with *Tingey* alongside. One bright afternoon the destroyer slowly backed away from its mother ship and with infinite care, its whistle constantly "bleating," began to thread its way through the heavy boat traffic toward the harbor mouth and the open sea beyond. The destroyer's slowly revolving propellers churned up "wonderful quantities of shrimp and garbage for the yelping gulls," while on its bridge Commander S. T. Howard, a serious-faced man in his late thirties, nervously smoked a cigarette and watched his ship's progress. Local lore had it that the sea devils who hung about seeking to bewitch unwary sailors and fishermen could be killed if one's junk or skiff passed sufficiently close to an on-charging vessel so that its bow would cut off the unseen ghoul. Daredevil sailors thus sought to pass directly under *Tingey*'s bow without being hit. "It's fine when they make it," Howard told Worden, "but when we were coming in this morning, one fishing boat misjudged. We picked up the skipper and other fishermen got the rest of the crew, but the boat sank. I'll be writing reports about it for a month."

Tingey at last reached the open sea "with guns manned, radar searching and sonar gear already pinging for" Soviet submarines that never appeared. "Cut-off devils presumably howled down both rails but there was no other problem. The fog was thin, the sea calm and the fishing boats remained well scattered," as *Tingey* headed for its sixty-mile-long patrol station somewhere off the China coast.

Howard's job was nearly impossible, though neither he nor anyone outside the highest circles of government guessed just how impossible it might be. Eisenhower had hinted at a new policy in his March 16 press conference when he stated that in "any general war in Asia" the United States would use tactical nuclear weapons against purely military targets. The president and Dulles agreed that tactical nukes would also be employed if the decision was made to defend the Jinmens and Mazus, since such weapons "alone will be effective against mainland air fields." Despite the administration's statement to Chiang that U.S. defense of the offshore islands was "off the table," Dulles told Senator Walter George nine days before Eisenhower's press conference that "under the present circumstances," it would be "impossible" for the United States to just stand aside and let the Communists march into Jinmens and the Mazus. If these islands, no more than five to twenty miles off the Chinese mainland, were allowed to fall to Beijing, "the psychological repercussions on Formosa and Southeast Asia," where the French were battling Vietnamese and Laotian insurgents, "would . . . make it almost certain that most of Asia would be lost to us. . . . [E]ffective defense of these islands would require the use of atomic weapons," Dulles continued, "because it would not be possible to knock out airfields and gun emplacements with conventional weapons in the face of Chinese manpower and capacity to replace and rebuild." Dulles assured a clearly shaken senator that the United States now possessed "missiles" that "had practically no radio-active fall-out and were entirely local in effect."[46] How local, the secretary did not say. Dulles never thought small, and anxieties about the communization of Asia never left him.

Howard and his men thus put to sea enormously burdened. One slipup, one miscalculation, one overeager response to an unclear situation, and they might create an incident that could easily escalate to a nuclear World War III. Destroyer sailors had already asked themselves and each other the ultimate question: "Would the United States go to war for one destroyer, if the communists decided to sink it without warning in the Formosa Strait?"

Howard's task was to avoid provoking a war while still patrolling with sufficient aggressiveness to make the American presence deeply felt. Ever shifting diplomatic and political assessments over which he had no control constantly changed the emphasis of his job. On one day he might be preoccupied with the Communists, ensuring that Mao's forces were not about to stage a sudden massive amphibious assault by junk across the strait and onto Taiwanese beaches. The following his chief task might be to discourage a too powerful Nationalist attack on the mainland. Here was the loneliness of command writ large. Howard and his sailors often experienced a sense of unreality as they steamed day after day on a racecourse pattern up and down the strait. Early in the cruise *Tingey*'s radar picked up a large target on radar through fog. As the heavy mist lifted, it revealed a freighter ahead, loosely surrounded by a collection of junks and small trawlers. Flying past the scattered collection, the destroyer came up astern of the big, clean ship displaying a British Union Jack painted on its side. Howard ordered signal flags displayed, as his warship's sharp bow came abreast of the freighter's blunt forecastle only a hundred yards away. Staring up at the bigger ship's bridge, Howard and his men made out the name: *Hoonah*. Another quiet order, and *Tingey*'s forward guns moved to train on *Hoonah*'s bridge. For long moments the freighter's Chinese crew lounging on the forecastle or standing in superstructure hatchways stared impassively at the destroyer alongside, as did several European officers in the pilothouse. At last, one spoke over his shoulder, and the destroyer's signal queries were answered by "a rash of pennants" from *Hoonah*. "Bound from Shanghai to Hong Kong," *Tingey*'s signal officer said. "She's the same one we saw out here last time." Howard hesitated for a moment, then shrugged. "Well, wish them a pleasant trip. It's all we can do. Take a picture and then get back on our base course."

Several nights later, the evening bridge game in the wardroom having "been fought to the last bitter rubber," and the last letter writer having collected his final cup of coffee, "the business of the Formosa patrol picked up" once again. Radar detected an unidentified aircraft a dozen miles away, no recognition signal, and closing on the destroyer's course "altitude a little low for comfort." Howard rushed out of his sea cabin, suddenly confronted with a problem that "makes his job in some ways more wearing on junior commanders involved than would be a patrol in all-out war." What was the captain to do? Fire on the stubbornly silent plane to protect his command from possible attack, only to start World War III if it proved to be Communist Chinese—or even Soviet? Do nothing and be bombed? And what if the aircraft was a "friendly"? Thirty-three years later another American skipper provided with a high-tech warship unimaginable to the men of 1955 would make the wrong decision in the Persian Gulf, and *Vincennes*—Robo-cruiser to critics—would send more than two hundred people to their deaths when the ship's Aegis surface-to-air missile downed an Iraqi airliner.

On this March night in the Taiwan Strait, Captain Howard chose to play it straight and as safe as possible. He ordered fire control to lock the five-inch main batteries on the aircraft, then called a Chinese Nationalist naval officer riding the ship as a trainee to take over the radio and attempt contact with the aircraft. But Commander Chai hailed from Hunan; perhaps the pilot came from another distant province. In any case the distant aviator replied, but in no way that Chai could understand. Finally, the pilot did what he should have done, giving his course and speed in English (then, as now, the international language of air traffic), even as he crossed *Tingey*'s course and flew on. "He never did say who he was, though. And if he ever had known the correct identification procedure, he gave no sign." Captain Howard earned a lifetime's pay that night.

Still later, *Tingey* ran into days and days of fog so thick that Howard slowed his swift warship down dramatically and stationed lookouts in the bow supporting the radar's constant search for junks and sampans. At one point the ship ran through a cluster, barely visible. Howard once again became nervous when the radar officer informed him that several of the sampans appeared to be motorized. Signalmen and officers crowded the bridge wing and signal deck, straining to make out the precise composition of the nest. Could it be hiding one or two Communist motor torpedo boats? "Motor torpedo boats got a nat [Nationalist warship] last fall," Howard told Worden soberly. "They were hiding in a bunch of fishing boats." Fortunately, the sampans began to scatter "like sparrows frightened on a street corner," and as the destroyer glided slowly past, its bridge people saw that all the boats had the Nationalist flag painted on their wooden sides. What these fishermen were doing "a bare thirty miles off land closed to them" was anyone's guess, but not *Tingey's* responsibility. Howard had again used his head in a potentially disastrous situation and averted a crisis. Nine and a half years later in the Tonkin Gulf, two other destroyers, *Maddox* and *C. Turner Joy,* on an intelligence mission to provoke North Vietnamese radar operators into revealing their location and system capabilities, were not so careful or so lucky. On a dark, moonless night, the two captains allowed themselves to conclude on the basis of what one later described as "freak weather effects and overeager sonar men" that they had been attacked by North Vietnamese torpedo boats when in fact no weapons had been fired at them. Pentagon carelessness and overeager interpretation of events by a Johnson administration anxious to bloody Hanoi for its support of Vietcong rebels in South Vietnam escalated the alleged incident to the point that it became one of the two foundations of the most controversial and arguably most humiliating war in American history.[47]

Never again would Lyndon Johnson or any other president permit local commanders, especially those of relatively junior rank, to set or frame national policy. But in a time before ultrasophisticated electronic communications encouraged Washington to manipulate distant battlefields and crisis spots, Howard and his fellow destroyer skippers in the Taiwan Strait continued to enjoy such latitude, though within the context of clearly defined policy. Fortunately, they employed the limited power at their disposal with restraint and discretion. Within days of the sampan incident, *Tingey* returned to Kaohsiung harbor, dodged the small boats hoping to use the ship as a devil killer, and tied up at its buoy. Within moments the first tired sailors were being skiffed ashore for another round of R & R, Far Eastern style.

Tingey's experience, replicated a thousand times and more during the lifetime of the Taiwan Strait patrol, was nothing more nor less than a routine exercise conducted by an imperial navy. Under different circumstances, river gunboats like *Luzon* and *Panay* had done similar enforcement work on the Yangtze for three generations before World War II, albeit much of their time in the tumultuous years of the Chinese Revolution after 1926 involved protecting or evacuating Christian missions. Destroyers and smaller vessels, both U.S. Navy and Coast Guard, would do the same kind of intercept and interdiction work in the coastal waters off Korea, Vietnam, and, much later, the Persian Gulf. The work was always dangerous, provocative, and potentially disastrous. Shortly before *Tingey* completed its patrol, another destroyer found itself "a few miles" off the mainland coast when Nationalist planes suddenly staged a raid on a nearby Communist port. One of the aircraft was badly hit and headed for sea, the pilot bailing out over the water just before his plane crashed. "In international law, the right of a neutral to make rescues is clear." The destroyer was, ostensibly, a neutral, though Chinese and American boys had stopped killing each other in Korea just short months before. So "without hesitation" the destroyer raced in at flank speed to pick up the downed pilot "somewhere in the water a few hundred yards from" the Communist "shore." The downed pilot's wingman, who should have remained long enough to indicate a precise location, flew over his downed colleague once, waggled his wings, and raced for Taiwan with antiaircraft fire bursting about him. Searching blind, the destroyer itself soon came under intense fire from enraged Communist gunners. "For long moments the skipper kept his bow headed in until geysers—perhaps only antiaircraft shells falling short, perhaps coastal guns more directly aimed—were reported by lookouts on both sides." Seeing his small, delicate ship being straddled, the captain reluctantly hauled around and left the area. As the destroyer showed its stern to the putative enemy, lookouts high in the superstructure saw fishing boats that had put out from shore hauling the limp body of the pilot out of the water.

The Seventh Fleet worked hard to stay atop a technologically changing cold war world. In February 1956 more than seventy warships and support vessels converged on Iwo Jima from all points on the compass for a "gigantic atomicage amphibious operation," nearly eleven years to the day after the marines had landed on the tiny island in World War II. Plans called for simulated use of atomic weapons for "softening" the beach defenses. The landing forces "will also practice defense against atomic attack." To simulate the real event, plasticcased projectiles were dropped over the task force to simulate nuclear air bursts, exploding harmlessly about a thousand yards overhead to create a mushroom cloud. The invasion armada was positioned in "new and complex" ways to avoid bunching them in so small an area that one bomb could wipe out the entire force. Three carriers, three cruisers, four destroyers, and several submarine radar picket ships constituted the striking and covering force, while an "enemy" group consisting of a single carrier and a handful of supporting vessels would seek to disrupt the movement toward Iwo.[48]

By the summer of 1958 global conditions had changed drastically. The ever growing Soviet arsenal of both tactical and strategic nuclear weapons, the Kremlin's impressive capabilities in missiles (two Sputniks had already been successfully launched into low earth orbit), and its steadily advancing submarine technology, now on the verge of nuclear propulsion, markedly diminished the power and effect of conventional military forces. There was widespread feeling in the Pentagon that although the strategic and tactical nuclear arsenals were sufficient, the country's limited conventional forces were being stretched too thinly in the face of heightened Sino-Soviet activity. On the eve of the Lebanese crisis, which would tie the Sixth Fleet to the eastern Mediterranean for many weeks, Arleigh Burke told Congress that "the mutual capacity to annihilate each other as we have seen is not a deterrent to Communist aggression by other means. It is in fact likely that the Communists will channel greater effort into the cold war. . . . Massive [nuclear] destruction will not prevent this type of creeping aggression."[49]

Despite the Seventh Fleet's power and responsiveness, the White House continued to fret intermittently over the situation in the Far East. Eisenhower had urged Chiang during the first strait crisis to abandon the Mazus and Jinmens along with the Dachens; the generalissimo had adamantly refused. Stuck with an ally who was at once unwelcome yet, in overriding cold war terms, essential, Washington determined to make Taiwan, at least, impregnable. The latest air-to-air missiles were shipped to Taipei, permitting Nationalist pilots to sweep the skies above the strait and the offshore islands clean of Chinese Communist MiGs. Eight-inch howitzers capable of lobbing nuclear-tipped shells onto the mainland were sent to the Jinmens and Mazus, though the nuclear tips stayed in the United States. But what the Eisenhower administration saw as a reluctant necessity to defend, Chiang interpreted as a mandate to attack. Back in April the generalissimo had begged for help in establishing guerrilla bases on the mainland. When Washington rejected the scheme, Chiang fell into despair. Early in August he told the head of the U.S. defense command on Taiwan that "strategic control" of the strait had been lost, and a "tactical" threat to the offshore islands was "imminent." Khrushchev had just concluded an abruptly scheduled visit to Beijing when, on the seventh, CIA director Allen Dulles informed the National Security Council that "the situation in the Taiwan Strait was 'heating up.'" Communist and Nationalist naval vessels had begun to clash with increasing frequency, and President Eisenhower was informed that "Sabre jets of the Chinese Nationalist Air Force began encountering Soviet built MiGs with more frequency." Officials in both Washington and Taipei took due note of Khrushchev's sudden appearance in Beijing, and though Dulles suggested correctly that it might reflect a degree of tension and rivalry between the two Communist camps, conventional cold war thinking assumed that the Soviets and Chinese were collaborating in a new initiative to destabilize the Western world and its allies.[50]

In fact, Mao detested Khrushchev, who had about run out of patience with his Chinese "comrade." The origin of the Soviet premier's hasty trip to China at the end of July 1958 lay in a proposal that began among the Russian naval advisers attached to Beijing's tiny fleet. In a burst of enthusiasm, the advisers told their hosts that all China had to do to obtain the newest Soviet nuclear submarine technology was to send a cable to Moscow asking for it. At the end of June, Premier Zhou Enlai did just that, requesting that Moscow "provide technology and documentation for construction of Chinese nuclear submarines with SLBMs [sea-launched ballistic missiles]." The request provoked a remarkable counterproposal from Moscow. The two great Communist powers should make a naval pact, including establishment of a Soviet naval radar station in China "to help Soviet submarine and surface fleets operate against the U.S. Navy in the Pacific" and establishment of "a joint Sino-Soviet submarine flotilla, operating under Soviet command." This "joint ownership and operating agreement," as Mao chose to characterize it, would permit Soviet submarines, including the first nuclear-powered boats, now in the pipeline, to deploy from ports along the entire Chinese coast. The Soviet fleet would at last be free of the historic geographic shackles that had kept Russian navies forever pent up in the Baltic and Black Seas and behind the island barriers of the northwest Pacific.

Late in July Mao summoned the Soviet ambassador and to Pavel Yudin's undoubted chagrin delivered a blistering rejection of the whole idea. He was withdrawing his navy's "request for [obtaining] nuclear powered submarines," Mao said. "Your navy's nuclear submarines are of a [top] secret advanced technology. The Chinese people are careless in handling things. If we are provided with them we might put you to trouble." Mao's latent sarcasm then turned to open anger. The Soviet comrades had exercised world power for forty years and well knew how to manipulate and exploit those with whom they cooperated. Under Stalin the Soviets had demonstrated in China as well as elsewhere that partnerships with the Soviets always redounded to their benefit, but no one else's. "You never trust the Chinese!" Mao burst out.

You only trust the Russians! [To you] the Russians are the first class [people] whereas the Chinese are among the inferior who are dumb and careless. Therefore [you] came up with the joint ownership and operation proposition. Well if [you] want joint ownership and operation, how about them all—let us turn into joint ownership and operation our army, navy, air force, industry, agriculture, culture and education. Can we do this? Or [you] may have all of China's more than ten thousand kilometers of coastline and let us only maintain a guerrilla force. With a few atomic bombs you think you are in a position to control us through asking for the right of rent and lease.

Mao continued in this vein for another several moments before dismissing Yudin, who promptly sent what must have been a quietly frantic cable to Moscow that brought Khrushchev winging in to Beijing within the week on a damage-control mission ordered by the Politburo.[51]

Mao held firm. There would be no joint operating agreement; the Soviet proposal had literally put him off his feed and left him sleepless, Mao told his visitor. Khrushchev quickly backed off, alternately denying the proposal's seriousness and stating that it was a dumb idea. There is no evidence from Soviet or Chinese files to date that Mao informed Khrushchev of the rain of shells that would soon descend upon the Jinmens and Mazus. Clearly, there was no Sino-Soviet plot or agreement to try to wrest the islands from Chiang's grasp, thereby threatening a third world war.[52]

Mao himself gave an explanation of policy when he addressed the Standing Committee of the Chinese Communist Party on the evening of August 23, just hours after the People's Liberation Army began its heavy shelling of the offshore islands. He had indeed been following American military deployments and had concluded that Washington was so involved in Lebanon that it could not and would not respond effectively to a new offshore-islands crisis. Mao and the party's Central Committee had therefore decided well before the Khrushchev visit "to conduct certain military operations in the Taiwan Straits to support the Arabs' anti-imperialist struggle as well as to crack down on" Chiang's "frequent and reckless harassment along the Fujian coast across from Jinmen and Mazu." As early as August 8, American intelligence had learned that the Chinese were deploying their best MiG-17 jet fighters to airfields near the offshore islands. In mid-July Chiang had put his own garrisons on extreme alert. Surely, Mao concluded, he, too, was up to something. Better that Beijing strike first. Later, Mao took aside Wu Lengxi, editor of the party's chief newspaper, the *People's Daily,* and amplified his remarks. "The bombardment of Jinmen, frankly speaking, was our turn to create international tension for a purpose. We intended to teach the Americans a lesson. America had bullied us for many years, so now we had a chance, why not give it a hard time?" Washington had "started a fire" in the Middle East, and now Beijing was doing the same in the Far East. "In our propaganda, however, we still need to condemn the Americans for causing tension in the Taiwan Straits." The Yanks had two large air bases on Taiwan and a big naval base in the Philippines. "Their largest fleet, the Seventh Fleet, often cruises in the Taiwan Straits. . . . The chief of staff of the American navy [presumably a reference to CNO Burke] had stated not long ago (around 6 August) that the American armed forces were ready anytime for a landing campaign in the Taiwan Straits just as it did in Lebanon. That was eloquent proof [of America's ambition] Mao said."[53]

The breaking crisis forced Eisenhower and his advisers to turn their attention from Lebanon to Taiwan. During the previous three years Chiang had, contrary to U.S. advice, deployed some eighty thousand troops to the offshore islands. The Nationalists had committed the "heart" of their military and naval establishments to the defense of the islands, Burke told the National Security Council. "Consequently, they had acquired a new strategic importance." Thus, Chiang was on the verge of drawing his American patrons right into the middle of the ongoing Chinese civil war. As news reached the States of the sudden bombardment, administration officials, including Dulles and Burke, immediately emphasized that the United States would go all the way in defending Taiwan. Privately, they thought defense of the offshore islands against attack would require use of tactical nuclear weapons. Eisenhower was determined to avoid hostilities if possible and, if Washington was forced to intervene, to restrict action to the immediate battle area. But he recognized that combat, once begun, might lead to a wider war, and if that occurred, Ike later wrote, the United States might at some point have to begin launching attacks into the Chinese interior as a "punishing" operation. Dulles publicly urged Mao not to invade the Jinmens or Mazus. "Any such naked use of force would pose an issue far transcending the offshore islands and even the security of Taiwan. . . . It would forecast a widespread use of force in the Far East which would endanger vital free world positions and the security of the United States."[54] As the shelling continued day after day and Chinese patrol boats laid virtual siege to the Jinmens, preventing essential supplies and reinforcements from reaching the embattled islands, it became clear that Mao's strategy was not to invade but simply to starve the garrisons out. Overt combat would be avoided, making it difficult for Washington and Taipei to find sufficient excuse for military and naval action.

Washington, however, refused to play Beijing's game. It surged Seventh Fleet carriers to the edge of the strait and cruisers and destroyers into the waterway itself. On the night after Chinese Communist batteries had begun firing on the islands, aircraft from two carriers made supersonic sweeps very near the off-shore islands. "Chinese complaints soon indicated that they had gotten the message," but Beijing radio defiantly continued to announce "an imminent invasion of Quemoy." By August 28 three carriers were "deployed in a fan-shaped formation to the north, east, and south of Taiwan." Eisenhower and the Pentagon then called Mao's bluff, announcing that the Seventh Fleet would be reinforced with carriers not only from California but also from the Sixth Fleet in the Mediterranean (where the Lebanon crisis had by now measurably eased). Moreover, Seventh Fleet units would begin escorting Nationalist convoys to within the universally acknowledged three-mile limit of Chinese coastal waters, which practically meant onto the beaches at Jinmen. Mao promptly raised the ante, reminding the world that China's territorial waters extended twelve, not three, miles from the coast.[55]

The mood in Washington was somber. In a September 4 memo to the president that in fact confirmed an existing consensus within the upper reaches of State, Defense, and the intelligence community, John Foster Dulles set forth the kind of cold war scenario that his brother, CIA director Allen Dulles, had rejected just days before in suggesting at least a degree of tension and rivalry between Khrushchev and Mao. Now, "Foster's" memorandum insisted that "events in the Taiwan Straits indicate that the Chicoms, with Soviet backing, have begun tentatively to put into operation a program, which has been prepared for over the past 3 years, designed initially to liquidate the Chinat positions in Taiwan and the offshore islands, and with probably even more far-reaching purposes." Later that day Dulles wrote to British prime minister Harold Macmillan about "the Sino-Soviet strategy" that was "designed to put strains upon us at many separate places and our various commitments to NATO, in Korea, to individual allies, are spreading our forces too thin for comfort."[56]

The Soviets, meantime, tried with increasing desperation to determine their Chinese comrades' mood and direction. Khrushchev and his colleagues were convinced from the start that Mao wanted to seize the offshore islands, and when the Americans began rattling their nuclear sabers, the Soviet premier on September 7 wrote Eisenhower invoking the Sino-Soviet Treaty of 1950 that regarded an attack on either ally as an attack on both. But all Soviet efforts to penetrate Chinese intentions were rebuffed. When Foreign Minister Andrei Gromyko flew to Beijing the first week in September, ostensibly to coordinate

positions at the forthcoming UN conference but really to probe Chinese thinking, he got a decided mixed message. Zhou assured him there would be no war,
but government-stimulated war hysteria was sweeping the country, and at one
point Zhou warned Gromyko that the USSR should stay out of the Taiwan fracas
in case the Americans employed tactical nuclear weapons. Khrushchev was left
twisting in the wind. Was Mao testing his friendship and loyalty? Or dragging
him into a possible Sino-American war without telling him? "After deliberating
for almost twenty days," during which Beijing called for ambassadorial talks to
defuse the crisis, the Soviet Politburo "sent a special message . . . on 27 September,
'thanking' the Chinese for their noble attitude, but affirming its intention to
consider" a possible Western war against China "a war with the entire Socialist
camp."[57] Khrushchev had kept his temper and his nerve. The old schemer began
to see a glimmer of some hope for Soviet foreign policy in the growing strait
muddle. But first he and Mao had had to endure some difficult moments.

The turning point in the crisis came during the first week of September
when the Seventh Fleet made clear to Beijing just how far the United States was
willing to go in supporting the Chinese Nationalists. In the steadily intensifying
political-military poker game between Beijing and Washington, the Americans
called China's bluff regarding territorial waters. As logistics experts at home, at
Pacific Fleet headquarters in Honolulu, and on Taiwan scrambled to determine
minimum supply requirements for the besieged islands, the Pentagon announced
that the Seventh Fleet would escort convoys to Jinmen. Just how close American warships would come was left unclear. Beijing got the message, and on the
sixth Zhou called for ambassadorial talks "to make another effort for the defense
of peace." The Americans did not relent. The following day the first coordinated
convoy under U.S. escort, two heavy cruisers, one of them *Helena,* and six destroyers, sailed "to within four miles of the beach at Quemoy. . . . Grey-helmeted
gun crews stood ready to go into action if the Communist shore batteries
opened fire." They never did. "The usual fleet of Chinese fishing junks scattered
and disappeared as the warships approached." Radar picked up three Communist aircraft that promptly veered off some thirty miles away. "There was no sign
of the Communist torpedo boats that had successfully broken up most of the
Nationalists' previous attempts to bring in supplies." Torpedo boats "don't live
long in the presence of destroyers," declared Vice Admiral Wallace M. Beakley,
the task force commander. The American warships stood quietly off the beach as
the convoy went in, unloaded its cargo, and came back out. Then the little fleet
steamed back to Taiwan. The next daily convoy did not fare as well. U.S. escort
vessels, including a cruiser, stayed well out of range, and the Nationalist supply

ships encountered heavy and effective shelling as they approached the beach, achieving "only limited success." But the Seventh Fleet had made its point. At any moment several big cruisers with eight-inch-gun main batteries could choose to come in very close to Jinmen, leaving Communist gunners with the alternatives of either keeping silent or starting hostilities in which they would doubtless be the first victims.[58]

The American media, if not the government, clung to the belief that Beijing's "over all strategy" had been "worked out by Red China's Mao Tse-tung and Russia's Nikita S. Khrushchev during their recent Peking meeting." In fact, Khrushchev had no control over the Chinese Communist Party chairman. Despite Zhou's call for talks, Mao himself wanted to prolong the crisis as long as possible. "It became clear to me," a Soviet diplomat recalled long afterward, "then just a young China specialist, that the [off-shore] islands were not the issue. The issue was domestic, not foreign policy." Chinese peasants were working in their fields with rifles stacked nearby. "The war preparations also explained to people why they had to eat less and work harder." When Soviet diplomats decided to place themselves in the middle of the Sino-American dispute, their ostensible Chinese friends reacted with anger. At one point in September, after consulting Washington informally, the Soviets informed Beijing that a deal might be worked out in which the Chinese army would cease shelling the islands in exchange for a renewed American effort to persuade Chiang to remove his troops. "We do not need any [of your mediating] mission with the Americans!" Mao retorted. "This is our business." Beijing would prolong the crisis as long as possible as "a means of educating all the peoples of the world, first of all the Chinese people," on the need for discipline and sacrifice to achieve material progress.[59] Soon enough, however, the Great Leap Forward faltered; outright famine loomed, and Mao let the second strait crisis sputter out like the first.

The first signs of easement came early in the morning of October 6, 1958, when Mao's defense minister, Peng Te-huai, broadcast a message to "compatriots in Taiwan" stating that "out of humanitarian considerations," the "bombardment on the "Fukien front" would be suspended for seven days. "Within this period," Peng added, "you will be fully free to ship in supplies" to the Jinmens and Mazus "on condition there be no American escort." Eisenhower and his people, realizing that they had won, ordered an immediate suspension of Seventh Fleet convoying. The silence lasted far longer than a week, and on the twenty-fifth Peng sent another message winging out into the strait to Taiwan noting that the continued "refrain" from shelling "is still conditional on not in-

troducing American escorts."[60] Soon thereafter, the Chinese did resume sporadic shelling, but let Taipei and Washington know that it would bombard the
offshore islands at most every other day. In each interim, Nationalist supply
ships could safely unload. Having made the point that he could shell the islands
as long as he wished, and Chiang could resupply them as long as he wished,
Mao let the siege die out with steadily diminishing intensity and ever more inter-
mittent shelling until at last the guns of Xiamen fell silent.

Khrushchev, having seen Mao's "shock therapy" succeed in part, promptly
moved the axis of crisis to central Europe, demanding that the Western powers
leave Berlin. Many at the time linked Taiwan and Berlin as part of a coordinated
Sino-Soviet Communist strategy to destabilize the entire world, but they were
quite wrong. By this time, Khrushchev and Mao worked apart, not in tandem,
though the cumulative effect in terms of world tension was roughly the same.

The exercise of sea power lay at the heart of both Taiwan Strait crises, and
overall Washington played well the predominant force at its disposal. The
essential throughout was the preservation of Chiang's Taiwan regime, but it was
enormously complicated by Chiang's own impulses; the existence of numerous
offshore Nationalist garrisons in the Dachens, Jinmens, Mazus, and elsewhere;
the possible use of nuclear weaponry; the provision of intelligence data to the
"Nationalist" government; and mounting tensions between Khrushchev and
Mao. Having determined in early 1955 that Chiang could not defend the
Dachens, Eisenhower ordered the Seventh Fleet to evacuate the islands, then
stood aside as Beijing sent its forces in. Having determined in both 1955 and
1958 that the Jinmens and Mazus were vital to U.S. and "free world" interests
(they were not), Eisenhower not only threatened the use of nuclear weapons,
which he himself admitted could alienate world opinion, but also moved the
Seventh Fleet into the strait in a show of force. He kept it there during moments
of peak crisis and, at last, dispatched a powerful cruiser-destroyer force right up
to the beaches of Jinmen as a show of American resolve not to let the offshore islands fall. In so doing he challenged—and broke—the Chinese air and
artillery blockade. In the end the force applied was sufficient to realize the
desired result: Mao's troops not only would never see the beaches of Taiwan but
would not even seize islands that, according to Chinese law (and, with the
future Law of the Sea Treaty, international law as well), clearly belonged with
national territorial waters. The only point at which the Eisenhower-Dulles
team faltered was in allowing Chiang's tiny navy to seize Communist-bloc vessels and eventually even a Soviet tanker. Any tacit encouragement of the gener-

alissimo was dangerous; to encourage him in this endeavor was foolhardy, and Ike was fortunate that the Kremlin, still bedeviled by post-Stalin power struggles, did not push its legitimate cry of piracy further.

By the time the second Taiwan Strait crisis wound down in 1958, the United States had already fought one major war in East Asia and was not that many years away from fighting another. The pretext in both instances was Communist aggression, an indubitable fact in igniting the Korean conflict, a more dubious proposition with respect to Vietnam. Both wars, however, imposed surprisingly similar patterns of experience and frustration on the Seventh Fleet.

CHAPTER 4

The A-frame Factor and Other Frustrations

Korea and Vietnam

THE MORE AMERICA'S cold war admirals planned, built, and trained for sophisticated strategic warfare against the Sino-Soviet bloc, the more their fleet was deployed on tactical wartime missions against small and comparatively primitive Asian states whose allegiance to Communism was unmistakable but whose ties to Moscow and Beijing were often tense and tenuous.

The Korean and Vietnam Wars were waged firmly within the cold war struggle, but their implications for American sea power ultimately transcended that context. After the first six months of movement, the Korean conflict settled into a stalemate that resembled nothing so much as the trench combat of World War I on a somewhat less intense scale. Vietnam was from the start a fluid, essentially guerrilla, war. Neither of these prolonged conflicts could have been prosecuted without "absolute control of the sea. . . . If our control of the sea had been contested just a little bit," Admiral Arleigh Burke recalled, "Korea would have been lost very fast. If there had just been some submarines or something like that." The Soviets possessed reasonably sophisticated U-boats by 1950, and "with a submarine you never know what nationality it is under there. If there had just been a torpedo launched from a Russian submarine and we would never have been able to prove it, or mines, or things like that. They put their mines in too

late. They were caught without using all the things that they could have used."[1]
The same was true of Vietnam—on both sides.

But in both wars, control of the sea-lanes to and around distant battlefields
did not translate into consistently effective power projection ashore. When not
in direct tactical support of ground forces, naval power in Korea and Vietnam
was employed in endless and frustrating aerial and surface interdiction campaigns
against the transportation and communication infrastructures of industrially
weak but militarily stubborn enemies who were sustained and doubtless encouraged by Washington's unwillingness to seek outright victory in a cold war
environment.

When the North Korean People's Army erupted across the thirty-eighth parallel on June 25, 1950, and Harry Truman rallied the United Nations to stop it,
Douglas MacArthur, the Supreme Allied Commander in the Far East, was confronted with a major problem. He had an army on occupation duty in Japan,
but how to get it across the narrow seas to Korea? And how was he to evacuate
American citizens from the battle zone? Aircraft could not do the massive job;
only ships could. Fortunately, MacArthur did not share the disastrous prejudices of senior army people in Washington. Just days before the invasion he had
invited Rear Admiral James H. Doyle, commander of the Pacific Fleet's amphibious force, to bring his handful of attack cargo, transportation, and command
vessels to Japan to train elements of the Eighth Army how to assault enemy-
held coasts from the sea. These ships together with a few big landing ship tank
(LST) vessels already in Japanese waters were thus immediately available to
transport the Eighth Army and critical supplies to the far southern Korean port
of Pohang-dong where blocking positions were established to hold the North
Korean tide until further reinforcements from a drastically drawn-down American military establishment and other UN countries could be poured in. "Nearly
every soldier sent to Korea from Japan, together with 99 percent of the logistical
support" went "by sea" during the crucial early days and weeks of the conflict.[2]
Sea power had saved what soon became a MacArthur-directed United Nations
Command from disaster.

For ten weeks American and UN troops grimly held on to an ever shrinking
semicircular perimeter above the port of Pusan at the very southern tip of the
peninsula while North Korean forces battered and pounded them daily with
artillery, tanks, and infantry assaults. Following initial air strikes against enemy
airfields in and around Pyongyang and a large oil refinery in the Wonsan area,
navy and marine fighters and fighter bombers concentrated on providing close
air support for the desperate defense of the perimeter and later the breakout

and pursuit by Eighth Army and the Tenth Corps to the Chongchou River, the Chongjini reservoir, and the coastal area above Hungnam.[3] Fighter-bomber directors aboard the carriers of Task Force 77 experienced "a lot of trouble... during the whole Korean war" coordinating close air support of frontline troops with the air force. The navy had accepted the marines' system of relying on the frontline troops to directly call in air support against enemy-troop formations, often as close as one hundred yards or less. Flying off both fleet and smaller escort carriers sailing close to shore and thus to the battle lines, U.S. Navy and Marine Corps fliers were but minutes away from responding to any call for help. The air force, however, relied on small planes flying above the battlefield to spot danger points. As a consequence, "If a soldier with a group of Army forces wanted close air support, he called his boss, his commander, and then the commander called the Air Force liaison, and the Air Force liaison called the... controlling aircraft.... Then they brought in the combat planes.... This was one of the big troubles around the Pusan perimeter, because there they had to have close air support and it had to be close because the troops were being pushed back." Moreover, in the war's initial stage, air force fighter bombers were based in Japan, "three or four hours away," which meant their loiter time over the battlefield was often little more than half an hour.[4] Fortunately for the Allies, the besieging North Koreans had no air support whatsoever, relying on artillery and manpower.

In shipping the Eighth Army to Korea with efficiency and dispatch, Admiral Doyle had won MacArthur's undying trust, and navy brass leveraged that relationship vigorously. As American and UN forces settled into their increasingly strong defense perimeter at the foot of the peninsula, MacArthur informed Doyle that he wanted the navy to land the First Cavalry Division at Inchon. Doyle and the commander in chief, Pacific Fleet (CinCPac), Arthur Radford, were able to convince MacArthur to employ the First Provisional Marine Division as the spearhead of the assault because it had been blooded in combat at the perimeter and was experienced in amphibious operations. But when the division was pulled out of line, the North Koreans rushed in, threatening to overwhelm the marines' poorly trained replacements. General Walton Walker tried to get the marines back, and General Ned Almond, who would command the Tenth Corps once ashore at Inchon, backed him up. Radford and Doyle once again had to expend precious bureaucratic chips to get the leathernecks reinstated, and once again MacArthur supported them.

At home a huge, frantic build-up of men and equipment began. By early September the rapidly augmented Seventh Fleet was ready and able to support a dramatic counterstroke against North Korean aggression. Fleet commander Arthur D. Struble "used his authority directly" to prevent the air force from participating in the Inchon operation. Struble did not want the crowded skies above the narrow beachhead filled with planes reporting to different commands and committed to different mission responsibilities. The admiral later wrote that he "was wary of the elaborate coordinating arrangements which always seemed necessary when Air Force units took part in invasions." Struble wanted the experienced navy carrier pilots of Task Force 77 and especially the marine flyers based aboard the smaller escort and light fleet flattops to operate without hindrance. Eleven weeks of unremitting war had given these men an intimate familiarity with the kind of close air support essential for successful amphibious operations. He got his way, but the navy would pay a price for humbling the air force.[5]

On September 15, 1950, Doyle's amphibians boldly landed one marine and one army division at Inchon, a small port town ten miles west-southwest of Seoul lying far behind enemy lines. The assault was arguably the most audacious—if not foolhardy—amphibious operation of all time. The build-up in Japan was quickly reported to both Beijing and Moscow. Chinese authorities immediately passed the word to Pyongyang with the suggestion that Inchon was a prime target. Soviet military advisers repeatedly warned their North Korean hosts of the same thing. Finally, the presence of a small and foolishly active American–South Korean reconnaissance team in the area should have been a tipoff to the Reds that something major was about to take place at Inchon. But Pyongyang had good reason to be complacent. The town was situated above formidable sixteen-foot-high seawalls. Between those seawalls and the ocean lay several miles of mudflats that were either inundated or exposed by tides that reached more than thirty feet at flood to minus half a foot at ebb. A single low-tide channel through the mudflats was dominated by a small but high island called Wolmi. An amphibious assault could be mounted only at high tide, and the first invaders could be stranded and destroyed by alert and determined defenders above the seawalls with no hope of early reinforcement or resupply. However, MacArthur, now Supreme UN Commander, was determined to take the risk and with the inestimable aid of Lieutenant Commander Eugene Clark's small reconnaissance team, the U.S. Navy, Army, and Marine Corps made the operation good.[6] Although two days of preinvasion bombing and shelling gave the operation away, marine shock troops were able to land below the seawalls, scale them, clear the surrounding buildings of enemy troops, and establish an ever expanding beachhead for the seventy thousand soldiers and marines that followed them ashore. With the town secured and air supremacy ensured, the expeditionary force could be sufficiently resupplied and reinforced through the one low-tide channel through the mud flats at any time during the day or night.

Once ashore, leathernecks and soldiers brushed aside weak resistance and raced to Seoul, which was recaptured on the twenty-fifth. Fully aware of the sudden danger to their rear, the North Koreans on the perimeter began a rapid withdrawal, chased by Walton Walker's rejuvenated UN forces. Caught in a trap between the UN forces breaking out of the perimeter and the soldiers and marines of the Tenth Corps at Seoul, the North Koreans scrambled frantically to get back over the thirty-eighth parallel before they were squeezed to death. While Walker's Eighth Army and its allied UN divisions moved toward Seoul and on across the parallel to Pyongyang, MacArthur ordered most of the Tenth Corps reembarked and sent by sea around the other side of the peninsula to Wonsan, where a more routine but nonetheless well-executed amphibious assault (which had to await the tedious clearing of an enemy minefield) placed it on the right flank of the now thoroughly routed North Korean army. Had the Eighth Army at Pyongyang and the Tenth Corps at Wonsan thrown a cordon of armor across the waist of the Korean peninsula that October of 1950, the West would have registered a smashing victory against the Communist world, perhaps altering twentieth-century history decisively. Tragically, MacArthur and his superiors in Washington succumbed to hubris and sought to destroy Communist North Korea and neutralize Chinese concerns about a capitalist enemy on their border without either the military muscle or the diplomatic means to do so. As UN forces approached the Yalu on both the eastern and western sides of the peninsula in pursuit of the last remaining vestiges of the North Korean enemy, Beijing intervened with devastating effect, sending half a million soldiers across the now frozen river to rout the Americans, South Koreans, and other elements of MacArthur's United Nations Command.

The Chinese intervention of November–December 1950 led to a third, and final, decisive employment of sea power in the Korean War. Elements of the Tenth Corps and the South Korean army trapped in the eastern portion of upper North Korea rushed or bitterly fought their way through gruesome winter cold and snows to the port of Hungnam. There the battleship *Missouri*, together with a handful of cruisers and destroyers supplemented by air strikes from several carriers, laid down a steel curtain of shell fire and bombs behind which more than a hundred thousand troops and ninety-one thousand Korean refugees were evacuated to the south. Hungnam was America's Suvla Bay, its little Dunkirk. The circumstances were quite different, of course. Hungnam was evacuated by day and night, not just night, as at the Gallipoli beaches. Unlike Dunkirk, enemy airpower was never a factor, and with pinpoint accuracy carrier aircraft from the U.S. Navy's Task Force 77 devastated Chinese positions on the hills and ridge-lines dominating the evacuation routes, allowing American marines and South Korean army units to fight their way to the port where the evacuating fleet and forces were never in danger of annihilation. But like the British imperial forces at the Dardanelles thirty-five years before, America's soldiers and marines at Hungnam experienced for the first time the bittersweet feeling of a successful evacuation before the superior forces of a non-Western enemy.

The navy's evacuation of Hungnam was so well done that few have noticed or commented on the prescience and advanced planning required to make it work. C. Turner Joy, commander, Naval Forces Far East (ComNavFE), and his staff people (including the ubiquitous Arleigh Burke) became uneasy about the war as early as October. Burke was told by Kichisaburu Nomura, the retired Japanese admiral who had been ambassador to the United States at the time of Pearl Harbor, that Communist China would permit neither UN forces nor a non-Communist North Korea on the Yalu. Joy and his people got their intelli-gence estimates from MacArthur's determinedly upbeat people. By the first week in November, however, even army intelligence was becoming alarmed by evi-dence that more and more Chinese forces were entering northern Korea. Joy consulted with army and air force counterparts, then ordered Struble to take his Seventh Fleet carriers north to support the ongoing UN offensive on both coasts. "Notified General Hickey [on MacArthur's staff] that the carriers were going up to fight and not to act only as a reservoir if needed," Joy told Struble. Hickey concurred, then told Joy confidentially that the 10 to 15 percent of North Korea "outside U.N. control was to be destroyed since back of enemy resistance must be broken quickly." For the next two weeks, Beijing said and apparently did little, and euphoria again gripped MacArthur's headquarters, while Burke prudently began placing navy transports in reserve status, "foreseeing the possibility that the troops and their equipment might well have to be evac-uated if the Chinese struck in force." Thus, the navy was ready for disaster, whereas the "Army still buoyantly hopeful war will be over by Christmas." Joy cabled those words to Washington on the twenty-sixth as the Eighth Army in western North Korea and the Tenth Corps on the east coast were in the midst of their last offensive push to the Yalu. Less than forty-eight hours later, an obscure lieutenant commander attached to the Eighth Army's Twenty-fourth Infantry Division dispatched a chilling for-your-eyes-only message back to ComNavFE.

"Situation here becoming critical. Borders on desperate. Could result demand for evacuation plan Chinnampo," a west coast North Korean port, "or further north. Request for all Navy air may be made and needed. Not my business, but you should know." Within hours MacArthur's people confirmed that the Chinese had entered the war with several hundred thousand men and shattering effect. Tokyo fell rapidly into outright defeatism; MacArthur himself briefly went into seclusion. Korea could not be held. Beijing was out to humiliate, then destroy, all American ground forces in Asia and was willing, perhaps eager, to risk World War III in the process. Nonsense, Burke and others responded. The Tenth Corps if not the Eighth Army could hold long enough to withdraw troops southward to evacuation ports. Everyone could agree on one point: in the freezing cold, winds, and snows of upper Korea, American and UN forces could not remain where they were. Burke's and Struble's foresight gave them a way out, and whereas the Eighth Army simply outran the Chinese offensive down the peninsula's west coast, the soldiers and marines of the Tenth Corps fought their way to the Hungnam beaches and safety. When they got there, Burke recalled, panicky army representatives on the beach asked Struble "to leave their heavy equipment, leave their tanks, but Jim loaded all the damned works. . . . We had all the merchant ships. Nearly 100 ships went out of there that he loaded. And he loaded them fast. He made the army work like hell. He did just a magnificent job."[7]

There were no Inchons or Hungnams in Vietnam, a war the navy approached with skepticism and waged with even more frustration than Korea.[8] Vietnam eerily resembled the American War for Independence nearly two centuries before, with U.S. "grunts" reprising the role of British redcoats, the North Vietnamese Army (NVA) that of Washington's Continental army, and the Vietcong (VC) the militiamen of the Carolinas and Virginia who sprang from their homes to contest the passage of enemy forces down their roads and across their meadows and fields. Both the late-eighteenth-century war in North America and the late-twentieth-century war in Southeast Asia seemed to last forever, with dramatic reversals of fortune on all sides. Geographically (if not climatically or topographically), the two battle areas were hauntingly similar, comprising long, comparatively narrow territories that required far more men to conquer than to defend. Indeed, neither General William Howe in 1776–1778 nor General William Westmoreland in 1965–1968 sought to physically seize and permanently control vast stretches of territory; such an objective was clearly beyond their resources. Rather, both generals tried every expedient to bring an elusive enemy to decisive and ruinous battle. In the end both of these highly competent but by-the-book soldiers were defeated by a combination of physical and political factors beyond either their control or, in some respects, their comprehension.

Just as the British firmly controlled Boston, New York, Charleston, and the surrounding seas between 1775 and 1780, so the United States controlled South Vietnam's cities and its navy ruled the waters off both North and South Vietnam between 1964 and 1975. The soldiers under Howe and Cornwallis were as well supplied (for their time), as initially keen for battle and victory, and, in many ways, as venturesome, if not nearly as mobile, as those under Westmoreland 190 years later. But in Vietnam as in revolutionary America, the enemy fought along interior lines of communication and at times and places of his own choosing. All that George Washington and Vo Nguyen Giap had to do was maintain (however precariously) an army in the field to attract and hold the world's attention and ultimately gain its recognition. This they did, and their enemies, never truly beaten, became exhausted and disheartened, eventually withdrawing.

Once the Korean campaign settled into essential stalemate and Vietnam into steady, intense guerrilla warfare, Chinese and North Vietnamese military leaders attempted to supply their field forces by sea. The U.S. Navy quickly responded by establishing highly effective inshore interdiction programs.

In Korea interdiction efforts were enhanced through occupation of the off-shore islands that ringed nearly all the North's important east and west coast ports.[9] Forced to rely thereafter on comparatively primitive road and rail corridors that either ran across the peninsula's mountainous, riverless terrain or along its narrow, rocky coasts, Communist generals found their supply lines fearfully vulnerable to both sea and air assault by the Seventh Fleet. From January 1951 to July 1953, Task Force 77 constantly maneuvered in the Sea of Japan above the thirty-eighth parallel its two or three rotating fleet carriers, dispatching flocks of aircraft on interdiction missions over North Korea. Periodically, escorting battleships, cruisers, and destroyers would peel off to form temporary "bomb" or "gun" lines either to blast rail installations and warehouse facilities in enemy ports such as Hungnam and especially Wonsan or to provide gunfire support for beleaguered UN forces ashore.

Heavy gunfire support brought the battleship back to prominence. Elmo Zumwalt who served aboard *Wisconsin* recalled many a mission that began with marines ashore "suddenly feeling pressure from artillery or an offensive infantry attack," calling out for "the 16-inch guns." If the battleship was nearby it could line up quickly and start firing. Otherwise, "our response was immediately to go to general quarters and ... to dash at maximum speed [27 knots] from wherever we were to the bombline." The captain would "put the rudder over hard, 1,000 yards from the bombline, and slow, so that by the time we got around, we'd killed most of our speed from the hard turn and were essentially down at the bombardment speed." The gunfire team would then "get a very accurate fix by both visual cuts and radar cuts," position the sixteen-inch guns from those navigational positions on the target, "and report that we were ready to fire." At one point, Task Force 77's commander, Seventh Fleet, Admiral Harold M. Martin, who "didn't believe much in the efficacy of naval gunfire support," sent a message to the marine commander ashore "in which he asserted he had real doubts about whether or not the naval gunfire was doing any good. A very strong message came back that the naval gunfire was far more effective than naval air support" and that on one occasion *Wisconsin*'s heavy gunfire had forced an entire Chinese division out of the front lines. The "surge of morale" among the ship's company was doubtless further enhanced by periodic but careful trips through Communist minefields to bombard Wonsan. "It was a psychological plus for all of us to feel that we're so damn good and tough and unassailable that we can go right into the heart of what was the enemy's major port" and shoot it to pieces with heavy artillery.[10]

Task Force 95, operating in the Yellow Sea off Korea's west coast, got no such publicity. The British and American carriers, destroyers, and occasional cruisers were the blue-collar component of the sea war in Korea, largely unseen but charged with the dangerous and important missions of providing direct air support and sea-based interdiction to the allied armies ashore. For these purposes relatively small flattops whose limited plane-carrying capacity was offset by limited displacement proved a perfect fit. "Light" and "escort" carriers could venture close inshore "where the larger CVA carriers could not go," giving "the fleet tremendous flexibility. . . . The CVAs almost never ventured to the west coast of Korea" with its shallow waters and treacherous shoals. But "light carrier[s], plus four escort destroyers," easily "rotated the task of operating Marine squadrons" over the peninsula's nearby battle lines for months at a time. The marines flew F4U Corsair propeller-driven aircraft. Too slow and unwieldy for the kind of tactical and strategic bombing assigned the F9F Panther jets of Task Force 77, the Corsairs were among the finest and most powerful battlefield support planes ever built. In this role, they "alternated tours between carriers and land bases."[11]

As soon as possible, Task Force 95 also established its own gun lines to disrupt enemy roads and rail installations. On the night of July 15, 1952, the destroyer

Orleck was patrolling near the coast "when we heard a train racing south. We sent up a star shell and in its light we saw a train." The ship's five-inch guns quickly swiveled on to the target area and within moments "shot up the tracks in front of and behind the train," derailing most of it. The engineer managed to get his locomotive away before the tracks disintegrated and tried to hide it in a nearby tunnel, "but we hammered it from midnight to daybreak" until aircraft from a nearby carrier arrived to destroy it, presumably skip-bombing ordnance into the tunnel. *Orleck*'s sailors boasted that they were now members of the "United Nations' 'Train Buster Club.'" They had a right to be pleased, having destroyed "fourteen cars of ammunition, one car carrying tanks, and five more cars loaded with heavy artillery" that ignited in a series of deafening explosions. Two weeks later the *Orleck* "busters" destroyed another enemy train by gunfire.[12]

Vietnam's peculiar geography and warfare forced both the North Vietnamese and the U.S. Navy to employ sharply different tactics than in Korea. Hanoi had no interest in an army-to-army, toe-to-toe clash with American might, as the North Koreans and Chinese had fifteen years earlier. The one time Ho Chi Minh and his generals were tempted, their Tet offensive of January 1968 came to disaster. From the outset Hanoi chose rather to wage a bushwhacker's war— combat waged with stealth and cunning in which Vietcong guerrillas or regular North Vietnamese Army units emerged, often abruptly, from jungle or on river- bank to engage in brief but brutal combat on their terms before breaking off and disappearing at the first hint that the tide of battle was turning against them. This kind of conflict placed a premium on infiltration as a means not only of offensive warfare but of resupply and reinforcement as well.

As the American build-up began in 1965, strategists at Military Assistance Command, Vietnam (MACV), in Saigon worked in a "frontier-like atmosphere where all seemed possible and nothing appeared beyond reach." Westmoreland quickly seized all naval assets in South Vietnam and its coastal waters that be- longed to the Seventh Fleet and had them placed under his own MACV banner under the rubric "Commander, U.S. Naval Forces, Vietnam." Formally estab- lished on April 1, 1966, this command assumed the major burden of coastal and riverine interdiction operations to the onset of "Vietnamization" in 1969.[13]

U.S. sailors together with their Marine Corps allies had at hand three dis- tinct ways and means of disrupting the infiltration into and concentration of enemy troops and supplies within South Vietnam: coastal surveillance and bom- bardment by fleet units; quick amphibious strikes and helicopter sweeps, often far inland, to disrupt enemy formations; and coastal and riverine interdiction. The latter activity consumed by far the majority of the navy's "in-country" resources in Vietnam and pointed to a major reorientation of roles and mission responsibilities for the service as a whole. In the century after the Civil War, the United States Navy had grown into the world's greatest blue-water power, accustomed to steaming, fighting upon, and dominating the vast, empty reaches of the world ocean. With a few minor exceptions, the navy had been content to project its power from the world ocean onto but not within the landmasses of the earth. In Vietnam the historic imbalance between blue- and brown-water operations began to redress, prefiguring the growing commitment to and pre-occupation with "littoral" operations in narrow and restricted waters (notably the Persian Gulf) that continues to define the service's mission responsibilities to this day. In-country naval warfare proved as costly to sailors as soldiers. According to one authoritative source, 2,558 sailors and 7 coast guardsmen were killed in coastal and riverine operations.[14]

Initially, the navy had to rely on a sister service for much riverine and coastal interdiction work. Historically, domestic coastal, lake, and river patrol work was the mission responsibility of the U.S. Coast Guard. As early as the spring of 1965, Chief of Naval Operations David McDonald requested coast guard commandant Edwin J. Roland to "provide cutters and expertise" for the coastal interdiction campaign, which the coast guard promptly did. Within three months, the first eighty-two-foot WPB fast patrol boats—arguably designed for port security and search-and-rescue work—were on duty and exchanging fire with Vietnamese shore positions. Subsequent firefights between junks and WPBs indicated that the traditional coast guard white-paint scheme was "highly visible at night under flares," and by September all WPBs had become camouflaged with dark-gray paint. The cutters proved too big and unwieldy for the intense riverine warfare that broke out in the Mekong Delta that autumn, and navy planners soon concluded that "purpose-built" navy patrol boats should shoulder the burden. By 1966 it was clear that the enemy was throwing so many resources into riverine and coastal supply and warfare activities as to overwhelm the coast guard's limited resources. But before the navy appeared in significant numbers, the "coasties" had some exciting and productive moments. During Operation Jackstay in early 1966 the WPBs were directed to clear all enemy forces from the delta's Soi Rap River. As the vessels moved inshore, "they engaged in firefights with junks, sampans, and ground troops." One lieutenant received the Silver Star for gallantry. As the navy came in greater numbers, the WPBs were shifted to gunfire-support missions, and "the interdiction and inspection of the estimated 50,000 junks that sailed the coast of South Vietnam on a daily basis." The WPBs together with the coast guard's larger, 311-foot high-endurance cutters

(WHECs) and the navy's "swift boats" also were "very successful in stopping North Vietnamese trawlers" that hugged the southern coastline as they attempted to supply North Vietnamese Army forces over the beach. Whatever their work, coast guardsmen, like their navy counterparts, found patrols "grueling." The "boarding evolutions required the participation of most of the crew. On patrol for days at a time, with round-the-clock boardings, . . . crews got little sleep. The oppressive heat and humidity, sometimes reaching 120° Fahrenheit and normally remaining above 90°, made the work extremely demanding; fortunately, the WPBs were air conditioned."[15]

On the comparatively few occasions when NVA or VC units ashore concentrated for offensive operations or resupply near the coast, they became as vulnerable as their Chinese allies in Korea to naval gunfire from U.S. cruisers, destroyers, and for one brief period in 1968 the battleship *New Jersey*. The huge naval shells invariably disrupted and often decimated enemy formations. But interdiction by naval gunfire was distinctly limited by the comparative short range of even *New Jersey*'s big sixteen-inch main batteries, the fluidity of the battlefield compared to Korea's static lines, and Washington's strict rules of engagement that precluded assaulting North Vietnam's comparatively few ports and coastal installations. Quick strikes and sweeps from the sea by the Seventh Fleet Amphibious Ready Group (ARG) and the marine Special Landing Forces (SLF, which usually enjoyed naval gunfire support) were more effective. Although minuscule compared to the great amphibious fleets that mustered off Normandy, Okinawa, and even Inchon, the "ARG/SLF" styled itself a powerful, versatile, and mobile force capable of attacking not only any point on the South Vietnamese coast but also far inland through "vertical envelopment" by helicopter. But the group was severely limited by size. It usually comprised four ships: a big amphibious assault ship deploying a transport helicopter squadron, a troop-carrying attack transport, an LST, and an "amphibious transport dock" (LPD), the latter two vessels loaded with supporting armor, artillery, communications, and engineering gear. MACV ordered no fewer than sixty-two amphibious assaults from the sea directly upon enemy-held or -infested coastal areas between 1965 and 1969. Although most involved the ARG/SLF, other marine amphibious-force units and even some South Vietnamese troops were employed as well, especially in the I Corps area just below the seventeenth-parallel border with the North. For the most part, however, MACV chose to employ the army's larger vertical-envelopment forces against the VC and NVA, even in coastal areas. MACV soon became bewitched by the speed and mobility of helicopter-borne warfare, and the navy's ARG simply did not have enough "choppers." Helicopters were a much faster alternative to slow-moving armor, which was largely confined to South Vietnam's mostly wretched and sketchy road network. Also, copters could bring to bear deadlier and more sweeping firepower. MACV brass insisted that although helicopters could be heard some distance away, they often could not be seen, especially through thick jungle canopies, until they were immediately overhead, laying down devastating bursts of fire. In fact, helicopter losses from all causes in Vietnam were consistently high.

If Hanoi was truly to make all South Vietnam a battlefield (unlike the fixed combat zone of conventional armies confronting each other on a jagged line across the Korean Peninsula), it would have to exploit all of the opportunities for mobile warfare that lay open to it not only along the coasts but up South Vietnam's great rivers and their numerous tributaries as well. Early on, Hanoi turned to the use of the ancient, ubiquitous, and nearly unsinkable junk and its river counterpart, the sampan.

Drifting in their scores of thousands across the coastal waters of East Asia, junks were extraordinarily difficult to differentiate and had been for centuries a prime vehicle for the clandestine transportation of people and illicit goods. To counter this classic mosquito fleet, the U.S. Navy itself went small. It quickly developed and deployed a "coastal surveillance force," designated Task Force 115 and composed of fast patrol craft (the famous "swift boats"), slightly larger patrol gunboats, and both coastal and oceangoing minesweepers. These forces were supplemented by U.S. Coast Guard patrol craft together with an aerial surveillance umbrella made up of big, long-range SP2H Neptune and P3A Orion patrol planes as well as helicopters. An "outer screen" composed of five big, 311-foot coast guard cutters and navy destroyer escort radar picket ships was also put in place some twenty miles or less offshore "to prevent an end run by the Communists."[16]

At the beginning of 1966 between 70 and 75 percent of enemy supplies were still reaching the field by coastal waters. Operations Market Time and Stable Door made enemy resupply and infiltration efforts along the South Vietnamese littoral such "a hazardous adventure" that a year later the figure had been reduced to 10 percent.

Coastal surveillance and interdiction work was always tedious and often frustrating. According to a 1968 official navy publication about the war, the destroyer escorts, swift boats, coast guard cutters, and patrol boats stopped up to a thousand junks, sampans, and related craft each day. "During routine searches, identification cards and cargo manifests are checked by Vietnamese National Maritime Policemen who are carried as liaison men and interpreters. If manifests or identification papers are out of order, the boat or persons are further investigated by Vietnamese or U.S. Intelligence authorities."[17] But if the vessel was attempting to smuggle arms or people into the South, the first indication that anything was remiss might be the blast of machine-gun or rifle fire. Those engaged in the earliest, most intense "junk patrol" efforts in 1965–1966 spoke of "nine months of never knowing whether the 'friendly' Vietnamese" they were "advising are VC sympathizers or never knowing from one second to the next whether the bullets that are an accepted part of every day's activities" would find their mark. One young officer told a friend of "the five VC who shot at his boat and how he and his crew fired back until the boat and all its occupants were slipping silently below the surface." The friend replied that he himself had to go on watch shortly. "Last night we shot 160 rounds of naval gunfire (160 naval projectiles) at the VC . . . but surely not all of the dead and injured will be VC. . . . [T]here'll be civilians . . . and animals . . . and homes . . . and gardens . . . and rice paddies." From the beginning, most South Vietnamese sailors displayed little stomach for or interest in such work. Despite a "Vietnamese sea force and junk force" that had been in continuous existence since the time of the French–Indo-China war of 1946–1954, they often exhibited the same kind of distaste for civil warfare and lack of commitment in working with the Americans that with a few exceptions characterized the South's war effort from start to finish.

Increasingly frustrated in its coastal-infiltration programs, Hanoi naturally turned to the mighty Mekong and smaller Saigon Rivers with their intricate systems of tributary streams and canals to sustain and expand its varied and numerous offensives. Along the Saigon River connecting South Vietnam's capital with the sea, the Rung Sat region, an "area of dense mangroves," became a veritable Vietcong bastion.

The Mekong, which extends into Cambodia and could be tapped into as a supply route at a hundred places throughout northwestern South Vietnam, was a guerrilla leader's dream. The countless villages along and close to the river's edge could easily be invested, intimidated, and turned to the enemy's purposes. Moreover, the river's great delta was South Vietnam's rice bowl. Deny it to Saigon, and the country's economy and society would be crippled. In 1965, as the U.S. war effort in Vietnam became pronounced, the Vietcong already had seventy thousand guerrillas in the Mekong Delta, organized to provide one squad for every hamlet, one platoon per village, one separate company per district, and one battalion per province. "The communist forces were generally well-trained, professionally led, and adequately armed."[18]

Westmoreland and his planners were alive to the danger; practical surrender of this area to a progressively infiltrating enemy was inconceivable. MACV soon determined not only to contest the VC presence but also to root it out. The delta and adjacent Ca Mau Peninsula thus early on became a major theater of combat, designated the IV Corps. A full army division was assigned to the delta, two of its three brigades based ashore, the third afloat aboard self-propelled barracks ships. The objective of this force was to carry the war aggressively to the enemy deep in the heart of his own base and staging areas. Thus was born the Mekong Delta Mobile Afloat Force, an idea formulated in early 1966 but not brought to fruition before the "first afloat deployment . . . on 11 June 1967." The force comprised several river-assault flotillas—or groups—commonly known as RAGs, that were made up of half a dozen shallow-draft troop carriers, four fast (twenty-five- to thirty-knot) assault-support patrol boats or ASPBs, and several converted World War II Higgins-built LCMs (landing craft mediums), originally designed to ferry army tanks from ship to shore. These latter seventy-five-ton vessels were reconstructed and employed either as heavy fire-support ships or command-and-communication vessels. Air support was emphasized, and the bigger vessels often carried one or two quick-response Seawolf helicopter gunships. As the assault flotilla moved on the waterways toward an objective, the ASPBs "would escort the flanks and rear of the formation," then join army fire-support ships in covering the landing. When lodgment was achieved, the fast little river boats sealed off any enemy withdrawal routes.[19]

Operations were partially successful at best. The big assault craft proved ungainly and difficult to maneuver in restricted waterways, especially in times of low water. Troops in the thinly armored assault boats were vulnerable to enemy rocket-fire fragments. Most exasperating were the Vietcong, whose discipline was remarkable. The VC stood and fought for as long as they pleased, then vanished into the countryside their people knew so well, often leaving behind a half-dozen expendables to hold the Americans at bay and pick off their wounded and those going to the rescue. Such problems and tactics became routine aspects of Mobile Afloat Force activities between mid-1967 and the end of the program in 1969, as they indeed were of the entire American–South Vietnamese effort.

Moreover, large-scale amphibious operations proved feasible only when VC units were discovered in reasonably sized concentrations, which they seldom were. And such operations failed to address the critical interdiction question.

To really break the VC grip along the Mekong and in the delta required daily patrol and intercept activities on the river itself. Westmoreland and his people recognized the problem early on, and in September 1965 the navy established a permanent patrol force on the Mekong and its tributaries known as Operation Game Warden. Initially, the navy got by with what it could scrape together in South Vietnam, but by mid-1966 Game Warden was enforced by roughly 120 PBRs (patrol boat river). Later the PBRs would be joined by their nearly identical PCF swift-boat sisters. Neither of these tiny craft measured up in size, speed, or offensive punch to their "PT boat" predecessors of World War II. One veteran of the river war described the first generation of PBRs, hastily shipped to Southeast Asia in March 1966, as "basically off-the-shelf commercial cabin cruiser/sport fisherman hulls, painted green, loaded down with machine guns and ammunition and sent to war." The vessels were designed by Willis Shane of the Hatteras Yacht Company in North Carolina. Shane came up with the idea of linking a 220-horsepower General Motors truck engine to a set of Jacuzzi water-jet pumps and placing them in "a 31-foot fiberglass pleasure boat hull" costing no more than a one hundred thousand dollars per copy. River-war veteran Wynn Goldsmith recalled that the government furnished guns, ceramic armor, and radios from ancient, left-over stocks. "Some of these venerable guns . . . had been fired by 8th Air Force gunners on B-17s over Nazi Germany and by Army infantry or armored personnel in Korea." Strapped as always for cash, the Pentagon kept its equipment costs for each riverine patrol craft to "probably less than $5,000 per boat." Although the armored upper works provided some protection from machine-gun fire, the entire boat was vulnerable to VC rockets, while the Fiberglas hull would shatter at the first contact with a VC mine. Late in 1967 the builders shipped more than two hundred improved versions of the PBR.[20]

The navy soon discovered what the army had already learned; the lumbering, old shallow-draft LSTs of World War II vintage that had served in a variety of capacities ever since made superb "mother ships" and barracks for the PBR and later PCF squadrons since they could be moved far upstream, along with their broods, to wherever enemy activities—or suspected activities—were the greatest. Unfortunately, they were also highly vulnerable to Vietcong swimmer-sappers who destroyed at least one (YRBM-16) late in 1967 by attaching flotation explosives to the vessel's hull.

Like the broader conflict ashore, the interdiction war on the Mekong and South Vietnam's other river systems soon degenerated into primitive, desperate combat by ambush, fought with advanced technologies of deadly force if not accuracy and defined by identity papers, cargo manifests, and free-fire zones. On the big rivers dusk-to-dawn curfews were imposed on thousands of increasingly sullen Vietnamese river people who might at any moment reveal their true loyalties with a burst of concealed gunfire or the explosion of a grenade or bomb against the PBRs charged with enforcement. This kind of battle, waged day after day and soon night after night, inevitably led over time to hair-trigger reactions. To read John Kerry's extended apologia via writer Douglas Brinkley and then to turn to Kerry's swift-boat critics is to enter a world awash in ambiguity, tension, and tragedy. Those (like this author) who were not there can only record as best as possible the dimensions of what happened and leave moral judgment on the actors to those who shared the scene with them.[21]

Opinions are as divided about the intensity and importance of this effort as they are about all the other elements of the Vietnam War. Wynn Goldsmith's gripping account of PBR warfare on the Ham Luong and My Tho Rivers in 1967–1968 suggests a very high and intense level of warfare. The battles for Ben Tre (the town that famously had to be destroyed to be saved) and Vinh Long during the first days of the enemy Tet offensive of January–February 1968 were as sustained and violent as any combat in World War II or Korea.

When the first batch of improved PBRs arrived in the delta in the autumn of 1967, they were dispatched ever farther upriver to interdict suspected VC traffic and provide a security presence along the waterway. Eighty more vessels soon followed. Each day as dawn lit the river, two-boat PBR patrols slipped away from their mother ship and roared up the brown waters rapidly filling with junks and sampans heading for early-morning markets in the various towns and villages along the riverfront. PBR commanders selectively stopped and searched various vessels for contraband. When such aggressive patrolling forced the VC to begin moving and supplying only at night, the navy moved right with it, imposing 8 P.M. to 6 A.M. curfews, harassing and disrupting VC waterborne supply activities as best it could through aggressive patrolling. The VC then pulled back from the Mekong into its tributary streams and canals. The navy followed, often employing British-designed air-cushion vehicles as patrol vessels.

Given VC strength in the delta, and the cunning and determination of the VC leadership, riverine operations by boat alone would have been foolhardy. The PBRs were too small, light, and vulnerable and their interdiction responsibilities too great to operate independently against the VC either on the water or ashore. When Wynn Goldsmith arrived aboard YRBM-16 in 1967 to serve as senior patrol officer, he was told that the nearby Ham Luong River "could be dangerous if the boats started chasing sampans up the little canals off the main river. . . . Ambush Alley, a crossing corridor just a mile and a half south of where the YRBM-16 was anchored" was especially hazardous. The American PBRs were winning the war simply by their presence, "causing the Viet Cong prob- lems in moving men and supplies." Goldsmith was told to leave outright chas- ing of the VC to the river assault groups and the South Vietnamese Army.

Nonetheless, the VC was more than capable of luring the small American riverine patrol boats into ambushes from onshore or less often from sampans. From the beginning, army (and, if available, navy) helicopter gunships were essential adjuncts of patrol work. If a boat or a two-boat PBR patrol got into real trouble, army and navy jet fighters were also often around to lend assis- tance within minutes. But as contact with the VC steadily grew and firefights between the enemy on canal or riverbanks and PBRs offshore often became daily and nightly occurrences, the navy rightly claimed there was never sufficient close air support; the patrol boat crews were often on their own.

There were occasional striking successes. Because PBRs were so small, the navy gave command of one or even two or three PBRs to senior enlisted people, chief petty officers and even first-class POs. The officers who supervised opera- tions were unstinting in their praise of the men. Small-boat command required people who knew the water intimately, whether it be blue or brown. They also had to have had combat experience and, equally important, demonstrate both personal pride and professional competence. Throughout 1965, '66, and '67, the Pentagon culled its files for boatswain's mates with Korean War service. Quartermasters and gunner's mates who had also risen "from the deck" over the past twenty years were equally welcome.

The senior enlisted people more than justified the faith placed in them, proving to be at once capable and aggressive. One day in late October 1966, Boatswain's Mate First Class James Elliot Williams in charge of two boats was cruising the My Tho River when he spotted two sampans "loaded down with enemy soldiers."[22] Williams gunned his two boats into high gear and raced after the motorized sampans, guns blazing. One of the enemy craft sank, but the other turned into a canal that was too narrow for the PBRs. Refusing to give up, Williams, who had closely studied the complicated systems of water- ways in the area, left the My Tho and rushed into a maze of adjacent streams "determined to head the sampan off by an alternate route." Rushing along the twisting, turning river maze at the "harrowing speed" of twenty-five knots (roughly thirty miles per hour) the two PBRs rounded a bend to find them- selves in a broader river area crowded with sampans laden with troops and weapons. The riverbanks "bristled with fortified gun and rocket emplacements." Trapped, the Americans did the only thing they could do, rushing forward full throttle at the sampans while letting loose with every gun and grenade aboard at the wooden craft and the riverbanks. The fire-spewing PBRs literally ran over several low-riding sampans while the astonished enemy began firing back so chaotically that a number of his troops were killed by friendly fire. Reaching the end of the broad river with bullet-holed hulls but no casualties, Williams radioed for helicopter gunfire support from a nearby navy Seawolf "chopper," then headed back into the enemy concentration, brown water curving away from his hulls and blasting out in heavy foam behind. This time Williams and his men did not try to escape. Racing and roaring about the broad river area for several hours with helicopter gunfire support, they destroyed an estimated sixty-five enemy sampans and killed seven hundred troops. Williams got a piece of shrapnel in his side; one of his crew was shot in the wrist. Only when the enemy ashore was silenced did Williams and his two small boats race away from the devastation. President Johnson later awarded the boatswain a Medal of Honor, and in 2003 a guided-missile destroyer bearing his name slipped down the builder's ways.

Equally often, however, aggressive patrolling led to near or real disaster. Late in 1967 orders came down from Saigon that the PBRs must begin "showing the flag" on all the delta rivers controlled by the enemy. The order was foolhardy, because by this time the VC had begun listening to American radio traffic. "They recognized call signs," Wynn Goldsmith later wrote. "Perhaps they recognized individual voices of the men on the radio. Twice, later on, English speaking voices taunted me on our radio channels, and once there was a sniper who fired rounds only at me." Goldsmith was not paranoid. "Others were targeted" also and several wounded. Within hours after the orders had come down from Saigon, two PBRs from River Section 522 reaped the consequences. Goldsmith had taken one of the first patrols up the Ben Tre River and an excitable South Vietnamese policeman riding aboard claimed to have spotted several VC. Rushing to the bow fifty-caliber machine guns he opened up on the suspects. Goldsmith immediately shut him down and returned to base, pleading with his superiors to let the area alone for a while, since the enemy was now doubtless alerted and waiting for the next patrol. His pleas fell on deaf ears, and the following morning someone ran in to the comfortable air-conditioned wardroom aboard the LST mother ship "to announce that there was a major action up the Ben Tre River and two 522nd boats were in trouble" within view. Racing on deck, Goldsmith saw several helicopter gunships already orbiting an area filled with smoke. Cruising up and into the Ben Tre River, the first PBR had taken a rocket through its Fiberglas hull and into the fuel tank. The little craft had promptly exploded, and began to sink. Amid a sheet of machine-gun and small-arms fire from the riverbank, its sister came alongside to rescue and was hit in the main cabin by another rocket. The desperate commander called in the gunships, which promptly appeared, along with several jet fighters, to lay down suppressing fire while boat two took the remains of boat one in tow back to base. Four sailors were medevacked downriver, though none were killed. The only person missing was the Vietnamese policeman on Goldsmith's boat the previous day who had opened wild fire on the suspected VC positions. After a long search through the "black ashes" of boat one's burnt-out hull, someone found his "badly melted" pistol. "Then portions of a human skull were recognized. That was all that remained of the feisty little Vietnamese cop who had been on my boat the previous day."

Early on, Goldsmith was "impressed and disheartened" to learn how much he was part of a "dirty war." One day in late 1967 he was induced to take aboard two young SEALs eager for action. Finding no enemy, the SEALs proposed to booby-trap with fragmentation grenades some sniper holes on a river island. Determined not to squander innocent civilian lives, Goldsmith asked how the SEALs could be sure the grenades would kill only Vietcong.

> "Suppose some little kid falls into a hole and sets off the grenade?"
> "Well, lieutenant, then we got a VC dead before his prime. What the hell this is war. We got to do unto them before they do unto us. Anybody checking out spider holes on the river bank will be at risk. If old mama-san and her kids get wasted so much the better. There will be fewer fighting holes being built."
> A young PBR sailor heard these SEAL words and contributed a few of his own.
> "Fucking A. Fuck up every firing hole and every dead gook body with grenades. That will teach them not to fuck with us."[23]

The PBRs went out day and night for three years. Each patrol lasted a minimum of fourteen hours. Supervising officers went out on at least five patrols a week, then got twenty-four hours off. The enlisted crewmen went out for two weeks at a stretch before they could expect a scant twenty-four-hour relief. As with every other American in Vietnam, a tour of duty lasted a year. Firefights with the enemy ashore almost invariably resulted in shot-up boats, often returning with torn and ripped sailors. A 75 mm recoilless rifle round contained enormous energy "that turns into thousands of bits of white-hot shrapnel when it explodes." Deaths were comparatively few; Purple Hearts were many. "But there are wounds and there are wounds," Goldsmith philosophized. "Some guys got a couple of Bronze Stars on their original Purple Hearts for scratches. Some guys were disabled for life when they earned their first."

By the autumn of 1968, authorities in Saigon and Washington determined that the time had come to turn the river war over to the Vietnamese. Zumwalt, an admiral now and commander of Naval Forces Vietnam, decided to send the American effort out with a bang. Following the urging of numerous sailors from the PBR flotillas upward, he concocted Operation SEA LORDS ("Southeast Asia Lake, Ocean, and Delta Strategy) in which South Vietnam's vast river system would be employed to throttle the enemy's crucial transit and resupply routes through adjacent Cambodia. The operation lasted well into 1969, but at the end of the previous year, the impatient, imaginative Zumwalt concocted a more focused plan, a six-week offensive known as Giant Slingshot. The admiral brought elements of the Operation Market Time coastal interdiction program, including swift boats, up the delta's rivers and canals to join the PBRs, river assault groups, and supporting air elements in sealing off the Cambodian border where it jutted far into South Vietnam at the infamous "Parrot's Beak." The six-week offensive made the earlier Tet battles "seem like a walk in the woods." The "river rats" found themselves up against some of the best units in the North Vietnamese Army who daily and nightly ambushed and fought and fell back before appearing the next day or evening in virtually the same spot. Battle erupted with suddenly blazing gunfire from the shore and turning and twisting little motorboats firing back amid blood-and-gut-churning fear on both sides. The Americans never flinched, fighting with habitual bravery and efficiency; they suffered heavy casualties, though fortunately most were counted in Purple Hearts, not caskets.

In April 1969, as the American effort neared its close, Commander Paul Yost led a group of nine PCF swift boats, each laden with South Vietnamese marines, on a proposed one-day excursion up a narrow river on the Ca Mau Peninsula to clear out enemy bunkers along the banks. A U.S. ordnance team was along with tear gas to render the bunkers unusable for weeks if not months. Yost and his sailors were coast guardsmen who by this time had become an absolutely essential component of the interdiction campaigns along the South Vietnamese coast and up its adjacent rivers. For several hours the mission was routine and boring as the South Vietnamese marines and U.S. ordnance team periodically jumped ashore to neutralize empty bunkers amid jungle stillness.

As the flotilla approached the end of its designated action area, a U.S. Marine Corps major along as an adviser to the South Vietnamese approached Yost. "I haven't seen anything that even looks like a Viet Cong. No activity. It's hot. It's sweaty. Going is hard. Do you have any problem with inserting us another mile up the river?" "Major," Yost replied, "my job is to insert you where you want to be inserted." To be on the safe side, Yost radioed back to the LST for immediate deployment of the two helicopter gunships as a covering force and received a laconic response.

Moving along the river "fat, dumb, and happy," believing the gunships would be overhead in ten or fifteen minutes, the flotilla abruptly came under deadly fire from both riverbanks. "I thought the end of the world had come," Yost remembered. "B-40 rockets were exploding. All at once all nine boats had their .50 calibers [machine guns] chattering, 'Boom, boom, boom, boom, boom, boom.' Everybody who had a weapon was firing it at something." The patrol craft skippers "two blocked" their engines to full ahead as Yost tried through the din to order dispersal to both sides of the river and the exposed South Vietnamese marines fell like tenpins dead or wounded on every deck. As the flotilla raced out of the ambush and regrouped, Yost realized that one of his boats was still back in the ambush area. He ordered the two PCFs alongside his to go back for rescue. We can't, their skippers replied, too many wounded aboard. So Yost and another captain turned their swift boats around and raced back to find the missing PCF "high and dry on the bank. The water intakes were out of the water, and the engines were running full speed. A B-40 rocket had gone through the pilot house and killed the skipper," who had his engines going full bore when he was destroyed. The swift boat promptly went out of control and "at full speed" raced halfway "up a slick mud bank." The survivors had leaped off and huddled "in about knee- to waist-deep water behind the boat" while the Vietcong fired down on them from high on the bank. The men "couldn't stick their necks out" and had lost most of their weapons in the melee. Yost's men and those aboard the other PCF promptly cut loose with their heavy machine guns, driving the VC back into nearby bunkers. "Nobody was going to have their heads out with .50 calibers going. Just the sound of them is enough to scare you to death, let alone the ruckus they make when the rounds are hitting. So the Vietcong were suppressed."

After rescuing the corpse of the dead swift boat captain, Yost got the survivors aboard, then screamed on the radiophone for the gunships to come in and finish off what intelligence later determined to be a Vietcong heavy-weapons company. Only then was he told the choppers were still aboard the LST, though about to launch. Yost could not convince the South Vietnamese (through the marine major) to go after the enemy, who promptly disappeared before the gunships arrived. As with all too many such operations, hours of planning and moments of blood, sweat, tears, and bravery yielded little but casualties.[24] By the autumn of 1969, Vietnamization had taken hold; the river rats gave all their boats, monitors, river barracks vessels, and armored troop carriers to the South Vietnamese and headed home.

From the start, the effort against an elusive but determined and imaginative foe had been frustrated by profound cultural differences among the allies. The rift between South Vietnamese and Americans became particularly acute in the latter stages of the war as the U.S. effort wound down. In 1970 William Crowe, a navy captain who would become Ronald Reagan's chairman of the Joint Chiefs of Staff, was appointed senior adviser to the now wholly South Vietnamese–run riverine war. A handful of American sailors stayed around to help him. Sensitive to cultural nuances, Crowe quickly concluded that Vietnamese history and sociology had not created a warlike people. The individual adhered to the family unit and structure; it was nearly impossible for him to transfer his loyalties to a larger social entity, such as an army or navy, or to feel for the plight of his fellow soldiers and sailors. Revolutionary North Vietnam had overcome its instinctive passivity with a cause to fight for. Most South Vietnamese never developed such a fervor. If someone shot at a fellow soldier or sailor, that was the other fellow's problem. Crowe once encountered one of his American advisers cleaning heavy mounted machine guns aboard a PBR while South Vietnamese sailors slept in the hot sun all around him. When Crowe expressed his dismay, the gunner's mate replied, "You know, sir, when we get on the canals tomorrow they'll be great. They're good fighters and they'll man the guns. But they don't like to clean them." When Crowe asked what would happen if the Americans weren't around, the sailor said, "Well, sir, if I wasn't around they'd clean them or die." Crowe promptly took all advisers off the boats while they were at base and told his South Vietnamese counterpart that henceforth South Vietnamese sailors would care for their boats. Crowe finally concluded that his often frustrating experiences reflected the entire American effort in Vietnam. "In the end we could only be as effective as we were persuasive, and we never learned to be adequately persuasive. . . . The underlying corruption, thuggishness, and cronyism of the South Vietnamese government strangled the war effort in a dozen ways, yet Washington seemed powerless to bring about any change."

The results of this prodigious effort, like the rest of the war, were in the end unavailing. The VC and NVA combined simply wore down their better-equipped foes through evasion, hit and run, harassment, and, above all, sheer, stubborn existence. And the riverine war proved to be a heavy financial drain. "The energetic General Westmoreland enjoyed ready access to America's resources. These were used with lavish hand to build ports and airfields and to provide vast quantities of arms and equipment of all types." Riverine warfare demanded not only new strategic concepts and new tactics but above all new warship types. The PBRs, the "fast boats," and the other craft that were either built or modified for operations on the Mekong and its larger tributaries, though not expensive individually, added measurably to the cost of the war in the aggregate. Once the war was over they were useless for any other work and were left behind.

The Asian wars of 1950–1953 and 1964–1975 were equally hard on the naval air arm, largely diverted from its preferred strategic mission into a tactical bombing role either as part of inconclusive aerial interdiction campaigns or in direct close air support of ground operations. Only occasionally in Korea and Vietnam were carrier pilots invited by the Far Eastern Air Force to participate in or to initiate heavy raids against enemy installations that could be described as of strategic importance.[25] The impact on pilot morale was cumulative and in some cases devastating. "Militarily this war is a tragedy," Admiral George Tarrant tells doomed carrier pilot Harry Brubaker in a quiet moment off Korea in 1952. "Imagine the United States navy tied down to a few square miles of ocean. The marines are worse. Dug into permanent trenches. And the poor air force is the most misused of all. Bombers flying close air support." Tarrant and Brubaker were fictional characters in James Michener's celebrated novel about Task Force 77, *The Bridges at Toko-Ri*.[26] But Tarrant's complaint was an accurate reflection of armed forces opinion about Korea. Vietnam was no different. One morning in 1965, James Bond Stockdale, commander of the air group aboard the carrier *Oriskany,* called his men together before their first strike mission "and made a super-spectacular speech two hours long." At one point Stockdale told his pilots:

> If any of you guys are saving yourselves for a big war—don't. This is it. Limited war means to us that our target list has limits; our rules of engagement have limits. But that doesn't mean there is anything limited about our personal obligations as fighting men to carry out assigned missions with all we've got. Don't ask for Hollywood answers to "What are we fighting for?" We're here to fight because it's in the interests of the United States that we do so, which may not be the most dramatic way to explain it, but it has the advantage of being absolutely correct.[27]

When the Korean War settled into stalemate in the spring of 1951 the aerial interdiction campaign came into its own. The air force was given overall command of the air campaign, and assigned the navy the eastern half of North Korea. While the air force's own tactical fighter and fighter-bomber wings concentrated on Communist rail lines running down to Pyongyang and the battlefront as well as the bombing of potential airfields for MiG-15s across upper North Korea, naval aviation was given the task of destroying the Korean rail system from the Yalu to Hungnam and from Wonsan to the front. In 1944 tactical and strategic airpower had succeeded in isolating the Normandy battlefield by cutting the bridges over the Loire and Seine and destroying enemy railroad-junction points across all of northern France. But in Korea and Vietnam the opponents were not industrial powers requiring masses of supplies to fight a highly mobile war but Third World states with the most primitive industrial base. When the Vietnam air war began air force chief of staff General Curtis LeMay was famously quoted as saying that his boys would bomb the North Vietnamese back to the Stone Age. He never realized that economically the Vietnamese had never emerged from the Stone Age, that the most advanced industrial military powers could be confronted and contained by primitive military forces in a limited field of battle. Historian David Rees's 1964 conclusion about Korea would apply equally to Vietnam:

The pre-war daily capacity of the western [Korean railroad] net was estimated at 6–9,000 tons, cut down to 1,000–1,500 tons by air attack [from the Fifth Air Force]. The eastern net could handle 5,000 tons daily before the war, but the aircraft from TF 77 had reduced this to 500 tons, so perhaps the Communists were receiving about 2,000 tons daily by rail in early 1951. This seemed immensely successful until the demands of Chinese logistics were calculated. Each UN soldier in Korea required at least sixty pounds of supplies a day: but the Communist soldier needed only ten pounds, so that a CCF [Chinese Communist Forces] division of 10,000 men consumed fifty short tons daily.

During 1951–52 there were about ninety Communist divisions in Korea, and about sixty of these were at the front so only about 3,000 tons daily were needed by the Communist forces facing the Eighth Army. Over half this requirement could still be supplied by the railways, and the balance was easily made up by road transport and human bearers each of whom could carry about forty-five pounds for twelve miles overnight. Hundreds of thousands of North Koreans were recruited for this purpose.[28]

Eighteen months into the Korean War, the Chinese and North Korean commands had stationed repair crews every four miles along rail lines capable of restoring destroyed or damaged tracks in two to six hours. Extensive tunnel and cave systems were built near the front to stockpile food and supplies between offensives. Fifteen years later, in Vietnam, the Hanoi government "overcame the loss of bridges, rail lines and oil-storage depots through the use of 'bicycle brigades'" and the "dispersal of oil storage facilities in 'thousands upon thousands' of fifty-five gallon drums" cached along highways and in villages, rice paddies, and anywhere else fertile military minds could think of.[29]

"Above all," as Arleigh Burke summed up years later:

> there was no realization of the importance or the effectiveness of the [enemy's] A-frame logistic system. Nobody ever realized—and I didn't either, nobody did that I know of—how an army can be supplied on the backs of people at night, without very many trucks, and carrying just one load on an A-frame they could really support an army, and they did. All the aircraft and everything else couldn't stop it.... [W]e didn't recognize that it could be done in Korea. We never recognized the same thing—not the same thing, but similar things—in Vietnam later. What men can do with very crude equipment, very crude systems. This A-frame logistic system was marvelous that they could do that. They had wonderful organization to be able to do that. They had a disciplined group of people.[30]

For three years in Korea and eight years in Vietnam, American airmen from all three branches insisted that if only they were totally unleashed against enemy supply lines and bases, airpower could win the interdiction war as it had in Normandy in 1944. They chafed and cursed those who restrained them, without realizing that somehow, someway, a primitive but clever and disciplined enemy could continually defeat them. As the flyers of the Fifth Air Force and Task Force 77 whittled down North Korea's railroad network in the first half of 1951, the Communists sharply increased their truck traffic from an estimated seventy-three hundred to fifty-four thousand vehicles. Air force strategists then came up with Operation STRANGLE, a bombing, rocket, and strafing campaign designed to sever North Korea's road network from the battlefront by obliterating all highways, tunnels, embankments, bridges, defiles, and choke points across one degree of latitude above thirty-eight degrees, fifteen minutes. The area was divided between the Fifth Air Force, Task Force 77 carrier planes, and the First Marine Air Wing. The operation failed. As failure became more evident, tacticians and flyers simply stepped up the process. At one point, crater overlapped crater for more than two miles. But nothing kept the foe from keeping his front lines resupplied. Railroad tracks and roads could be knocked out for a day at most, bridges for as much as a week. But night after night thousands of docile human bearers ran along with their loads toward the front. Despite the employment of almost 100 percent of the offensive air potential aboard the carriers of Task Force 77 and 70 percent of the offensive power of the Fifth Air Force's and Far East Air Force's bomber command, the enemy was no weaker in June 1952 than he had been a year earlier. In the first two years of the Korean War the American Navy and its Marine Corps flying element expended more ordnance than during the entire Pacific war. More than two hundred marine and naval aircraft were lost to enemy ground fire. But the enemy kept eating and fighting, a fact that even Admiral Radford publicly admitted several months after the armistice.[31]

What went wrong in Korea? After-action assessments pointed to one crucial factor: if the military front remained stable, even the most vigorous air campaign against enemy supply lines and communication routes would fail. The Communists could lose up to 90 percent of their supplies to bombing, but so long as the remaining 10 percent got through, they could hold a static front against anything less than a full-scale offensive by UN forces. This became fully evident during the last six months of the war in the spring and early summer of 1953 when the Communists, seeking to expand their front lines before an inevitable armistice was signed, did begin moving troops and supplies to the battlefront during daylight hours. UN Air Force, Navy, and Marine Corps pilots suddenly found plentiful targets and happily blasted away with gun and rocket. Thousands of enemy soldiers were killed, an equal number of vehicles were destroyed, and mountains of supplies perished. But Chinese and North Korean forces stubbornly continued their pressure against the UN lines.[32] Interdiction simply could not work in a stalemated war. After the spring of 1951 the Allied objective in Korea was to hold the line, not to rout and chase the Chinese and North Korean armies from the peninsula. There would be no Normandy in Korea.[33]

Nor in Vietnam. No part of that prolonged, agonizing struggle has generated more heated debate than the air war against the North, which formally began with Operation Rolling Thunder in July 1965 and continued with several major breaks to assess Hanoi's reaction until March 1968, then resumed again in 1972 with the Pocket Money and two Linebacker bombing campaigns. Between 1968 and 1972 the navy and air force turned to concentrated attacks— designated Commando Hunt—against enemy supply lines, especially the Ho

Chi Minh Trail through Laos and western South Vietnam. It was "the longest air interdiction campaign in the history of warfare." In December 1968 alone, carrier aircraft flew over Laos more than thirty-seven hundred times. Such "production line bombing" had by 1972 transformed a jungle-clad country into a "wasteland."[34] Liberals and "doves" emphasized the indiscriminate nature of aerial bombing with presumably vast civilian casualties and the fact that every escalation drew in more ground troops in support. They argued that an unlimited air war could so antagonize North Vietnam's patrons in Beijing and Moscow as to eventually force Soviet and Chinese armies into battle, thereby igniting a global holocaust. Conservatives and "hawks"—including most of the air force and many elements within the army and navy (including Admiral U. S. Grant Sharp, CinCPac)—bitterly complained that the air war was being constrained by the White House and civilian elements in the Pentagon so as to preclude a victory that could be won through a combination of wearing North Vietnam down while heightening South Vietnam's will to resist.[35]

Few if any paid attention to military men seasoned in the nation's two previous wars. In 1967, at the height of national debate over the Vietnam bombing offensive, Matthew B. Ridgway, the veteran World War II paratroop commander who had gone on to lead UN forces in Korea, wrote in wonderment about the persistent attraction of attrition warfare. Even in World War II the Germans had been able to maintain twenty-six divisions in Italy for two years by supplying them through two narrow Alpine passes despite unquestioned Allied air superiority across the region. "In Korea, where we had air mastery over practically the whole peninsula, MacArthur himself acknowledged our inability to isolate the battle area by air bombardment or to choke off the flow of reinforcements and supply. In Vietnam, results to date have repeated this lesson: rails and bridges are repaired and functioning within a few days of a bomb attack, and infiltration routes have not been cut off."[36]

The problems that had plagued "limited" interdiction warfare in Korea not only resurfaced in Vietnam but took on new and disturbing dimensions. Whatever sins of omission or commission had been committed in Korea, they did not include close tactical direction of the war from Washington. But from the beginning, Lyndon Johnson insisted on calling even the most innocuous shots in Vietnam. He would control the pace and direction of the war as he controlled the pace and direction of his Great Society at home. All three armed forces suddenly found themselves victims of the iron law of unintended consequences. The splendid C3I systems that by 1965 allowed battlefield commanders to direct their forces with unprecedented speed and efficiency and in unprecedented detail could now be wielded by a distant commander in chief and his political advisers to subordinate local or regional military imperatives to distant (read domestic) political necessities. Johnson once boasted that his air force, navy, and marine flyers in Vietnam "can't even bomb an outhouse without my approval."[37] The president was not kidding. However reluctant he was to get into a major war in Southeast Asia, he eventually succumbed to pressures from the Joint Chiefs, most of his civilian advisers, and General Westmoreland in Saigon to do so. But he never trusted or truly believed the military. In moments of crisis he was fully prepared to control it right down to the unit level, as he dramatized one January day in 1968. The nuclear-powered supercarrier *Enterprise* had been diverted from taking up station on the "bomb line" off Vietnam because of the North Korean seizure of the spy ship *Pueblo*. For several days, the carrier and its task force cruised the Sea of Japan as a show of force. One evening, as the task force commander, Admiral Horace H. Epes, was watching a movie in his quarters, Captain Kent L. Lee, commanding the *Enterprise*, was summoned to a phone on the carrier's bridge and found himself talking directly to the president of the United States ten thousand miles away. As Lee later recalled, the president asked, were "those fellows from the north . . . giving us a problem?" No, sir, Captain Lee replied, they did not seem to be giving anyone a problem at the moment. There seemed to be no further danger to American interests in the seas off Korea. Fine, Johnson replied. He wanted the carrier task force to "turn south and head out of the Sea of Japan" immediately. The call was being monitored by the duty officer at CinCPac headquarters in Honolulu. After the president hung up, the duty officer asked Captain Lee if he fully understood what his president had directly ordered him to do. Despite the fact that there had been absolutely no authentication that Lee had actually been talking to the president, the captain assured CinCPac that he had understood Johnson's order and that *Enterprise* and its escorts were about to turn south toward Tsushima Strait. Only at that point did Lee interrupt Epes at his movie to tell the understandably nonplussed task force commander what had transpired. Epes had no desire to question the order, and he soon transferred to another carrier, *Ranger,* and released the *Enterprise* task force to sail to the Tonkin Gulf. On several other occasions during the Kennedy-Johnson years, naval analyst Norman Friedman assures us, "the White House situation room actually sent out rudder orders, which were deeply resented—but which were obeyed."[38]

Speed of communication could not overcome isolation from the Vietnamese battlefield, however. Executive decisions were often hopelessly out of date or irrelevant by the time they reached U.S. Army or Marine Corps field commanders in South Vietnam or navy task force and air group commanders aboard the air-craft carriers on Dixie and Yankee Stations. The frustrations of Korea wherein civilian authority prevented airmen from bombing key enemy installations and airfields across the Yalu or following enemy aircraft in "hot pursuit" into Soviet or Chinese airspace were extended in Vietnam to include rigid exclusion by Washington planners of most of Hanoi and nearly all of its chief port of Haiphong from systematic bombing. The Cambodian port of Sihanoukville was likewise kept off the bombing lists. As a consequence, a steady flow of Soviet cargo vessels kept the modest but unremitting North Vietnamese war effort well supplied while U.S. Air Force and Navy flyers hunted and pecked around the edges of the enemy's internal transportation and supply lines.[39]

Admiral Thomas Hayward, who commanded the carrier *America* during the war, and thereafter became, progressively, commander of the Seventh Fleet, commander of the Pacific Fleet, and chief of naval operations (under Carter and Reagan), articulated the navy's three "great frustrations" in Vietnam. First was use of the marines as just another army division. The corps should have been employed in short surprise amphibious assaults against North Vietnam to keep the enemy constantly off-balance. Second was Washington's unwillingness to allow the navy to intercept the sea route by which the Warsaw Pact countries rearmed and resupplied North Vietnam throughout the war. According to Ad-miral Hayward, Soviet and other Communist-bloc vessels on their way to the North Vietnamese port of Haiphong often brazenly steamed right through the carrier task forces on Yankee Station. Finally, until 1972 Washington refused to permit an aggressive mining of North Vietnamese harbors and anchorages as a means of further drastically reducing the flow of supplies on which the North Vietnamese war effort was almost totally dependent.[40]

As early as the summer of 1967 it was clear from congressional testimony that Robert McNamara—and apparently Johnson as well—had no intentions of winning the Vietnam War. They simply intended to hang on until the Com-munists could be teased or finagled or exhausted into coming to the peace table.[41] The secretary and his president had reason by this time to exercise extreme care and caution in prosecuting ground and especially air operations in Southeast Asia. The specter of another massive Chinese—and limited Soviet—intervention as in Korea could never be discounted, though all evidence suggests that the U.S. military, air, and naval chiefs in Washington and the Pacific did just that. Such radical diversion of strategic assumptions quickly led to poison-ous cross-purposes in waging the Vietnam War. Sharp soon became convinced that McNamara had become a sinister éminence grise behind the president, "a muddlehead who wanted it both ways": to strike the Communists without really hurting them so badly that they would surrender. Such a strategy, if such it could be called, led, in Hayward's view, to "colossal errors . . . driven by political, not military factors." As the bombing offensives sporadically continued, the decisions coming out of the Tuesday White House luncheons became more and more erratic. Rules of engagement and targets were "added, dropped, restricted, or qualified for the most ephemeral of reasons." At one point, "'pilots learned that they had authority to strike moving targets such as convoys and troops, but could not attack highways, railroads, or bridges with no moving traffic on them.'" To pilots flying off *Midway* in the summer of 1965 and on a later deployment at the end of the war eight years later, prohibitions against attacking enemy aircraft unless they shot first or North Vietnamese fishing boats moving toward downed flyers were nothing short of criminal. Under the stress of combat, the flyers simply ignored both prohibitions.[42]

Sharp and those in Saigon understood that "North Vietnam was undeveloped, with a weak economy based on growing rice. The Pentagon could find only ninety four significant military targets in the whole country. Baltimore probably had more than that." North Vietnam was not Nazi Germany, and it was folly to risk valuable planes and invaluable pilots in a highly dubious war of limited aerial interdiction.[43]

But that was precisely what Washington demanded of those flying off the navy's carriers on Yankee Station as well as from air force bases in Thailand and South Vietnam. Essentially, Johnson and McNamara bought the "dovish" arguments, especially with respect to the Communist superpowers. Should F-8s or F-105s sink one or two Soviet cargo vessels unloading war material at Haiphong or kill Chinese engineers and technicians working to maintain supply and communication lines between South China and North Vietnam, there was no telling how Beijing or Moscow might react. Better to conduct the war in such a way that they would have no pretext to react. High-altitude "strategic" carpet bombing of broad urban and industrial areas such as had been undertaken over Germany and Japan in World War II was thus out of the question in North Vietnam. Precision low-level "tactical" bombing to knock out specific targets (without killing nearby civilians) was what the White House and Pentagon insisted would bring Hanoi to the bargaining table. Even then, the few undeniably key targets like the great Paul Doumer Bridge built by the French outside of Hanoi in 1902 were off-limits. McNamara apparently felt that the bombing must be exquisitely balanced between hurting the North Vietnamese war effort, on the one hand, and not destroying what little modern facilities Hanoi had, on the other.

Precision bombing of questionable targets could lead only to a useless expenditure of American lives. In the best book about the air war over Vietnam,
Zalin Grant says of the carrier attacks against the North: "Dive bombing was
unquestionably more accurate than the carpet bombing done by the B-52s inside
South Vietnam. But the F-8 pilots had no illusions about hitting the target
with absolute accuracy. Even under the best conditions, in practice, with no
one shooting at him, and with the aim point perfectly visible, a tactical pilot
was satisfied if his bombs fell within a radius of fifty feet of the target." Admiral
John Hyland remembered with anguish and bitterness the air war during his
days as Seventh Fleet and later Pacific Fleet commander. Air policy was "just
completely ridiculous and terrible. I thought it was one of the great sins to ask
those pilots to try to do anything under the rules of engagement that were
then in force." Flyers could defend themselves only if attacked. Promising but
unlisted targets on the ground could not be bombed or strafed unless they posed
a direct and immediate threat to the aircraft. Long-range Sparrow missiles, the
most advanced ordnance in the naval arsenal, could not be used for fear that in
one case out of a hundred a distant but unidentified aircraft might be a Pan
Am airliner or a foreign aircraft that had strayed into an aerial battlefield by
mistake. (Given the tragic shootdown of an Iranian airliner by the cruiser *Vincennes* two decades later, this latter restriction made sense.) The restrictions
"came essentially from our old friend McNamara and the 'whiz kids.'... To
them apparently it was a very fascinating thing to try this and try that. Of
course, our people in our airplanes were just pawns in this game that these men
in Washington found so fascinating."[44]

Another senior commander recalled with equal bitterness that on the few
occasions when Task Force 77 flyers did make unauthorized raids against North
Vietnamese port installations, such as an attack on Cam Pha, "all hell broke
loose" at the Pentagon. A Polish freighter had been in port at the time, and
although not hit, "The Commies, as usual... immediately brought pressure to
bear, and the pussycats in Washington saw fit to cancel the second strike" with
a "direct flash" message to the bridge of *Kitty Hawk*.[45]

Nothing angered pilots more in the early years of Rolling Thunder than the
order to resist attacking surface-to-air (SAM) missile sites unless shot at first.
SAMs were "a brand new threat" in 1966–1967. "It took quite a bit of doing to
develop ways of handling those things," Hyland recalled, "because a pilot
often — and I guess most times — couldn't see the missile coming." Before proper
electronic countermeasures were mounted in strike and reconnaissance aircraft,
"there was little likelihood" that a pilot "could duck it even if [he] could see it."[46]

For seven long and terrible years, the pilots of Task Force 77 routinely assumed the role as the ongoing "large support force for the Army and for the Marines" that their fathers and older brothers had in Korea. Hyland remembered "many times" at the height of the air war against North Vietnam that "on board carriers I'd go down and talk to a whole bunch of" pilots "assembled and try to tell them how well they were doing, and how we were trying to get the whole thing squared away so all these lucrative targets would be available whenever we could get at them." There were always questions for the admiral, who recalled one young flier asking "quite sarcastically, 'Admiral, if I get a couple of bullet holes right through my body, can I assume that I can take retaliatory action?'" Hyland took no offense and "didn't shut him up." All the admiral could do was tell his charges to keep flying while he and others sought to change Washington's changeless policies.[47]

As the air war in Vietnam intensified, command and control became chaotic. General Westmoreland in Saigon demanded a share of the decision making in those portions of North Vietnam adjacent to the South Vietnamese battle areas, and his staff recommended that he obtain total control over all air operations in South Vietnam. "Westy," Sharp, and Admiral Roy Johnson, Sharp's successor while Hyland still commanded the Seventh Fleet, waged a long and bitter if quiet struggle over the matter. Hyland recalled talking to Admiral Johnson "on a daily basis about this." Johnson's instructions to his subordinate were blunt and to the point: "'Don't let the Seventh Fleet come under the operational control of MACV in Saigon.'" As a consequence, the command-and-control system that emerged for the air war in Vietnam—if, indeed, it could be dignified as a "system"—was

> mind boggling in its complexity and inefficiency. . . . Not only was there a three-way split in operational control of the strikes on North Vietnam [between Washington, Honolulu, and Saigon], but the naval [carrier] task force in the Tonkin Gulf reported to Admiral Sharp [and later Johnson] in Hawaii through the Seventh Fleet, while the air force went through a different channel. Later, when B-52's became involved in the bombing, the Strategic Air Command set up its own control system.

Even this arrangement did not take into account the occasional tactical and strategic bombings of Laos and Cambodia. Nor did it account for early naval aviation operations in Dixie Station off South Vietnam in support of hard-pressed U.S. and South Vietnamese ground troops. "Rationality called for an Indochina-wide allocation of resources under a single commander, so that airplanes could be employed in an efficient manner." Instead, "there was a hodgepodge of five or six separate command and control systems."[48]

In the combat-flying environments of Korea and Vietnam, "staying loose" was an absolute requirement for a pilot. "If a man tended to tighten up on Yankee Station," Frank Harvey wrote in describing carrier operations off North Vietnam as early as the summer of 1966, "he'd strip his emotional threads and crack up in a short time." But the tension of flying often questionable interdiction missions against Communist supply and communication lines was ferocious. Men came back from the flak-filled skies of Korea and the missile-filled skies over Vietnam "pale and shaken."[49]

One of the worst experiences was night flying over Korea off the straight decks of the relatively small, unmodernized *Essex*-class carriers of the early 1950s.[50] The handful of Skyraider pilots and aircrews found that "loneliness... is their constant companion" as, singly or in pairs, they groped along in pitch darkness at 250 knots through mountain passes and down steep valleys with only obsolete Japanese charts as guides, looking for stray gleams of dim light from truck convoys or the sudden spark from a railroad engine. The men rose from bunks in officers' country or sleeping racks in the crew's quarters just as the last daylight flights returned at dusk from striking bridges, marshaling yards, and military installations in southern North Korea. By the time the night crews "breakfasted" at 1800 (6 PM), the carrier wardrooms and mess halls had largely emptied of officers and men finished with supper. The few flyers, ship's officers, or crewmen who remained had nothing in common with the night airmen who soon trooped into empty ready rooms that immediately took on "a somber air. Night flyers have too much on their minds," one recalled at the time, "for any of the usual horseplay and ribbing." Once airborne in their propeller-driven aircraft, the pilots relied completely on instruments—artificial horizon indicators, altimeters, air-speed indicators, and turning needles—as they flew over snow-covered mountains or down icy passes into the black hole of a suspected valley. Visual contact with the world outside the cockpit could readily lead to disorientation, and many a night crew slammed into mountains or failed to pull out of a dive. Frank Metzner, who flew off *Princeton* during the winter of 1950–1951, recounted several times when his plane brushed treetops before he realized exactly where he was or what his plane was doing.

Once a truck convoy or train was sighted (the best time was on moonlit winter nights with a snowy ground cover that made them relatively easy to spot), the flyer's ordeal had just begun. The Communists soon developed some evil tricks to lure unwary airmen to their doom, stretching heavy copper wires between mountains over valley floors or deliberately leaving an empty truck with lights on sitting on a roadway whose sides were lined with twenty-millimeter guns. Roaring in to strafe or rocket a train or truck convoy might lead to momentary fireworks, to the realization that there had been nothing there in the first place, or to sudden, violent death in the dark.

Returning to the carrier wallowing in stormy, night-blackened seas demanded every ounce of flying ability a pilot could muster at the end of a long, frightening mission. Once aboard, pilots and aircrews returned to their strange routine of daylight sleeping in preparation for yet another night of lonely work. Metzner wrote obsessively about the unreality of the job.

In the winter and spring of 1952, popular novelist James Michener went out to Korea on press assignment to see the strange war for himself. He rode *Essex* for several weeks, observing its air group, and returned convinced its carrier pilots were the most heroic men among a group of unsung heroes. It had been easy to fight well and feel appreciated on Guadalcanal or at Normandy; the country was 100 percent behind the war effort. Nobody at home seemed to care about Korea. "When the men of Marsh Beebe's squadron go forth to hold the enemy, they are, I am ashamed to say, alone."[51]

The air interdiction campaigns in both Korea and Vietnam were frighteningly dangerous without being especially productive. In Korea increasingly dense enemy flak batteries were constantly upgraded with ever more precise radar-guidance systems operated by Soviet and Chinese technicians. In Vietnam SAMs were a terror to every aviator. Operation STRANGLE and other bombing campaigns in Korea carried out by both land- and carrier-based aircraft essentially involved a return, day after day, week after week, month after month, year after year to the same railroad-marshaling yards, the same well-defended valley bridges, the same roads and supply build-up areas. What the aviators knocked down or exploded or ruined on one day, the enemy would usually have rebuilt or resupplied by the next. Concentrated attacks on manufacturing facilities and transportation choke points, when they occurred, were often devastating but just as often too late, as the enemy learned to disperse his factories and expand his transportation net so that few critical targets remained. Not until the summer of 1952 did B-29s and navy Skyraiders and Panthers knock out the last of North Korea's concentrated industrial works, and heavy bombing and strafing of the North Korean capital of Pyongyang by navy and air force planes at the same time was too late to seriously affect enemy morale. Only near the very end of hostilities, in May 1953, did air force target planners tumble to the fact that destruction of North Korea's irrigation dams might make a decisive difference in the war. But by that time all outstanding differences were rapidly being negotiated, and an armistice was signed at the end of July.[52]

Korea had come at the end of a long period of progressive disarmament, so the sudden military and naval build-up required a major infusion of World War II veterans. This situation caused a crisis in air force ranks that peaked in 1951–1952 as a substantial number of voluntarily and involuntarily recalled reservists (and their wives) tried to invoke "fear of flying" as a means of avoiding combat. Navy pilots, however, seemed able to stifle whatever grievances, fear, and bitterness they may have felt and went about their jobs. Each carrier squadron in Task Force 77 between 1951 and 1953 was heavily leavened with a number of "retreads" who provided an atmosphere of tough, experienced professionalism. Bill Mauldin, who had won fame as a young, fresh-faced war correspondent and cartoonist in Europe during World War II, visited Korea in 1952. Aboard the unconverted fleet carrier *Antietam,* Mauldin was transfixed by "those souped up meteors" that the navy was flying. "I was curious to see what kind of wild eyed kids the navy hires to hell around" in the F-9F Panther jets. He was dumbfounded to discover that when the pilots pulled off their crash helmets the sun bounced off "so many bald heads." Tim Donohoe, a thirty-four-year-old lieutenant commander, told Mauldin, "Nearly all of us are reserves that flew in the last war." Donohoe, who suffered from gout, had left a wife and four children back in Chicago. Lieutenant Warren Hubbard from Abilene, Texas, added, "A bachelor under 30 is a curiosity around here." After several days aboard the carrier, Mauldin concluded that a "pretty big chunk of this war is being fought by guys who carry pockets full of pictures of their wives and kids while they bounce on the deck in an airplane shot full of holes."[53]

What kept both novice and veteran carrier pilots flying despite apathy at home was personal integrity, a strong determination not to let their buddies down, and patriotism. The men believed that what their country was doing in Korea was right. "I doubt if you could find men less eager for war—more acutely aware of what they have surrendered to participate," Michener wrote. "But they go out day after day over the icy seas, over the high mountains" and into the deadly, gun-ringed valleys. And when *Essex* and its air group at last went home after six or eight months on the line, "other men like them, reserves yanked from their homes and their jobs, will be coming out here on other carriers to fight this lonesome, forgotten war."[54]

In the early winter of 1952, Ensign Norman S. Broomfield of Salt Lake City was catapulted off *Valley Forge* and with his squadron went after a bridge in

North Korea. He was hit and crashed in the snow-covered mountains nearby. At first his mates above thought him dead, but they waited around long enough to see him crawl painfully out of his ruined fighter, both legs obviously broken. As enemy soldiers closed in on the helpless youngster, a squadron of propeller-driven Corsairs appeared to establish a "canopy of fire" around him. A helicopter was dispatched from the cruiser *Manchester* off the coast to effect a rescue. But the chopper went down near where Broomfield lay, whether from sudden mechanical failure or enemy fire no one could say. The two-man crew, Lieutenant Ed Moore and marine First Lieutenant Kenneth Henry, climbed out safely, found Broomfield, and calmly began fashioning a sled to carry him away as the enemy again closed in. Word was flashed to the fleet from the Corsairs detailing what had happened and also the fact that the planes were running dangerously low on fuel. A relief squadron was promptly launched from *Valley Forge's* sister carrier, *Philippine Sea,* and it roared in over Broomfield, Moore, and Henry to maintain ground suppression. The enemy fought back tenaciously, and one plane was badly shot up as it came in low on a strafing attack. Out at sea on the two carriers, "pilots insisted on going in to get their man" and his two would-be rescuers. Over the next several hours, other squadrons came in to take up rotational ground-suppression duties. At last an army helicopter managed to land on the only flat terrain near the beleaguered three, about two hundred yards away. Under enemy fire the helicopter pilot screamed at Henry and Moore to leave Broomfield and make a run for it. The helicopter could only take two men. Moore and Henry refused. The chopper pilot lifted off and daringly brought his craft right down near the three and again begged Moore and Henry to save themselves. Again the two waved him off, and after taking small-arms fire the pilot at last took his chopper staggering into the air and away from the cauldron. Darkness fell, but night fighters from the two carriers combed the mountainous area where they believed the three men were, "trying for one last miracle" to keep them alive. It failed. When the planes returned at daybreak all they could see were trails of blood in the snow and the tramping of many feet where there had been a fight. What happened to the three men no one could say. But a strange exultation swept through the carrier ready rooms. The fliers knew they had kept the faith with their downed, doomed comrades. If one of them should find himself in the same position, he knew he would not be abandoned until every last effort at rescue had been tried.[55]

The same spirit initially pervaded the carrier squadrons and helicopter rescue pilots off Vietnam. But it could not be sustained over the length of a seven-year conflict by officers and men far removed from the glory days of World War

II, burdened by doubts about their government's strategies and, in many cases, about the war itself. In 1965 and 1966 when pilots ejected over North Vietnam superhuman efforts were frequently made to find them and get them out. By the following year spirits began to flag, in part because the Americans were being victimized by their own advanced technologies. When Butch Verich was shot down during a mission off *Oriskany,* opinion on board was sharply divided over whether to even attempt a rescue that might cost further lives. North Vietnamese troops had gotten wise to the survival radio beacons each pilot carried and were beginning to use captured instruments either to lure would-be rescuers into a trap or to complicate their search. Overruling two staff captains, the commander of the air group and the admiral determined to try a mission just to let the squadron know that risks would still be taken to find downed airmen. But the helicopter pilot who went in and daringly made the snatch in the midst of enemy ground fire told Verich on the way home that had the downed flyer missed the rescue sling one more time he would have been left.[56]

By 1969 veteran carrier pilot John B. Nichols noted a decisive sea change in morale, as many navy and air force pilots openly questioned both the wisdom and the morality of the war. A few turned in their wings and left the service. Some frankly admitted their fears and frustrations and were persuaded to stay on. Those who did the persuading were often the flight surgeons, who saw their traditional role as monitor and healer expand to counselor, father confessor, and psychologist. By the time *Midway* deployed on its last wartime cruise in late 1972, "the number of . . . crew needing a psychiatrist had become overwhelming." The medical staff was counseling not only flight crews but nineteen-year-old members of the ship's company who were "homesick, lonely, or simply scared of not surviving" the frantic pace of fourteen- to eighteen-hour nonstop flight-deck and air operations. Dr. Donald Vance recommended that a trained psychiatrist be assigned to the huge carrier, at least for a time. Request denied. Vance was later haunted by one "private talk" in which he convinced an experienced jet pilot to remain on flight status, only to have the man crash and die several weeks later.[57] Not for another thirty years would the navy admit that carrier duty in general and flight operations in particular imposed the kind of inhuman stress that often required psychiatric counseling.

The war's ambiguities proved literally killing for some. Pilots could accept flak- and missile-suppression missions; that was going one-on-one with an armed enemy. So were the endless interdiction missions against truck parks and ammunition dumps on the Ho Chi Minh Trail and railroad installations in the North. But if a flyer strafed or bombed a junk in a river near Haiphong, Hanoi, or Hue, had he sunk a small combatant or killed an entire peasant family? If four or five pajama-clad figures were cut down in a rice paddy somewhere in either the North or South, had one killed enemy soldiers or peaceful farmers? Increasingly, the risk of death, maiming, or capture did not seem to be worth the squalor of the target, and many a mission as early as 1966 ended abruptly with the planes dumping their bombs and scuttling back to the ship.[58]

William Lawrence, who made two tours to Vietnam in 1966–1967 and was shot down and incarcerated in Hanoi for nearly six years, "remember[ed] vividly how we hoped so much between cruises that the war would end" and "how disappointed I was when" after a month's pause in early 1967, "we started the bombing again because we just didn't want to go back." Night flying over Vietnam in F-4 fighter planes searching for enemy supply trucks to bomb and shoot up was dangerous and frustrating as well. The F-4s did not possess the radar capabilities to pick up the trucks on their own and had to rely on EA-3 Skywarrior electronic-warfare aircraft. Once an EA-3 picked up an enemy truck formation or even a single unit, the trailing F-4 would roar in at high speed to drop an illumination flare prior to attack. "The flares often didn't work," Lawrence later wrote, "and when they did illuminate, they obliterated any horizon that you had and destroyed your night vision, making instrument flying much more difficult. Then, of course, you couldn't really see anything on the ground. In two combat cruises in Vietnam, I've yet to see my first truck on the ground, but I sure hurled a lot of bombs at the ground." Such was the result of Washington's unwillingness to mine Haiphong Harbor or allow American airpower to cut the rail lines between Hanoi and China.[59]

The rigors of flying in both Korea and Vietnam were compounded by the hardships of carrier life "on the line." The ships were invariably noisy, crowded, and busy and often either freezing cold or blistering hot as they steamed their mind-numbing racecourse patterns off Wonsan, Hungnam, or Haiphong, ceaselessly conducting air operations. In Korea the navy had been forced to wage war largely with World War II fleet carriers only marginally capable of supporting and deploying jet aircraft. One young ensign aboard *Bon Homme Richard* remembered the ship's "underpowered, WWII-style catapults. . . . 'When the winds were light it was necessary to strip a rocket or two from each wing in order to better assure getting the F9F Panthers safely into the air.'" Catapults were always tricky, and pilots were aware that any mission in either peace or war could terminate fatally at inception due to various malfunctions, collectively referred to off Vietnam as "a cold shot."[60] Catapults were also fatal to restful sleep. In both the *Essex*-class carriers and the later *Forrestal–Kitty Hawk*–class

supercarriers, pilots and officers of the ship's company lived and slept up forward where catapults boomed out day and night. Off Korea and Vietnam carriers frequently "unrepped" at night, and the sounds of heavy machinery and
cargo being dragged across hangar decks and down passageways were further barriers to restful sleep for stressed-out pilots. The winter air and seas off Korea
were icy, and flight-deck crews were often blinded by blowing snow and sleet as
they horsed heavy jets into launch or parking positions on slippery decks.

   Even summer weather in the Sea of Japan could be frightening. June 1953 was
a dreadful month. On the seventh, a flight of four propeller-driven Skyraiders
was returning in late afternoon to *Philippine Sea* from a canceled ground-support
mission "when low clouds, rain, and wind conspired to make flying conditions
difficult." As Robert F. Dorr and Warren Thompson later related, visibility near
the carrier dropped to nil, as the Skyraiders groped through murk and gloom
to find the flight deck. Automated light-and-mirror landing systems supported
by radar guidance were still some years away, and in any case the *Phil Sea* was a
straight-deck, unmodernized World War II–era carrier. There was no chance of
a pilot's "flying the ball" down a perfect glide path through the murk onto the
ship. With fuel rapidly dwindling, the Skyraiders made three passes before one
ditched in the water (the pilot was rescued), while the others (one of which was
fortunately "blessed" with radar) set off with an equally lost Corsair to reach a
friendly airfield on the nearby coast. Soon the radar-carrying Skyraider ran out
of fuel and ditched near a fishing boat. As darkness closed in, the last three aircraft found airfield K-18, where an F9F jet had recently overshot the runway
and ended up a crumpled heap at the end of the tarmac. The Corsair landed
first and flipped over, but the pilot walked away. The two remaining Skyraiders,
"operating on fumes," landed in one piece. Lieutenant William Barron later
"wrote in a shaky hand that it was the 'hairiest hop I've ever flown.' On that
day, he had never seen the enemy."[61]

   If cold, snow, and cloud dogged the pilots off Korea, the enemy in Vietnam
was heat—and rapidly aging ships. Dick Wyman recalled that in the Tonkin
Gulf he and his roommate, the squadron flight surgeon, shared a small compartment "underneath the flight deck between the two catapults" aboard the
upgraded *Essex*-class carrier *Oriskany.* "When the catapults fired, the room shook
like an earthquake had hit it. We found an air conditioner and kept it running
full-time but the coolest the room got was ninety-two degrees Fahrenheit."
Temperatures aboard *Oriskany's* equally antiquated *Essex*-class sister, *Shangri-
La,* off North Vietnam in the spring, summer, and autumn of 1970 routinely
exceeded one hundred degrees, forcing a squadron commander to allow his

pilots to sleep in their ready-room's deep chairs. "Sitting in the airplane waiting to be launched, I and every bit of my clothing would be soaked," Wyman remembered.

> Guys got sick to their stomachs with the heat and the exhausts from the next plane ahead flaming back. Even though we weren't supposed to, I would take off my flight helmet after I was in the air and knock the sweat out of my eyes. You smelled so bad after a flight you had to bathe, but fresh water was so scarce we had to take salt-water showers, which left us sticky and itchy. I would shower and return to my room and fill my small sink with fresh water, and put a towel on the floor and sponge myself off.

Frank Harvey aboard the supercarrier *Constellation* in 1966 wrote of the crew coming out on deck during the night to escape the stifling heat of un-air-conditioned quarters.[62]

Aboard all the carriers, thousands of crewmen "rolled themselves out of sticky bunks ... that smelled of mildew every morning in the Tonkin Gulf." Aboard *Midway*, Rick Janes, "a skinny youngster from Minnesota," often was assigned "the bizarre task" of maintaining the steam catapult canal just below the flight deck. "The steel cooked in the sun" and in "sweltering tropical humidity" Janes swathed himself from head to toe with heavy clothing to prevent any part of his skin from touching the scorching metal. In a literal frying-pan-into-fire scenario, however, the young sailor risked heat stroke.

> Whenever Janes squeezed into the long, narrow catapult chamber, a chief petty officer stood by and insisted that Janes keep talking as he worked so the chief knew Janes had not passed out from the heat.
> "Janes, you okay?"
> "Yeah."
> "Janes! Are you all right? You still breathin' in there? Speak up son!"
> *"Yes, sir."*[63]

As was true of all the carriers, and like any comparable-sized small city of forty-five hundred or five thousand souls, *Midway* was a collection of disparate—and separate—communities. "The primary loyalty of most young men repairing jet engines, mixing kegs of bread dough, or monitoring hundreds of gauges in engineering rested with their department and the men who shared their cramped, musty quarters." "Snipes" toiling in broiling-hot propulsion spaces at the bottom of the ship felt little kinship with and some resentment toward those who worked "on the roof" or "punched the holes in the sky. . . . Deep inside the hull, well below the waterline, daylight was a rarity, a wisp of fresh air a faded memory." The succession of twelve-hour shifts day after day for a month on the combat line brought such numbing exhaustion that men went from work to food to sleep and back to work. After a month at sea the precious five- to seven-day liberties in Subic Bay or, much better still, Hong Kong were prized beyond measure.[64]

For officers and pilots, liberty, especially in the Philippines, included numerous privileges not accorded the enlisted people. Perhaps the most precious was the right to purchase "up to five fifths of hard liquor a month and an unlimited amount of beer." Navy regulations clearly stipulated that "no liquor at all will be kept aboard U.S. Navy ships," but no one checked at the officers' gangway. Jim McBride, who flew an A-4 Skyhawk jet fighter off the carrier *Shangri-La* in 1970, "usually kept two cans of beer hidden" in the equally unauthorized little refrigerator he had hidden "next to the washbasin underneath a beach blanket." Some and possibly a great deal of heavy drinking occurred in carrier ready rooms and officers' countries at sea during World War II and off Korea, but was never reported by the Micheners and Mauldins because, like illicit sex among prominent public figures, it was considered beyond the pale of legitimate reportage. In the growing let-it-all-hang-out atmosphere of the late 1960s, however, both the formal illegality of onboard drinking and bans on its discussion were widely considered unrealistic and hypocritical. Combat flying off carriers in a seemingly endless war was unimaginably dangerous and frustrating; if pilots required heavy doses of restoratives to retain morale and fighting trim, so be it. While few if any pilots drank before missions, beer and liquor parties while proceeding to or from the combat line went on "for as long as the war had and they would continue until the last U.S. ship left Vietnam for good." Relaxing in their squadron ready rooms on the way to or from Subic Bay, pilots "would pull out a bottle of Chivas, Johnnie Walker Red Label, or a six-pack or two of beer." Since ice was nearly unobtainable under way, pilots and ship's officers aboard at least one carrier, *Kitty Hawk,* chilled their beer by putting it in a garbage can that they then "sprayed ... with a fire extinguisher." When McBride brought his by now ancient, accident-prone Skyhawk aboard *Shangri-La* for the last time in November 1970, he joined "a number of parties.... [W]e had champagne in the senior officers' bunkroom, the first time for the bubbly."[65]

In both Korea and Vietnam, carriers were dangerously overloaded with ordnance, and shipboard fires caused either by internal accidents or by plane crashes on the flight deck were potentially lethal. No ship was lost, but off Vietnam *Forrestal* suffered horrendous casualties and severe damage, and other carriers, including *Oriskany, Midway,* and *Enterprise* (undergoing final training exercises off Hawaii), were badly fire damaged.

However lonely and unreal carrier duty was in Korea, a firm consensus existed that "international Communism" had to be stopped there (or in Europe) before it flooded down Main Street USA. Moreover, the carriers were still fairly new, even if some had seen hard service during World War II. As a consequence, the ships' companies as well as the air groups were of relatively high caliber, morale was good, and the ships were well run once acceptable manpower levels were reached. Moreover, the Korean War, far more than Vietnam, brought U.S. forces in perilously close contact with the Soviet military machine, which provided an added sense of importance to the overall commitment. Korea really seemed to be on the cutting edge of the anti-Communist crusade at a time when that crusade was coming to preoccupy ever larger and noisier segments of the American public. It is now well known that Russian pilots flew MiG-15s and -21s against B-29s and jet-fighter aircraft in the skies over North Korea, and as early as September 1950 a Soviet Tupelov bomber "ventured close" to the American carrier fleet offshore. When a combat air patrol from *Valley Forge* intercepted the plane, its tail gunner opened up, and an F4U-4 pilot promptly shot the twin-engined aircraft out of the sky. A nearby destroyer recovered one Russian survivor who soon died. "Messages then flew thick and fast to Pearl Harbor and on to Washington." President Truman was about to address the United Nations on Communist aggression against South Korea, Donald Engen remembered, and Task Force 77 had just shot down—in international airspace—a Soviet plane that may or may not have harbored hostile intent. According to Engen, a jet pilot aboard *Valley Forge,* the incident was perceived as so embarrassing that the Soviet corpse was quickly transferred to the fleet flagship "where it was temporarily interred in the refrigerated meat locker" before being sent on to a morgue in Sasebo, Japan. Forty-seven years later Engen thought the corpse might still rest there in "limbo." The Russian air build-up in adjacent Manchuria late in 1952 and the incursion of Soviet aircraft into international airspace off Korea and even into skies near Japan deeply concerned the UN command in Korea and the government in Washington. No one was more skittish than the commanders and air crews of Task Force 77 who flew about 275,000 of the more than 1 million individual missions during the war. As interservice cooperation in the air war improved markedly in the latter stages of the conflict, the carrier admirals off Korea fretted that "even with alert combat air patrols," they could not "effectively defend" their fragile ships "against attacks by MiG-15's or IL-28's [Ilyushin bombers]."[66]

Another crisis took place in November 1952 after Far East Command, following concurrence by the U.S. Joint Chiefs of Staff and State Department, ordered UN aircraft to engage any and all Russian planes that entered their airspace. Seven Soviet MiGs from Vladivostok openly attacked a combat air patrol of F9F-5 Panther jets from *Oriskany* over international waters. The Soviets were badly bloodied, at least one pilot having to eject before his plane crashed into the frigid seas. According to one recent source, "Probably fewer than half the enemy jets made it back to base, though the Navy was disappointed because faulty plotting had foiled any chance for the UN to finally grab a Russian airman." UN Command headquarters did not publicize the incident, and the Russians never repeated it, probably because they feared the loss and capture of one or more of their pilots over international waters.[67]

Off Vietnam, lack of an equally powerful rationale for commitment and sacrifice, a declining national financial base for maintaining the war and upgrading the fleet, growing morale problems in the officer corps, and a drastically changing lifestyle among the young Americans enlisted for naval service produced a new kind of sailor and naval aviator. In the late sixties more and more youngsters appeared at recruiting stations simply to escape the draft. Better to spend four years at sea, even aboard a dangerous fighting ship, than a year in a Vietnamese rice paddy or hilltop waiting to be killed in the next ambush. Service loyalty among such recruits was often practically nil.

Once in uniform, the indifferent recruits realized just how hard and lonely life could be. Ideally, the navy strove to maintain operating schedules in which ships would spend one-third of their time in overseas deployment, one-third training in the waters near their home ports, and one-third at dockside, allowing people to be with their families. But the demands of war, cold and hot, shot this ideal to pieces. As early as the late fifties, one deputy Atlantic Fleet commander tried to ameliorate the growing problem of deployment imbalances by having ships' companies do their training ashore on first-generation electronic simulators. He thought the effort "fairly successful" in maintaining the skill levels of "anti-submarine warfare specialists, radar men [and] combat information center people." But his efforts were undermined by fleet commanders who, rightly, wanted training done at sea."[68] Vietnam's high operating tempo overwhelmed all efforts to maintain humane operational scheduling.

At the same time, the reformed officer promotion and retirement system that had seemed equitable and promising in the small prewar naval service had gotten out of control after 1945. Annapolis doubled its size in the early postwar era, while naval ROTC programs and officer candidate schools increased the flood of commissioned officers. Only a fortunate handful of men had real chances at full careers. Many promising young officers left at the end of their initial service obligations; others who did remain were ultimately forced into premature retirement while still in their productive years. The whole chaotic system led, in the words of one embittered, if moderately successful, naval officer, to the retention of "an illogical few."[69]

Admiral Alfred Ward, who divided his later career almost evenly between Washington and command at sea, recalled that while he was in the Plans and Policy section of the Pentagon during Vietnam, "we had carriers...that would be out in the Western Pacific for more than a year at a time, and you cannot maintain personnel strength and personnel morale if a young man or a young married officer has to be away from home for more than a year." Ward remembered different times when he was himself a young officer in the thirties. In those comparatively quiet years between world wars, ships were deployed to the Pacific and even the small Asiatic Fleet for years at a time. But officers, and even some senior enlisted men, could take their families with them. "The families would go on transports and set up homes in Shanghai and the Philippines or somewhere else and the ships would operate from those places, so there was no break-up of family life. It was a very pleasant experience for them."[70]

Aging ships and aircraft rapidly deteriorated under the constant and high operational tempo of the Vietnam war, becoming "old technologies" in the space of a few short years (the A-4 was a prime example), contributing further to the fears and frustrations of combat. Jim McBride "felt bitter and cranky" as the upgraded World War II carrier *Shangri-La* came off its initial "line tour" on Yankee Station in May 1970. Missions had often been canceled by aircraft malfunction, the Skyhawk with its "dumb" ordnance was unsuitable for the pinpoint work of interdiction, and machinery aboard the carrier tended to break down or remain marginally effective. "If the *Shang* were truly a trim fighting carrier one might take pride in the thought of returning again" to the bomb line "and really being a contributing force to the war effort," McBride wrote in his lengthy diary on the way to Subic Bay. But a month of flight operations "shows the carrier to be an old ship barely managing to meet her combat commitments." Things got progressively worse aboard the twenty-six-year-old vessel. In June, during its third line period, one of the carrier's evaporators went down, and the liquid-oxygen plant soon followed. "The *Shang* finally gave out for good" on July 2 when a shaft coupling sheared off, effectively stopping a quarter of

the propulsion system. Within hours the big vessel was limping toward a Japanese shipyard for major repairs. When it returned to Yankee Station a month
later, nothing seemed to work. Wardroom meals were occasionally served on
paper plates, there was never any ice to cut the still terrible heat, and showers in
officers' country were invariably warm, salty, and sticky when they worked at
all. Conditions in the crew's quarters could only be imagined.[71]

As Vietnam dragged on, morale was further sapped by a spirited antiwar
movement both beyond and even within the navy. Service towns and port cities
were flooded with counterculture broadsides and newspapers advocating sabotage
and outright mutiny. Popular motion picture stars like Donald Sutherland and
Jane Fonda held rallies outside military and naval bases exhorting soldiers and
sailors not to go to Vietnam. A Pentagon sailor named Roger Priest began printing an antiwar propaganda sheet and dared the navy to take away his basic First
Amendment right to say and print what he pleased. From the midsixties onward, war protesters passed out broadsides on the streets of navy towns, invited
sailors to picnics and private parties, and tried to get Fonda onto naval bases
and ships to exhort the sailors to rebel. By 1972 the antiwar movement in the
San Francisco Bay area had reached such a pitch that the captain of the carrier
Hancock ordered general quarters just before the ship sailed under the Golden
Gate Bridge on its way to a final Vietnam deployment. Looking up, the crew
"could see traffic backed up for miles, the bridge being kept clear lest protesters
drop explosives on the flight deck." One aviation-squadron commander "stalked
down" to his stateroom, threw himself across his bunk, "and cried."[72] In terms
of desertion rates or the formation of clandestine societies within the naval
establishment the antiwar efforts failed miserably. And on the carriers during the
early years off Vietnam, the flight-deck, maintenance, and catapult crews essential to sustaining effective air operations generally performed magnificently.[73]
But the growing antiwar mood of the country after 1968 had a decidedly adverse
impact on traditional reenlistment rates and, eventually, on morale throughout
the fleet.

By late 1972, when the newly refurbished *Midway* began a comparatively
comfortable final cruise off Vietnam, enlisted men were permitted to wear beards
and enjoyed a "private lounge" where no officers were allowed. Rumors swept
the huge craft that recruiters were under heavy pressure to relax standards and
that some had made deals with local small-town judges "to accept petty crimi-
nals into the service as an alternative to a few months in the county jail." Older
sailors remembered a time when a man could leave valuables in the open; no
longer. When the average sailor's time in the Vietnam-era navy was up, he went

out with a sigh of relief. Understaffed with key personnel, the navy strove to keep a man at sea as long as possible. This meant that when his enlistment ended, a sailor was promptly flown off the ship to home, creating one more vacancy in an important rating.[74]

Decreasing numbers of highly trained men raised the danger level steadily aboard the ships of the surface fleet, especially on the highly vulnerable aircraft carriers. A steady rise in drug use compounded the crisis alarmingly. According to one source, the navy discharged 150 sailors for drug use in 1965; four years later, thirty times and more that many were charged and separated. More rumors "swept" *Midway* in 1972 that one West Coast destroyer could not meet its deployment schedule because nearly half the crew had been busted. "The drug culture was no less insidious aboard Midway. Prodigious amounts of drugs were consumed ashore on liberty, especially in the Philippines. For many, 'speed,' 'smoke,' and 'grass' topped the list of most popular drugs." LSD was smuggled aboard "as microdots hidden under stamps." The rumor mill had it that several marines were primary dealers, but no one dared "rat" on a shipmate and either face the consequences from his enraged buddies or be implicated as a druggie.[75]

The growing financial crisis in the national security area added yet another burden. In March 1968 Vietnam commander General William Westmoreland asked for an additional 206,000 troops. Westmoreland rightly believed that North Vietnam's just-concluded "Tet" offensive had been both a total failure and a reflection of growing desperation in Hanoi. But Tet was erroneously depicted by the American media as a smashing Communist victory, and the general's request was interpreted as itself a gesture of discouragement if not despair. Treasury secretary Henry Fowler bluntly told President Johnson that if Westmoreland's request was granted, deep cuts would have to be made not only in other areas of national defense but in the president's cherished domestic spending programs as well, and even then the dollar would suffer. "It was a significant turning point in American history," British journalist and historian Paul Johnson has written, "the first time the Great Republic, the richest nation on earth, came up against the limits of its financial resources."[76]

At last, in the spring of 1972, what might have been had sea and airpower been fully employed in Vietnam from the beginning was demonstrated when the Communists launched a surprise Easter offensive while participating in desultory peace talks far away in Paris. A suddenly infuriated Richard Nixon determined on an unprecedented retaliation to bomb the North into suspending its offensive and beginning serious negotiations. The president lifted nearly

all constraints against bombing in the North, including the key strategic facilities and installations in and around Hanoi and, eventually, Haiphong. Whether he and Pentagon planners acted on chance or design, they hit on the only way to neutralize the A-frame factor: constant and increasingly indiscriminate bombing of central supply and distribution points that forced Hanoi's Communist suppliers to recalculate the cost of their support. By May 9 nearly all of North Vietnam, "excluding a buffer zone thirty miles deep along the Chinese border and a number of other sensitive targets, had been opened to Navy and Air Force attack." Day after day for five months as Washington progressively narrowed the bombing exclusion zones, navy and air force fighter bombers and B-52s flung every kind of ordnance they had, including new laser-guided "smart" bombs, at an ever widening circle of enemy targets. Bridges, railroad installations, small vessels, and truck parks throughout the country were subject to sustained, savage assault, while A-6 Intruders and A-7 Corsairs—initially from the carrier *Coral Sea*—dropped hundreds of magnetic-acoustic sea mines in "the river approaches to Haiphong" and, shortly thereafter, "other major ports . . . as well." As soon as the North Vietnamese swept these minefields, carrier aircraft promptly "reseeded" them. All of these operations complemented daily air strikes by air force and navy jets in support of beleaguered South Vietnamese units.[77]

The operational tempo was frantic and unceasing. Between May 9 and September 30, the navy's carriers alone launched an average of 4,000 missions per month, day and night, "reaching a peak of 4,746 in August." The enemy offensive against the South was brought to a halt as early as June, but the bombing continued for another three months until North Vietnamese diplomats in Paris began to demonstrate an interest in serious negotiation. But the cost had been high. Hanoi met the determined Linebacker I and Pocket Money fliers with nearly 2,000 SAMs and a flock of MiG interceptors. On May 10 alone, forty-one MiGs rose from their airfields to contest air force and naval fliers. Twenty-eight naval aircraft were lost during Linebacker and Pocket Money; thirty air crews were rescued "in the North Vietnamese theater of operations," both ashore and, for the majority who could make the sea, afloat. In August U.S. warships bombarded Haiphong itself, and by September the North Vietnamese had been bombed back to the conference table, their infrastructure and their supply lines into China at least temporarily ruined. One aviation historian has concluded that these operations "gradually destroyed Hanoi's ability to prosecute the war." Perhaps, but the North Vietnamese proved stubborn and feisty enough to require another massive dose of airpower in December (Linebacker II), which resulted, among other things, in the carpet bombing of downtown

Hanoi and the reseeding, by naval aircraft, of the North Vietnamese ports. Hanoi retaliated with another 1,250 SAMs that brought down fifteen B-52s, while four carrier planes were lost to antiaircraft fire and sporadic MiG attacks. By the end of the month, however, the air force and navy had succeeded in destroying nearly all North Vietnamese SAM sites. Within days Hanoi began to seriously negotiate what seemed to be an end to the war. In fact, it proved merely a truce long enough for Hanoi to rebuild its war-making base and gather its forces for the final climactic drive that would conquer a South now bereft of American protectors.[78]

For at least a generation, Vietnam and its loss remained the wound in the American heart. The country was not used to failure, and with a few long-ago exceptions, history had given it a pass. The army and guerrillas let loose by Ho Chi Minh and his successors between 1964 and 1973 at last brought the nation face to face with the limits of power not only on the ground but at sea as well. By the early seventies, the United States Navy was as worn out as the army, ground down by twenty-five years of incessant steaming and frequent battle. As it staggered into the post-Vietnam era, it found itself faced with a formidable new foe born of a humiliation that had taken place a decade before.

CHAPTER 5

Crisis and Consequence

Cuba, 1962

BY 1960 THE COLD WAR had become the defining fact of international life. The incessant contest between Communist "East" and democratic-capitalistic "West" transcended simplistic explanations of economic competition, territorial expansion, or even the clash of rights and interests. Rather, it closely resembled Karen Armstrong's compelling depiction of the Crusades, "fueled on all sides by myths and passions that were far more effective in getting people to act than any purely political motivation."[1] As Moscow and Washington jockeyed ceaselessly for local, regional, and global mastery across an increasingly complicated politico-military chessboard, no revolutionary or insurrectionist movement, however obscure, was safe from interference and absorption by either side.

Geopolitically, the United States, long dominant on the American world island, had managed to ring the vast Soviet-dominated Eurasian heartland with bases and sea power. Together with its democratically inclined allies in Western Europe, Washington contained Josef Stalin's newly emergent Soviet empire within the confines of old czarist Russia and immediately adjacent territories to the west conquered by Soviet arms in 1944–1945. Growing ideological if not political rivalry during the fifties had also created great and ultimately unbearable strains between Moscow and its "fraternal comrades" in China. The ostensible partnership between the world's largest territorial nation and its most populous—both fervently committed to the ideology of global revolutionary struggle and change—caused deep apprehension throughout much of the international community that had endured two ghastly and devastating global conflicts in the space of thirty-one years. Growing evidence that the Sino-Soviet bloc had become an illusion, a fabrication—and possibly always had been—was usually dismissed in Washington, though European diplomats and intellectuals occasionally glimpsed the truth.

Nikita Khrushchev knew better. A turbulent, unstable man, largely unlettered, and often too shrewd for his own good, Khrushchev understood as well as the old masters of the movement that the Communist impulse must expand or die. Somehow, somewhere, in some way the Kremlin must break out of the capitalist encirclement, must probe for weak spots in the surrounding ring of diplomacy and steel and exploit them. Egypt and Syria looked promising in the late fifties; so did Indonesia. And suddenly, late in 1959, there was Fidel Castro's new regime in Cuba.

Whether Castro was a dedicated Communist or an equally dedicated opportunist has been a matter of sharp debate. Certainly, the Eisenhower administration and the American media expressed skepticism about his movement and his motives from the outset, and when the Cuban leader failed to provide the proper answers he was dismissed and branded a threat. Less than a year after seizing power, Castro joined Khrushchev in New York for a United Nations session, and the two were depicted on the cover of *Time* as "The East Side Rockets."

Time's satire owed its pungency only in part to a contemporary Broadway hit about New York City street gangs. This was also the short-lived age of the "missile gap" in which the Soviet Union, largely due to Sputnik and other early space spectaculars, was assumed to possess sufficient long-range weaponry to overwhelm the United States at the outset of a major confrontation. The notion of Soviet superiority in offensive long-range, nuclear-tipped missiles understandably terrified the American public, adding immeasurably to cold war tensions. In fact, the missile gap was a myth in two ways. First, the Kremlin did not possess numerical superiority; the United States did. Second, even when the Soviets years later did produce and deploy a substantially larger missile arsenal, their chronic inability to develop an efficient guidance system meant that their Rocket Force posed as great a danger to itself and its immediately adjacent allies as it did to the West.

But Cuba as a Communist base only ninety miles from American shores possessed both strategic advantages and drawbacks. On the one hand, it might give Washington pause in pursuing its own cold war initiatives. At the same time, the island was highly vulnerable to both invasion and blockade.

As soon as Washington turned away, Castro took the plunge, revolutionizing cold war relations by agreeing to sell or barter to Moscow the entire Cuban sugar crop that had hitherto routinely gone to American buyers. It was Nasser and Egypt all over again, as Soviet arms shipments soon began flowing to Havana. Washington analysts quickly concluded that the shipments might not only bolster the Castro regime but also provide the Kremlin with an advanced base to attack the United States directly. The Eisenhower and Kennedy administrations reacted as expected, and if they hadn't a rising chorus of congressional voices was there to remind them: Castro could not be allowed to exist. The cry was taken up by an eager band of exiles yearning to return home and, in the name of democracy and the free world, restore the good old days under Fulgencio Batista. The CIA laid plans to invade the island with this ragtag group, but Eisenhower left office before the plan could be carried out. The Kennedy administration decided, with growing misgivings, to carry on. In April 1961, just weeks after the new administration took office, several thousand exiles stormed ashore at the Bay of Pigs on Cuba's southeastern shore, expecting to generate an immediate uprising by a grateful people.

Instead, they were greeted by withering defensive fire and a population far from inclined to welcome them as liberators. Within moments the assault became a fiasco. The men were poorly trained, air cover consisted of a few hasty bombing runs over the beach by obsolescent aircraft that promptly disappeared never to return, and the handful of war-surplus invasion craft were shot to pieces, thereby precluding a fighting withdrawal back to sea. As frantic messages for help reached Washington from the front, Kennedy, wisely seeking a measure of plausible denial, decided not to compound the felony by permitting air strikes from the nearby carrier *Essex*. But everyone knew who had sponsored the disaster.[2]

The most regrettable feature of the botched raid from Washington's perspective was that it catapulted Castro firmly into the Communist camp. Neither Washington nor Moscow nor Havana could turn back. Kennedy and his people promptly, foolishly, turned once more to the Cuban exile community in Miami, as well as to CIA resources and even the Mafia, which had done quite well for itself in Batista's Havana. The result was a series of feckless attempts to assassinate or overthrow Castro by a variety of means, the most extreme of which were given over to a clandestine buccaneer named Ed Lansdale and code-named Operation Mongoose. Although the Soviets were apparently never aware of Mongoose as such, Soviet ambassadors in Havana and Washington reported throughout late 1961 and early 1962 frequent "landing[s] of counter-revolutionary spies and arms" on the Cuban coast together with "constant acts of provocation," all of which provided Khrushchev with a morally and politically justifiable pretext to defend his new ally by force.[3] The premier's precise motives in subsequently dispatching nuclear weapons and medium-range ballistic missiles to Cuba have been the subject of equally searching debate. Did he merely mean to make the island impregnable? Or did he wish to turn it into a launching pad with which to threaten nearly the entire United States with a quick-strike capability, thus neutralizing with one bold stroke Washington's lead in long-range, highly accurate ballistic missiles? No matter; it was an act of incredible folly.

Late in 1961 Khrushchev began a "prodigious buildup" of conventional Soviet arms on the island: more than forty Soviet-piloted MiG fighters, forty-two IL-28 light bombers, forty-two thousand Red Arm combat troops and assorted technicians, together with several new *Komar*-class "fast attack missile craft." The *Komar*s were large (sixty-ton) motor torpedo boats that could whip across the waves at forty-five knots (roughly fifty-two miles per hour) and could theoretically sink enemy warships from onboard missile launchers. Five years later, a *Komar* sold to the Egyptian navy did just that during the June 1967 Six-Day War, sinking the Israeli destroyer *Eilat* with three Styx missiles at a range of more than a dozen miles. Khrushchev also ordered dispatched to Cuba short-range, AS-1 Kennel shore-to-ship cruise missiles.[4] Given the state of the cold war, this activity in itself could be said to constitute a casus belli, but then and for many long months thereafter Washington restrained itself, knowing full well that any kind of military retaliation against Cuba could risk World War III. The following May, after fifteen months of constant sparring with Kennedy, Khrushchev ordered a dramatic escalation. His generals were "to deploy on the island of Cuba a Group of Soviet Forces comprising all branches of the Armed Forces under a single integrated staff." At the heart of this group was the Forty-third Missile Division with a total of forty R-12 and R-14 launchers for intermediate-range nuclear ballistic missiles. The rockets were capable of covering a broad arc of targets that included every major urban area in the United States with the exceptions of Portland, Oregon, and Seattle.[5]

As the Soviet build-up gathered force throughout the summer, the Kennedy administration became alarmed. American dominance of the world ocean (and of the heavens above where first-generation spy satellites were routinely photographing wide swaths of the Soviet Union daily and in detail) ensured that the Kremlin would not be able to clandestinely slip substantial offensive or defensive weapon systems onto the island. Western analysts at the time pronounced the Soviet Navy "mediocre," and in most ways it was. To the bafflement of America's sailors and the equally mystified editors of the authoritative *Jane's Fighting Ships,* a Soviet submarine threat that had been impending ever since midcentury had failed to materialize, and the Russian surface fleet had grown only marginally. Since 1957 fewer than a score of small missile-carrying destroyers had appeared whose weapons were confined to short ranges and surface-to-surface employment.[6]

Nonetheless, the Soviets were clearly up to something that summer of 1962. U.S. spy satellites picked up increasing activity around Baltic Sea and Black Sea dock areas. Within days, the Sixth Fleet and U.S. naval air patrols over the eastern North Atlantic spotted the first elements of the Soviet sealift. As the lift continued, America's dense, sophisticated surveillance network folded around it. "Operating from bases in Greece, Sicily, and Spain, Sixth Fleet patrol squadrons watched the increasing flow of outbound Soviet merchantmen, as did their counterparts based in Scotland, Iceland, Nova Scotia, the Azores and Bermuda. Long-range patrol planes tracked the arms-laden freighters through the Mediterranean and Baltic seas strategic choke points and across the Atlantic."[7] Khrushchev was surely arming his new friend, but it all seemed well within the limits of acceptable international practice, however deplorable it might be to excitable anti-Communists in and out of Congress. As late as mid-September, when in fact nuclear warheads for midrange missiles and Il-28 medium-range bombers were already deployed in Cuba, all evidence in Washington's hands continued to point to the conclusion that the Soviets were arming their Cuban clients with conventional weaponry, solely to repel a widely expected American invasion—a second Bay of Pigs on a much larger scale. JFK cautiously accepted the presence of SAMs as part of the Soviet strategy. On September 13 a CIA Intelligence Memorandum concluded that "a review of all available evidence" suggested "that the suspect missile site near Banes, Cuba is a facility for launching cruise missiles against ship targets at fairly close range." Six days later, Special National Intelligence Estimate 85–3–62 reached the same conclusion. The Soviets valued their position in Cuba "primarily for the political advantages to be derived from it," and therefore "the main purpose of the present military buildup . . . is to strengthen the Communist regime . . . against what the Cubans and Soviets conceive to be a danger that the US may attempt by one means or another to overthrow it. . . . In terms of military significance, the current Soviet deliveries are substantially improving air defense and coastal defense capabilities in Cuba."[8]

Kennedy nonetheless took no chances. He queried his service chiefs about the prospects of another and much stronger armed invasion of the island and was dismayed when air force chief of staff Curtis LeMay and Chief of Naval Operations Admiral George W. Anderson exhibited "an apparent lack of unanimity. . . with respect to aircraft losses that might occur in attacking an SA-2 site." The air force–navy disagreement was neither surprising nor especially significant in terms of historic interservice rivalries. Ground-to-air defensive missiles were still new and their effectiveness generally unknown. Kennedy's suggestion that the Pentagon build a model of an SA-2 site for training purposes was a reflection of his growing concern that Khrushchev was deliberately deceiving him.[9]

When routine U-2 spy-plane flights over the island during the second week in October revealed to expert photo interpreters the beginnings of a serious missile build-up, Kennedy reacted immediately, focusing decision making in the National Security Council (NSC) and an even smaller, informal, crisis-management team called the Ex-Com. After a series of intense, occasionally heated, and wide-ranging discussions, the NSC decided late on the afternoon of October 21 to impose a naval blockade of Cuba as a first step in forcing Khrushchev to back down short of nuclear war. One senses how eager the navy was for this moment. After years of frustration the service could at last demonstrate what it could do in a major national security crisis; McNamara's "whiz kids" could be taught a lesson on the value of naval power, and the ships and aircraft of the Atlantic Fleet would spearhead a dramatic effort to humble if not eradicate Communism on America's doorstep. And there was the matter of Castro himself, who had been a major irritant to naval operations from the beginning, periodically threatening to cut essential services to the navy's main training and support base at Guantánamo Bay ("Gitmo") on Cuba's eastern tip.

Kennedy, an old navy man himself and a voracious seeker after every relevant fact, quizzed Admiral Anderson closely on how the blockade (publicly labeled a "quarantine" in a diplomatic effort to calm fears) would work. Anderson replied that the navy was fully prepared; no reserves needed to be called up. In fact, the CNO had prepared and positioned his sailors perfectly to respond to any Soviet threat. "For example, we had all our available Polaris submarines at sea, we had a line of defensive submarine barriers across the Atlantic, we had our [aircraft] patrol squadrons scouring the Atlantic from the best available bases for reconnaissance of ships, particularly for Russian submarines." Moreover, the marines were in "a high degree of readiness." Several battalions had gone to sea, and some were moving down the Pacific coast toward Panama and the canal. "In all, we had some eleven marine battalions committed in varying degrees of proximity to Cuba." No fewer than forty surface ships of the Atlantic Fleet "were already in position" off eastern Florida, including the brand-new supercarriers *Enterprise* (nuclear powered) and *Independence* and their support vessels. Each flattop had on board an eighty-plane-plus air group.

Anderson had just pulled *Essex* (recently converted to an antisubmarine carrier) and its group out of Gitmo and sent them to the surface quarantine line. The carrier would be joined by its sister ship, *Randolph.* Anderson did not miss a thing. At one point, he sent an action message to Atlantic Fleet headquarters to ensure that every ship on the blockade line had at least one Russian-speaking officer or enlisted man aboard.

Moreover, "the Navy knew the positions of twenty-seven to thirty ships enroute to Cuba." Anderson added that he hoped the first intercept would be by a large, impressive cruiser rather than a more modestly sized destroyer. Kennedy had already decided to reveal the Soviet missile build-up and the American response in a speech the following evening. Anderson recommended that Khrushchev be given a twenty-four-hour grace period after the address "during which the Russians could communicate with their ships, giving them instructions as to what to do in the event they were stopped by United States ships." Anderson concluded by assuring his president that "we had a capability to protect United States ships in the Caribbean. If the Komar [missile] ships took any hostile action they could be destroyed, thereby creating a new situation." Anderson requested permission to shoot down any Russian or Cuban MiGs that appeared over the blockading fleet and to sink any Soviet submarine known to be en route to Havana. According to Anderson, Kennedy responded, "Admiral, this is up to the navy." Anderson replied, "Mr. President, the navy will not let you down."[10]

The NSC meeting had broken up shortly after dinnertime on the twenty-first. That evening, "in anticipation of the presidential proclamation" regarding offensive missiles in Cuba, the commander in chief of the Atlantic Fleet, Admiral Robert L. Dennison, issued operation order 45–62 establishing a specific blockade task force (TF 136) and designating the commander of the Second Fleet, Admiral Alfred G. Ward (responsible for the western Atlantic and Caribbean areas), to command "about 46 ships, 240 aircraft, some 30,000 personnel." "None of us knew what would happen," Ward recalled. "We did not expect any numbers of Soviet warships, but we did not know the reactions that the Soviet ships might take." Ward and his people "did not know" there were Russian submarines approaching the quarantine area. "We discovered them."[11]

Within hours, the carrier task forces surged toward their designated blockade points. Task Force 136.1, composed of two cruisers and fifteen destroyers, took up stations on an arc (code-named "Walnut") five hundred miles from the southeastern tip of Cuba, "set up," according to Admiral Dennison, "outside of the reasonable range of any land-based aircraft from Cuba." Each of the twelve stations on the arc was forty-seven miles apart. Task Force 136.2 including *Essex* and four destroyers was stationed to the west of the center of the arc, and the *Enterprise* and *Independence* lay still farther back in a position of wide intercept possibilities. A logistics group of several oilers and ammunition ships escorted by two destroyers steamed near the arc, ready to reprovision the blockading ships whenever necessary. Dennison also ordered all Atlantic Fleet submarines to load for wartime operations; the few strategic-ballistic-missile submarines based at Holy Loch, Scotland, had already deployed to their battle stations "deep under the sea." Finally, Dennison and his army and air force opposites began intensive amphibious exercises in Florida to prepare for a possible invasion of Cuba should the "quarantine" prove ineffective. The following day, October 22, as Kennedy addressed the nation, Marshal Rodion Malinovsky, carrying out Khrushchev's order, put all Soviet forces on a high state of alert, canceling all leaves for Soviet Rocket Force and submarine personnel.[12]

CNO Anderson, no less than LeMay, believed that Castro was now in a position to carry out the dream of his Kremlin masters to subvert much of Latin America to Communism. The man and sponsors had to be taught a lesson. Cuba should be invaded, Anderson believed, and the Soviet troops there sent home. Castro could not stand up to such an event; the Kremlin seven thousand miles away dared not. "This is what I tried to emphasize to McNamara personally," Anderson recalled, "but he was really preoccupied with something else, I guess, at the time and I didn't get it across to him." Anderson's contempt for his boss and the civilian "whiz kids" surrounding him became total. Although the admiral emphasized the need to keep Kennedy fully informed of all developments relating to the blockade, "We did not want, and I had it pretty well set up to prevent, any intrusion by McNamara or anybody else in the direct operations of any ship or squadron or anything of the sort."[13]

Those who called for a "surgical strike" against the Cuban missile bases (and the Soviet personnel who manned them) as a first step toward probable invasion never grasped the fact that sea power had already finished off Khrushchev's reckless dream. The central fact of the 1962 missile crisis was Cuba's vulnerable position not only because of its proximity to the United States but also because of its susceptibility to strangulation and submission at any time Washington and its allies chose. And Washington soon attracted allies. Not only did the Organization of American States support the blockade, but its members actively participated in it. The Soviets could have broken or contested the quarantine only with a fleet of comparable size and capability that could have forced the U.S. Navy to back down and permit not only the shipment of missiles (and soon offensive aircraft) into Cuba but also the food, fuel, and men necessary to man and maintain them. Khrushchev evidently did not grasp this fundamental fact when he decided to dispatch nuclear weapons to the island, and neither, apparently, did his military people.

What the Soviet premier did know was that the admittedly inferior Soviet Navy was more formidable than the West believed. By the eve of the Cuban missile crisis, the Soviet submarine force included not only the first generation of missile-firing boats but also another nuclear weapon system capable of triggering Armageddon. Russian scientists had recently managed to rig nuclear tips onto torpedoes, and in August 1962, as the CIA was issuing its first direct alerts to Kennedy about possible missiles in Cuba, Rear Admiral Leonid F. Rybalko was ordered to clandestinely send four diesel-powered boats with such weapons into Cuba as an added layer of support for the missile build-up and deployment. Rybalko's captains were directed to fire their nuclear torpedoes at any American ships that "attack you submerged, or force your units to the surface, or upon receipt of orders from Moscow." The young junior admiral was appalled. Not only did his orders "virtually give his submarine commanders personal authority to begin a nuclear war with the United States," but to his knowledge few if any Soviet submarines had ever even test-fired atomic weapons at sea. And none had carried the distinctly purple-painted nuclear torpedo tips on patrol. Common sense suggested that any submarine firing such a weapon at an enemy would itself be destroyed by the blast. Admiral Sergey Gorshkov, the commander in chief of the Soviet Navy, personally assured his anxious subordinate that a Soviet U-boat had indeed recently "fired two live nuclear torpedoes off Novaya Zimlaya, one subsurface burst and one surface burst" without incident. Rybalko's skippers were unceremoniously dispatched to the Caribbean with their diesel-powered boats and deadly weapons. Once at sea, the captains discovered that they were the advance force for seven more submarines— diesel-powered, missile-carrying *"Golf"* boats capable of firing one of their three onboard birds every four minutes.[14] When completed, Khrushchev's medium- and short-range ballistic-missile build-up in Cuba, crude though it was, would be formidably multidimensional. Weak as he was at sea, Khrushchev could thrust nuclear war upon the world if he chose. The Soviet premier was gambling with stakes that Kennedy's sailors did not even suspect he possessed. Once again, as on a number of occasions throughout the twentieth century, a reckless tyrant was ready to use his inferior fleet to force the pace of events and dictate the dimensions of crisis.

Nonetheless, as the Cuban build-up came closer to completion, the realities of sea power began coming clear to Khrushchev, Malinovsky, and the rest of the Kremlin leadership. Responding to Khrushchev's initial directive, Malinovsky and his planners dispatched a small surface fleet to Caribbean waters in September, just as the missile build-up was getting under way. Two cruisers and two of the new, small, missile-firing destroyers, together with two conventionally armed destroyers, would accompany the seven Soviet *Golf*-class diesel-powered, missile-firing submarines to Cuba as a further demonstration of Soviet strength and resolve. During the summer, however, Khrushchev became aware how violent the American-controlled waters around Cuba had become. Although Moscow remained unaware of "Mongoose," Soviet intelligence informed Khrushchev in mid-September that "the piratic raids by the so-called 'Alpha 66' group (composed mostly of Miami-based exiles) on the Cuban coast and on several vessels near Cuba are being carried out, not from a base on the American mainland but rather directly from the sea, from American landing ships, carrying the corresponding cutters [that is, small fast, motor vessels]." Moreover, "the American ships carrying these cutters maintain a constant readiness for military action, and meticulously care for the technical condition of the cutters, performing repairs in case of damage. During this time, the American instructors on these ships direct the training, both tactical and otherwise, of the Cuban [that is, exile] crews who carry out operations directly on the cutters."[15]

On September 25 Khrushchev personally canceled the order for the fleet of cruisers, destroyers, and *Golf*-class submarines to sail to Cuba.[16] It was a wise decision. The force might well have proved provocative without in any way being decisive. With no control over the sea-lanes from Russia to the Caribbean, the only way Khrushchev could hope to get missiles to Cuba was either through open acknowledgment and an emphasis on the need to defend the island in any and all ways from further American aggression or clandestinely. In choosing to pursue a clandestine policy, Khrushchev added deceit to folly. It was a measure of the man's desperation that he chose that course.

With the second-echelon fleet deployment canceled, the only Soviet naval elements remaining near Cuban waters after Kennedy's October 22 quarantine announcement were Admiral Rybalko's four diesel boats, each carrying a single nuclear-tipped torpedo with orders to fire if fired upon. But here, too, the Soviets had begun pulling back. The boats were originally ordered to the small port of Mariel, just west of Havana. As evidence mounted in Moscow in mid-October that the Americans might be catching on at last to the nature and dimensions of the missile build-up, orders were sent out to the four vessels to break off steaming and take up patrol positions in the Sargasso Sea, several hundred miles east of the Bahamas and north and east of the island of Hispaniola. They would thus be in a position to join, and possibly protect, the Soviet freighters approaching the arc of the American "Walnut" distant blockade line above Cuba.[17]

Kennedy was far from happy with the blockade. Too many things could go wrong, and only a single miscalculation could send the world kiting down the road to nuclear war. The navy was to avoid a major confrontation at all costs. Initially, he insisted that no freighters could be boarded, for if they were there might be resistance, death, and outright war. Kennedy insisted that the most extreme measure that Dennison's warships could take if a freighter refused to stop was to shoot out its rudders and propellers. Still the president fretted. Suppose a Cuba-bound Soviet vessel was shot up? Well, McNamara replied, it would not have to be boarded, but merely towed into Jacksonville or Charleston, South Carolina. But at some point it *would* have to be boarded. "What would you do then," Kennedy asked peevishly, "if we go through all this effort and then find out there's baby food aboard it?" Dennison solved his president's problem. He later claimed that on his own initiative he ordered his people to board the Lebanese-flagged freighter *Marcula* inbound to Cuba. "It carried a nonsuspicious cargo," Dennison remembered, "and really I did it to show that we could and would" board if necessary. "Of course, they didn't know that we already knew what was in that ship. It was little more than a stunt, a demonstration that we were effective." If ships did not stop, as *Marcula* readily did, air force and navy surveillance planes and photo interpreters ashore would have to identify as positively as possible those Soviet vessels evidently carrying military cargo.[18]

The crisis wound down in agonizing stages over several long weeks that no one who was alive and aware at the time would ever forget. Khrushchev was in an impossible bind, and Kennedy let him know it. At the same time, the Americans remained keyed to a fever pitch. Matters almost spun out of hand when the navy insisted on disabling a Soviet vessel that would not stop. Anderson and his sailors were not convinced that the first Soviet vessels to turn around were deferring to the blockade. "The Navy... had a more sinister interpretation. They suspected that the ships had altered course in order to pick up more Soviet submarines as escorts." The Soviet submarine menace was the navy's great preoccupation. If the missile crisis provided U.S. sailors with an unmatched opportunity to show their stuff, it obviously provided Soviet submariners with the same opportunity. Would they take it? The Atlantic Fleet had deployed most of its formidable antisubmarine resources to make sure they did not.

Tempers were thus at the breaking point when on October 24 McNamara suddenly appeared at the navy's Flag Plot in the Pentagon to oversee events. He "began to question Anderson sharply and in detail—who would make the first interception, were Russian speaking officers aboard and so on" and then proceeded according to one bystander to "direct where to place the carriers and what we were to do with our ships." Anderson, according to some accounts, did his own imitation of a ballistic missile. In a "bitter exchange," he all but told McNamara to stay out of the navy's professional business. Neither man backed down, but Anderson had to admit that his civilian chief had asked pertinent questions. The navy promptly issued a worldwide Notice to Mariners (Notam), carefully setting forth procedures it would take when encountering a submerged submarine near, at, or within the blockade line. Planes or ships would drop four or five small grenades near the submerged vessel that would constitute an order for it to surface "on an easterly direction." Further requests and directions might or might not be made of the submarine "in the 8 kc [radio] frequency range." Aside from issuance of the Notam, however, Anderson "didn't interfere with my operations at all," a grateful Admiral Dennison recalled. Running Atlantic Fleet operations "through my own staff set-up" and working closely with Second Fleet commander Alfred Ward ("He was perfectly marvelous"), Dennison remembered that Anderson "was responsible for keeping a lot of people and things off my back."

Unbeknownst to the Americans, the procedures outlined in the Notam, designed to defuse or at least define the nature of any encounter with Soviet submarines, in fact provided the basis for nuclear combat. Although the grenades could not materially damage a submarine, they sounded very much like depth charges, and Soviet commanders, under orders to fire their nuclear-tipped torpedoes if attacked, might well respond. The Soviet Naval Staff in Moscow promptly compounded the crisis by reacting to Kennedy's announcement of the blockade of Cuba with paralysis. Under Gorshkov's express orders, none of the four Soviet boats were informed of the nature and dimensions of the maturing crisis, nor were they given clear orders as to their role within it, beyond patrolling provocatively near the Walnut line in the midst of the heavily armed blockading fleet. Most inexcusably, Gorshkov refused to pass the American Notam on to the boats. At last, Admiral Rybalko, grossly exceeding authority, did just that, giving the U-boat commanders a clear idea of what they could expect.

Rybalko's action also carried with it an implicit plea not to use the nuclear tor-pedoes except in a moment of extremis. Rybalko's courageous act cost him his career, but it very possibly saved the world from all-out nuclear war.

As Anderson issued the Notam on October 24, the navy made the first of its many Soviet submarine contacts far out in the Atlantic, beginning what one enthusiastic American admiral called "an absolutely magnificent anti-submarine workout." The nature of that "workout," however, is unclear, as is its "mag-nificence." Even now, authorities differ on dates and places of intercept. Most recent scholarship suggests that none of the four nuclear-torpedo-carrying boats were detected before October 30, and by that time the immediate crisis had been defused. Second Fleet commander Admiral Alfred G. Ward told an interviewer in 1972 that his destroyers "detected four submarines. There may have been more, but we detected four and this was just by chance." Several Soviet freighters kept steaming toward the Walnut blockade line, and the navy was forced to fire toward one of them to gain its adherence to the quarantine. But no Soviet surface vessels were disabled or even directly shot at, and Anderson later said that none of the missile-carrying freighters ever "got much beyond the Azores."[19]

Having made his point with Khrushchev and the Kremlin, Kennedy eased the pressure, allowing certain freighters and other ships to proceed through the quarantine. The president also agreed back-channel to a later pullout of obso-lete Jupiter short-range missiles from Turkey in exchange for an immediate and internationally monitored removal of Soviet missiles from Cuba. Khrushchev still had to be nudged diplomatically; a promising first letter from the premier received a cautiously optimistic reply, whereas a second, harder, message was ignored. At last, the premier publicly declared that he would remove his offen-sive missiles and did so under international Red Cross supervision. But now Kennedy aggressively pushed his advantage. Maintaining his naval quarantine, the president insisted that not only would all offensive missiles have to be pulled out of Cuba but so too would the Ilyushin-28 bombers that Khrushchev had dispatched to the island. Robert Kennedy, acting on behalf of his brother, took the lead in deflecting subsequent Soviet insistence that the aircraft had been sent for defensive purposes only; they would have to go. Several further exhausting weeks of diplomacy ensued until at last the bombers followed the missiles out of the island, and Washington at last lifted its blockade.[20]

As the Soviet ships steamed away from Cuba with their crates of missiles and bombers prominently displayed on deck, American sailors "wished [them] God speed and good sailing and happy return home." On one occasion, the pilot of a surveillance helicopter from the cruiser *Newport News,* loitering briefly over a Russian freighter, gave way to impulse, pulled the clasp from his tie, and lowered it by hydraulic cable to the deck below. Taking the tiny package, the Soviet sailors gestured to have the cable returned, tied a bottle of vodka to it, and sent it aloft.[21]

But as we now know, the crisis was not yet over. Between October 30 and November 4, Rybalko's four submarines, B-4, B-36, B-59, and B-130, were all detected by U.S. antisubmarine ships and aircraft. The destroyer *Blandy* ambushed B-130 on the surface at 0300 hours on October 30, forcing the sub into a frantic crash dive. Thereafter, *Blandy* grimly followed the Soviet submarine's every evasive movement and maneuver for the next seventeen hours, while conditions inside the Russian boat swiftly deteriorated. The main diesel soon fell out of operation, forcing the cooling system to shut down. At one point Captain Nikolai Shumkov thought the enemy might have launched depth charges, and he wondered if the two nations might be at war. He had heard just enough from Moscow during brief message bursts to know that a real crisis was brewing. But war? Moscow's inexcusable blunder in not keeping its submarine commanders up-to-date on world affairs nearly cost that world its life. Fortunately, Shumkov had received Rybalko's message about the American Notam. Several hundred feet below the Caribbean, Shumkov considered his response. Should he fire at his tormentor? And what about his nuclear-tipped torpedo? Submerged in tropical waters with no air-conditioning, and an increasing lack of oxygen, B-130 soon filled with the smell of human sweat and other foul odors. Shumkov and his crew struggled to maintain their poise and competence, while on the surface the excitable American destroyer captain determined to force his prey to submit and surface. In a last, desperate bid to shake off his pursuers, Shumkov released a decoy that for a long moment sounded to the Americans like a torpedo. Then, his batteries critically low, his boat crippled by the loss of two of its three diesel engines, Shumkov took the path to peace, not war. Relying more on the contents of the Notam than on what immediate circumstances might suggest, he surfaced. Aboard *Blandy* some fool ordered the forward 5-inch gun mount trained on the sub until Captain Edward G. Kelley furiously countermanded the order.

As each of the four nuclear-tipped torpedo-carrying Soviet submarines was detected and either did or did not escape, their captains displayed amazing composure. Each knew he was in a crisis situation, yet Moscow had said little or nothing about the state of events. Tracked by determined adversaries, any one of the four skippers would have been justified in firing at least conventional weapons. Yet none did, even when forced to the surface and taunted by their adversaries with the usual message, "Do you require assistance?" McNamara's insistence on clarifying the situation and Rybalko's decision to transmit that clarification to his submarine skippers may well have prevented World War III. The Americans enjoyed their antisubmarine "workout," and the world escaped Armageddon.[22]

Early in November Khrushchev dispatched Anastas Mikoyan, then a member of the Soviet Presidium, to Havana to calm an infuriated Castro. The Cuban leader demanded to know why he, a Communist in good standing, had been so coldly sacrificed to purely Soviet interests. Mikoyan told him why. "We can't use our Air Force or Navy forces in case of a blockade of Cuba." "Political maneuvering," diplomacy, and the United Nations were the only ways out when Kennedy called Khrushchev's bluff. The lack of sea power was decisive. "We could not blockade American bases in Turkey in response because we have no other exit to the Mediterranean. We could not undertake such steps; neither in Norway, nor in England, nor in Japan. We do not have enough possibilities for counter-blockade." Only in Berlin could "countermeasures" be undertaken. But even there, American power, sustained by the North Atlantic lifeline and guaranteed by Western European allies, could be projected in sufficiently measured terms to preclude the kind of clear-cut Soviet triumph that might have mitigated the Cuban humiliation. One American newspaper caught the significance of the Cuban crisis perfectly, editorializing, "Perhaps the key lesson . . . is that sea power remains the dominant force in the world's affairs."[23]

Khrushchev and his military people agreed. They had learned their lesson. To American sailors, the very fact that Soviet submarines had for the first time been detected "so far away from home and so close to our coast" indicated the seriousness of the Soviet effort in the western Atlantic. "It's quite an important matter," Dennison told an interviewer in July 1973, "when they start deploying that kind of weapon so close to our shores. They must have known the reaction would have been violent. So it isn't just a minor matter. I think it's a matter of major significance in this whole picture." If by the "whole picture," Dennison meant the cold war, he was quite right. Shortly after the crisis was finally resolved and the last Ilyushin-28 was in its crate bound for home, "a senior Russian official" in New York told his American counterpart, "Well, Mr. McCloy, you got away with it this time. But you will never get away with it again."[24]

One answer to the Cuban humiliation, of course, was a crash effort to bring the Soviet missile program up to parity with America's, and beyond, and Khrushchev and his people did that. But missiles alone could not break the capitalist encirclement of the Eurasian landmass. Khrushchev had tried black-mail through bluff, and it hadn't worked. Only a formidable blue-water navy could materially and routinely project Soviet power to the ends of the earth while keeping America's formidable war fleets well away from Soviet waters. In 1963 Khrushchev began to construct such a force. His successors would continue the effort for nearly a decade thereafter without interruption.

CHAPTER 6

Red Fleet Rising

THE SOVIET-AMERICAN naval contest that emerged after 1963 was like no other in the twentieth century. No fleet engagements ever took place. The challenging (Soviet) maritime power rested on a shoddy industrial base totally unknown in early-twentieth-century Britain, Germany, Japan, or the United States. Soviet ships were often poorly constructed and always poorly maintained. Soviet sailors in general suffered from a "low level of technical and navigational education," and a deliberately fostered high turnover rate of enlisted personnel resulted in a much too small pool of long-serving, experienced senior people. Moreover, even as the Soviet surface and submarine fleets grew to enormous size in the early seventies, their commander in chief, Sergey G. Gorshkov, argued that sea power had been of marginal importance in the global war just past.[1]

The rapid collapse of the Soviet Union between 1989 and 1991 led many observers and commentators to question whether Communist Russia had *ever* been a truly *great* force. As early as the mid-1980s, some dismissed it as "Upper Volta with missiles"—a blundering, incompetent military superpower sustained only by access through espionage to Western (especially American) science and technology, while its infant mortality rate and other indices of social deprivation "were at Third World levels." According to one account, as late as the 1980s Western naval attachés visiting "front line Soviet ships" making routine port calls in Yugoslavia and a special visit to Boston found them in shocking disrepair. "From a distance the vessels bristled with heavy weapons, a hallmark of Soviet ship design" by that time. Closer inspection revealed that the tops of the surface-to-air and surface-to-surface missile launchers for nuclear and conventional weapons "were rusted shut." Some were "dinged up so badly" that the attachés "doubted missiles could be fired at all." Soviet designers and builders had "done a terrible job . . . putting those ships together." The cold war image of a malevolent, omnicompetent Soviet Moloch was the creation of Western political and military analysts who indulged in "threat inflation" year after year merely for selfish budgetary and professional purposes.[2]

There was much in the Soviet naval record to support this view. Often hastily conceived from original German designs seized following the war, thrown together in huge quantities by a poorly trained and motivated labor force, frequently operated in ignorance and seldom maintained adequately, Soviet naval vessels, especially the huge submarine force, were plagued with frightful malfunctions, mostly to their diesel and later nuclear propulsion systems. In 1956 alone, three diesel-powered Soviet submarines went to the bottom after onboard fires or catastrophic system failures with nearly 100 percent loss of crew. Many more would go down as the cold war progressed. The often gallant but usually half-trained sailors who manned these vessels had chilling names for them: "Widow Maker" and "Cigarette Lighter." Some submarines, like the notorious K-19, were saved several times in their careers only by the most heroic and usually fatal efforts of crew members.[3]

Poorly constructed nuclear reactors and badly maintained nuclear weapons resulted in a flurry of "small Chernobyls" at sea and ashore. In 1962 conventional weapons aboard a submarine docked at the northern naval base at Polyarny exploded with such force that "pieces of the submarine and tanks of compressed air could be found some kilometers away from the pier, in the flats of frightened people." Twenty-three years later a nuclear ammunition dump exploded and burned near Northern Fleet Headquarters. Numerous submarines were lost at sea and in port to crippling accidents. The frequent failure of primary coolants aboard the nuclear boats led to hideous radiation deaths for at least a portion of their crews. Surface ships were not immune to folly and ignorance. Once the cruiser-carrier *Kiev* suffered a navigational accident when high winds drove it away from the mooring buoy—its usual anchorage in Severomorsk. Many American naval officers were convinced that collisions at sea with Soviet vessels were not always the result of aggressive design on the part of Russian captains so much as their navigational incompetence. Recalling a litany of woes, Vladimir V. Stefanovsky, the former Soviet deputy submarine-force commander, writing in 1992, asked in despair: "How can the fleet maintain its reputation in the eyes of the world community and its potential adversaries if it cannot keep itself afloat? How can we stop this chain of accidents, stop throwing out national resources, and stop killing [our] submariners?"[4]

The chronic crises within the Soviet fleet climaxed in October 1986 and April 1989, with the losses of the obsolete *Yankee*-class strategic-missile submarine K-219 south of Bermuda, as it sought to maintain its patrol box off the eastern seaboard of the United States, and the K-278 *Mike*-class submarine *Komsomolets* in the high North Atlantic near Jan Mayen Island. K-219 and the American attack boat *Augusta* were involved in dangerous—indeed foolhardy—close-in maneuvers when a small but long-neglected leak in K-219's missile compartment reached the liquified fuel in missile number 6 and touched off an explosion of nitric acid that progressively destroyed the sub's ability to function. Only the heroic efforts of an obscure Russian seaman, Sergei A. Preminin, who shut down the ship's two nuclear reactors from inside at the cost of his own life, prevented K-219 from erupting in a nuclear fireball that at the very least would have spread contamination by wind and water up and down much of the East Coast of the United States. Two and a half years later, with the cold war nearing its end, the submarine *Komsomolets* (the second so named after the first had sunk years before) went down after a series of severe internal fires with the loss of forty-two men. Launched five years before, it had never had a refit or repair.[5]

When the Soviets began an "intense fleet renewal" in the late fifties based on nuclear power for both propulsion and warheads, their sailors handled the new element "with little concern for consequences." Because Soviet political doctrine mandated a short-term conscript military establishment, no real effort was made to form large pools of highly trained, extended-service cadres. Even if such an effort had been made, the Soviet Union lagged tragically behind the West in technological literacy and competence.

The United States Navy's own chronic short-term service problem was never as severe and in any case was far less acute because American boys (and many girls) were accustomed to being around and comfortable with rather complex machinery from an early age. An open society had long allowed and encouraged youngsters to tinker, to experiment, and to learn by doing. Soviet society was far more restrictive. The top 2 or 3 percent of Soviet scientists, mathematicians, physicists, and technicians could hold their own with any colleagues in the world. Below this elite group, however, the scientific and technical proficiency of the Soviet citizen fell off drastically.[6] As late as the 1980s, huge areas of the Soviet Union remained essentially unmechanized.[7] Advanced technologies were known to only a comparative few.

Soviet naval conscription, originally for four years, was soon reduced to only three. Each of the four regional fleets (Northern, Baltic, Black Sea, and Far Eastern) conducted its own superficial basic training of four to five weeks, followed by five months of technical specialist training for most conscripts before assignment to the fleet. But the specialist trainees seldom if ever worked with adequate equipment. Once in the fleet, they usually found their ships to be poorly repaired, with tired engines, worn-out equipment, and questionable emergency survival and salvage gear. Maintenance became a major problem amid a chronic shortage of spare parts, supplies, "and elementary engineering support." No efforts were made to develop the quality controls essential to anticipate and avoid accidents. Although this was a fleetwide problem, it was particularly acute in the submarine service. As Stefanovsky noted, "The fleet fathers, having ordered all ships to sea, organized crew training only after an accident. It was the submariners themselves, the captains and the engineers, who were held responsible for the accidents. The deputy political commanders were always blameless."

The poor quality of professional training and compulsory military service combined to work against crew safety. "Since submarine crews often included people with little interest in or care for the sea," Stefanovsky later observed, "the accident rate was hardly surprising." The problem was compounded by a chaotic manpower situation. Because the rapidly expanding Soviet Navy was dominated by Russian officers who mistrusted the ethnic minorities, there was always a scramble for manpower. "Often," Stefanovsky continued, the crew of a boat departing for sea was "complemented by sailors from different fleets, with different levels of training. For example, submarine #574 of the Pacific Ocean Fleet sank in 1968 with all her crew. The crew roster and number of victims are still unknown."[8]

Personnel weaknesses were not confined to poor training. Though the American armed forces were plagued by 1970 with the curse of racial disharmony, Soviet forces were even more so. Beneath the Kremlin's steady barrage of patriotic exhortation and bombast, behind its constant appeals to national loyalty, lurked a disastrous Russian ethnocentrism. There existed a "historic friction between ethnic Russians and other nationalities, like Georgians, Armenians, Lithuanians, or Uzbeks who now comprise a majority of the Soviet population and who often privately resent the Russification of their minority republics." If the ethnic "minorities" felt themselves dominated by arrogant Russians, *New York Times* Moscow bureau chief Hedrick Smith wrote in 1976, "the Russians felt themselves and their culture besieged by a rising tide of ethnic influence within the Soviet Union. Russians believed their own sense of nationality was being sacrificed to the greater idea of a Soviet federation." The dramatic decline in the Russian birthrate added to the growing sense of peril. By the mid-1970s, wartime memories and experiences as a propaganda instrument binding all Soviet peoples into a single harmonious whole had begun to wear thin.[9]

Gorshkov soon found that manning ships with mixed ethnic complements was a prescription for continual turmoil and even disaster in a navy (and society) chronically cursed with low pay, crowded conditions, indifferent and frugal rations, and a tendency to follow the national trend in drowning individual sorrows and frustrations in copious amounts of vodka. Reports of an attempted mutiny on a Soviet nuclear submarine in 1969 were followed by rumors of another aborted attempt on a diesel submarine three years later. In 1975 the ethnically mixed crew aboard a Soviet *Krivak*-class frigate in the Baltic rebelled against their Russian captain and eventually sought to take the ship into Western waters. The ringleader, who happened to be the onboard party political officer, apparently revolted from a sense of idealism and revulsion at the treatment of the lower deck. But some U.S. government analysts quietly maintained that ethnic frictions also played a role. The rebels were quickly run down by ship and plane before they reached Swedish waters, but their attempt represented the kind of open mutiny that the twentieth-century United States Navy never had to deal with in its worst moments.[10]

The stubborn presence of ethnic intolerance and prejudice was greatly enhanced by the decidedly spartan lifestyles of the vast majority of Soviet sailors together with deep-seated corruption within the officer class. Living conditions aboard Soviet warships "resembled those in British and American ships of the 1930s. Older ships lacked a general mess." Visitors to the helicopter carrier–missile cruiser *Moskva*, completed in the late 1960s, found "limited space, Spartan living conditions," and rudimentary equipment. Aboard the large group of *Kotlin*-class destroyers, drinking water for the crew was available only from "a portable metal barrel with a community drinking cup." First-term conscripts not only existed on low pay and simple food but were also hazed unmercifully by the third-year men about to get out and were granted almost no "liberty," as Western and especially American sailors had become accustomed to. A submarine veteran later wrote of "the dismal prospect of shore life" with its cold, overcrowded barracks ("which usually are occupied by three or even more ships' companies at a time") and endless watches and patrols. In only one area did Soviet sailors seem to have an edge on their American counterparts: the families of first-term servicemen were given some special privileges, including tax exemptions for married couples with no children, and the state did help in finding work for the wives of enlisted men.

Officers' wives, however, were fair game for the *zampolit*, members of the navy's "political" section, who were Communist Party hacks and zealots officially charged with ensuring the ideological purity of the fleet. When ships, and especially submarines, deployed on lengthy cruises, the *zampolit* ashore demanded— and often got—sexual favors from bored and frustrated officers' wives, in return for passes for the women to travel from the bleak northern port towns on vacation trips to Moscow or Leningrad. The *zampolit* were already widely despised as at best incompetent meddlers and toadies and at worst as informers. Their presence on every major Soviet warship was itself a source of cynicism and low morale. When they proved to be seducers as well, shipboard morale plummeted even further.[11]

The *zampolit* reflected a Soviet Navy stifled and suffocated inside a Communist ideology that was at best irrelevant to operations and at its worst dangerous to both personal and operational safety and efficiency. "By the end of 1948," a Russian officer proudly noted thirty years later, the Soviet armed forces had established "a vast political education system" for the more than 270,000 party members in the army and navy. The system included more than 2,600 political schools, more than 4,000 "groups for the study of Lenin's biography," 6,000-plus groups engaged in mastering the history of the Communist Party, "690 divisional schools for party activists," and 142 "evening universities for the study of Marxism-Leninism." In addition, nearly 600 party newspapers were published within the Soviet military establishment "at the district, fleet, army, division, and other levels." Throughout the 1950s and early '60s the deadening hand of the Party gripped the Soviet military ever tighter.[12]

Since Lenin's time, the party had mandated success; because it represented the wave of the future—indeed, defined that future—it could not fail. Therefore, when things went wrong, paralysis inevitably resulted. When the huge *Oscar II*–class submarine *Kursk* blew up deep below the surface of the Barents Sea in August 2000, Russian naval and civil authorities initially reacted according to their Communist training. Northern Fleet commander Vyacheslav Popov "had been trained and groomed under the Soviet system. He knew the two golden rules were never take or admit responsibility for failure; and never be the one to give bad news to your military or political bosses. Life still wasn't that different nine years after the collapse of communism." Confronted with growing evidence of a huge disaster, "Popov did what a long line of senior officers and politicians had done before and after him. He did nothing." The admiral reasoned, quite correctly, that any survivors were doomed since the Russian navy no longer possessed "a deep sea rescue capability to speak of."[13]

Reviewing the intelligence data that had come to light by the summer of 1992, Rear Admiral Thomas Brooks identified four specific areas in which the Soviet submarine force (and, by implication, the surface navy as well) suffered crippling defects. First, inadequate repair facilities never kept pace with fleet construction. There were many instances of new classes of submarines with unique maintenance requirements serving in the fleet for nearly a decade before docking for repairs. Second, poor leadership permitted and in some cases even encouraged evasion, lying, cover-ups, and corruption in the running and repair of the fleet. Third, as a result of financial constraints, essential training was chronically sacrificed to the need to build more and more ships. Not only was shoreside training neglected, but as time passed more and more Soviet ships spent fewer and fewer days at sea, despite occasional spectacular exercises such as *Okean 70* and *Okean 75,* in which nearly the entire Soviet Navy sortied for several weeks of very well-coordinated exercises across the North Atlantic, Baltic, Mediterranean, North Pacific, and even Indian Oceans. Finally, Soviet sailors were simply not up to the standards of their Western counterparts despite numerous pictures of clean-featured, well-scrubbed, slender lads smiling broadly for the cameras. "A system of short-term conscripts, poorly led and marginally trained, will not be able to sustain a navy," Admiral Brooks wrote, "against a force of well-trained, well-led, and well-equipped professionals." Thirteen years later, respected naval analysts and historians Gary E. Weir and Walter J. Boyne condemned Gorshkov without reservation. Coming to command of the Red Fleet in 1956, lashed by the Kremlin leadership to produce a large, sophisticated, ultramodern fleet instantly, the man had demanded development of nuclear submarines, missiles, and torpedoes "at the earliest possible date with a minimum regard for nuclear safety and no regard for human life," then insisted that the fatally flawed undersea weapon systems be accepted and operated "by the very naval commanders whom he knowingly sent to sea in fatally inadequate equipment."[14]

But those who criticize the possibly exaggerated Western response to Soviet power are themselves guilty of both exaggeration and a bit of amnesia. In retrospect, much of the Nazi military machine was overrated; so was the Japanese. The Luftwaffe's frontline aircraft, except for a few advanced models, were clearly inferior to those of the Anglo-Americans by 1943 at the latest. The German army, even at the height of its mechanized power and mobility in 1940–1942, relied heavily on horse-drawn transport, which was being phased out of the British and American military. The striking technical and operational limits of the German U-boat arm have been amply documented. Yet Hitler was able to wage aggressive war on his neighbors and to conquer most of the European continent at one time or another, while Karl Dönitz's young men on several occasions strained Britain's Atlantic lifeline to the breaking point. "The Japs can't fight" was a staple of American and British thinking in 1940–1941. It was one thing for the soldiers and airmen of Japan to rape, bomb, and bayonet helpless Chinese, but wait until they ran up against real fighters. Pearl Harbor decisively changed that perspective. As Japanese forces flowed across Asia and Oceania, the Americans responded with an exaggerated respect that crippled a truly creative strategic approach to the Pacific war. Responsible Western political and military officials after 1945 (and especially after midcentury) could neither dismiss nor ignore the Soviet Union's massive military and naval power when combined with the Kremlin's always aggressive propaganda and diplomacy.

Moreover, the Soviet naval establishment was somewhat better than it looked at the beginning of the cold war. Although Moscow welcomed Nazi naval architects, scientists, and some of the latest U-boat designs as war booty, the Soviet Union had boasted the largest submarine fleet in the world in 1940, and of the roughly 250–260 boats just 15 or so were of older types. Nonetheless, the submarine fared poorly during the war because of what historian Donald W. Mitchell characterizes as "material disadvantages," including lack of ready access to open seas and ice conditions in the Baltic and Arctic Seas. Mitchell adds to these natural problems poor administrative organization and "lack of a clear and mature concept of how to employ undersea boats," which he not unjustly attributes to a closed totalitarian mind incapable of thinking beyond well-worn grooves. "In a highly technical field, undeviating loyalty to Marxist doctrine is of no assistance in discovering solutions to difficult and demanding problems," a criticism that Mitchell extends to Soviet "naval warfare in general." But he also argues that lend-lease shipments and indigenous industrial output allowed Soviet naval aviation to reconstitute "so effectively" that by 1944–1945 "it was overwhelmingly stronger than the Luftwaffe." Moreover, Soviet marines made at least twenty significant assaults in the Baltic and Black Seas in support of the Red Army and more than one hundred more modest landings, most of which were "impromptu affairs which involved short distance movements of troops, improvised landing craft, minimal naval support following the landing and very low logistic support for the troops landed." Little wonder that many of these impulsive expeditions proved "outright failures." Like their Red Army compatriots, the Soviet sailors and marines knew how to die. But the war did lay some foundations, especially in aviation, for a rapid, indeed forced, draft expansion of postwar Soviet naval power.[15]

And just about the time Western analysts concluded that the entire postwar Soviet military machine *was* irremediably crude and inferior, its engineers and technicians would suddenly unleash a stunningly new and effective system of advanced technology. The MiG-15s and MiG-21s of the Korean War and immediate postwar era, followed by Sputnik, were but two outstanding examples; nuclear submarine–based long-range missiles and the hyper-speedy "Shkval" torpedoes that appeared in 1977 were others. Moreover, Russian tactical and technological weaknesses were replicated just often enough in the West to drive home the realization that the incredibly high-tech weapon, electronic, and propulsion systems employed by both sides in the nuclear power–guided missile age were subject to catastrophic failure.

Finally, Gorshkov's sailors came at the U.S. Navy full bore from the moment the admiral felt comfortable in having them do so. Account after account of Soviet naval disasters emphasize the almost bovine dedication of the average Soviet sailor, and his officers, to the ship, its mission, and the nation. They *would* succeed, or literally go down trying. Half or even three-quarters of Soviet missiles at sea might not work because of comparatively primitive radar and tracking devices or faulty weapons. But when Soviet fleet units closely tracked the Sixth Fleet in the eastern Mediterranean, or the carrier formations of Task Force 77 off Vietnam, the quarter or half of weapons on board a missile cruiser or destroyer that did work could have horrific effects on American sea power. With the burden of twentieth-century history, especially Pearl Harbor, before them, Pentagon analysts dared not err on the side of either optimism or contempt.

Much of the confusion in Western naval and intelligence circles about the Soviet Navy and its objectives reflected ongoing debates and rivalries within the Soviet military machine, where the Red Army reigned supreme but the lure of blue-water power and adventure was never far from Kremlin thinking. In the early and mid-1930s, as great navies continued to operate on the Soviet doorstep in both the Baltic and North Pacific, Josef Stalin, newly installed in power, dreamed of re-creating a substantial Russian fleet composed of large, powerful surface ships, submarines, and after a time even aircraft carriers. Indeed, one recent cold war historian has emphasized Stalin's "obsession with Soviet naval power."[16] Stalin had to overcome strong resistance in the navy itself, for in the wake of the Washington and London Naval Conferences, a "young school" of officers had emerged, arguing that with the apparent demise of the battleship after Jutland, "small defensive naval forces" were all that Soviet Russia required. The youngsters dethroned their "old school" elders who had clung to traditional command-of-the-seas doctrines and entrenched themselves in the highest echelons of the navy. Stalin could not dislodge them until the Great Purge of the late thirties, but as early as 1936, with diplomatic relations between Washington and Moscow restored, the Soviet dictator approached American firms requesting designs for a new class of battleship and offering to pay for the prototype vessel to be built in an American yard. To ensure official support for the deal, Stalin also expressed a willingness to station one of the battleships in the Soviet Far East where its presence was certain to tie down substantial elements of the Imperial Japanese Navy. Negotiations dragged on for three years before high officials in the U.S. Navy Department killed the project. "It is probably fair to conclude," one recent history states, "that the Soviet Union's extensive campaign of espionage in the U.S. (including attempts to acquire plans for major combat ships and other industrial secrets), which kept the Office of Naval Intelligence (ONI) very busy in the 1930s, contributed to the Navy Department's wariness in dealing with the Soviet Union."[17]

By 1940 Stalin was well on the way to building battleships of his own. Several new hulls were already on the building ways, and the Soviet dictator planned to augment the remnants of the old czarist fleet, consisting of three reconditioned dreadnoughts, five cruisers, two dozen destroyers, eighteen submarines, and a force of auxiliary ships roughly divided between the Baltic and Black Seas, with a new fleet to be divided between the Baltic and the Pacific, comprising 4 to 5 seventy-five thousand–ton battlewagons, 6 heavy or battle cruisers, 30 light cruisers, 7 or 8 aircraft carriers, and more than 250 submarines.[18] Mounting prospects of a German invasion caused the Soviet dictator to cancel production of any weapons that would not contribute directly to an impending land war. The Nazi assault the following year ended whatever possibilities there may have been to complete at least a portion of "Project 23." But the dream never died in Stalin's mind, despite the fact that "Soviet naval operations from 1941 through 1945 were restricted almost entirely to supporting the Army ground forces in what was essentially a continental war for the Soviet Union." Russia's enormous submarine fleet performed poorly at best, and its surface navy was so powerless that at the height of hostilities against Germany nearly half a million sailors were drafted to serve as foot soldiers at Stalingrad, Kursk, and elsewhere. Most naval operations were confined to the Black Sea estuaries and coastal inlets under Gorshkov's direction, though near the end of the war Soviet submarines were active and effective in the Baltic, as the German army and navy attempted to evacuate the East.[19]

By midcentury Stalin was again striving to create a major world navy whose surface force would include four carriers and an equal number of battleships, plus

supporting vessels, together with many hundreds of submarines. Capture of
advanced Nazi U-boat designs, especially the Type XXI, together with a handful
of old and small cruisers, suggested that, as in rocketry, Soviet naval designers
might be able to leap forward to match or even possibly exceed their Western
antagonists within a few short years. In the autumn of 1952, Stalin approved
Project 627, the development of a nuclear-powered submarine, as high priority.
The old tyrant's death the following March led to a brief period of intense theorizing about the naval future of the Soviet Union that paralleled much earlier
soul-searching in Imperial Japan and Germany about the place of sea power in
national destiny. Several schools of thought contended for supremacy over the
Soviet naval mind, each explicitly or implicitly accepting coastal defense as the
basic mission role and responsibility of the navy. Beyond that, blue-water strategic thought posited the need for control of much if not all of the world ocean
as the best means of guaranteeing national security. Such control would require
great numbers of large, technically complex capital ships, that is, attack aircraft
carriers. The "limited command" or "control" school, based to a great degree in
wartime experience directly supporting Soviet ground operations, ultimately
argued for a fleet bereft of carriers but large and powerful enough to be capable of
effective sea control in a limited area "to permit the carrying out one's own operations while preventing the adversary from carrying out his." Such control could
not long be maintained in the face of NATO's overwhelming naval strength.
But with a sufficient fleet, it could be gained and employed for enough time to
secure the seaborne flank or flanks of any operations that the Red Army might
need to undertake in Western Europe or even the Far East. In calling for a "release" from the restrictions of coastal warfare, the limited-control school hinted,
suggested, but never clearly stated that one initiative against preponderant Western naval power might be a Pearl Harbor–type strike against "the ships of the
basic forces of the adversary in their bases and at sea . . . thereby depriv[ing] them
of the possibility of being employed for combat missions." Another school was
defined as "tactical command of the sea" gained through "'offensive' operations
by establishing scene-of-action superiority of naval forces or from defensive operations by use of man-made defenses (i.e. minefields and coastal artillery)," in other
words an even more spatially and chronologically marginal sea control that might
gain the army time to complete some sharply circumscribed operations.

Like Japanese and German sailors of an earlier age, Soviet naval thinkers were
always aware that they labored under the thumb of the army. They constantly
sought ways to educate colleagues obsessed with ground combat in Eurasia on
the fact that in any war "evasion of a [naval] battle . . . was fatuous, indeed,"
because as one theorist wrote in 1955, "if strategic command of the sea is held

by the enemy, operational [or limited] command of the sea [for a specific time and for specific purposes in support of the Red Army] cannot always be gained in whatever zone would be desirable." In short, cold war imperatives demanded that the Soviet Union could neither avoid building a large fleet nor ignore the demands of flexibility in its construction and deployment if the heartland was to be secure from assault from the West or should politico-diplomatic imperatives require a limited military offensive in central and western Europe. Such thinking ultimately led to the proposition that a successful war against the West would require Soviet fleets to gain "'strategic' command in key theaters in wartime." The notion of at least a small flotilla of immense attack aircraft carriers thus crept back into Soviet naval calculations.[20]

The steady elaboration of sophisticated missile and submarine technologies after World War II expanded the dimensions of inquiry. Submarines were invulnerable at sea, while in port they could be dispersed in such a way that many could survive even a nuclear attack. Pursuing an essentially defensive role two to five hundred miles out on the world ocean, Soviet submarines could seek out and hunt down enemy carrier battle groups charging in to attack Soviet cities and installations. Analyst Robert W. Herrick suggests that by 1955 this had become "the real thrust" of Soviet naval strategy, and that carrier killing became a prime mission responsibility of the Soviet submarine and surface fleets from that time on. Although work was actively beginning on the first Soviet and American strategic-ballistic-missile submarines, it was far too early to construct elaborate theories as to their employment. "The main role in modern warfare for surface ships was stipulated to be for antisubmarine defense," which suggests that Soviet naval planners had a very clear idea of the kind of horrific nuclear warfare that was looming on the horizon.[21]

Soviet naval planners and philosophers thus provided Gorshkov with a doctrinal base sufficiently broad to permit pursuit of a number of courses as chance, circumstance, and developments warranted. But first, the admiral had to endure years of Khrushchev's erratic leadership and the ambitions of design engineers and naval architects whose reach exceeded the grasp of the Soviet labor force and most Soviet sailors.

When Khrushchev attained a strong measure of power in 1956, he set about drastically reducing the entire Soviet military machine, with the navy bearing a disproportionate share of the cuts. His objective, however, was not disarmament and peaceful coexistence but modernization. The navy had come to resemble Grandma's attic, in which every type of ship of every age had managed to survive. Khrushchev found a perfect pretext to drastically prune the service when in 1957 the battleship *Novorossysk,* the former Italian vessel *Giulio Cesare* acquired as spoils of war, exploded at its pier. The premier demanded a massive reorientation of his sea forces. Surface ships were out; submarines were in, but not just any submarines. Khrushchev insisted that all new boats be nuclear powered. Stalin's people had already laid the foundations for such a fleet with the *Zulu*-class diesel-powered submarine that first came into service in 1952. "The world's first ballistic missile submarine," *Zulu* was by 1955 modified to carry one or two missiles in launch tubes faired into an enlarged conning tower or "sail." These missiles were eventually tipped with nuclear warheads. On September 16, 1955, an advanced German V-2 rocket, designated the R-11FM missile, designed by Sergey Korolyov and propelled by kerosene and nitric-acid liquid fuel, roared aloft from its launch tube aboard B-67. Three years later, working from a feverishly accelerated schedule, the first dedicated Soviet ballistic-missile submarine, designated by NATO analysts the *Golf* class, took to the water carrying "Shraddock" missiles with a range of roughly 350 miles.

After that, ambitious Soviet planners, designers, and builders raced ahead with no fewer than three classes of nuclear-powered ballistic-missile submarines—which Western sailors called *Hotel, November,* and *Echo I* and *II*—the lead units of which were commissioned between 1958 and 1960. They proved disasters, too hastily built and perhaps too ambitious in design for their era. According to one respected source, at the time of the Cuban missile crisis the entire first generation of Soviet nukes were in dry dock being retrofitted. Several of these crudely conceived and built vessels had either suffered fatal fires, exploded at their docks from faulty torpedoes, or sunk at sea. The rest suffered severe damage to their nuclear reactors. Many of the diesel subs that still composed by far the largest part of the Soviet undersea fleet were more or less crippled by problems with their propulsion systems.[22]

Nonetheless, Khrushchev and his admirals pushed on, heedless of system failures and loss of life, though the premier did complain often and heartily of the great cost incurred by his seagoing "metal eaters." As the missile submarine force grew and developed, the Soviets turned back to the surface navy, determined to build ships dramatically new in conception and design. In 1960 Raymond V. B. Blackman, editor of *Jane's Fighting Ships,* noted uneasily that a blending of nuclear power with the missile technologies already in the Soviet sea arsenal could not be long delayed. Completion of the nuclear-powered icebreaker *Lenin,* a cruiser-sized vessel, provided Soviet naval architects, marine engineers, and physicists with all the technological data and scientific experience necessary to build a powerful nuclear-powered surface fleet. Moreover, "it is obvious that the Soviet Navy has the intention of launching guided missiles from submarines for, according to the American Chief of Naval Operations, the United States has photographs of Soviet submarines which have ballistic missile tubes in them and it is only common sense to assume that the U.S.S.R. is working very hard on the missiles themselves."[23]

Blackman also commented on the changing nature of warships. Fifteen years of rapid postwar technological advances in propulsion and armaments had created new classes of war vessels never thought of before. The battleship was all but extinct, and traditional cruisers were following them to the breakers' yards. "Today we have attack ships, command ships, assault ships, support ships, deterrent ships, commando ships, task ships, anti-submarine warships, amphibious warfare ships, early warning ships, anti-aircraft ships, aircraft direction ships, and amphibious force flagships."[24]

Soviet sailors gratefully embraced the newest revolution at sea. In terms of advanced technologies it was 1900 and 1906 (or 1896 when the French introduced the armored cruiser) all over again. "We have had to cease comparing the number of warships of one type or another and their total displacement (or the number of guns in a salvo, or the weight of this salvo) and turn to a more complex, but also more correct appraisal of the striking and defensive power of ships," Gorshkov wrote in 1972, "based on a mathematical analysis of their capabilities and qualitative characteristics." Whether fulfilling Khrushchev's orders for a massive submarine fleet complemented by a relatively small but powerful surface fleet to counter Western naval strength or responding to Brezhnev's later aspirations for a full-fledged blue-water global navy, Gorshkov ordered vessels bristling with ostentatious armaments. "The USSR is no longer copying and emulating," Blackman wrote in 1971. "She is initiating and inventing. Regularly there appears a new class of warship peculiar to Soviet requirements. Each year for the last few years a new type of rocket cruiser or missile destroyer has appeared. Each year a new class of submarine has been observed, either nuclear or conventionally powered."[25]

Gorshkov and his people were both clever and innovative. Disdaining to build up to or outbuild their American antagonists in terms of similar ship types (as Kaiser Wilhelm II had tried and failed to do against Britain in the years before World War I), the Soviets built *against* the American fleet, particularly its fast carrier task forces. The formidable Russian missile-cruiser and missile-destroyer flotillas that began to appear after 1965 were designed to closely shadow American carrier task forces, aided greatly by intelligence-gathering trawlers that sailed right through American naval formations, even during flight operations. According to one alarmed observer in the early '70s, if in a time of crisis in the narrow waters of the Mediterranean or off East Asia Soviet missile cruisers and destroyers chose to strike first, "they could launch a coordinated volley of surface-to-surface cruise missiles with no tactical warning. By assumption, we would not be able to take any action against the enemy. . . ships until their missiles had already been launched." Moreover, the ships *looked* grand and were indisputably new. Defense analyst Barry M. Blechman wrote:

> Ton for ton, the newest Soviet destroyer—the Krivak—is said to be the most powerful warship ever built. Fifty per cent of the cruisers, 40 per cent of the destroyers, and 50 per cent of the escorts have become operational since 1958. These new ships incorporate advanced capabilities in propulsion, detection, communication and weapon systems. Surface-to-surface and surface-to-air missiles have become fairly common. Anti-submarine capabilities have been improved with the introduction of new sonars and torpedoes, ship-borne helicopters, and large numbers of anti-submarine rockets.

All in all, it was a very formidable, increasingly large, force. One American admiral characterized it as "the most modern in the world."[26]

By 1972 Gorshkov boasted that his fleet and sailors "can not only break the attack of an aggressor but also inflict annihilating blows in distant oceans and deep in enemy territory. . . . The flag of the Soviet Navy now proudly flies over the oceans of the world. Sooner or later, the United States will have to understand that it no longer has mastery of the seas." These were no idle boasts. Starting in the late 1960s and throughout the following decade, Gorshkov flexed the ever growing naval muscle at his command to shape Third World developments in the Kremlin's favor. Soviet warships cruised the eastern Mediterranean during the June 1967 war and off Jordan during its civil war three years later. Another Soviet flotilla visited Port Said, Egypt, in 1967, and early the following year a small Soviet task force built around a cruiser, a missile destroyer, a nuclear submarine, and an oiler undertook a four-month journey with "courtesy visits" to Iraq, Somalia, India, Iran, Ceylon, and Yemen—which had just become the South Yemen People's Republic. In the spring of 1970, Gorshkov sent fleet units on "prolonged port calls" to Somalia, and that December the Soviet Navy patrolled the western African coast off Guinea. The previous year, Gorshkov and his masters had practiced a bit of classic gunboat diplomacy at the expense of nearby Ghana, whose government had seized several Soviet fishing trawlers for alleged arms smuggling. When diplomatic and economic pressures failed to stir the Ghanaians, three Soviet warships appeared off the coast, and the Russian fishermen were promptly released. During the Angolan civil war of 1975–1976, Gorshkov dispatched another small fleet to African waters both as a show of support for the Soviet-backed faction there and to protect Russian merchant ships supporting it. The Ethiopian-Somali War of 1977–1978 brought forth another show of naval strength as Soviet fleet units established temporary control over the southern Red Sea and the eastern Gulf of Aden because the western powers chose not to intervene. The following year the Kremlin demonstrated its firm support for a now united Vietnam in its brief conflict with China by dispatching a significant portion of its strong Pacific Fleet to the South China Sea. From that moment on, Soviet warships were guaranteed use of the comparatively lavish repair and recreation facilities of the huge former American naval base at Cam Ranh Bay. Cuba remained a safe haven for Soviet fleet units, usually submarines and small but missile-equipped surface combatants. These units could deploy all over the Caribbean from the island, though burdened by the knowledge that their every movement was being monitored intensely from close by. Only when the Americans chose to surge massive fleet reinforcements, as they did twice in the Indian Ocean in response to the Indo-Pakistan War of 1971 and the Iranian hostage crisis eight years later, did Gorshkov order his forces to back off.[27]

The most dramatic escalation of Soviet naval presence and power in the mid- and late sixties occurred in the eastern Mediterranean and western Pacific against the Sixth and Seventh Fleets. Soviet diplomacy had begun penetrating the Near East in the late fifties through the successful exploitation of Arab grievances against Israel, widely perceived then as now as a U.S., indeed Western, client. Thereafter, the Kremlin concentrated its attention on wooing what it perceived as the more "progressive" or "advanced" "socialist" states—Egypt, Syria, Algeria, and Iraq. Gorshkov's sailors first followed the diplomats and the military aid missions in 1964, when the admiral sent "about eight" cruisers and destroyers through the Dardanelles toward the Lebanese and Syrian coasts.

Dramatically expanding the surface and submarine fleets did not exhaust Gorshkov's ambitious agenda. Continuing the strong tradition of Soviet land-based naval aviation that emerged during the latter stages of World War II, the admiral began in the late fifties to deploy large numbers of long-range, land-based naval aircraft—Bulls and Badgers and later Bisons and Backfires—into the world's sea-lanes to track and harass American naval task forces. As soon as possible the aircraft were equipped not only with standard bomb ordnance but also with standoff air-to-surface missiles. When deployed from bases in friendly Egypt and Syria, as well as in the Crimea, these aircraft further circumscribed

Sixth Fleet operations. Even before Khrushchev's departure in 1964, the Soviet Navy was not only expanding its surface missile forces but also building hundreds of small ocean surveillance and intelligence vessels that soon appeared all across the world's sea-lanes to harass and spy upon American naval task forces.

By the early seventies Soviet naval presence in the Mediterranean was "albeit reluctantly, nevertheless accepted rather routinely by most of the Western powers." In fact, the Red Fleet now tacitly divided the Middle Sea with the U.S. Navy. Few Soviet fleet units ventured west of Sicily, where they would have been constantly under the thumb not only of Sixth Fleet units but of numerous NATO air bases in Italy, southern France, and Spain and, for a time, the huge Wheelus Air Force Base in Libya. The Sixth Fleet correspondingly stayed away for the most part from the Lebanese-Syrian and Egyptian coasts where the Soviet Navy found its anchorages and the Soviet naval air force enjoyed deployment rights at several airfields. After June 1967 the Sixth Fleet also had to consider the admittedly remote possibility of independent attacks by Syrian or Egyptian air forces. Sixth Fleet commanders countered critics who accused them of leaving the eastern Mediterranean to the Soviets by claiming that "adequate maneuvers of sea and air units are hazardous . . . on account of the low ceiling for commercial aircraft." Such arguments may have persuaded some, but knowledgeable observers knew the rapidly emerging realities of Soviet-American naval affairs. In 1976 Chief of Naval Operations James L. Holloway made an astounding admission. Because its fleet had recently been overcome with bloc obsolescence as the magnificent World War II vessels at last wore out or simply could not accommodate the new technologies, the U.S. Navy was operating "with the fewest ships . . . since before Pearl Harbor." As a consequence, the Americans enjoyed, at best, "a slim margin of superiority over that of the Soviets." In the event of war, Holloway continued,

> we could retain control of the North Atlantic sea-lanes to Europe but would suffer serious losses in both U.S. and allied shipping in the early stages. Our ability to operate in the Eastern Mediterranean would be uncertain at best. Our fleets in the Pacific could hold open the sea-lanes to Hawaii and Alaska, but, because of the shortages of sea control and mobile logistic support forces, we would have difficulty in projecting our sea lines of communication into the Western Pacific.[28]

In 1967 the first of the Soviet *Yankee*-class strategic-ballistic-missile submarines put to sea. Sixty such vessels would appear during the next fifteen years.[29] By 1970 the Soviet Navy comprised 20 strategic-ballistic-missile submarines, 112 short-range cruise-missile undersea boats, 2 new helicopter carriers, 8 guided-missile cruisers, and 29 guided-missile destroyers. Buried in all these impressive statistics were the first Soviet medium landing ships and LSTs—which seemed to mark a serious commitment at last to amphibious warfare—and the steady growth of the Soviet merchant marine, or MORFLOT, which by 1985 comprised 1,700 vessels, including container ships, roll on–roll off cargo carriers, tankers, passenger liners, and more. According to one authoritative American source, the Soviet Merchant Marine was a "carefully directed . . . fleet that can perform a commercially competitive peacetime mission and satisfy military logistics requirements in crisis or war." Each vessel was "constructed to military standards" containing such features as chemical-biological-radiation warfare protection, "increased endurance and service speed," and identification-friend-or-foe systems. As MORFLOT proudly announced on the seventieth anniversary of the "Great October Socialist Revolution," the "technological level of the modern Soviet fleet makes it possible to maintain steady seaborne links with any coastal country, to call at ports of any continent on the globe."[30]

Within the Soviet Navy, often innovative weapon systems were complemented by an ever more elaborate command-control-communications-intelligence structure. By the end of the sixties, Soviet naval intelligence was collecting an enormous amount of information about the U.S. fleet and its movements on, above, and beneath the world ocean. The chief collecting agents were aircraft, space satellites, radio intercepts, surface ships, undercover agents, and, of course, submarines. U.S. aircraft carriers on their way to Vietnamese or Japanese waters were routinely overflown by long-range Soviet reconnaissance aircraft in mid-ocean. The Americans responded by scrambling their latest jet fighters to fly close escort to the intruders, often holding up for appreciative Russian flight crews the latest copy of *Playboy* with its celebrated centerfold "bunnies."

Not a day went by that American fleet units were not dogged by small Soviet trawlers laden with electronic surveillance and detection antennae. A score of these intelligence collection ships, like the notorious *Gidrofon* off Vietnam, eavesdropped on American fleet transmissions, observed air operations and underway replenishment exercises, took notes on American fleet exercises, and hovered near underwater ballistic-missile firing areas off the Florida coast. *Krivak*- and *Kashin*-class destroyers and submarines were also used as data-collection ships. As early as 1967, with the Soviet naval build-up well under way but far from complete, frigates and destroyers of the Russian fleet often steamed within a hundred yards of American carriers conducting flight operations in the Mediterranean or western Pacific. Occasionally, the audacious Soviets even brushed against American warships, causing a flare-up of tempers and tensions that threatened to get out of hand. On one occasion during the Arab-Israeli Six-Day War that year, Vice Admiral William I. Martin, commander of the Sixth Fleet, messaged a Soviet destroyer sailing in the midst of his formation, "Your actions for the past five days have interfered with our operations." Continuing his message, which was transmitted by voice radio and flashing light in both English and Russian, Martin added:

> By positioning your ship in the midst of our formation and shadowing our every move you are denying us the freedom of maneuver on the high seas that has been traditionally recognized by seafaring nations for centuries.
>
> In a few minutes the task force will commence maneuvering at high speeds and various courses. Your present position will be dangerous to your ship, as well as the ships of this force.
>
> I request you clear our formation without delay and discontinue interference and unsafe practices.[31]

The Soviet captain never replied, and Martin, like Sixth Fleet commanders before and well after, had to maneuver around the stubbornly positioned Soviet vessel. Tensions rose steadily on both sides. Vietnam was no help. Several times during the war, excited American air force and naval pilots shot at Soviet merchantmen unloading supplies in North Vietnamese ports. By 1973 both sides realized the potential for a major conflict arising out of unintended—and more than once deliberately reckless—behavior by both navies. Soviet and American officials worked out an uneasy arrangement for the avoidance of collisions at sea, but more often than not, INCSEA (the Incidents at Sea talks) was honored in the breach. Times of special tension and deliberate provocation, such as the entrance of American warships into the Black Sea in the 1980s, brought forth more confrontations and incidents that ended only with the life of the Soviet Union.[32]

Soviet intelligence compiled a flood of information from such activities and gathered it into a comprehensive ocean-surveillance package that was correlated at the command centers of the four fleet headquarters and at naval command in Moscow. Since defense of the homeland was the primary strategic concept and function of the Soviet Navy (indeed, of any navy) the centrally collected intelligence was intended to be used to coordinate and control attacks against any enemy forces nearing Soviet coasts.

As Soviet fleets approached quantitative parity with their American antagonists in the late 1960s and early '70s, Gorshkov and his admirals not only swung firmly behind the doctrine of limited control over those seas adjacent to the Eurasian landmass that lay on the flanks of any possible Red Army offensive but also boldly tested the idea of strategic control over ever widening areas of the world ocean. This new policy was most dramatically demonstrated in two great naval exercises conducted at the height of America's involvement in Vietnam. In the first, conducted between April 14 and May 6, 1970, Soviet surface warships, submarines, naval aircraft, and naval infantry sailed into the Atlantic, Pacific, and Arctic Oceans "according to a unified plan" called simply *Okean,* or Ocean. Nearly the entire Soviet Navy spent several weeks conducting very well-coordinated exercises. Several units even steamed into the Indian Ocean. According to one Soviet source, Pacific Fleet maneuvers were conducted "in the immediate vicinity of the hotbeds of U.S. military aggression in Southeast Asia, in the zone of war activity of the U.S. Navy." Okean 1970 and its successor, Okean 1975, not only demonstrated the surge capabilities of the Soviet Navy's variously scattered fleets but also showed Moscow's ability to tightly control and coordinate activities and exercises. The two Okean exercises thus suggested that Gorshkov was pursuing, or at least planning for, both offensive and defensive warfare. Norman Polmar, the highly respected American naval analyst, wrote in 1983 that the admiral and his Kremlin superiors "appear to view the sea in wartime as a 'jungle' with all or most warships at sea subject to rapid destruction." But a powerful Soviet fighting fleet *could* pursue major mission objectives in both war and peace. During wartime it could surge its forces to control temporarily a particular maritime sector close to home in order to execute a given operation. During peacetime various fleet units would exercise political influence in the Mediterranean, Caribbean, South Atlantic, and Indian oceans. Much as Admiral Alfred von Tirpitz had dreamed of the kaiser's warships reawakening a sense of "Germandom" in émigré populations from New York to Santiago in the years before World War I, so the Soviet Navy in its peacetime role would advance the influence and physically display the armed might of Marxism-Leninism throughout the Third World. Significantly, Soviet fleets visited about "a dozen foreign ports on four continents" at the close of Okean 1970.[33]

But Gorshkov was no Tirpitz. He possessed far greater vision and ability to go with an equal amount of energy. It was not enough just to send a few gunboats here and there to show the flag as the old German admiral had done, or to dispatch several obsolete armored cruisers to a China station. The Soviets conducted full-scale fleet exercises across the world ocean, not just off Scandinavia. And in the seventies, before the advent of the really big ships, Gorshkov placed semipermanent flotillas of rocket cruisers, missile destroyers, and the occasional helicopter carrier in the Mediterranean, while conducting yearly naval exercises in the Caribbean near Cuba.[34]

The world was stunned by this sudden eruption of modern naval power, whose only precedent had been the rise of the German High Seas Fleet sixty years before. What it portended no one in the West could quite say. When Alfred Ward took command of Amphibious Forces, Atlantic Fleet, in August 1961, he discovered that the Soviets were coming out into the Atlantic more frequently with both surface ships and submarines. Nonetheless, "most of their surface ships would remain north of Iceland or in their land-locked water areas, or, out in the Western Pacific, they would normally not come down below Japan. . . . Their merchant marine was greatly expanded." Increasing traffic into Cuba convinced some within Ward's circle as well as the admiral himself that "some kind of a battle for the supremacy of the Atlantic was underway, particularly in the merchant marine." That same year, young Bobby Ray Inman became an operations intelligence analyst at the U.S. National Security Agency outside Washington, D.C. "I was an analyst for thirty-three months," Admiral Inman later recalled, "looking at the Soviet Navy as my prime occupation in a complete all-[intelligence re]source environment." Every piece of information on the expanding Soviet fleet that might even tangentially interest Inman was passed to his desk. In the months before the Cuban missile crisis, Gorshkov "rarely sent any ships two hundred miles beyond their waters." Those that ventured farther "frequently broke down and had to be towed back." By the time Inman left in 1964, the Soviets had developed "a permanent presence in the Mediterranean and off West Africa, and they were building a framework for their presence in the Indian Ocean." While Vietnam absorbed more and more of Washington's attention and gobbled up more and more of the national resources, the United States Navy began to suffer, while its Soviet counterpart raced to parity. Between 1966 and 1970 only 88 new ships joined the American fleet; during the same period the Soviets built 209 combatants and auxiliaries.[35]

Blackman wrote in 1971:

> It seems that once in her stride there is no stopping the Soviet Union in her naval progress. . . . There is no hiding place from the Hammer and Sickle. . . . The Soviet merchant fleet has expanded from 1,000 ships aggregating 2,300,000 tons gross in 1955 to 7,000 ships aggregating 16,000,000 tons gross in 1970. The increase in the fighting fleet has been no less spectacular, particularly in the later 1960s. . . . The expansion of Soviet maritime power was a military phenomenon of the 1960's which looks like rising to a flood tide in the 1970's.

Blackman proved correct. Far from slackening the pace of construction in the seventies, Gorshkov accelerated the building of his fleet. The 1976 appearance of the 37,000-ton carrier-cruiser *Kiev,* followed over time by three sisters together with the nuclear-powered-missile battle cruiser *Kirov* and two other units, represented an impressive advance in Soviet naval architecture and engineering. As Polmar observed, these ships were substantially larger and more complex than any previous Soviet naval vessels, "requiring a significant amount of industrial capability and other resources."[36]

What all these observers correctly saw and emphasized was the *totality* of the Soviet thrust into the world's sea-lanes. Communist Russia had become not only a naval power but a massive maritime presence: it can be plausibly argued that in the coherence and central direction of its various components, the Soviet Union in the quarter century after 1960 became a holistic sea power in a way and on a scale achieved only by eighteenth- and nineteenth-century Great Britain. "The most impressive thing about Russia's maritime ambitions is not their specific impact but their scope; the fact that they embrace every aspect of sea power and are based on such a broad programme of research and education," an admiring British scholar noted in 1971. Not only were the Soviet Merchant Marine and Navy growing steadily in size, but they were also deploying all over the world. "The apparent co-ordination of the various elements—research, fishing, commercial, naval—is a major test of Communist state planning," David Fairhall continued. The political direction of this effort had momentous consequences, for it tested the Communists' ability to match Western capitalism "as an instrument of worldwide imperialism. Russia, the great land power, has curiously chosen to fight the ideological battle at sea."[37]

Whether the Kremlin leadership directly orchestrated its naval and especially maritime build-up with an increasing awareness of the ocean, and particularly the deep seabed, as a source of wealth is unclear. Certainly from the late fifties onward, the international community began serious debate about national jurisdictions over continental shelves and adjacent seas, international fishing rights, management and conservation of living resources, and seabed mining. The First UN Conference on the Law of the Sea took place between February and April 1958; a second was held between March 17 and April 26, 1960. Seven years later, the Maltese foreign minister asserted the principle of the deep seabed with its rich nodules of manganese and other critical resources as "the common heritage of all mankind," touching off a third and prolonged international search for a comprehensive Law of the Sea treaty. Soviet spokesmen and delegates were actively involved in the process from the beginning, and, in my experience on the U.S. delegation to the Third UN Conference on the Law of the Sea during its 1980 deliberations in New York and Geneva, Russian diplomats played a leading, highly knowledgeable, and self-assured role in negotiations.[38]

By the early seventies Gorshkov's fleet was demonstrating a growing technical and operational competence as it pursued various short-term and usually short-range missions across the world ocean "with imagination, ingenuity and flexibility," prompting the editor of *Jane's Fighting Ships* to ask, "Who *is* policing the world now?" The world's two super sea powers shared "a situation which is neither peace nor war, both holding the flints and the sparks which could touch the explosive ingredients in the hands of Egypt and Israel." And, according to Hyman Rickover, the Soviet Navy was about to surge ahead of its American rival in the number of deployed ballistic-missile submarines. In September 1971 President Nixon reportedly told Soviet foreign minister Andrei Gromyko that "he did not criticize the Soviet Union for continuing to build up its offensive submarine-launched ballistic missiles—he said he would, too, in their shoes."[39]

Nixon's admirals did not enjoy the luxury of such thinking. As early as 1967 much of the U.S. war fleet was obsolete and exhausted, slowly but steadily declining in strength as the World War II–vintage vessels—run to death throughout the consistently high-tempo cold war years—began to fall apart. Moreover, many sailors in the Pentagon got the distinct impression that Defense Secretary Robert McNamara and his civilian "whiz kids" "never really believed you needed much of a navy. And so they not only were against nuclear propulsion for the aircraft carrier, they were against the aircraft carrier per se." Fortunately, navy secretary Paul Nitze "outpoint[ed] them in the battle for McNamara's mind," partly because of Rickover's relations with Congress and partly because some of McNamara's key associates had earned their reputations in Rickover's program.[40]

When Elmo Zumwalt became chief of naval operations in 1970, the anti–Vietnam War movement was at full tide, while the revolutions in race, dress, and style sweeping the civilian world were beginning to exert unprecedented social pressures on a naval service that had always been successful in hermetically sealing itself off from the outside. It was not a time to seek rejuvenation of the navy. Had Zumwalt tried, McNamara and Congress would doubtless have slapped him down hard. An intelligent, thoughtful man, Zumwalt concluded that the best way to preserve as much of the service as possible was to downplay the carrier's cherished status as a tactical strategic nuclear power–projection platform and return the fleet to its classic sea-control responsibilities. "From his point of view," one highly knowledgeable naval analyst has written, "it was particularly advantageous to minimize power projection because many Americans identified it with the failed war in Vietnam." The CNO was "uncomfortably aware" that the public would demand a peace dividend, leading to the kind of bitter interservice rivalries that surfaced back in 1945–1949. The only way to avoid a repetition of interservice bloodletting was to advocate a navy with more surface ships of lesser quality and capabilities. The new navy of the late seventies and eighties would comprise scores of frigates instead of dozens of destroyers, eight or ten much smaller, and slower, "sea control ships" embarking a comparative handful of helicopters and marginally capable Harrier "jump jets" in place of one or more new supercarriers. In effect, the United States Navy would drastically downgrade, if not abandon, any tactical nuclear role it had pursued to concentrate primarily on antisubmarine warfare. However realistic Zumwalt's proposals may have been in light of prevailing budgetary stringencies and the public mood, they caused an outburst of anger and a crisis of morale not seen within navy ranks since the "revolt of the admirals" over armed forces unification a quarter century before.[41]

Declining power and morale, together with rising Soviet presence and harassment across the world ocean, may well explain why the more aggressive factions within the U.S. Navy—especially the submarine force—waged implacable and at times foolhardy competition with their Soviet opposites from the late sixties on. Lurking outside Soviet sub-Arctic anchorages to dog outbound Russian submarines for hundreds or even a few thousand miles, crowding, chivying, and taunting their crews with infuriating tactics, daring the Russians to respond in some way so that more and more intelligence could be gleaned about Soviet submarine and antisubmarine capabilities, methods, and tactics, American submarine captains made their own substantial contributions to a consistently tense and hostile cold war at sea. Occasionally, such exercises culminated in high-speed chases and counterchases in ever tightening circles that resembled nothing so much as the famous "dogfights" between two aviators over the World War I trenches and in the 1940 Battle of Britain. On one occasion these clashes came close to destroying vessels on both sides.[42] Although never expressly stating the idea, American submariners—and the surface navy as well—believed it was imperative that they not only never give up command of the world ocean but also constantly demonstrate total professional superiority over their upstart opponents. Despite the enormous efforts put forth by Tirpitz and his kaiser, the Royal Navy in 1914 clearly exerted such an influence over its German opposite. Admirals Isoroku Yamamoto and Chuichi Nagumo just as clearly suffered from inferiority complexes in confronting the American fleet in 1941–1942, despite substantial disparities in sea power during the half year between Pearl Harbor and Midway, and in local power at Guadalcanal.

Western and Soviet publics were unaware of the more chilling aspects of the cold war beneath the seas. Only once after the Cuban crisis of 1962 did open naval combat between the two great sea powers appear imminent, and that was during the October 1973 Arab-Israeli Six-Day War.

Following the 1967 Arab-Israeli War that so devastated Moscow's Arab clients, Gorshkov escalated Soviet fleet deployment in the eastern Mediterranean to close to seventy vessels and never again let the number fall below forty. The following year he formally created the Fifth Eskadra, designed specifically to maintain continuous surveillance of the Sixth Fleet (especially its carriers), detect U.S. ballistic-missile submarine-deployment zones, and disrupt U.S. sea control. On an average day in 1968, the Fifth Eskadra deployed thirty ships. Five years later this number had risen to fifty-six, usually including ten to fifteen missile cruisers and destroyers, often screening one of the two new helicopter carriers, *Moskva* or *Leningrad,* together with eight to ten submarines and a variety of amphibious ships, auxiliary craft, and intelligence gatherers. The Kremlin was able to provide diplomatic support for its new Mediterranean armada through exploitation of its friendships in the Arab world. By 1973 the year of the Arab-Israeli October war, the Syrian port of Latakia, Port Said in Egypt, and even Mers el-Kébir in distant Algeria, right under the nose of NATO's westernmost European members, had become important anchorages and bases for Soviet naval flotillas. As in the Caribbean, Gorshkov and his admirals now cared little if their fleet units were under immediate and intense surveillance in the far western Mediterranean; they had penetrated the NATO naval shield there as elsewhere.[43]

The two navies were obviously on a collision course to test relative fleet superiority, and the October 1973 war provided a suitable pretext. A distinguished student of East-West relations has recently argued that the 1968 confrontation over the Soviet invasion of Czechoslovakia convinced military people on both sides that, all planning to the contrary, no "conventional" superpower war could be certain. After 1968 "the adversaries still kept planning for a military contingency in which they could use their conventional forces without having to resort to nuclear weapons." Swept up in onrushing events, both Soviet and American generals "showed a prudent disposition to underestimate their own strength and overestimate the strength of the adversary." They concluded that any military conflict, no matter how limited at the outset "was wrought with so many uncertainties that it could not be planned with any reliability."[44] In October 1973, however, the two powers became so fixated on the plight of their respective Mideast allies that a naval war—conventional or otherwise—became for a moment a distinct possibility, with fingers on both sides hovering near hair triggers.

Following their 1967 defeat, Egypt's Gamal Abdel Nasser and his Syrian allies, rejecting any negotiations with the enemy, determined to drive Israel out of its newly occupied territories on the Golan Heights, in Jordan's former West Bank (including East Jerusalem), and from former Egyptian holdings in the Sinai peninsula and Gaza Strip. Nasser died in 1970 and was succeeded by Anwar Sadat, who soon concluded that the Soviets were of little help except as arms suppliers and military technicians. In 1972 Sadat became thoroughly disenchanted with Leonid Brezhnev when the Soviet secretary-general failed to achieve any diplomatic breakthrough for his Arab client during a summit meeting with Nixon. Concluding that diplomacy had failed and the alliance was not worth pursuing, the Egyptian leader decided that the only way to resolve the Israeli problem was by means of another war. (When he learned that hostilities had broken out, Secretary of State Henry Kissinger muttered that "what may have happened is the Soviets told the Egyptians . . . that there will not be any progress unless there is stirring in the Middle East, and those maniacs have stirred a little too much.")[45]

Sadat harbored no illusions that he and the Syrians could win another go-around with the Israelis, but he hoped battle would lead Jerusalem to disgorge all or a significant portion of the occupied lands. He expelled most of the Soviet technicians (to maintain the fiction that he was not a Soviet client, though, in fact, he maintained close ties with Moscow), then began active preparations for conflict. On several occasions he publicly stated his intent to commence hostilities at a time of his own choosing. Brezhnev warned President Nixon during a visit to the United States in June 1973 that "the Arabs were planning for war." Nonetheless, Washington and Tel Aviv were both caught flat-footed when war came.[46] Nixon, Kissinger, the Pentagon, the CIA, and, astonishingly, the government of Golda Meir all believed that no responsible Arab leader would go to war against qualitatively superior Israeli forces, and Kissinger was seeking to normalize Mideast relations through backdoor diplomacy.

Early on the afternoon of October 6, the Egyptian army, "massively equipped" with Soviet tanks, planes, and artillery, plunged across the Suez Canal, while the Syrian army raced up the Golan Heights. The two nations promptly declared wide areas off their coasts dangerous to foreign shipping. Washington immediately alerted the Sixth Fleet, and despite Kissinger's testy prediction that it might take commanders "a week" to get their men back from shore leave and their scattered vessels assembled, the carriers and their supporting vessels were ready to surge eastward toward the battle front within twelve hours. Kissinger, who hoped to gain Soviet collaboration rather than face Soviet threats, later claimed to have told the Kremlin that "our only protection is to be extremely tough and to teach the facts of life to people who like to make great speeches. I will be very brutal. That will be our strategy."[47]

But Moscow was spectacularly unimpressed. Cold war politics dictated that the Kremlin not abandon Sadat or the Syrians, and the Soviet fleet that cruised the Mediterranean in 1973 was a far stronger and more varied force than ten or even six years before. In September 1969 a mass naval exercise with the Syrians and Egyptians had led to the imposition of "a protective shield of over 100 ships . . . to deter intervention by the United Kingdom" when a sudden coup d'état took place in Libya.[48]

On the second day of the war, Kissinger told Nixon that the Russians appeared to "have withdrawn their fleet in the Mediterranean," including eleven submarines, several cruise missile–equipped cruisers and destroyers, and a formidable array of support ships, including medium landing craft, minesweepers, frigates, corvettes, and supply vessels. At first, Kissinger continued, "ours went east and theirs went west," coming in close proximity, but then "they have moved back and we have moved up." But the Egyptian offensive developed with horrifying speed and success. Israeli diplomats told the Americans early in the morning of October 9 that "losses to date had been staggering and totally unexpected. . . . The real shocker was the loss of five hundred tanks, four hundred on the Egyptian front alone." Israel had mounted a weak counteroffensive on the Suez front the day before; it turned out to be "a miserable failure." The Israelis begged Kissinger to keep the information tightly controlled; only the president must know—otherwise, the rest of the Arab world might suddenly join in to deliver Israel "a knock out blow." So frightening had Israeli air and armor losses become that according to one source, the panic-stricken defense minister, Moshe Dayan, begged Prime Minister Meir to authorize the use of nuclear weapons because the nation's very existence was at stake.[49]

With its client suddenly on a spectacular war path, the Kremlin changed politico-military course sharply. Kissinger received reports that "Soviet diplomats were urging heretofore uninvolved Arab states to enter the fray," and on the morning of the tenth the Pentagon learned that Soviet resupply operations to Egypt and Syria had "gone overt." Gorshkov supported this effort by dramatically surging a powerful naval force out of the Black Sea through the Bosporus to reinforce the Fifth Eskadra.[50]

Fighting for its existence, Israel nonetheless refrained from directly attacking Soviet ships or aircraft en route to either Egypt or Syria. But on the tenth Israeli warplanes struck at Syrian airfields, destroying several Soviet transport planes and forcing others to return to their southern Russian and Georgian airfields. On the twelfth the Israeli Air Force sank a Soviet cargo ship while attacking Syrian warships in the port of Tartūs. Gorshkov immediately countered by concentrating most of the Fifth Eskadra on a line between the eastern tip of Cyprus and the Syrian coast. "For what was probably the first time since World War II, the Soviet Navy moved combat forces into an active war zone." Thereafter, Moscow sent several "clear signals to the White House that any 6th Fleet interference with 5th Eskadra operations would be met by force." Gorshkov further escalated tensions by ordering his "anti-carrier groups" to closely track the two independently steaming U.S. carrier battle groups as well as the cruiser-destroyer force built around the Sixth Fleet command ship, *Little Rock*.[51] By October 24 the Soviet Mediterranean Fleet totaled an astounding eighty ships built around several surface-action groups composed of missile cruisers and destroyers plus sixteen nuclear submarines. The entire force possessed a first-launch capability of 40 surface-to-surface cruise missiles, 250 torpedoes, and 28 surface-to-air missiles. The cruise missiles were of particular concern to American sailors, because they employed a new kind of infrared guidance system that the U.S. Navy had as yet been unable to counter, despite a number of surreptitious submarine spy missions into Soviet waters to pick up missile fragments off the ocean floor after test firings.[52]

The Israelis had always planned—and conducted—short, sharp, successful wars against their Arab enemies, but this conflict threatened to drag on for weeks. Combat was fierce, and losses in men and equipment were ruinous on both sides. The Israeli Air Force was particularly hard-hit by mobile Soviet-supplied SAM-6 missiles sites in Egypt. By the end of the first week of the war, the Israelis had lost 20 percent of their air strength. If the United States did not counter the Soviet air- and sealifts with one of its own, Israel could well perish—or go nuclear. Mindful of ever growing American and Western dependence on Mideast oil, Defense Secretary James Schlesinger openly worried about antagonizing the Arabs. But the increasingly desperate Israelis frantically lobbied Congress while Kissinger dithered, hoping that a civilian airlift under Defense Department charter would provide adequate reinforcement. With gloomy news continuing to flow in from the battlefronts, however, the administration at last caved in and on October 13 agreed to commence an immediate nonstop military airlift to Israel. Now Kissinger decided that American air- and sealifts would do more than just save the Israelis; they would send a message to the Kremlin about American resolve. "Our only interest in this semi-confrontation situation is to run the Soviets into the ground, fast," the secretary told fellow members of the Washington Special Action Group on the sixteenth. "Give them the maximum incentive [to help arrange] a quick settlement. Bring in more [to the battle-fronts] each day than they do." As a "rough guideline," Kissinger asked that the American resupply effort remain "at least 25 percent of the Soviets." Unfortunately, the American effort soon proved so spectacular that it antagonized Brezhnev and his colleagues. Kissinger, fearing that Washington might provoke the Kremlin into World War III, changed tactics once more, seeking to "fine-tune" the crisis to a stalemate so that both the Arabs and the Israelis would be sufficiently weakened by the bloodletting to be amenable to a long-term regional peace package.[53]

The Sixth Fleet was suddenly on the firing line. Its ships and aircraft would have to guarantee safe passage of the big air force C-5s and C-130s across Mediterranean skies to Israel and also counter whatever moves Gorshkov's large naval task force might take. In addition, the amphibious group of eighteen hundred marines that was also part of the Sixth Fleet could at least act as a trip wire if not deterrent should the Soviets be foolish enough to try to decide the outcome of the war with their own forces. By this time the supercarrier *Independence* had left Greece and was steaming north of Crete. *Franklin D. Roosevelt* had departed Barcelona and was holding east of Sicily. A third carrier, *John F. Kennedy,* sister ship of *Independence,* was ordered down from a port call in Scotland to maneuver in the Atlantic just off Gibraltar. The amphibious group remained at Suda Bay, Crete. The Kremlin was very much aware of this powerful naval force. Even before Washington formally initiated its airlift, Soviet ambassador Anatoly Dobrynin at a "testy luncheon" objected to the eastward deployment of the Sixth Fleet. Kissinger made no reply. Within hours after Washington's decision to massively resupply Israel, the three carriers became an essential part of another critical airlift, the delivery of F-4 Phantom fighter jets to the Israeli Air Force. Flying out of fields on the East Coast, the rugged but short-range aircraft were refueled once in flight before they reached the vicinity of *JFK* where they were again refueled in flight by tankers launched from the carrier. The fighter jets then flew on to *FDR*, where they landed aboard for the night, then were launched the next morning for the last leg of their journey to Israel after one more in-flight refueling from tankers off *Independence.* Just seventy-two hours after Nixon ordered the massive reinforcement of Israeli air and ground forces, Kissinger told Senator Stuart Symington that the Phantoms "are going in about six to eight a day."[54]

The Israelis launched their major counteroffensive on the Suez front as the first Phantoms and C-5s landed at Tel Aviv. Thereafter, as the American-supplied Israeli arms build-up continued, Israeli armored columns drove into Egypt, while other Israeli forces surrounded Sadat's finest troops on the east bank of the canal. Suddenly it was 1967 all over again, and Brezhnev's sole concern was not to be humiliated by yet another defeat of a client. Initially, the Soviet leader avoided Kosygin's mistake six years earlier of trying to rescue a client through the unilateral imposition of Soviet military power. He would work with, not against, Washington. Nixon and Kissinger, having made their point, were perfectly willing to join in pressing both sides into negotiations. The Kremlin and White House thus managed to cobble together one, then another, fragile cease-fire, but both broke down in the excitement and despair of changing fortunes on the battlefield.

By October 24 Brezhnev had had enough. As the Israelis began a hard squeeze on the Egyptian forces stranded in the Sinai, he proposed the imposition of a joint Soviet-U.S. peace through the dispatch of troops from both countries to Egypt. In a tough, "very urgent" message to Nixon through Dobrynin, Brezhnev urged the president to join Moscow "to compel observance" of a cease-fire "without delay." If Washington refused, Brezhnev continued, the Soviets might have no choice but to impose peace on the Middle East unilaterally. "I just had a letter from Brezhnev," Kissinger told White House chief of staff Alexander Haig late that evening, "asking us to send forces in together or he would send them in alone." "I was afraid of that," Haig replied. Several moments later, Kissinger ruefully admitted to Israeli ambassador Simcha Dinitz: "I just think we turned the wheel yesterday one screw too much" on Brezhnev's Cairo client.[55] The Soviet secretary-general backed up his threat by issuing several substantial troop alerts, and Washington analysts concluded that Soviet soldiers might soon be air- or sealifted the short distance to the Middle East battlefronts. Late in the evening of the twenty-fourth, following a hastily called meeting of the National Security Council, the Pentagon issued a limited DefCon (Defense Condition) III alert and ordered the Eighty-second Airborne Division at Fort Bragg, North Carolina, to be ready to move. The B-52 intercontinental bombers of the Strategic Air Command took up advanced positions around the Soviet Union. Within hours *JFK* raced into the Mediterranean to join *FDR,* rapidly steaming to team up with *Independence* south of Crete. The amphibious group at Suda Bay was also placed on alert, and the helicopter assault carrier *Iwo Jima* steamed east-ward through the Straits of Gibraltar. The Soviet admiral in the Mediterranean ordered several of his warships, including an amphibious landing craft, to move toward Egypt.

Once the American airlift began, Gorshkov's sailors escalated the tension and kept it at a high level. Normally, only a single Soviet destroyer trailed U.S. carrier task forces in the Mediterranean. But after October 16 two Soviet guided-missile cruisers with two admirals and two "other command authorities" aboard, together with a guided-missile destroyer and a submarine tender, began stalking *Independence* and its escorts, designated Task Force 60. After the twenty-fifth another Soviet missile cruiser and destroyer joined the forces monitoring the carrier's activities. The following day the Soviets began intensive anticarrier warfare exercises against Task Force 60, employing both diesel- and nuclear-powered guided-missile submarines in mock exercises. The exercises continued on the twenty-seventh, as *Independence* was joined by *JFK* and *FDR,* and for six nerve-racking days thereafter both sides locked themselves tightly into a pos-sible preemptive-strike scenario.

> Gravely threatened by Soviet cruise missiles, the U.S. carrier groups would have needed to preemptively destroy the weapons system radar in the masts as well as the missile and gun mounts, or to otherwise have sunk every Soviet warship within range before Soviet missiles reached their decks. Meanwhile, 5th Eskadra commanders would need to sink or incapacitate as many U.S. carriers as possible before U.S planes and ships had sufficient time to retaliate.[56]

Never before and never again would the United States and Soviet navies be closer to nuclear war. Never before and never again would carrier admirals, captains, and sailors be steaming within visual range of their enemies whose fingers lingered as close to the nuclear triggers as their own. It was more than Cuba; it was much worse, though as in 1962, the publics on both sides were never told so.[57]

On the last day of the month, Sixth Fleet commander Daniel Murphy re-ported to the Pentagon that Soviet fleet strength had risen to 96 ships, includ-ing 34 surface combatants and 23 submarines possessing a first-launch capability of 88 surface-to-surface missiles, 348 torpedoes, and 46 surface-to-air missiles. "The U.S. Sixth Fleet and the Soviet Mediterranean Fleet were, in effect, sitting in a pond in close proximity," Murphy later told his superiors far away in the Pentagon, "and the stage for the hitherto unlikely 'war at sea' scenario was set.

This situation prevailed for several days. Both fleets were obviously in a high readiness posture for whatever might come next, although it appeared neither fleet knew exactly what to expect."[58]

In one sense, the Soviets won the showdown. Gravely weakened by the mounting Watergate crisis at home (the "Saturday-night massacre" of Attorney General Eliot Richardson and Special Prosecutor Archibald Cox had just occurred) and perhaps lacking sufficient military force abroad, Nixon and Kissinger were forced to acquiesce in Soviet demands that the Israelis draw back from the encirclement of the Egyptian Third Army on the right bank of the Suez Canal. As the Israelis withdrew, so did the Sixth Fleet from the eastern Mediterranean. "From a tactical perspective," Lyle Goldstein and Yuri Zhukov have written, "this decision was made to provide the [carrier battle] groups with more room for maneuver, and to complicate targeting by the Soviets. On a strategic level, the White House was certainly sending the Soviets a signal that the U.S. was returning to a more relaxed posture."[59]

But in another and deeper sense, the Americans won the day. Kissinger's suggestion that he *wanted* to weaken the Israeli clients sufficiently to induce them to pursue a lasting peace with their Arab neighbors has the ring of justification after the fact, but it did conform with the generally ruthless—and often self-defeating—realpolitik that the secretary loved to practice. Certainly, he had no desire to see Egypt utterly crushed militarily by the Israelis. In fact, both the Soviets and the Americans were saved by the United Nations, which in Resolution 340 called for an immediate cease-fire and a return to the status quo ante.

The Soviet Navy tried to defeat its Sixth Fleet rival through intimidation—and failed. Throughout the crisis the Americans coolly performed the essential mission of guaranteeing shuttle flights of critically needed F-4s from the United States to Israel, as well as protecting the C-5As from possible Soviet sea-launched missiles. But the Soviets had come a very long way from the humiliation off Cuba little more than a decade before. Whether their surface missiles and submarines could have destroyed all three Sixth Fleet carriers and thus driven American sea power from the Mediterranean (however briefly) is a question without answers. Certainly, any such attempt, whether initiated deliberately or coming about through miscalculation or accident, would have brought about a general nuclear war. Undoubtedly, Gorshkov had ensured that his best ships, boats, and crews were stalking the American flattops off Crete. If Zumwalt is correct, the demands of Vietnam had, by 1973, substantially if not drastically reduced U.S. antisubmarine warfare capabilities. But as defense analyst Robert G. Weinland has written:

The United States would not permit the Soviets to determine the outcome of the conflict either indirectly, through resupply efforts, or directly
by deploying their ground forces into the combat area. The initiation of
U.S. sea and air lift operations conveyed the first of these messages to the
Soviets. The worldwide U.S. military alert [including the surge of the *JFK*
task force and the *Iwo Jima* assault group into the Mediterranean] called
Soviet attention to the actions that transmitted the second of these messages. When it called its alert, the United States also insured that it, rather
than the Soviets, had the superior military capability in the critical place
at the critical time: it reinforced the Sixth Fleet and concentrated it athwart
the Soviet's sea and air lines of communication to the Middle East making
Soviet intervention in the conflict, at best, potentially very costly, and at
worst, militarily infeasible. The Soviets got that message.[60]

Whether the United States did indeed project a "superior military capability
in the critical place at the critical time" may be questionable; that the Soviets
chose not to find out is incontestable. Gorshkov had written at one point that
his fleet was "an instrument . . . for deterring military adventures and firmly
counteracting threats to security from the imperialist states." One notable Russian analyst interpreted this to mean that "the Soviet Navy could be a deterrent
in crisis situations in various parts of the world."[61] In 1973 it carried out that
function, possibly saving its Egyptian client from total defeat at the hands of
the Israelis. But Gorshkov and his superiors went no further, clearly restrained
by American power, the tip of which was the Sixth Fleet. Even under the provocation of having their planes destroyed on Syrian airfields, the Soviets did not
intervene anywhere in the war anytime for any reason. The Sixth Fleet, as sorely
pressed in the peacetime tensions of the high cold war as the British fleet had
been in the wartime emergencies of World War II, kept the strategically critical
Mediterranean open for the exercise of American interests. That in the end is
what sea control—and sea power—is all about.
     Although the Soviet Navy had nearly achieved the power to obtain "local
command" in a crisis setting, the strategic—and geographic—cards were still
stacked heavily against it. Even in relative decline, the United States Navy remained a mighty force with long experience on, under, and over the world
ocean. And it could rely on the not insignificant sea power of its NATO allies,
more or less friendly neutrals like Sweden, and the eternal, brute realities of
geography to help keep the Soviet sea challenge barely within bounds. Fourteen
years after Marshall Plan aid, a dozen years after the formation of NATO,
Western European naval power had grown substantially. France (with two new

fleet carriers in commission) and Britain could field moderately powerful carrier task forces, and their submarine flotillas were growing in size. Both nations were dedicated to building several nuclear-powered subs. Italy was moving quickly to construct a small fleet of guided-missile cruisers and destroyers. In times of crisis, these three nations stood ready under the NATO banner to provide the U.S. Navy with substantial assistance. But it was neutral Sweden and NATO member Turkey, lying astride key choke points in the Baltic Sea and the Sea of Mamara/Dardanelles, that held the real keys to suppressing Soviet sea power. By 1962 Sweden deployed not only a small but modern and powerful cruiser-destroyer force but also a dozen relatively new, Schnorkel-equipped submarines, almost exactly the size and dimensions of the Class VII World War II Nazi U-boats. Turkey possessed no fewer than ten former U.S. *Balao*-class fleet submarines built in 1944–1945.[62]

Nine years later, as the Soviet Navy surged out into the world ocean, Allied naval power had grown apace. Britain, no longer a significant surface navy, nonetheless deployed four nuclear-powered, sixteen-tube ballistic-missile submarines, together with eight other nuclear-powered boats. France, although no longer a part of NATO, was, despite frequent Gallic grumbling, still very much a part of the always fractious European community. In times of tension and crisis, Gorshkov and his American opposites knew where France would be. Three SSBNs were on the building ways; three more would soon follow. It mattered little if Moscow or Kiev was annihilated by French or British sea-based intercontinental ballistic missiles or those launched by the United States. The two French *Clemenceau*-class small fleet carriers capable of deploying fifty to sixty jet aircraft were still very much in service to make conventional—perhaps tactical nuclear—strikes against Soviet ground forces moving westward across the North German plain. They would be screened by a modest but reasonably up-to-date collection of cruisers and destroyers. Of equal importance was the new West German navy that could put no fewer than seventeen small hunter-killer submarines into the central and western reaches of the Baltic, close to or even within that sea's exit choke points. Italy continued to build up its guided-missile-cruiser flotilla in the Mediterranean, while also completing the first of several hunter-killer submarines. Sweden commissioned small hunter-killer submarines throughout the sixties, together with a few fast destroyers to go with its twenty-year-old light cruiser, while Turkey deployed its still capable ex-U.S. submarines.[63]

Taken together, these relatively small naval forces composed a layered defense in depth that Gorshkov could not ignore. In peacetime his Baltic and Black Sea Fleets would be under constant surveillance as they moved through the tight bottlenecks of the Dardanelles and Store Strait–Øresund to gain the broad sea spaces of the world ocean. In times of outright war, Turkish, Swedish, and West German surface and submarine forces might destroy or damage perhaps 10 to 30 percent of these fleets as they fought their way through, only to come in contact with the U.S. and British navies in or near the North Sea. Lack of standardization among NATO fleets was a common complaint a quarter century ago as the Soviet challenge reached its apex. One reason for the lack, of course, was the unwillingness of the Americans to share their advanced technologies, which became an obsession under President Reagan.[64] But even acting on their own with their own weaponry, the geography of the Baltic and Mamara-Dardanelles so favored Swedish, West German, and Turkish surface and sub-surface forces as to constitute in and of itself an enormous multiplier effect in favor of Western seapower.

Nonetheless, Gorshkov and his colleagues were able to successfully obscure serious flaws and weaknesses behind a flood of ships, planes, rockets, surveillance systems, and communication networks that seemed on the cutting edge of novelty and usefulness. Soviet submarine technology in the seventies and early eighties continued to advance dramatically. Both missile and attack boats attained a surprising degree of operational quietness, essential to effective deployment on the world ocean, whereas America's attack submarines, ghosting about off the coasts of the Soviet Union, found themselves detected with increasing frequency. Construction of major combatants continued. The Kremlin's decision in 1983–1984 to resume building heavy ships led to construction of the sixty-five thousand–ton supercarrier *Tbilsi*. This ship (renamed *Admiral Kuznetsov*) represented another quantum leap in Soviet naval technology. It entered service in 1989 well ahead of U.S. naval intelligence estimates.[65]

By the mideighties, strategic-missile submarines of the vastly improved *Delta* class appeared, together with the first of the huge *Typhoon*s, near battleship-size undersea craft with no fewer than twenty intercontinental ballistic-missile tubes. The Red Flag continued to find friendly anchorages everywhere from Port Said to Cam Ranh Bay. Fainter hearts in Washington, fixated on U.S.-Soviet détente, were intimidated. In 1978 President Carter and his people declined to send a carrier task force to the western Indian Ocean in support of Somalia, which had just thrown out Soviet advisers and closed down a strategic Soviet naval base adjacent to the Red Sea. When nearby Soviet client Ethiopia threatened the Somalis with invasion, the Carter administration decided that it "did not want to engage in 'a bluffing game'" with the Ethiopians that "would be perceived as a defeat for the United States" if the Soviet fleet suddenly appeared in force to back their African ally.[66]

A few individuals in the U.S. naval intelligence community suspected something sinister might be behind growing Soviet naval capabilities, especially in undersea warfare. But not until early 1985, when a woman named Barbara Walker reported to the FBI that her ex-husband, John, their son, John's brother, and a handful of other people had formed a Soviet spy ring, were suspicions corroborated. Since the late sixties John Walker, former submariner, watch officer at the U.S. Atlantic Fleet headquarters in Norfolk, and communication expert, had been passing to the Russians information on U.S. submarine technology, operating schedules, and communication lists that "had given America its priceless edge" over the rapidly expanding Soviet Navy. When a high-ranking KGB official defected in the summer of 1985, he told his American debriefers that the Walker spy ring "was the most important espionage victory in KGB history." It soon transpired that Soviet naval technology had also been immeasurably assisted by Norwegian and Japanese firms, including a Toshiba subsidiary that had surreptitiously sold the Russians large computer-guided milling machines that made smoother and quieter propeller blades.[67]

Still, despite these intelligence setbacks, Gorshkov and his sailors seemed poised to sustain the astonishing status they had won over the past decade and a half. The momentum of massive construction continued unabated. Yet within five years the Soviet fleet would begin a decline as swift and remarkable as its rise, while the revolutionary country that sustained it crashed in ruins.

CHAPTER 7

Reversals of Fortune

WHEN THOMAS HAYWARD became chief of naval operations five years after the U.S. withdrawal from Vietnam, he found the navy in "the worst condition . . . in my lifetime." Whereas the submarine force remained well supported and of high morale, the surface fleet was in disarray. To begin with, the ships were in increasingly poor material condition after years of wartime overwork. The navy had a C1–4 criterion for assessing vessel capability. C-1 was fully combat ready; C-2 acceptable; C-3 major deficiencies in people, parts, training, equipment, and ammunition but minimally capable of advanced operations; and C-4 wholly unready for such operations. In 1978 not one major surface combatant—not even the huge attack carriers—could be classified other than C-3 or C-4.

Hayward had commanded the Pacific Fleet before going to Washington. At the time, all of his attack carriers had one of their four fire rooms shut down, which meant the vessels were operating on just three screws, not four. One day, when *Kitty Hawk* was cruising off Guam a minor engineering casualty quickly cascaded into a major crisis. The engineering officer asked the captain for permission to in effect take over the ship. The captain agreed, and the engineering officer ordered the great carrier to "all stop." This was a disastrous decision, for seawater flowing through the main induction system stopped, causing steam pressure in the pipes to build dangerously. Before the problem could be corrected by getting the ship under way again (a time-consuming process), the main induction system failed, causing seawater still in the pipes to flood one of the three online fire rooms. *Kitty Hawk* limped on to Subic Bay and the repair facilities at Cubi Point. The ship's entire deployment was spent in the yard getting repaired. The same incident occurred on an Atlantic Fleet carrier in forward deployment to the Mediterranean. The problems, Hayward maintained, were due to personnel shortages and undertrained people forced to manage emergencies in which they made mistakes. The retention rate in those immediate post-Vietnam years was so abysmal that many chief petty officer billets were unfilled. Throughout the fleet at all levels below command, willing and eager but poorly trained junior people were forced to fill senior positions. They "tried hard and worked hard," Hayward recalled, "but there were not enough experienced leaders."[1]

"When we came out of Vietnam," the admiral added, "the Soviets were significantly better than we." Although the U.S. Navy struggled with a horrendous retention problem and "lots of small, worn-out ships," the Soviets "had modern ships, had developed over-the-horizon cruise missiles and they had a very competent submarine force" supported by long-range Bison, Bear, and Backfire long-range strike and surveillance aircraft.[2]

Half a year later, Ronald Reagan came to power determined to infuse the Pentagon with new energy and direction. He brought with him as secretary of the navy a young man named John Lehman, who shared his every view, and in Hayward a chief of naval operations already working in that direction. The Ethiopian-Somalia crisis of 1978 in which the Soviets had, for a brief time at least, gained practical control of the southern Red Sea because of Western naval weakness had stirred the Carter administration to begin a modest fleet-rebuilding program, and Hayward's immediate predecessor, James L. Holloway, had gotten the naval establishment to agree that enough was enough; it was time to regain superiority over Soviet sea power.[3]

Indeed, the crises of the seventies, the Vietnam failure, a declining fleet, and the rising Soviet challenge across the length and breadth of the world ocean, had stirred academics within and beyond the naval establishment, together with "OpNav" (the director of navy program planning) to seriously rethink naval strategy. What emerged were four basic concepts to guide current and future navy planning. First, classic dictums of sea power should be folded into a much broader, holistic concept of national maritime strength, embracing such "law of the sea" considerations as exclusive national economic zones, transit rights, the specific problems of huge oil tankers, antipollution regulations, and exploitation of the resources of the global water column and deep seabed. Second, strategy, whether devoted to land, air, or sea power, should thus "become more than merely a military concept." It should "tend" instead "toward the coordinated execution of statecraft." Third, no matter how regrettable or distasteful the thought might be, warfare itself should be considered an ongoing phenomenon of contemporary international life. The challenge for naval planners and theorists—as for their ground and air colleagues—was to understand the impact and dynamics of conventional warfare while examining "variations" in a possible nuclear war, from sharply limited exchanges of tactical nuclear weapons all the way to all-out thermonuclear warfare. Finally, as far as the navy was concerned, such thinking should be grounded in the simple objectives— first set forth in the midseventies by the department's civil and uniformed leadership—that the service must strive for superiority at sea against the Soviets, concentrating on a forward strategy to fulfill its mission goals and objectives.[4]

Hayward went several critical steps further when he became CNO in June 1978. Command of the Pacific Fleet had given him the first opportunity to significantly affect servicewide thinking and morale. He had no desire to develop an official new sea power doctrine; his successor, James D. Watkins, would do that. But he was determined to revive a demoralized service and revive its offensive mentality "even before the resources were available. You couldn't wait until everything was perfect." The navy had developed "a highly defensive mentality" since Vietnam. "We lacked confidence in ourselves."[5] The service badly needed a sense of direction and a revival of professionalism, in which future naval leaders "would be well-versed in the role of naval forces in national policy and strategy." At Pearl Harbor, Hayward had set his planners to work on a "Sea Strike Strategy" proposal that at once restated but modified Forrest Sherman's Maritime Doctrine of 1946–1947. Determined to rein in defense spending, the Carter administration insisted throughout its single term that any conceivable conflict with the Soviets would be confined to the Warsaw Pact–NATO front in central Europe. Naval forces would not have a substantial forward role to play in any such limited war beyond keeping the sea-lanes open between the Old World and the New. Hayward and his people rejected such thinking. The United States should play not the Russians' game but its own. The fifteen-carrier battle groups still in operation allowed it to do so. Sea power, imaginatively deployed, could play a major role not only by delivering strong flanking blows from the Norwegian and Mediterranean Seas against a Soviet surge through Germany and Austria but also by striking hard against important enemy strategic assets elsewhere. Assaults against southern Russia and even as far away as the Sea of Okhotsk against enemy ballistic-missile submarines and their nearby bases would force the Kremlin to deflect strong air and naval forces from the European front to peripheral areas, thus seriously diluting any European offensive.

Hayward's Sea Strike Strategy dovetailed with a "Seaplan 2000" exercise simultaneously under way at the Navy Department. Secretary Graham Claytor and Holloway got behind the two efforts, which really took off after Hayward went to Washington in June 1978 as Holloway's successor. Experience with the Pacific Fleet and the shocking state of overall service readiness and morale had already convinced Hayward that fiscal obsessions underlay much of the navy's problems. Since Zumwalt's time, the armed services had been budget driven. The White House developed funding levels, Congress provided what it thought it could, and the navy and its sister services fashioned force-level and mission responsibilities accordingly. This proved disastrous for the navy, as military spending in general grew only slowly through the inflation-plagued seventies, while more and more of the fleet became obsolete.

Hayward abandoned the fight for particular force levels, working instead for a highly ready, adequately manned service, letting Congress worry about how big that navy should be. Not surprisingly, given his experiences in the Pacific, Hayward emphasized funding for spare parts, ammunition, pay, and benefits. He then turned to questions of strategy, emphasizing that the central front in Europe was not the only problem for the United States. "The country needed a war-winning strategy." Hayward not only lobbied Congress vigorously on behalf of his ideas but also established a series of strategic studies and planning groups in the Pentagon. When Reagan came to the presidency, the navy was thus positioned to reconsider the whole question of American sea power in the nuclear age. Hayward soon drew the talents and prestige of the Naval War College into the planning exercise. He created a Center for Naval Warfare Studies at Newport and a CNO's Strategic Studies Group within his own Pentagon shop. "Our objective is to make this Naval War College respected around the globe as the residence of the finest maritime strategic logic of our time," Hayward explained. "A related objective is to provide the Chief of Naval Operations and our senior military officers with stimuli relative to strategy and tactics in order to make certain that regardless of the perception of those less informed, our Navy will never, never be found 'sailing backwards.'" Civilian experts and senior service people flocked to Newport, where they engaged in a series of yearlong academic studies all directed at one objective: the development, or in practical fact restatement, of a forward maritime strategy. Unlike Sherman's earlier forced-draft efforts, undertaken in part to justify the navy's very existence in the early cold war era, the strategic exercises initiated by Hayward and carried forward enthusiastically by his successor, James D. Watkins, were comparatively leisurely. Participants were given time to ponder, weigh, and consider. The emerging strategy was first circulated in draft, then in classified form. Not until early 1986 did Watkins reveal it and summarize its main ideas in an article in the *U.S. Naval Institute Proceedings.*[6]

In the meantime, however, the navy had to confront Congress yearly for funding, and thus its emerging maritime strategy was gradually revealed by Lehman and others during the early Reagan years. One of the most acute critics of the navy's insistence that it had a vital role to play in any war—conventional or nuclear—with the Soviets was the young Chicago academic John Mearsheimer, who closely monitored navy testimony in order to eventually refute it. Mearsheimer, and others, believed that "the Maritime Strategy is not coherent or complete, and does not provide an adequate rationale for increasing the size of the Navy." The sailors had defined their strategy "in different ways at different times," giving it "an amorphous and elastic quality," shifting "rhetorical emphasis" to suit an immediate purpose. Beyond deterring a direct attack on the homeland, Mearsheimer wrote, the "central military objective" of the United States "is to deter the Soviet Union from starting a European war." Nothing in the navy's maritime strategy suggested that sea power had a major, or even important, deterrent role.

Once war began, Mearsheimer continued, the navy would play an important defensive role by controlling the sea-lanes of communication (SLOCs) across the Atlantic. Navy spokesmen decisively rejected such a mission, which smacked of World War II convoy activity by small combatants (from corvettes to escort carriers) in favor of an aggressive forward strategy—"offensive sea control." The outline of this strategy, which might also be styled a "barrier and the bastion" approach, became clear during the first Reagan administration. In its modest form, U.S. nuclear-powered hunter-killer submarines and Allied surface antisubmarine forces (that is, carriers and destroyers) would form a barrier across the Greenland-Iceland-Norway gap, destroying any Soviet submarines "surging" out of their bases in the Kola Peninsula to cut the SLOCs between the New World and the Old. In the more aggressive form that the navy insisted was vital to any effort against the Soviet Union, "offensive sea control" would begin the moment Soviet forces began a central European war. U.S. nuclear-powered hunter-killer submarines would do the "surging," rushing northward to the Soviet naval bastion that composed the Northern Fleet, its bases on the Kola Peninsula, and the adjacent waters of the upper Norwegian and Barents Seas where lay the Russian strategic-missile submarines and their hunter-killer protectors. The U.S. hunter-killer subs would destroy their Soviet counterparts and in so doing achieve two objectives. First, their ballistic-missile submarines now bereft of much protection, the Soviets might abruptly end their aggression, fearing that if hostilities went nuclear much of their arsenal would be open to instant destruction. Second, if the war continued, the U.S. Navy could safely surge its carrier task forces toward the Soviet bastion and destroy the formidable surface units of the Soviet Navy, thus denying the Russians opportunity for an uncontested invasion of Norway and opening the way for a "direct naval impact" on the European front itself through the use of carrier air-power together with the new long-range Tomahawk land-attack cruise missiles (T-LAMs) just coming into service.[7]

The new Reagan-Lehman-Hayward maritime strategy thus focused on Europe, and later iterations included suggestions that sea power might be employed even more directly to relieve the pressure of a Russian assault against Western Europe: the Baltic or Black Sea might be forced and amphibious landings made behind Soviet lines, and long-range carrier aircraft could be employed against Soviet troop and armor concentrations on the front itself but also against Moscow and other key Soviet politico-military centers. Subsequent elaborations went even further, reviving Hayward's interest in broadening the naval reach to global proportions.

> Horizontal escalation . . . calls for the Navy to threaten Soviet vital interests *outside* of Europe—for instance, Soviet Third World allies such as Cuba or Vietnam, or Soviet naval bases in East Asia. The Soviets, it is assumed, are particularly vulnerable in the Third World or on their own periphery. When struck there, they would be forced either to draw units away from Europe or simply to make concessions in Europe because of the grave threat to these other areas.[8]

However expressed, however broad its reach, the new forward maritime strategy was sequential in nature, designed to fold Zumwalt's modest defensive sea-control doctrine into a broader restatement of global power projection. It replicated much of the thinking and conclusions that had gone into Sherman's 1946–1949 maritime strategy. But it depended—critically so—upon two new assumptions. The first—that no conflict with the Soviets would involve the immediate use of nuclear weapons and might be confined throughout to conventional warfare—was mercifully never put to the test. By the early 1980s, so the argument went, the stockpiles on both sides of the iron curtain were so immense that no rational human being would ever think of using them. "Limited nuclear war" had lost its meaning. Perhaps it had, but it might suddenly become appealing to the losing side in a future conventional conflict. Mearsheimer reflected this thinking when he suggested that the very act of destroying the Soviet hunter-killer subs protecting the ballistic-missile-submarine armada might induce the Kremlin leadership to go nuclear at once before their most precious strategic asset was itself destroyed. The second assumption, developed after years of dedicated intelligence gathering and analysis, was that for all its formidable blue-water *potential* and showmanship, Gorshkov's imposing fleet was essentially defensive in character. The first analyst to seriously argue the point was Robert W. Herrick, who wrote as early as 1968 that Gorshkov's strategy really differed little from the czars' in assuming an essentially defensive posture. This argument took many years to percolate up the naval chain of command and through the planning structure. But by the time Hayward reached the Pentagon, analysts detected a shift in Soviet naval strategy. If Gorshkov had ever truly dreamed of a true blue-water navy sailing the seven seas in a determined effort to dethrone American sea power, the effort had been abandoned in favor of a "withholding strategy"—a bastion philosophy, if you will—in which air and naval forces would concentrate on defending Soviet ballistic-missile submarines in "protected" waters near home, namely, in the upper Norwegian and Barents Seas and the Sea of Okhotsk. As Polmar observed in 1983, "the most significant point" about the postwar Soviet naval mission "has been and remains, the defense of the homeland, with the perimeter of that defense continuously expanding outward" as possibilities arose or events dictated. Central Intelligence Agency analysts generally shared Polmar's view. In a secret National Intelligence Estimate completed in March of that year, the agency concluded that the Kremlin's recent "ambitious naval construction" had yielded "larger ships with increased endurance and technologically advanced weapon and electronic systems" that allowed the Soviet fleet to engage in "sustained conventional combat and distant area deployments." Nonetheless, "within the Soviets' overall wartime strategy . . . the primary initial tasks of the Navy remain: To deploy and provide protection for ballistic missile submarines in preparation for and conduct of strategic and theater nuclear strikes. To defend the USSR and its allies from strikes by enemy ballistic missile submarines and aircraft carriers."[9]

We now know that the shrewd guesses indulged in by American analysts were being confirmed even as they wrote. From 1971 onward, U.S. spy submarines had managed to tap into Soviet communication cables, first in the Sea of Okhotsk, and much later in the Barents Sea off the main Soviet Northern Fleet base at Murmansk. In 1985, with the cold war having reheated to dangerous levels, the spy submarine *Parche* returned from its latest wiretapping mission with "the crown jewels." Recordings of critical Soviet naval communications since 1983 revealed that analyses about Soviet naval doctrine collected through human intelligence (that is, spies) in the late 1960s and throughout the seventies "had been dead wrong." Should an ultimate world crisis brew and general war appear imminent, the sole task of both the surface and subsurface elements of the Red fleet had now become the protection of the new *Delta*-class intercontinental ballistic-missile submarines as they launched their *second*-strike weapons against the West either from home waters or from the marginal ice zones of the Soviet Arctic (where Western hunter-killer attack subs found detection of the enemy extraordinarily difficult). The writings of Soviet military analysts and theorists—including Gorshkov himself—had always hinted at that fact.[10] But they had been sufficiently couched in and surrounded by a rhetoric suggesting forward deployment as to obscure the essential message in the minds of Western interpreters determined not to be responsible for another Pearl Harbor. For all his faults, Khrushchev had provided his sailors with the foundations of strategic force and doctrine by his grasp of the importance of both nuclear-powered and ballistic-missile-carrying submarines. Gorshkov and his Kremlin masters, however, were loath to risk their ships, aircraft, and submarines in major fleet engagements on the high seas far from home.[11]

Confirmation seemed to come—Lehman thought it did—with the arrest shortly after the Walker case broke of Ronald W. Pelton, a former cryptologist for the National Security Agency who had been passing information on the U.S. submarine spy missions to his Soviet masters. Rather than abandoning their "bastion" strategy once it had been revealed to the West, the Kremlin proceeded to confirm and continue it. According to Lehman, the "intelligence failures" revealed by the Walker and Pelton cases led to "unexpected benefits. . . . The Soviets shifted their naval strategy from one of challenging the West around the world by means of a 1,700 ship blue-water Navy to a defensive 'bastion strategy,' pulling back into the northern seas and under the polar ice cap to protect their missile subs." Lehman understood that Soviet strategy and doctrine presented him with the carte blanche he needed to embrace an aggressive forward maritime strategy should World War III materialize.[12]

A close reading of the 1983 CIA report suggests that perhaps Gorshkov did yearn for something more. The *"primary initial"* responsibility of the Red Fleet in a time of war would be defensive, Langley's analysts emphasized. But once Russia's submarines had launched their second-strike missiles, the Soviet Navy, or its presumably substantial remnants, might well be set free to pursue an offensive role.

Such caveats aside, if the analyses of the mid- and late Reagan years were right, the United States Navy could resume its role as a significant power projector, and Watkins's 1986 exposition of the new forward maritime strategy reflected a newly restored, indeed onrushing, confidence, within the service.

The admiral began with the observation that the world had been living since 1945 in an era of "violent peace," characterized by continuing and widespread local conflicts and crises, "mostly in the Third World, but often with global implications." In 1984 "millions of people were involved in more than 30 armed conflicts throughout the world." Since a key component of Kremlin strategy was to exploit Third World instability in order to turn it to Soviet advantage, frequently employing Cuban, North Korean, and Libyan "proxies," a "fundamental component of the nation's success in deterring war with the Soviet Union depends upon our ability to stabilize and control escalation in Third World crises." For this reason, the navy now maintained a continual presence not only in the traditional forward-deployment areas of the Mediterranean and western Pacific but in the Indian Ocean, Persian Gulf, and Caribbean as well. This "international setting" was enormously complicated by the steady proliferation of "modern high-technology weaponry in the Third World" and the emergence there of state-sponsored terrorism. Effective sea power was simply essential to achieving any sort of mastery over this turbulent global environment.

"The heart of our evolving Maritime Strategy," Watkins continued, "is crisis response" across the entire world chessboard. Between 1946 and 1982 American military forces had been employed no less than 250 times, and "naval forces constituted the principal element of our response in about 80% of the crises." But as the Soviet Union remained the locus of world instability and tension, a third world war could result at any time from its inability to control a crisis of its own making. Thus, the heart of American maritime strategy had to remain the defeat of Soviet surface, submarine, and naval air forces and the destruction of its submarine-based intercontinental-ballistic-missile force.

Watkins stated the new strategic realities clearly. Despite its striking achievements in blue-water power projection in the late sixties and seventies—Okean 70 and 75, the threat to the Sixth Fleet during the October 1973 Arab-Israeli war, the unchallenged control of the southern Red Sea at the time of the Ethiopian-Somali crisis as recently as 1978—Gorshkov was now bringing his fleet home. "While Soviet ground and air forces conduct a massive offensive" in Western Europe or, perhaps, even Northeast Asia, a critical Soviet Navy role in a future conflict would be to protect the Soviet homeland and their ballistic missile submarines which provide the Soviets with their ultimate strategic reserve. Consistent with its overall stress on the nuclear balance, Soviet doctrine gives high priority to locating and destroying Western sea-based nuclear assets, including aircraft carriers, ballistic missile submarines, and Tomahawk [missile]-equipped platforms.

Of course, the Soviets were particularly keen to knock out the American ballistic-missile submarines together with the ten similar boats deployed by France and the Royal Navy. But Gorshkov's people "lack the antisubmarine warfare capability to implement such a mission."

Under the forward–maritime strategy scenario, a limited East-West conflict would most likely develop out of a Soviet effort to "rectify" European borders in the Kremlin's favor. The limited and conventional nature of this thrust would probably guarantee a conventional response. Western navies would *not* rush pell-mell in a charge-of-the-light-brigade surge toward the Kola Peninsula and Soviet Northern Fleet bases. Rather, they would "seize the initiative as far forward as possible" not only in the Norwegian Sea adjacent to the German and Austrian fronts but in the Mediterranean, western Pacific, and Indian Oceans as well, countering the first enemy salvos, wearing down his sea forces, protecting sea lines of communication, and preparing for amphibious operations. "We must defeat Soviet maritime strength in all its dimensions including base support," Watkins emphasized. Such efforts would require defeat of Soviet submarine forces, tactical and even strategic carrier air strikes against Soviet ground facili-ties, antiair- and antimine-warfare, amphibious operations, and the like—in short, a total expenditure of modern sea power in all its many dimensions.

The objective of this furious activity would go far beyond defeat of the Soviet Navy. Amplifying Hayward's earlier thinking, Watkins argued that Amer-ican sea power, broadly exercised, would help "dilute" the enemy's limited Euro-pean offensive by diverting the attention of Soviet generals from their attacks against Austria and West Germany to countless other areas around the Soviet periphery where amphibious assaults and air attacks threatened the integrity of the homeland. As the Soviet offensive weakened and waned, American sub-marines and carrier airpower would step up the operational tempo, working in close cooperation and coordination with U.S. ground and strategic air forces to pound the enemy unmercifully (as was done in the case of Japan in the late spring and summer of 1945) in order to force enemy capitulation on whatever terms Western civil authorities deemed appropriate.[13]

Translated into practical terms, the main Soviet naval units would likely be found lurking either near their bases in the Murmansk area or in the adjacent Norwegian Sea as the first level of a formidable Soviet layered-defense system. Hundreds of ship- or airborne missiles launched by both sides would arc across blue-gray northern skies to crash with hideous effect upon flight decks, upper works, and hulls, killing scores of ships and thousands of sailors. Others would dive into frigid waters to become homing torpedoes circling in a restless search for enemy submarines until the faint signal was picked up and they raced in toward frantically maneuvering vessels whose crews realized that in all probability, their last moment had come. Soviet cruiser-carriers, rocket cruisers, missile destroyers, and land-based naval aircraft would perish, while Western attackers would pay a dear price but would not be driven from the seas. Freed from the menace of Soviet naval air and rocket attack, Western antisubmarine forces would then surge into the Barents Sea and Sea of Okhotsk to hunt down the last of the enemy ballistic-missile submarines that had escaped destruction by U.S. and NATO hunter-killer submarines.

While fleet units from the Pacific would threaten Soviet territory in the Far East and the Sixth Fleet would send aircraft and missiles against southern Russia, surviving American carrier task forces in the Atlantic Ocean and Norwegian Sea would race into the waters immediately adjacent to Western Europe where they would encounter the last formidable enemy defense layers. Fortunately, the Russians' best antiaircraft carrier submarines, the huge but characteristically trouble-prone *Oscar II* class (of which *Kursk,* launched in 1994, was one), did not appear in large numbers until after the Soviet Union had collapsed and Western navies had regained the edge in antisubmarine warfare. But before American carrier task forces in the North Sea and Mediterranean could begin launching air and missile strikes at the flanks of enemy ground columns advancing westward through Germany and Austria, they would have to contend with the formidable remnants of enemy airpower and its standoff weaponry.[14] In the climactic battles of a third world war, the safety of Allied naval forces would depend absolutely upon—and could be guaranteed by—a remarkable new fleet-defense system.

Whatever contribution Reagan's "Star Wars" program may have made to the collapse of the Soviet Union, the Aegis fleet ballistic missile defense system more than matched. Because for years it had fallen victim to other program imperatives, its appearance was abrupt and its success dramatic. Star Wars and Aegis each depended on highly advanced, incredibly rapid computers to track a multitude of enemy missiles or planes and destroy them with quick-launch, high-speed, deadly accurate defensive missiles. Unlike Star Wars, the Aegis system worked from the start, though skeptical senators and representatives grilled the navy hard on the question of platform stability and survivability. Along with the long-range T-LAMs that appeared in growing numbers in the fleet after the mideighties, the Aegis antiaircraft, antimissile umbrella was the United States Navy's ticket back into long-range-penetration modes of warfare.[15]

The centerpiece of the Aegis system was and is the "standard missile" (SM), an all-weather, ship-launched "robust area air defense missile" specifically designed to maintain a forward U.S. naval presence anywhere in the world, no matter how inhospitable or threatening. SM-1, "a single-stage, relatively short range" (fifteen to twenty miles) weapon, came into the fleet as early as 1970. The SM-2, "intended specifically for use aboard Aegis missile cruisers" and possessing "increased range, the addition of mid-course guidance and enhanced resistance to electronic countermeasures," became part of the navy's inventory eleven years later.

The SM-2 has been upgraded substantially since its introduction "to keep pace with the changing threat environment." The Block IIIA upgrade, introduced after the end of the cold war, was designed specifically against sea-skimming missile threats, whereas the IIIB upgrade adds "an infrared guidance mode to improve performance in a stressing electronic countermeasures environment," that is, to defeat enemy attempts to electronically jam the SM guidance system. Finally, the SM-3, introduced early in the millennium, is designed to counter ballistic-missile threats in near outer space. The missile contains a third-stage booster with a dual-pulse rocket motor to achieve low outer-space altitude "and a revolutionary Lightweight Exo-Atmospheric Projectile which is the kill mechanism for the final phase of the flight." The missile employs simple hit-to-kill technology, directly colliding with the target at a force equivalent to a ten-ton truck traveling at six hundred miles per hour, thus achieving ensured destruction by the sheer force of the collision. The first successful system test occurred in January 2002, and following two other successful intercepts in low outer space, the SM-3 was approved for production.[16]

Aegis was not only the essential ticket to a forward maritime strategy but also justification for the six hundred–ship navy, which was Lehman's dream. With Aegis missile cruisers and destroyers protecting them from enemy air attack, the fifteen-carrier task forces that Lehman fought for, Reagan authorized, and Congress reluctantly approved could theoretically rush right up to the Soviet doorstep to deliver devastating conventional and nuclear attacks.[17] Possessing newly developed T-LAM nuclear-tipped, cruise-missile strike capability, America's four revived battleships, together with numerous new Aegis-carrying *Ticonderoga* guided-missile cruisers, could roam the world ocean at will, projecting enormous force far beyond the traditional twenty-five-mile range of the battleships' sixteen-inch guns. Should all-out nuclear war come, the limited-war scenario would simply be ramped up accordingly.

Aegis thus lay at the heart of a sea-based challenge that the Soviet Union, beset by an eroding industrial base and increasingly restless populations at home, together with fractious "comrades" in neighboring states and an endless, debilitating war in Afghanistan, simply could not match. In the last months of 1986, the Gorbachev regime reversed forty years of Soviet policy, announcing that the Kremlin would no longer prepare for any sort of offensive war in the nuclear age, no matter what the rationale or provocation. Three years later the Soviet Union died under the weight of its long-accumulating political, moral, and industrial inadequacies, and with it ended the seventy-five-year era of total war and violent peace called the twentieth century. Once again, sea power, driven and defined by the latest products of an advanced technological and industrial society, helped determine the course of history, and the United States Navy was mistress of the world ocean once more.

Without a major enemy to fight, America swiftly turned away from its armed forces. The United States Navy, having come within half a dozen vessels of its six hundred–ship dream in the last years of the Reagan administration, began once again to decline, even as the Sixth and Seventh Fleets continued to carry out their mission responsibilities routinely.[18] But the long decades of dramatic East-West tension had obscured mounting turbulence in the "Third World" that had slowly, laboriously come into being in the fifties and sixties out of the wreckage of Western Europe's old imperial regimes. Throughout the cold war, Washington and Moscow had viewed these new nations and their peoples as mere pawns in the wider political-moral conflict between capitalism and communism. That was how the Vietnam and even Korea Wars had come to be, and it was what sent Soviet forces rushing into Afghanistan in 1980 to rescue a client government, only to run into bitter opposition and humiliating defeat.

Keener analysts in the United States sensed the possibility of disaster early on, but guessed neither its expression nor its dimensions. In the summer of 1959 political scientist and longtime government adviser Robert Strausz-Hupé wrote:

The issue now before mankind is the political unification of the globe. Two forces contest the future planetary order: Western democracy and Soviet-Chinese Communism.... With few exceptions the new nation-states of Asia and Africa are politically unstable and economically weak. Most of them are nation-states by international courtesy rather than ethnic or cultural homogeneity. In almost all of them, internal tensions, generated by racial and religious frictions, are being increased by population pressure. If massive forces are not brought to bear from outside, most of them will fall apart. The signs of dissolution are plainly visible. The fragments will be the bones of contention in tomorrow's conflicts.[19]

By the mid–cold war years, various Third World terrorist groups and a handful of allies in the West emerged to wage a new kind of low-intensity warfare against the international community. Dramatic airline hijacking escalated together with massacres at the Rome and Vienna airports. Western journalists and citizens living in the Middle East were kidnapped and either killed or held for long periods. In 1979 Ayatollah Khomeini's new radically religious regime in Iran complicated and confused matters by officially sanctioning mob action in Tehran that resulted in seizure of the U.S. embassy and forty-four hostages.

These events reflected an eruption of Islamic militancy that destabilized the entire Middle East–South Asian corridor. Washington's response to this largely unanticipated tide of unrest and terror was uncertain at best. While days stretched into weeks, then months, with the Iranian hostage crisis no nearer resolution, the Pentagon planned a special-forces rescue mission involving eight helicopters, designed for mine warfare, deployed from the supercarrier *Nimitz* in the Arabian Sea. These short-range craft would be supported by air force C-130 tanker-refueling planes flying out of Egypt. As the White House dithered, ambient temperatures in Tehran continued to rise, threatening the capability of the helicopters to execute the mission. Finally, in April 1980, President Carter authorized the mission. The result was disaster.

To the press, public, academic critics, and later historians, "Desert 1" represented the "absolute nadir of the U.S. military's self-confidence" in the post-Vietnam era: interservice coordination was poor, the mission commander knew little or nothing about transportation problems, and incompetence marked every level of planning and execution (no one, it was alleged, had studied the problem of desert flying, with its constant threat of local sandstorms). The botched operation reflected how demoralizing an experience Vietnam had been for all four services. By the time the rescue forces converged at their secret nighttime desert rendezvous point south of Tehran, three of the helicopters were unusable after running through sand-filled skies. Deciding to scrub the mission for lack of sufficient resources, the local commander allegedly ordered a panic withdrawal when it appeared the force had been spotted by local bedouins. In the resulting confusion, a fourth helicopter collided with one of the big air force refueling planes, and eight men died in the resulting fireball. A poll taken soon after the "abortive, farcical" mission revealed that only 25 percent of the respondents trusted the federal government to do what was right. Air force historian Richard P. Hallion subsequently asserted that Desert 1 was more destructive to America's military prestige than all the long years of the Southeast Asian conflict.[20]

In fact, Desert 1 failed not because of poor conception, planning, and incompetence, but because of heartbreakingly bad luck. CNO Hayward states that as the mission concept developed, interservice cooperation was "extraordinarily good" precisely because there was no joint command at the time. The air force, army, navy, and marines coordinated plans closely, working together to find suitable equipment that could meet the strenuous mission requirements, together with the best people to carry it out. Several months of dedicated training melded men and machines into tight teams. Aerographers and meteorologists studied satellite data and local weather history carefully and developed predictive models as to which areas of the Iranian desert were subject to sandstorms and which were not. Advance parties were dispatched to Iran surreptitiously to pick a suitable rendezvous site where the C-130s could refuel the helicopters before and after their dash into Tehran. Only after full consultation and careful consideration of all the factors in this intrinsically hazardous mission did the Joint Chiefs approach Carter as a group to recommend a "go." The president replied, "I hear you." Carter did not intervene thereafter, and the mission people were given carte blanche to execute matters as they saw fit.

When, despite all expectations, an unpredicted dust storm abruptly engulfed the navy helicopters flying low level at night, their pilots pushed on at greatly reduced speeds, reaching the landing zone far behind schedule to find the air force C-130s waiting and unaware of any difficulties. A handful of bedouins who had somehow stumbled onto the remote site were being held until the mission was completed. Landing without incident, three of the eight helos scheduled to fly on to Tehran with the special-forces rescue personnel were determined to be unreliable because of heavy dust damage. This sudden crisis required a change in tanker-refueling assignments, and while seeking to "marry up" with its new C-130, one of the helicopters rising aloft collided with one of the tankers on the ground and the fireball killed eight men. Seeing his mission collapsing amid a cascade of calamities—the bedouins, the unexpected dust storm, and now the fearful accident—the commander wisely aborted before disaster became outright catastrophe. Unfortunately, the flaming wrecks of the C-130 and the helicopter had to be abandoned, and with them the horribly charred bodies of the eight Americans. The Iranian government was, of course, delighted, and within days it released gruesome pictures of officials poking their walking sticks through the burnt remains of the airmen, whose flight helmets could still be clearly identified. Three and a half years later, 241 marines sent ashore by President Reagan and the Sixth Fleet to separate warring elements in Beirut were assassinated by a car bomb as they slept in their barracks. Reagan promptly withdrew the remaining American expeditionary force. A decade after that, eighteen U.S. soldiers were killed and the corpse of one dragged through the streets of Mogadishu when President Clinton's order to find and kill or capture a local Somali warlord, Mohamed Farrah Aidid, went tragically awry. Clinton, too, withdrew from chaos. Thus, thrice in thirteen years because of ill-fortune, insufficient resources, poor planning, or a combination of all three, America's armed forces were deprived of or driven from their objectives in the increasingly volatile African–Middle East region. From Algeria to Palestine to the Philippines, terrorists determined to drive out Western "crusaders" and their clients took due note.[21]

Saddam Hussein's 1991 invasion of neighboring Kuwait provided America's armed forces with a badly needed opportunity to arrest declining reputations. It also gave a once great foreign sea service the same chance.

Forced to share theoretical parity with the United States as early as 1922 and true equality after 1936, Britain's Royal Navy saw itself dramatically eclipsed by its American cousins ten years later. "The year 1953 marked an even more sinister stage in Britain's naval decline, when the Soviet Union became possessor of the world's second largest navy."[22] After the Suez debacle of 1956, Britain sank rapidly into second-class military/naval status. A defense white paper early the following year reduced the army to 1937 levels and the RAF to a small tactical-nuclear strike and defense force. The navy would retain just a few carriers and would reduce its commerce-protection forces.[23] The last of Britain's battleships soon disappeared. The four remaining *King George V* class had been decommissioned in the early fifties; all went to the breakers in 1958. *Vanguard,* a truly splendid 44,500-ton vessel with yachtlike lines, eight fifteen-inch guns, and close to a thirty-knot sustained speed that came into commission in 1946 was retired. What remained in the late fifties to spearhead a "now streamlined Royal Navy" were three small fleet carriers, a commando carrier, two light carriers, fourteen cruisers, and roughly fifty destroyers. At the apex of this modest fleet

were two large carriers, *Eagle* and *Ark Royal,* laid down in the middle war years
but not completed for ten years thereafter. Their tonnage approximated the
American *Midway* class, but their air groups were not the size of those aboard
the *Essex.* By this time Soviet fleet tonnage was about twice that of the Royal
Navy.[24]

Despite increasing impoverishment the Royal Navy strove to play an important role in world affairs well into the sixties. During the 1958 crisis in Lebanon,
Britain provided a strong supporting presence to the Sixth Fleet in the Mediterranean, lessening the U.S. load and complicating the possibility of any real
or symbolic Soviet intervention. Nine years later, during the Six-Day War between Israel and the Arab bloc, London again sent a carrier task force into
the Mediterranean, while another task group built around the light fleet carrier *Hermes* maneuvered just south of Aden at the entrance to the Red Sea.
The Royal Navy thus provided crucial support to the Sixth Fleet on either
flank.[25]

British maritime technology also continued to flourish for a time. In the
decade following the war, the Royal Air Establishment developed the angled
carrier flight deck, steam catapult, and mirror landing system, which "transformed
carrier design and made practical the wholesale use of high-performance jet aircraft." But it was the American carriers, not the smaller British vessels, that
would benefit most from these advances. The cost of maintaining a technologically advanced sea service ultimately proved too much to bear for an England
that insisted on fulfilling its NATO air and ground commitments on a rapidly
declining financial base brought about in part by the fall of the empire.[26]

The crisis point was reached in 1965, when the Royal Navy and Air Force
fought each other as they had in the early and mid-1930s for chronically scarce
funds. It had now become clear to the Labour Government that if *any* national
presence could be maintained beyond Egypt it would have to be done so on the
most cost-effective basis. The RAF stressed that seventy-five new F-111 fighter
bombers to be purchased from the United States—a third of which would be
based on Singapore—constituted the only viable "solution to the conundrum
of how to remain East of Suez on a limited budget." The Royal Navy countered
with the proposal for two new fleet carriers, CVA-01 and -02, which though
not supercarriers in the American mode would nonetheless be capable of formidable power projection. The two ships were designed to carry thirty-six strike
and defensive aircraft plus eleven ASWs and miscellaneous support planes. The
RAF replied that its twenty-five land-based strike aircraft at Singapore would
equal the power that a CVA-01 would be able to provide on station. As Eric J.

Grove later observed, "The real point . . . was finance. The total cost of a carrier force was put at 1.4 billion pounds over the next decade. This was a comprehensive figure, including the ship's running and refitting costs and aircraft, as well as the extra escorts and auxiliaries that would be required specifically for strike carriers. Infrastructure costs, e.g. dockyards, were excluded." But a minimum force of fifty F-111s (only a dozen of which would be deployed east of Suez) "costed out" at roughly 280 million pounds. Evidently, RAF planners assumed, probably rightly, that as configured CVA-01 could mount only one or at most two squadrons of strike aircraft at any one time. Thus, British land-based airpower in the Far East would cost only about 40 percent of carrier power.[27]

The RAF not only won the battle but also the war. In the face of such devastating figures, the government promptly decreed an end to all future aircraft-carrier building. "The decision to abandon CVA-01," Grove has written, "was perhaps the most traumatic shock to the Royal Navy of the entire postwar period. The fleet carrier had been central to the Royal Navy's plans and self-image for the last quarter century." Now the Admiralty Board "decided that 1966 was the right time for a fundamental in-house review of British naval policy." By 1970 Whitehall had reduced the Royal Navy "to its lowest ever peacetime level commensurate with the abdication of a world-wide role and super-power status."[28] What was left of the fleet, including *Eagle* and *Ark Royal*, was brought back to home waters, where its future role would be to roam the northeast Atlantic, guarding the western approaches to Europe in partnership with the United States and the smaller navies of the North Atlantic Treaty Organization. A decade later *Eagle* had been scrapped, and *Ark Royal* was on its way out of service. England was racked by class conflict and an antimilitary, antinaval sentiment that manifested itself in formal and unofficial industrial strikes in the defense industries and virulent left-wing opposition to defense spending in and out of government. Somehow, despite frustrating delays and inadequate budgeting, Whitehall managed to maintain a modest "downbuilding" program designed to further transform the navy into a very limited regional strategic force (a handful of fleet ballistic-missile and attack submarines) with a modest antisubmarine and antiaircraft capability built around three small helicopter carriers with a contingent of half a dozen Harrier vertical and short takeoff and landing jets. But construction completion dates were continually pushed back, which forced the navy to retain even the most modest vessels in service long after their obsolescence had been reached. At one point only two minesweepers in the British arsenal were less than twenty years old. "Meanwhile, despite the changes of mind of the politicians and the shipyard workers which hold back the building programme, the men of the fleet have reached an advanced pitch of professional ability as new training ideas bear fruit." But "the resultant efficiency can only be impaired by a sag in morale as these splendidly prepared and competent young men find their families suffering from pay anomalies . . . while they reflect on the fact that the whole structure of the fleet depends not only upon governmental support but also on the industrial efficiency and willingness to work of their countrymen ashore."[29]

By 1980 the Royal Navy seemed finished as a major armed force, and the next year Margaret Thatcher apparently determined to scuttle the service once and for all. She announced plans to do away with the Royal Marines and most of the surface fleet, including the three small helicopter and Harrier jet carriers at last coming into commission. When the navy minister spoke out against the cuts, Mrs. Thatcher—fondly known to her many enemies as "Attila the Hen"— promptly sacked him and then abolished the office itself to ensure that there would be no further mutinies. Looking across the Atlantic from Washington, American officials concluded that the Royal Navy had been reduced to the status of a coast guard. They were wrong in one crucial aspect, for Mrs. Thatcher did maintain Britain's long-term commitment to a modest strategic-ballistic-missile-submarine capability embodied in four sixteen-tube *Resolution*-class boats that closely approximated the U.S. *Lafayette* and its thirty sisters.[30]

The 1982 Falklands war rescued the Royal Navy from oblivion as a surface force even as it emphasized the grave weaknesses that had crept into the service.[31] "The first sea lord could not have wished for a better 'show,'" the critic James Cable wrote acidly the following year. "From the information so far available, . . . the Royal Navy were only just able to meet the Argentine challenge and at crippling cost to the naval readiness of NATO," which still relied heavily on British antisubmarine expertise and equipment, embodied in the three new helicopter carriers; the older, about to be decommissioned *Hermes;* and their escorts. The Royal Navy devoted fully 40 percent of its major surface combatants to the South Atlantic war. Since it no longer possessed a significant amphibious warfare capability, and its logistic-support ships were few, the navy had to appropriate civilian cargo vessels and cruise ships, including the giant *Queen Elizabeth II,* and employ them as combat transports to bounce the Argentine invaders from the Falklands. Underway refueling and replenishment rigs likewise had to be borrowed from the civilian sector. The overall commander of the campaign, Sir John Fieldhouse, conducted the battle from a London suburb, and even Max Hastings, that most uncritical of British military and naval observers, admits that C3I was far from satisfactory, leading to much confusion and ignorance in conducting the land campaign. Cable wrote of "those absurd weeks" of preparation in which "the Ministry of Defence were simultaneously organizing the permanent reduction and the temporary expansion of the Navy."[32]

The Royal Navy's fleet air-defense system was abysmal, its carrier airborne early-warning system nonexistent. So ignorant were fleet commanders of the most basic principles of air defense in the electronic age that they chose invasion sites in Falklands Sound that were beneath bluffs and cliffs that in the event provided no real protection against air attacks but did prevent long-range radar detection of incoming Argentine fighter aircraft equipped with deadly Exocet missiles. Fortunately, Britain's first helicopter-Harrier carrier, *Invincible*, had not yet been sold to Australia as planned, and its last modestly sized light fleet carrier, *Hermes*—which had taken fifteen years to build (1944–1959) while naval authorities dithered over what to make of it—had not yet gone to the breaker's yards (it was ultimately sold to India and renamed *Viraat*). The invasion fleet thus enjoyed a modest degree of air protection, though never air superiority, from the twenty to twenty-five limited-capability Harrier "jump jets" aboard the two vessels. In fact, neither *Hermes* nor *Invincible* was capable of true power projection or even fleet defense. Each was essentially an antisubmarine support vessel. Britain's narrow margin of air superiority was sustained only by the Argentineans' persistent inability to find the two ships and the superb flying qualities of the Harrier pilots. Admiralty authorities had agreed even before the Falklands invasion began that if either carrier were lost, the entire operation would have to be abandoned.[33] Fortunately, the ships managed to avoid detection, though in the midst of battle on May 4, the loss of a destroyer (HMS *Sheffield*) and a Sea Harrier convinced task force commander "Sandy" Woodward that "a too aggressive use of the battle group was dangerous given its technical weaknesses," which included not only a lack of airborne radar coverage but also faulty fire-control computers, poor damage control, and broken-down defensive-missile systems.[34]

A careful review of the seventy-five-day campaign in the South Atlantic leads to the inescapable conclusion that an always gallant British military establishment—including the Royal Navy—fought a war of much too narrow margins against an Argentine enemy that was in general poorly equipped, poorly led, and poorly inspired.[35] The one exception to Argentine ineptitude was in the air. An internal U.S. Navy assessment of the South Atlantic war that fairly drips with disdain for Royal Navy capabilities concludes, "Despite severe limitations of the attacking Argentine forces and the few Exocet launched, British casualties were significant," four ships sunk, sixteen damaged. "This is both a tribute to

the Argentine attackers and acknowledgement of the limitations of the British"
aerial-defense systems that "lacked defense in depth," including deployment of
electronic warning aircraft. As British ground forces prepared for the final successful offensive against Port Stanley,

> Admiral Woodward later made it clear that he was becoming worried about
> the condition of his command as wear and tear took its toll and the oper-
> ations margins became even narrower... "only one-eighth of the [air de-
> fense] systems were available to us. If the opposition had found us then
> we'd have been in a very poor way." For him and his ships and aircraft, the
> [Argentine] surrender on June 14 "came none too soon."

The U.S. chief of naval operations at the time, Admiral Thomas Hayward,
confirmed this assessment to me twenty years later. As the Falklands campaign
reached its climax, "Britain was on the edge. One more loss" of a naval combat
or support vessel, "and Thatcher could not have sustained" the war. A hidden
factor was the "brand-new" and well-trained Argentine submarine force. If one
of its boats had managed to put a torpedo or two into the *Queen Elizabeth* or
another vessel, "that was it." But combat revealed a fatal flaw in the torpedo-
control software system, and the submarines never came into play.[36]

When the naval task force returned to England, Mrs. Thatcher publicly wept
over her "gallant boys," and the government announced plans to keep *Invincible*
and its two sisters, still in the building stage, in service, thereby preserving a
moderately powerful antisubmarine and quite limited maritime-strike capability. This proved enough to maintain, indeed strengthen, the Royal Navy's long
heritage. According to Peter Nailor, the "core fleet" (Admiral Peter Stafford's
characterization) of three small antisubmarine carriers and their destroyer escorts,
together with a number of attack as well as strategic-ballistic-missile submarines
and a significant countermine capability, was "a much tighter, leaner, profession"
in 1984 "than that which I first knew" shortly after World War II. "It works
much harder, is resolutely technical in its preoccupations, is altogether more
serious and capable and very responsible in its objectives and its style." A good
bit of sheer "fun" had gone out of service life, "but in terms of professional
standards and accomplishments, it is a much better navy, and it is full of men
and women, who are carefully trained, constantly exercised, and more than fully
occupied."[37]

The Royal Navy still had important roles and missions to carry out, not only
in the adjacent North and Norwegian Seas close to home but in the distant Persian Gulf as well. For all that it lay well "east of Suez," the gulf as a critical tanker

route between the Middle Eastern oil fields and Western Europe constituted a decided national interest. During the long, frightfully costly, and inconclusive Iran-Iraqi War of the 1980s, Britain launched Operation Armilla, maintaining a gulf patrol of three or four frigates or destroyers in part to protect British shipping interests (the U.S. Navy, of course, did the same thing) but in part also to provide a continuing national presence in the area. The Royal Navy was thus well positioned after Iraq's August 1990 invasion of Kuwait to enforce UN sanctions alongside their far more formidable American cousins. When such efforts failed, the international community turned to other means.

In one hundred hours of brilliantly conducted warfare following weeks of careful build-up and pressure, fifteen Western and Arab allies united to drive the world's fourth-largest army out of Kuwait in bloody, headlong flight. No fewer than six U.S. carrier task forces, two large helicopter assault ships, and two battleship surface-action groups were involved, together with an amphibious force poised to free Kuwait by a classic over-the-beach assault. It was the largest battle fleet deployed by the United States since 1945.[38] And it did comparatively little. All of Lehman's promises of a revived service apparently had turned to ashes.

Any and every consideration of the first Gulf War must begin by noting the uncertainty that Hussein wrought by his sudden, unexpected lunge into neighboring Kuwait. The commander of all ground forces in the Gulf War, U.S. Lieutenant General John Yeosock, later recalled the first week in August 1990 when Defense Secretary Dick Cheney and others met with the Saudi leadership "to reach a basic agreement on victory objectives." To American military and political leaders, the "truth . . . *clearly* was" that the United States and its Mideast and Western allies had to pursue a policy of dual containment of both Iraq and Iran. Saddam would have to be bounced out of Kuwait, but thereafter matters were very unclear. There were "no documents exchanged, no memoranda of understanding, no codified alliances, no agreements, no nothing, other than a message conveyed by Secretary Cheney from President Bush that said, in essence, 'We will come if you ask, we will leave when you tell us.' That was the extent of the agreement." And, Yeosock added, the Saudis, not the Americans, "were the glue" that held a very fragile Arab-Western coalition together.[39] Within this broad framework, the four main field commanders under General H. Norman Schwarzkopf (Yeosock; General Walter E. Boomer, head of the Marine Corps forces in the gulf; Admiral Stanley R. Arthur, head of naval forces; and air force general Charles A. Horner, who commanded U.S. and allied air assets before and during the conflict) had to define what turned out to be a very confused "back of the envelope" command-and-control structure. And "if you think the top commanders were confused by the lack of guidance and information," a subordinate later said, "you should have been a division commander...sitting there trying to figure things out."

Horner later told a conference on the war that "the one thing you need to understand if you're going to understand Desert Storm" as the enormous—if sharply limited—victory it turned out to be was "the relationship of the four people at this table—Arthur, Boomer, Yeosock, and me." If Horner is to be believed, the men worked in nearly perfect harmony throughout the entire Desert "Shield/Storm" operations. Such a premium on personalities inevitably meant that one would dominate. Horner quickly assumed control because he thoroughly understood and was far better positioned to exploit the joint war-making doctrines and legislation at his disposal than Admiral Arthur, whose predecessor had remained at sea and thus failed to influence any of the early planning decisions made at command headquarters in Riyadh. Upon assuming command, Arthur did come ashore, but as he emphasized in the postwar conference, his major concern was in being a good and loyal staff man who properly worried more about his navy's inability to counter enemy oil spills and sea mines in the upper gulf than in its comparative role in winning the war. Iraqi mines not only damaged the guided-missile cruiser *Princeton* and the amphibious-assault ship *Tripoli* but also prevented an amphibious assault against Iraqi forces in Kuwait. "It is true," retired admiral and Joint Chiefs chairman William Crowe later wrote, that "our feinting and maneuvering off the coast caused the Iraqis problems, and the value of the deception was, of course, emphasized in postmortems. The fact is, however, that we would have liked to have the option of mounting an amphibious assault, but the mine danger was too serious."[40]

The sailors' disillusion with Desert Shield–Desert Storm began as soon as Saddam's troops flooded over Kuwait and threatened Saudi Arabia. If the Iraqis should lunge into the northern Saudi oil fields, Crowe told a television reporter, "There's not much the U.S. Navy can do. We'd have to get land-based air power into Saudi Arabia." That was precisely what the Bush administration did. A massive airlift of C-5 and C-141 cargo aircraft, together with several chartered DC-10 passenger jets, began delivering troops and supplies to northern Saudi airfields as soon as the frightened government in Riyadh asked for help. Air force F-15s, F-16s, and F-117s promptly deployed from the United States, refueling in air many times along the way to the Middle East. "Airlift proved critical, for it was the only rapid mobility tool that could deliver significant combat strength at long ranges within hours; sealift, while capable of carrying more, would obviously take weeks if not months."[41] The navy's traditional rapid-response capabilities apparently had been at last overtaken by advanced aviation technologies.

Others were not so quick to hail the end of sea power, or at least air-sea operations. After the war, allied field commander General Norman Schwarzkopf noted that once Saddam invaded Kuwait, the United States Navy was, in fact, first on the scene with both surface and airpower. Schwarzkopf believed that without the presence of a few navy carriers in the northern Arabian Sea and southern Persian Gulf Saddam might well have been tempted to add the Saudis to his list of captives. As for the continuing importance of sea control, Schwarz-kopf described Desert Shield as "the quickest and largest military sealift buildup since World War II, an 8,000 mile, 250-ship haze-grey bridge, one ship every 50 miles from the shores of the United States to the shores of Saudi Arabia." This bridge ultimately delivered more than nine million tons of essential fuel and equipment to UN forces waiting to pounce on Iraq.[42]

But once Desert Storm broke on January 17, 1991, the United States Navy—with one major exception—was relegated to a subordinate role. During the monthlong air war that destroyed Iraq's production, communication, and trans-portation infrastructures, carrier pilots found themselves jostled and shuffled in the midst of a campaign dominated by land-based fighter and bomber aircraft. What air force zealots like Stuart Symington and Frank Armstrong had been unable to accomplish in the late forties was achieved nearly a half century later by a piece of American legislation and the Saudis' provision of a network of sophisticated airfields. The Gulf War seemed to prove that all things being equal, late-twentieth-century land-based airpower had at last become superior to that which could be projected from the sea.

Saudi air bases allowed the United States and allied air forces to deploy far more and more varied strike aircraft than could be launched from the decks of the six available carriers. According to one source, more than 1,400 allied land-based aircraft of all types participated in the gulf air war versus 445 U.S. Navy aircraft. Moreover, the land-based aircraft were inevitably better and stronger planes. Because they are compelled to operate from small decks and endure the shock of catapult launches and mechanically arrested landings, contemporary carrier aircraft lack both the range and the payload of their land-based sisters. Throughout most of Desert Shield–Desert Storm the six carriers remained either in the Red or northern Arabian Sea or in the southern gulf. As a consequence, they had to rely on refueling from air force tanker aircraft to reach and remain on assigned patrol or attack stations.

Worse still for the Navy, it entered the Gulf War having failed to replace its Vietnam-era strike aircraft, the A-6 Intruder; it also lacked stealthy aircraft like the Air Force's F-117A, and had but a fraction of the kind of Air Force heavy and precision-guided ordnance that proved indispensable to destroying such key Iraqi targets as telecommunications centers in urban areas and hardened aircraft shelters and ammunition bunkers.[43]

According to one authoritative account, the best that the navy could offer in terms of contribution to the air war in the Persian Gulf was 35 percent of the power-projection missions flown, which perfectly reflected the 35 percent over-all contribution in terms of sheer numbers that the six carriers provided with their 445 planes. Other evaluators, however, placed the navy contribution much lower. One writer estimated that carrier-based air forces provided only 16 percent of the sorties during Desert Shield and Desert Storm, dropping 15 percent of the bombs, and accounting for just 8 percent of Iraqi aircraft downed. All analysts identified several inherent problems in carrier operations that inevitably reduced the navy's contribution. Carrier magazines simply could not hold either the amount or the variety of ordnance that could be stowed at air bases ashore, thus "Navy carrier deck loads were not optimized for the tasking that developed during the course of the Gulf War." Moreover, average daily carrier strike sorties were not as high as prewar predictions, and the unwillingness of the navy to move any carriers permanently into the lower gulf until the eve of battle meant that naval aircraft had to rely heavily on air force refueling planes to carry out their missions. This was especially true of the two carriers that remained in the Red Sea area throughout the conflict.

Although some sailors disputed the assertion, the navy was plainly unwilling to risk its carriers in upper-gulf operations until the last moment for a number of compelling reasons. The brown waters off Kuwait were considered a possible death trap for huge "super" carriers. They provided only the most restricted sea room, and their shallowness made them very minable. When *Tripoli* and *Princeton* were mined almost simultaneously, the carrier people took due notice. Wind patterns required high launch and recovery speeds, but the warmth of the waters resulted in high condenser injection temperatures that limited top speeds. Most important, hostile land areas were but minutes away, which meant a frightening lack of both "battle depth" and attack warning time.[44]

The limitations of sea-air power in an enclosed and shallow space were exacerbated by the Goldwater-Nichols military reform act of 1986 under whose provisions the Gulf War was fought. The genesis of the legislation lay in the suicide-bombing deaths of the U.S. Marines in their Beirut barracks on October 23, 1983, which revealed a shoddy and confusing command structure. "Jointness" in military operations had been a long-sought goal of the army and air force. Neither service had completely given up on the campaign for an ever more unified command structure both in the Pentagon and in the field. A major step in this direction had been taken in 1958 with amendments to the basic 1947 National Security Act, essentially requiring that naval-, air-, and military-force levels be justified on the basis of regional-command needs. The practical result, as far as the navy was concerned, was to take overall command and control out of the hands of the chief of naval operations and place them with regional commanders. Goldwater-Nichols took matters one or two steps further. According to one account, it was Lehman himself who soon after the Beirut disaster approached Barry Goldwater, the "conscience of the Republican Party" and soon to be chairman of the Senate Armed Forces Committee, with demands for a drastic reform of the national-security command structure. The crusty air force veteran agreed, but he detested Lehman for his pushy behavior and pork-barrel tactics in fighting for a six hundred–ship navy. Goldwater's legislation on Pentagon reorganization could be and was interpreted as subordinating naval airpower to that of the air force.[45]

In the Gulf War, for the first time since 1945, all U.S. air power was under a single "joint-force air-component commander," or JFACC. As JFACC, General Horner was in charge of all airspace in the combat theater. He exercised tactical control over every sortie made available by the various air force components under his command, including tanker-refueling operations and defense-suppression activities. Horner coordinated with the various components "and then put out the air tasking order that ratified the fruits of that coordination."[46]

By 1991 the air force was much better positioned than the navy to exploit the JFACC system. The service was well into an agonizing but highly fruitful reappraisal of its roles and missions after a prolonged period of post-Vietnam malaise. Air force theorists and strategists were in the process of at last abandoning the increasingly dubious distinction between tactical and strategic airpower in favor of a more holistic approach in which the mission of the air force was defined as "defend[ing] the United States through control and exploitation of air and space." Although this prescription was "deceptively simple, the statement," according to one air force scholar, "captures the comprehensive nature of an *Air Force* approach to airpower."[47] The navy, mired in its own post-Vietnam problems, had never found a comparable vision for its own flyers and unlike the air force (and the tactical pilots of the marine air wing) suffered as badly in the Persian Gulf as in Korea and Vietnam from a confused and uncertain sense of mission roles and responsibilities.

According to Admiral Hayward, weaponry also played a major role in the subordination of naval and marine airpower. "Smart" weapons—laser-guided precision bombs—had first been used by the navy and air force during the latter stages of the Vietnam War, and in 1991 the air force had managed to retain the great majority of them. On their missions, navy and marine pilots were forced to rely "mostly" on old "iron" or "dumb" bombs, at least ten of which—often more—were required to hit a target. In a rapidly emerging age of pinpoint warfare and precision intelligence in which the battlefield was increasingly resembling an electronic game board, the old method of bombing was not only sloppy, it wasn't "sexy." The air force gained many media points with its televised (from the launching aircraft) images of smart bombs obliterating a target on the first go.[48] Once the ground war began on February 24, the navy's role was further reduced. Whereas bad weather hampered tactical air support, Marine Corps units ashore in the desert spearheaded coalition forces in easily punching through Iraq's main line of defense. Schwarzkopf used the marines aboard the amphibious vessels off Kuwait City as a threat to tie down the substantial Iraqi garrison inside the city. The astonishingly rapid pace of the ground offensive rendered their use unnecessary.

Thus, for a variety of reasons, the United States Navy played a decidedly subordinate role in America's one unambiguously triumphant if truncated military operation to date of the long post–World War II era. In only one area did naval technology prove outstanding. The T-LAMs deployed from the battleships *Missouri* and *Wisconsin,* as well as from a number of cruisers, destroyers, and submarines positioned all the way from the Persian Gulf through the Red Sea and around to the Eastern Mediterranean, proved a critical ingredient in the most important aerial strike operations of the war. Without risking a single pilot, the fleet units were able to hit targets "with reasonable accuracy hundreds of miles from the sea in heavily defended Baghdad," thus adding a major new dimension to the traditional naval mission of power projection ashore. The T-LAMs were far from superweapons; their penetrating power proved weak, which meant that many failed to utterly destroy their targets. "Moreover, the Iraqis were able to shoot down some of the missiles." But most of the successfully launched missiles did do significant damage.[49]

Although naval aircraft did make "a special contribution to the air campaign" by their assistance in destroying the enemy's integrated air-defense network, the great victory over Saddam did not *require* either naval air or amphibious support, despite the fact that the campaign was, or should have been, a classic example of power projection from the sea over the beaches of a coastal nation.[50] This was all the more galling since prior to Saddam's seizure of Kuwait, the gulf region had been considered primarily a U.S. Navy and Marine Corps responsibility.

Lesser navies with their inventories of small combatants did much better. Blue-water fleets by their very nature do not do well in confined sea spaces. This was, of course, a constant source of bedevilment to the Russians who, to reach the open world ocean from bases in the Baltic and Black Seas, had to cross and squeeze out of narrow waters, even in the Mediterranean, where they became vulnerable to mines; small, fast torpedo boats; sudden air attack; and equally sudden assaults by small but modern and nimble coastal-defense submarines built specifically for the purpose. High-seas fleets do not, as a rule, concentrate on these forms of close-in warfare, whereas coastal navies must. The United States Navy had to learn and relearn and re-relearn to counter mines in World War II, Korea, Vietnam, and the Persian Gulf in order to fully realize the potential of power projection *from* the sea. It was not surprising, therefore, that as Desert Shield took shape in the summer of 1990, some dozen of the best small navies from Latin America and Europe—including the Argentines, the Danes, the Dutch and Norwegians and Spaniards, and now, too, Britain's relatively impoverished Royal Navy—dispatched between fifty and sixty (the numbers vary according to source) frigates, destroyers, and patrol vessels to a multinational force dominated by the United States that imposed a crippling five-month-long preinvasion blockade ("maritime interception") on Iraq, effectively severing that country's critical economic lifeline from the sea. While the Royal Navy sent one of its three small Harrier jet-helicopter carriers and escorts to the eastern Mediterranean to bolster the Sixth Fleet, mine-countermeasure surface and air forces arrived in the gulf from England in September, impressing everyone with their well-organized, -trained, and -equipped personnel. Built of glass, reinforced plastic, and nonferrous material, the *Hunt*-class mine hunters possessed "extremely low magnetic signature and they were equipped with some of the most modern search gear in the world," with crews highly skilled in how to use it. When the two American warships were severely damaged by mines in the upper gulf, the U.S. Navy virtually withdrew from the area until the outbreak of hostilities. The British supply ship *Olna* proudly steamed in harm's way, however, operating farther north than any other replenishment vessel, serving the needs of the light units near the Kuwaiti-Iraqi coast.

On the eve of Desert Storm and during the one hundred hours of its eruption, British Lynx helicopters staging from Type 42 destroyers *Cardiff* and *Gloucester*, operating both alone and with U.S. forces, were instrumental in forcing Iraqi naval and amphibious units to either stay home or be destroyed at sea. The Lynx crews shot up small Iraqi counterinvasion forces, fast patrol boats, and landing craft. At one point they even attacked an enemy antiaircraft battery.[51]

However well its small allies performed, the blue-water, high-seas U.S. fleet emerged from the Gulf War with its image diminished rather than enhanced. And within weeks after perhaps the most ambiguous war it had ever fought the service found itself caught in perhaps the most embarrassing and divisive position it had ever been.

U.S. Chief of Naval Operations Arleigh Burke addresses a Naval Academy football rally, 1960. (U.S. Naval Historical Center, NH 54900)

The origins of power *from* the sea. Air Force brigadier general James H. Doolittle leads a flight of 16 B-25 medium bombers off the deck of the USS *Hornet* to bomb Tokyo, April 18, 1942. (U.S. Naval Historical Center, 80-G-41196)

Inchon, September 15, 1950. First Lieutenant Baldomero Lopez leads Third Platoon, Company A, First Battalion, Fifth Marines over the seawall on the north side of Red Beach as the second assault wave lands. Lopez was killed in action within a few minutes assaulting a North Korean bunker. (U.S. Naval Historical Center, NH 96876)

Jet fighters parked on the flight deck of the carrier *Philippine Sea* during a snowstorm off North Korea, November 1950. (U.S. Naval Historical Center, 80-G-439871)

Blowing up abandoned facilities and abandoned supplies at Hungnam, North Korea, on the last day of evacuation, December 24, 1950. (U.S. Naval Historical Center, 80-G-K11771)

Cruiser USS *St. Paul* firing the final salvo of the Korean War against Hungnam, July 26, 1953, the day before the armistice was signed. (U.S. Naval Historical Center, 80-G-625880)

F2H-2 "Banshee" jet photographed from a sister jet as it makes its landing approach to USS *Oriskany* somewhere off San Francisco, February 8, 1955. (U.S. Naval Historical Center, NH 97412)

Cruiser USS *Salem* as Sixth Fleet flagship in the Canal Della Guidecca, during a visit to Venice, August 1951. Note fancy decorations around the awning, which suggests it is rigged for visitors. (U.S. Naval Historical Center, 80-G-K-12025)

Another routine day at the office for the Sixth Fleet in the fifties. Piasecki HUP-2 "Retriever" of Helicopter Utility Squadron 2 lowers guard mail to the forward deck of the cruiser *Salem* during operations in the Mediterranean, April 29, 1957, while in the background the carrier USS *Lake Champlain* and a destroyer are being refueled from the oiler USS *Caloosahatchee*. (U.S. Naval Historical Center, NH 97609)

South China Sea, March 24, 1965. USS *Coral Sea* steams past the USS *Ranger* during the earliest days of the air campaign against North Vietnam. Aircraft on the *Ranger*'s deck include RA-5C Vigilantes and several F-4B Phantom II fighters. (U.S. Naval Historical Center, USN 1110187-C)

That same day, an A-4 jet is launched from USS *Coral Sea* to seek out targets in North Vietnam. (U.S. Naval Historical Center, USN 1111691a)

PCF-94 of Coastal Division 11 fires its 81-mm mortar on Vietcong positions in the Gulf of Thailand, March 1968. (U.S. Naval Historical Center, USN 1130655)

Strategic-ballistic-missile submarine USS *Sam Rayburn* at dockside, Newport News, Virginia, ca. 1964–1965. Note the sixteen open tubes for the Polaris intercontinental ballistic missiles. The hatch covers are colored and numbered billiard-ball style. (U.S. Naval Historical Center, K-29910)

Fourth Poseidon advanced submarine-launched intercontinental ballistic missile clears the water after launch from the USS *Daniel Boone* in the Atlantic, September 21, 1970. (U.S. Naval Historical Center, USN 1145251)

CHAPTER 8

Rocks and Shoals

THE U.S. NAVY that steamed home victorious in 1945 was an institution steeped in traditions, habits, and customs that had prevailed since the earliest days of Fighting Sail. It was a white man's preserve, a white man's culture; women and racial minorities were present only in sharply circumscribed numbers and importance. The white citizen sailors who had projected American power across the Atlantic, the Rhine, the Pacific, and, indeed, most of the world, were as proud of themselves, their country, and their service as were their officers. Many of the veterans, of course, had no idea that the war itself had created a revolution of expectations that at once transformed and expanded the very notion of democracy. The white male lock on power across the globe that sailors from Alabama and Mississippi, Massachusetts, Illinois, and Idaho continued to take for granted had been shaken to its roots and suddenly became morally questionable.

The enormous manpower required to defeat Nazi Germany and Japan gave black Americans a real chance for the first time to combat racism. In some ways, the navy took the longest strides, though with great reluctance. In the weeks immediately following Pearl Harbor, as the United States became a garrison state oriented toward war, "Secretary Knox continued to resist subtle pressure from the White House to change racial policy," either ignoring FDR's express wishes or responding "with predictions of disaster if the status quo were changed." Not even the heroics of Doris Miller, a steward's mate who had carried his dying battleship captain to safety at Pearl Harbor before manning a machine gun he had never fired before, could shake Knox's prejudice. Finally, in March 1942, the president "lost patience with Knox and told him that the Navy would have to accept black recruits in a proportion acceptable to the White House." The secretary and his sailors first agreed to accept African Americans as stevedores as well as stewards—still a comparatively menial, and in the case of the ammunition depot at Port Chicago, California, deadly task. But the service did bow to pressure, commissioning a handful of black officers ("the Golden Thirteen") and filling one small combatant, the destroyer-escort *Mason*, with an all African American crew, commanded, of course, by white officers. Moreover, the demands of almost incessant fleet action began to dissolve racial prejudices aboard many a warship. When fighting desperate, deadly night actions off the Solomons or keeping Japanese kamikazes from ripping into the ship, white sailors wanted all the support and firepower from shipmates they could get, no matter the color of their skin, or the fact that their primary duty was to serve officers dinner and make their beds. Finally, many white sailors realized how foolish segregation had become when they had to go war at sea while black sailors filled a disproportionate number of billets ashore, even as many other qualified and eager young blacks were never drafted or enlisted at all. Knox's sudden death in the spring of 1944 brought James Forrestal to the secretaryship, and this civil rights activist promptly ordered the integration of blacks into the navy mainstream. But the naval bureaucracy, much of it from the South, fought back bitterly. Rear Admiral Randall Jacobs, chief of the bureau of naval personnel, not only successfully demanded a 10 percent "minority" limit on "integrated" crews but also insisted that African American sailors not of the steward rank be assigned only to noncombatant support ships—fleet oilers, ammunition ships, and transports. Forrestal and his reformers apparently won some battles, however, for according to one account by the autumn of 1944 some five hundred black seamen were serving as radiomen and gunner's mates on twenty-five combat ships.[1]

On July 26, 1948, President Truman at last ordered the complete desegregation of the armed forces. Executive Order 9981 told the national defense establishment to assume the moral imperative that civil society was as yet unwilling to embrace, to do what the civilian sector was as yet unwilling to do, namely, require white people to live with their fellow citizens of African, Latin, Asian, and Native descent on equal terms in an atmosphere of rigidly enforced equal rights. The armed forces were abruptly confronted with a revolution, one that in the navy's case, at any rate, would ultimately tax its very capability to wage effective war.

By the time I enlisted and went to sea in 1954, training ("boot") camp companies were fully integrated, as were ships and rates (though I never saw an Asian,

Hispanic, or Native American officer). I served on one vessel with a black second-class radarman and on another with a black second-class fire-control techni-cian. When a Louisiana white boy on my small auxiliary/combatant refused to "kiss that n . . . 's belly" during crossing-the-line shenanigans in 1956, he was ordered to go through the pollywog ordeal again and again until he did so. On the other hand, the ancient system of African American and Filipino mess stew-ards to serve the officers in the wardroom remained rigid, and on one occasion led to an experience that was embarrassing to me and humiliating to one African American sailor. A week or so before the crossing-the-line incident, I accompa-nied several officers ashore in Panama on official business, and when in early afternoon it was determined that the enlisted men's cafeteria at the naval base was closed, the officers ordered me to join them in their own mess and eat with them. What was meant as a kindness to me—at that time a brand-new third-class petty officer—swiftly turned into a gratuitous insult to the black first-class steward's mate who had to serve me as if I was his superior.

The navy proclaimed that bigotry and repression had no place within its ranks: one *could* be "black and navy." This was not so. As chief of naval operations, Admiral Elmo R. Zumwalt Jr. told his colleagues in 1972: "It is self-deception to think that the Navy is made up of some separate species of man—that Navy personnel come to us fresh from some other place than our world—that they came untainted by prejudices of the society which produced them. They do not."[2] And so although highly talented minority men and women quickly embraced careers in all the armed forces as the newest and perhaps best means of obtaining middle-class status and respectability in a white world, they still encountered all of the overt and subtle aspects of racism that continued to infect that world. White supremacy and racial segregation were ways of life in too many American towns and countrysides to die peacefully even under the lash of military discipline.

The strains of bigotry and desegregation could be more readily mitigated among airmen and soldiers who spent most of their time on large bases where opportunities (if nothing more than a long walk) existed to vent whatever frus-trations stemmed from unsavory prejudice. Close-order combat or the crisis involved in a long-range air mission forced each man to rely on his comrades, if only for the duration of the mission, thus reducing if not destroying racial antagonisms and stereotypes. But long deployments at sea, even on the biggest warships, provided little opportunity either for a change in personal contacts or for venting the anger and tensions that inevitably built up under the accumu-lating stress of constant air and sea operations. Aboard the carriers, only a tiny fraction of the ship's company could believe that it had any direct support role in the combat missions carried out by the air group, whereas the battleships, cruisers, and destroyers on the gun lines off Korea and Vietnam fired only sporadically at a usually unseen enemy. "Cruises" of six or seven months or longer aboard crowded, aging, overworked ships with stressed-out crews tending often faulty or obsolescent machinery in the midst of an interminable and apparently meaningless war inevitably abraded even the strongest nerves and left sailors prey to increasingly stormy emotions. When, in the sixties, the pace of revolution in American racial relations abruptly accelerated, often reluctantly enlisted sailors brought aboard ship with them all of the accumulating antagonisms and uncertainties that wracked civil life. The evil brew at last boiled over in the final Vietnam years.

Zumwalt saw the crisis coming and did what he could to mitigate it. He understood that with the antiwar movement at full tide and revolutions in race, dress, and style sweeping the civilian world, the navy would have to change. There was a widespread opinion among both the general public and the sailors, "having some basis in fact, that [the service] was a humorless, tradition-bound, starchy institution owned by and operated for the benefit of white males." But his efforts often shattered against entrenched interests and prejudices. The CNO's famous "Z-grams" — in effect, executive orders — were designed to reform service practices in four broad areas: loosening dress and grooming regulations and practices to conform more closely to the more informal standards of 1960s America; developing operational schedules, job-rotation systems, and homeporting facilities to reduce family separation, thereby encouraging a more stable and long-term enlisted pool; providing bright and ambitious enlisted men and officers with greater responsibilities and advancement opportunities, thereby increasing "job satisfaction"; and, most controversial, to make the service a truly color-blind "equal means equal" work and professional environment. Out of this dramatic blizzard of messages came a host of changes, including round-the-clock mess lines on aircraft carriers, beer machines in barracks ashore, permission for aviators to wear flight suits anywhere on shore bases, and authorization for enlisted men of all rates to stow civilian clothing aboard ship.[3]

Zumwalt was especially sensitive to African American complaints, concerns, and needs. He understood that many forms of racism are subtle and, however unintentional, devastate morale. One of his earliest directives, for example, ordered commissaries to stock African American cosmetics and music. Since it is a truism that dominant races and control groups often cannot understand the myriad forms of discrimination and degradation they impose on others,

Zumwalt's crusade was probably unintentionally condescending at certain times. But it was heartfelt and badly needed. The young American white sailors who in 1945 had insisted that the navy had to loosen up to survive at last found a spokesman twenty-five years later. It is a measure of American society that the reforms he imposed on race relations in the fleet and ashore alienated and embittered many wartime veterans, including those still on active duty.

Zumwalt's adjustments, derisively dismissed as "permissive" by his many critics in and out of uniform, came too late to prevent a number of ugly incidents in late 1972, as the long, futile Vietnam ordeal was at last coming to an end. Not surprisingly, the two most serious outbreaks occurred on Pacific Fleet aircraft carriers, and both reached the very edge of mutiny.

By this time, the entire American carrier fleet and its supporting cast of cruisers, destroyers, and support vessels had been run ragged by the unceasing demands and pressures of the cold war. Operations in Far Eastern and Mediterranean waters were always hyperintensive and conducted in a context of dread. As one veteran recalled, the ever present prospect of atomic or thermonuclear conflict with the Soviets "was never pretty. Air crews, intelligence personnel, and weapons people were all intimately involved, on a 24-hour basis when deployed. Security drills, loading drills, flight planning, and flight rehearsals were constant. In the early days, so too were the alerts, sitting in a loaded airplane on the flight deck awaiting a call to launch with a [nuclear] weapon rated at several kilotons or more." Cold war doctrine for carrier strikes against Soviet targets directed that the small propeller-driven Skyraiders of the fifties and the equally small jet-propelled Skyhawks who followed them a decade later were to proceed to heavily defended targets independently at low altitude, drop their single bomb load on a designated installation, "then return to a ship that might or might not be there." Pilots adopted a macabre motto: "One engine, one bomb, one target, one way." Off Lebanon in 1958, young Robert "Bud" McFarlane was appalled to discover that fleet operation orders designated the ancient, nuclear-armed Skyraiders aboard *Essex* as a contingency attack force against the Soviet Union. The bigger A-3 Skywarriors that deployed well into the Vietnam era "were expected to carry two weapons to two different targets and return." Vietnam's endless demands sucked in carriers from both the Pacific and Atlantic Fleets, whereas the Sixth Fleet in the Mediterranean was always on hair-trigger status as it sought to cope with both growing Soviet sea and airpower and recurring crises in the Middle East. Over the years Atlantic Fleet carriers like the *Saratoga* beat such a well-worn path to the Mediterranean and back that "a few individuals actually left their families in Europe and 'deployed' to the United

States instead of the more conventional other way round."[4] All too many families simply disintegrated under the relentless strain.

Early in 1972 a three-week inspection of *Forrestal,* then cruising in the eastern Mediterranean, uncovered grave racial and job-related tensions. Young John Lehman serving aboard *Saratoga,* then assigned temporary duty off Vietnam, recalled that no white officer would walk unescorted through the enlisted men's mess. In July fires were started aboard *Forrestal* and the Pacific Fleet carrier *Ranger.*[5]

Ironically, the violent rampages by several hundred black crewmen aboard *Kitty Hawk* in October, followed the next month by prolonged tumult on *Constellation* that climaxed in a dramatic sit-down strike on the North Island carrier pier by predominantly African American crewmen, were the result not only of escalating wartime and racial tensions but also of what officers, especially carrier pilots, interpreted as a positive change in fortune after seven frustrating years of operational limitations.[6] Nixon's determination to initiate unrestricted bombing of North Vietnam in reaction to Hanoi's 1972 Easter offensive against the South unleashed the Linebacker I (May–August 1972), Pocket Money (May 1972–January 1973), and Linebacker II (December 18–27, 1972) naval air campaigns that kept Seventh Fleet carrier crews operating full blast under inhuman strain in the spring storms and searing summer heat off Vietnam. *Kitty Hawk* was kept on the "bomb line" weeks past its scheduled rotation home, steaming, launching, and recovering, mind-numbing hour after hour and day after day.

Early in October the exhausted ship and crew were pulled off line for a hasty port call at Subic Bay. The squalid and often bizarre brothels and bars of Olongapo, teeming with people and blaring with noise, did nothing to calm nerves. By this stage of the war, Subic Bay's notorious "recreation area" was rigidly segregated between bars and brothels catering to white sailors, known as "the strip," and an identical area, known as "the jungle," catering to blacks. Drunken, stressed-out seamen, however, did mingle and mix waiting for and aboard the buses that brought them to and from their ships. At one point a nasty interracial brawl broke out. Tensions further escalated with news that because of damaging fires aboard *Forrestal* and *Ranger, Kitty Hawk* would definitely return to Yankee Station rather than heading home.

Early on the evening of October 12, back on Yankee Station off North Vietnam, the carrier's chief investigator summoned a black sailor to his office for questioning about the Olongapo brawl. The sailor came in with nine mates who, according to official sources, became "belligerent, loud, and used abusive language." They were not allowed to speak, and the sailor angrily refused to give testimony. All ten men, evidently seething in rage, were permitted to leave the compartment. Soon after, they and a growing number of disaffected mates began assaulting white crewmen in the big after-mess deck. As the mob swiftly grew to nearly two hundred (a sizable portion of the carrier's African American crewmen) the executive officer, himself black, called out the marine guard trained in riot control. In reaction the African American sailors, now crowded in the after-hangar bay, reached for heavy dogging wrenches, metal pipes, fire-extinguisher nozzles, and "tie-down" chains used to secure aircraft on the flight and hangar decks. Thereafter, the executive officer and *Kitty Hawk*'s white commanding officer tried, often at cross-purposes and amid growing confusion, to calm the disaffected sailors. Instead, the men began a rampage with their weapons, racing through below-deck berthing spaces, allegedly shouting, "Kill the son-of-a-bitch! Kill the white trash! Kill, kill, kill!" Others reportedly screamed, "They are killing our brothers!" Before it all ended, sleeping sailors were hauled out of their bunks to be beaten and punched, the executive officer thought for a time that the commanding officer had been killed, while "doctors and corpsmen working on the injured personnel" together with those waiting treatment were allegedly harassed by "another group of blacks." At last, about two in the morning, the disaffected seamen, excited but emotionally spent, congregated on the fo'c'sle where the executive officer managed to calm them and send them back to their quarters, "and for all intents and purposes violence aboard *Kitty Hawk* was over." In all, 26 black sailors were charged under the Uniform Code of Military Justice and received some sort of punishment. Forty-seven other sailors, "all but 6 or 7 of them white," were treated for injuries, 3 of whom required evacuation to medical facilities in the Philippines. "The ship fulfilled its combat mission" the following day "and for the remainder of her time on station, which included 177 days on the line in a single deployment, a record unmatched by any post-World War II aircraft carrier in a combat theater." A hastily convened congressional investigation concluded that the incident was provoked and sustained "by a very few men, most of whom were below-average mental capacity, most of whom had been aboard for less than one year, and all of whom were black." It was not a determination likely to sit well in the racially charged atmosphere of the time.

At the time of the riot aboard *Kitty Hawk,* its sister carrier, *Constellation,* was in San Diego, recently returned from Yankee Station and in the midst of a frenzied turnaround schedule, including a hasty dry docking followed by a fast-paced underway retraining schedule. The recent end of the draft had led to an abrupt

drop in navy enlistments, and Zumwalt, hoping to secure a more racially representative navy, had lowered both recruiting standards and basic training time
in order to staff the fleet with sufficient men of diverse racial background. Nine
hundred new recruits, many of them African American, came aboard the *"Con-
nie"* at just the moment during the yard period when the ship was the dirtiest,
most foul, and marginally habitable. The newcomers were naturally assigned
the poorest living quarters and the most menial, unpopular work. Aware of the
recent events on *Kitty Hawk,* some among the new men, joined by dissidents
already aboard, formed an angry faction to demand redress of what they characterized as racial slurs and oppression by the carrier's command structure.
Captain John D. Ward, anxious to get his ship back to sea, left the problem to
his executive officer and part-time minority affairs staff, who legitimated the rebellion by meeting with the protesters, who naturally escalated their demands
and eventually threatened a "bloodbath."

   Constellation was under a fast-paced working-up schedule that shuttled the
carrier rapidly back and forth between underway training and its pier at North
Island. Amid the confusion, Ward determined that his ship was 250 men over
complement and obtained permission to send that number ashore. A rumor
raced through the ship that the militants would be singled out, sent off, and
discharged as undesirables. In the resulting confusion of angry, threatening,
obscenity-laced meetings, a young black officer led 144 men, most of them
alleged militants (including 8 whites), off the ship and into barracks ashore.
Ward was immediately told to get the men back and solve the problem on board.
But when the protesters were bused back to the pier, they staged a sit-down
strike complete with clenched fists and inflammatory rhetoric in front of hastily
gathered press and media representatives.

   The entire navy was humiliated by this public display that, without stretching
the truth too far, could be construed as a mutiny, since the carrier was scheduled to depart on its next battle cruise at an early date. As the service command
structure from Ward to Zumwalt struggled to defuse the crisis, President Nixon
and National Security Adviser Henry Kissinger reacted with outrage to the
press stories and television images coming out of San Diego. Nixon, himself a
World War II navy veteran, called his chief of staff, H. R. "Bob" Haldeman at
home, "furious by a navy episode where Zumwalt had heralded on the blacks
that refused to sail on the *Constellation.* He's told Henry to have all the men
court-martialed and give them dishonorable discharges. Zumwalt instead gave
them active shore stations with Coca-Colas and ice cream."[7]

The CNO was able to turn presidential rage to his advantage, since immediate courts-martial would have violated military due process. Careful investigations of the incidents aboard both *Kitty Hawk* and *Constellation* led to the
trial and dishonorable discharge of a handful of militants and far lesser punishment for other participants, and the incidents were closed. But the image of
angry sailors brawling on *Kitty Hawk* and raising clenched-fist salutes of defiance
on the dock next to *Constellation* were the most dramatic reflections of a service
frightfully close to becoming out of touch with its own soul.

The practical end of U.S. naval operations in and off Vietnam the following
year gave sorely stressed sailors, captains, and admirals time to catch their breaths
and rethink their social as well as maritime mission responsibilities. Over the
following decade and more as America's sailors confronted their Soviet adversary around the world ocean, race relations smoothed out, and rancor was
replaced by wary trust and even fragile comradeship. Mutual suspicion and
lingering dislike, however, lurked just below daily life ashore and at sea. Vietnam cast many a long shadow, and none longer than the complicated issue of
gender relations that burst forth in the Tailhook scandal of 1991.

To its many bitter critics, "Tailhook" was a disaster waiting to happen. Since
at least the Reagan-Lehman buildup of 1981–1985, they charged, the United
States Navy had gotten completely out of control. A persistently bloated postwar officer corps whose flawed promotion system rewarded blind loyalty to
service above country had produced captains and admirals who were cynical,
secretive, manipulative, deceitful, sexist, and racist. Lehman's hasty, forced-draft
rebuilding of the service was based upon highly questionable assumptions both
about the pertinence and safety of equipment and the quality of the men—
and, increasingly, the women—behind it. Accident-prone sailors behaved in
unprofessional and even disgraceful fashion. The unnecessary—and unneces-
sarily prolonged—invasion of Grenada in 1983, the scandals involving the
destruction of an Iranian airliner by missiles from the cruiser *Vincennes* and the
explosion inside a sixteen-inch-gun turret aboard battleship *Iowa* were offered
as incontrovertible evidence, as was the case of the rogue naval aviators (one of
whom was such a rabid sexist that he circulated obscene poetry about his own
wife) who in 1986 tried to lure Iran into a sea-air war.[8]

If the officer corps seemed riddled with incompetents, the enlisted ranks were
apparently no better. The tensions and violence aboard the Sixth and Seventh
Fleet carriers in the early seventies could be traced in part to disastrous experi-
ments in social engineering not only by Zumwalt but also by earlier Defense

Secretary Robert McNamara, whose "Project 100,000" deliberately introduced
one hundred thousand less qualified recruits to all three services. Then, according to one recent critic, for a period of approximately four years in the early
eighties, the armed forces deliberately dumbed down (that is, "misgraded")
their vocational aptitude battery tests that profiled all incoming recruits. "The
result was that a pool of underqualified enlistees much larger than McNamara's
Project 100,000 was accessed into the enlisted ranks. One in four of these
enlistees was not qualified for the military occupation specialty assigned" them.
"When Congress discovered this fact, it requested that a study be done—the
Joint Job Performance Military Project. All of the services' studies concluded
that recruit quality matters: lower-aptitude recruits start out slower, take longer
to train, and never catch up to higher-aptitude recruits."[9]

Taken together, these incidents and developments reflected a service stressed
since midcentury to the breaking point by frequent crises, often meaningless
and always tension-filled missions, occasionally questionable if not criminal
military and diplomatic policies, interservice rivalries, congressional microman-
agement, steadily advancing technologies that demanded ever more sophisticated
skills to operate, and, most important, the growing insistence of an imperfect
society that its armed forces assume the burden of cutting-edge reforms in
racial, ethnic, and sexual politics. If the critics were to be believed, the United
States Navy had become a virtual mirror image of its Soviet antagonist.

The Tailhook investigation was as flawed as that concerning the explosion
aboard *Iowa*. Navy and Defense Department inspectors granted immunity
from prosecution to those male aviators whose lewd conduct (including streak-
ing and exposure) was the most egregious. At the same time, they scrupulously
refused to consider possible misconduct by female aviators and other women
"guests." That numerous women—most but not all of whom were active-duty
naval flyers—were physically mauled and sexually molested by a group of half-
or completely drunk male pilots at the annual convention of a quasi-official
organization devoted to the promotion of carrier air is incontestable. The Tailhook Association had been meeting annually for years, and earlier conventions
had been lewd and rowdy enough. But the president of Tailhook at the time of
the 1991 incident, Captain Frederic G. Ludwig Jr., ignited a crisis when he
freely admitted that in terms of gross and blatantly unprofessional conduct,
"Tailhook '91 was the 'Mother of all Hooks.'" Numerous hospitality suites in
the Las Vegas hotel became cockpits of wild drinking and loutish behavior that
culminated in a long "gauntlet" on the third floor through which women officers
were forced to run or crawl while being verbally and physically abused (includ-

ing having drinks thrown on them) and sexually degraded. Lieutenant Paula Coughlin, who first reported the incident, later told ABC News: "I went down that hallway where every man in that hallway got a shot at me. They knew I was an officer. They knew I was an admiral's aide. And I think that made the sport that much more rewarding." Whether some of the victims may have contributed to the obscenity by their own questionable behavior remains tantalizingly unclear.[10]

Tailhook was clearly a reflection of the ongoing cultural and gender wars that had rocked America's civil as well as military society for years; it was a case of the old navy warrior culture clashing with a New Age civilian culture. The bungled investigations generated a firestorm of anger, denial, soul-searching, and witch-hunting that shook the navy to its foundations and left scars that may never completely heal. Heated charges and countercharges of sexual harassment, racism, and favoritism in the service were carelessly thrown about that soon spread far beyond the Tailhook incident itself. Careers were destroyed, and basic trust in the service and one's shipmates and colleagues was badly compromised. After cursory consideration, President Bush abruptly fired Secretary of the Navy H. Lawrence Garrett III who found his thirty-year government career beginning as a enlisted man on the mess decks ending in disgrace ("It's as if someone had died," his wife confided to her diary). More than three hundred officers eventually left the service, including a chief of naval operations (Frank Kelso), thirteen other admirals, Coughlin herself, and Commander Robert Strumpf of the famed Blue Angels aerial acrobatics team.[11] New chief of naval operations Mike Boorda was eventually so caught up in the escalating and expanding tragedy over the nature and limits of service competence, loyalty, integrity, and conduct that he killed himself. As the century drew to a close, the navy's reputation with the general public remained low, and various advocacy groups for women, homosexuals, and other minorities, led by Minnesota senator David Durenberger, stood ready to pounce on any real or alleged shortcomings in naval conduct and discipline.

But all the finger-pointing at and within the navy over Tailhook begged many questions. Should military organizations be used as social laboratories or reform clubs? As Rudyard Kipling trenchantly remarked a century ago, "Single men in barracks don't grow into plaster saints." The same observation applies to those who live aboard and fly off of warships. Kipling's Tommy Adkins was rightly infuriated by hypocritical civilians who sent soldiers out to do society's dirty work, only to revile them for being dirty. "It's Tommy this, an' Tommy that, an' 'Tommy, 'ow's yer soul?' But it's 'Thin red line of 'eroes' when the drums begin to roll. . . . It's Tommy this, an' Tommy that, an' 'Chuck him out, the brute!' But it's 'Saviour of 'is country' when the guns begin to shoot."

The navy contained its share of primitives, though government social statistics would suggest that there were fewer than in civilian life. Certainly, the primitive kinds of wars the U.S. Navy and Marine Corps were asked to wage after midcentury brought such individuals to the fore. Tailhook was woven of three disparate strands: the All Volunteer Army that was forced into being with the end of the draft in 1972, the hypermacho attitudes developed as a coping mechanism by many Vietnam-era navy carrier pilots, and the writings of an influential government bureaucrat and popular novelist who eloquently proclaimed the virtues and defended the necessity of prejudice.

When Washington terminated the national draft near the end of the Vietnam War, the U.S. Army was forced to join the Navy, Air Force, and Marine Corps in recruiting an all-volunteer force. Competition for "bodies and smart people" in the antiwar atmosphere of the time forced all four armed forces not only to seek out unprecedented numbers of women but to open ever wider opportunities to them.

Women were first formally recruited into American naval and military ranks in World War I. Several thousand "yeomanettes" served largely in Washington as clerks, though the Royal Navy employed its "Wrens" in a variety of broader noncombatant tasks. World War II brought a dramatic increase in servicewomen and an equally dramatic expansion of their roles. In August 1945 the WAVES (women accepted for volunteer emergency service) totaled eighty-six thousand: pharmacists' mates, storekeepers, gunnery instructors, aerologists, and communication specialists. But unlike their army sisters, WAVES never served in combat theaters. A comparative handful of gallant navy nurses did, and some were captured (in the Philippines during the early stages of the war) and others killed aboard at least one brazenly attacked hospital ship. A vocal minority of GIs bitterly resented the presence of women at war, and especially any suggestion that they were making a significant contribution to the war effort. "I was disgusted when I opened the pages of a recent YANK and saw some silly female in GI clothes," a soldier wrote from New Zealand. "I detest WACs very thoroughly and I hope I never meet one. This is also the opinion of all my buddies." Another wrote from the New Hebrides urging an end to the "cock and bull and feminine propaganda . . . about some doll who has made the supreme sacrifice of giving up her lace-trimmed undies for ODs." The WACs he knew were not "overworked dears" driving trucks "or puttering around in a photo lab." Instead, they wrote about "the dances, picnics, swimming parties and bars" they attended. The postwar navy continued to recruit WAVES (and, of course, nurses) but until 1973 provided few opportunities to expand their role within the service. In that year, women constituted but 2 percent of the entire uniformed defense establishment. Twenty-four years later women composed 14 percent of the army, 17 percent of the air force, and 13 percent of the navy. The growing numbers of women in the military fueled demands by the women themselves and outside pressure and interest groups for greater and greater opportunities for females to serve in all military capacities, including combat. This unleashed a torrent of often confused and angry male reactions that masked some serious questions.[12]

It took many years and several scandals for thoughtful observers to realize that at the heart of the problem lay "something primal and sexual." For millennia, men had made war their special preserve, convincing themselves in the process that women loved warriors who would demonstrate their masculinity by protecting the ostensibly weaker sex. Now thousands of bright and ambitious young women were demonstrating by word and deed that they were no longer willing to conform to the wet-hankie-on-the-train-platform image that men had established for them. To many a proud male warrior, it seemed that the females in their midst were "trying to take war away from men."[13]

In the navy the growing numbers of women in more and more critical billets quickly ran afoul of the hypermachoism that carrier pilots had developed in Vietnam to cope with the constant terrors and tensions of combat in a no-win situation. The bad night in Las Vegas in 1991 was simply a replication of countless bad nights at "the zoo" at Cubi Point between 1965 and 1972 as they became hallowed in service memory, tradition, and folklore.

Military and especially naval aviation has always attracted daring and brutally competitive young men necessarily possessed of hair-trigger responses and often hair-trigger tempers to go with them. From the earliest days of World War II onward, army and navy flyers released the unbearable stresses of combat through drunken and half-drunken brawling. Between 1942 and 1945 the night streets of Honolulu were often disrupted by the sounds of bitter, well-attended fistfights between boozed-up combat pilots.[14] Twenty-five years later the ambiguous and violent war on the ground and in the skies over Vietnam would create its own unbearable tensions with the same inevitable result.

Flyers whose carriers sailed into Subic Bay for rest and recreation between 1965 and 1972 discovered that there were two officers' clubs, "but only one where the birdmen could flock together."[15] On the Subic Bay side "was a fine facility with formal dining, a nice dance floor—all the trappings. It was mainly patronized by the naval base personnel, refined individuals who pulled out their ladies' chairs when seating them, and generally behaved as Congress intended for officers and gentlemen." But real men from the world of aerial warfare disdained such civilized frippery. They were out to party and to revel, and they did at the nearby Cubi Point air station where another officers' club, aptly dubbed the zoo, allowed the flyers to be "pretty much on their own" as long as "the animals remained" confined within its premises.

The Cubi club quickly assumed the atmosphere of a third-rate bistro whose worn-out furniture was used to make piles of chairs and tables reaching to the ceiling. "There were food fights and fist fights. Pilots took the microphone from the Filipino singers and showed the local talent how it was done. The hoarse shouting that passed for singing among aviators had to be heard to be believed." The 0100 hours closing time was invariably ignored as the pilots and their Filipina dates drank and caroused until dawn, and if the manager insisted on making a formal closing announcement, "some tipsy aviator swayed on the stage announcing, 'No way, Jose. This joint closes when we leave.' On occasion that was the [carrier] air wing commander." If the navy's own officer of the day was foolish enough to attempt to enforce the closing ordinance, "he might find himself bound and gagged behind the bar. Not out of malevolence, you understand; merely in the interest of continuing the evening's entertainment."

The flyers knew that "alcohol fuels all wars. And the lads at Cubi never suffered a fuel crisis." Instead, they got "knee walking, commode-hugging drunk the first couple of days, then recuperat[ed] with golf, swimming, or deep breathing." Conditions finally became so bad at the zoo that the base commander decided to give the airmen a toy. A length of track was laid from the edge of the outdoor pond to a specially built shed housing a hydraulic catapult that propelled the nose section of one of the navy's big F-8 Crusader jets down the track at tremendous speed. The cockpit was fully equipped with flight instruments and throttle, neither of which exerted any control over the trajectory. The contraption also contained an arresting hook.

The object of the game was to drop the hook at the exact split-second the hurtling cockpit passed over a four-foot section of track equipped with arresting wires. Drop the hook too early and it skipped over the wires. Too late and you missed the wires entirely. In either case, you bolted directly into the slimy pool. To make a successful "landing" took a keen eye and a steady hand, neither of which was likely to characterize the occupant.

Inside the shed were hundreds of autographs left by both the pilots and their dates. "Every optimistic fool who ever rode that battered Crusader scrawled his or her name on the wall."

The inhuman tensions and demands of combat in Vietnam debased naval aviators as fully as they did soldiers and marines. And one highly influential figure emerged from the experience determined that America's necessarily brutal fighting men should not have their battlefield essence sapped by the presence of women.

James Webb was a highly decorated marine veteran of small-unit fighting who eventually parlayed a postwar career as a popular novelist and bureaucrat into the secretaryship of the navy. In 1979, well before he replaced Lehman at the Pentagon, Webb published an article in *Washingtonian* magazine titled "Women Can't Fight" that ignited two decades of bitter strife over the issue of the role of females—and by implication other minorities—in the military. Webb began by briefly describing the always sweaty, filthy, noisy, bloody, terrifying nature of ground combat in Vietnam. Women, he asserted boldly, simply were not equal to such situations. The brutality of combat—and the necessarily brutal training for combat—would bring out the worst in men while destroying women. No other country, Webb charged, not even the garrison state of Israel, seriously entertained thoughts of women serving in combat. Only the United States was pushing women toward the battlefield where they would be as brutalized by their comrades as by the enemy. American civil society was becoming ever more violent toward women, Webb maintained. The steady rise in rapes and wife beating attested to that. Where had this unwholesome trend come from? It was an inevitable result of the abrupt and complete "realignment of sexual roles." That realignment had now reached the military with disastrous effect. Webb charged that Bancroft Hall, the enormous dormitory on the Naval Academy campus at Annapolis, had become nothing but a brothel—"a horny woman's dream"—where the academy's four thousand male midshipmen vied for the sexual favors of their three hundred female counterparts; the women, in short, were whores. The conclusion was obvious: not only could women not fight, but they must not fight if the discipline and good order of the navy (and by implication the other armed services as well) were to be preserved. In the end, the issue came down to one basic fact: "Men fight better. . . . Man must be more aggressive in order to perpetuate the human race."[16]

Angry critics rightly charged that Webb's 1979 article, and his later writings on the same theme, represented a direct attack upon civilian control of the military no less than upon the coeducational policies of the Naval Academy. But of even greater importance, Webb was encouraging a breakdown of funda- mental discipline and, above all, respect within the naval establishment.[17] Cer- tainly, his devastating thesis opened the door to every bigot in and beyond the military to plead his or her own special case. If women could not or should not fight, then it was an easy step to proclaiming that other historically maligned and marginalized groups in national life who were seeking to better their lot through a military career—African Americans, for instance, or Hispanics or Native Amer- icans—could not fight, or perhaps could not fight quite as well as the macho white male elite. Since Americans of all races and ethnic groups have demon- strated military prowess time and again, the only result of Webb's crusade has been to inflame ancient prejudices and passions at a time when the country at large continues to struggle to resolve its lingering and bitter social ills.

But Webb found some surprising support. A popular 1997 motion picture about a young woman seeking against all odds to become the first female navy SEAL unleashed another blizzard of letters and articles. At least one woman who claimed to have served ten years on active duty with the navy, "including a brief deployment with a combat unit," was as derisive of women in combat as Webb. Lori Raff argued that in a ship under fire or missile attack, "nine out of 10 female sailors would be a hindrance, not an asset." In expressing horror over such opinions, politicians, pundits, and citizens all too often forget that the ultimate role of an effective military is to impose the national will through force and violence—with extreme prejudice. This ruthless fact led Fred Ikle, undersecretary of defense under Ronald Reagan, to boldly assert, "You can't cultivate the necessary commitment to physical violence and fully protect against the risk of [sexual] harassment. Military life may *correctly* foster the attitudes that tend toward rape." Such a view was surely draconian, especially in the increas- ingly high-tech navy where more and more violence was projected at the touch of a button that could be pushed as easily by a woman as a man. "In a nuclear submarine," military affairs expert Edward N. Luttwak correctly maintained, "all the jobs could be done by women with their left hand."[18] But whether women should *be* in submarines with men given the highly constricted envi- ronment on board might be another matter altogether.

Indeed, the highly constricted environment of warships creates a basic social problem between young male and female sailors that feminists and other defend- ers of women's rights simply refused to address: pregnancy. Officers, even those in training at Annapolis, enjoy a measure of privacy that enlisted people aboard ship do not. Thus, although Webb's depiction of Bancroft Hall as a brothel may be properly questioned, the fact that some vibrant, adventurous eighteen- to twenty-two-year-old boys and girls packed aboard a warship at sea will seek release from the nearly intolerable stresses and tensions of sixteen-hour workdays through quick, furtive sexual release is incontestable. By the end of the twentieth century, the navy admitted a pregnancy rate of about 10 percent for women at sea. Anecdotal evidence suggested a much higher rate on some ships. Pilots aboard the supercarrier *Theodore Roosevelt* during the air war against Kosovo complained of "the resource limitations we had to overcome," casually commenting on "girls getting pregnant having to leave the ship." Each pregnancy meant a drop in unit and servicewide combat readiness. Moreover, by the end of 1999 the navy was again contemplating the need to lower recruitment standards that would swiftly lead to "an enlisted force comprised, in ever increasing numbers, of the lower 50th-percentile mental categories" at a time of ever accelerating advances in cost-effective technologies. "The alarming trend of recruiting more females could also prove damaging as pregnancy rates among the less educated tend to be higher than those of the more educated."[19]

Whatever one's views, it was clear that the United States Navy and its sister services were in the midst of a battle with no end in sight. The forced resignation of Sara Lister from her Pentagon post because she criticized the Marine Corps as "extremist" for refusing to integrate male and female recruits in basic training was merely the latest incident. Outraged critics of Lister, Madeline Morris (the army's special assistant for "gender relations") and Lieutenant General Claudia Kennedy (who mounted a campaign to make the American military a kinder and gentler place where "common courtesy, decency, and sensitivity to the feelings of others" would predominate), charged that "the services have been commandeered by agenda-driven dilettantes, whose military experience can more or less be summarized by their belief that every fighting unit should look pretty much like the bridge of the starship *Enterprise*." The critics raised valid points: the navy had ceased drilling its recruits with rifles and, more disturbing, "issues them a 'blue card' to hand to their trainer if they feel discouraged" and wish to rest. Army physical training had become "gender-normed" to the point of irrelevance. Feminist reformers seemed determined to ignore (or even worse dismiss) the fact that the whole point of basic training in all the armed services was to inure recruits as much as possible to extreme stress so that in the inevitable horror of the battlefield or the tension of prolonged cruises in areas of international stress and conflict, mistakes such as the downing of Iran Air 655 by *Vincennes* and atrocities like My Lai could at least be kept to a minimum. Historically, it has been the poorly trained (and therefore comparatively weak-willed) soldiers such as Task Force Smith in Korea and Lieutenant William Calley's troops in Vietnam who have been guilty of deliberate atrocity against civilians, and it has been half-trained and confused sailors in a combat zone like those aboard *Vincennes* who have unwittingly consigned innocents to death. The United States Marine Corps, on the other hand, has compiled a sterling combat record. It was difficult to argue with the conclusion of one writer that when the next violent incident in the world occurred, "the hopeless and besieged" for a multiplicity of reasons "won't be looking anxiously over the horizon for a group of American troops liberated from their masculine constructs, polite and courteous, attentive to the sensitivities of others. They'll be looking for the Marines."[20]

At the end of the 1990s women and African Americans continued to clash openly and bitterly as they struggled to protect and expand their hard-won places in the naval hierarchy. Captain Everett Greene was slated to become the first black head of the SEALs until he was accused of making improper overtures to two white female subordinates while in charge of the navy's office of sexual harassment. Commander Robert Davis was summarily removed from command of the naval telecommunications center at Yokosuka, Japan, in 1991 by his immediate superior, Captain Katharine Laughton, after charges that he had made "lewd or leering" comments to several white women. Laughton wrote Davis a poor fitness report that terminated his career, and his subsequent lawsuit apparently had something to do with Laughton's decision to leave the navy, although she had in the meantime achieved flag rank. News accounts suggest that the entire affair was handled badly. Davis was quoted as stating bitterly: "In the navy we're told not to complain about racism, but its always there.... If you're an African-American and you're accused, it's over."[21]

Whether fair or not, the burden of resolving America's seemingly intractable racial and sexual tensions continued to fall on its armed services. The United States Navy, like all the great navies of this and other centuries, was a faithful reflection of the society it served. It could neither ignore nor escape that reality.

CHAPTER 9

Navy Imperial

WHILE THE U.S. NAVY struggled throughout the 1990s to reform itself even as it maintained a suitable fighting edge, old questions about the necessity for sea power reemerged. What use was the mammoth Reagan-built navy with its glaring forward maritime strategy when Soviet warships no longer plied and Soviet naval aircraft no longer patrolled the South China Sea, the Indian Ocean, the South Atlantic, and the Caribbean? When Soviet merchant ships no longer provided the bulk of supplies to insurgent groups and their Russian and Cuban advisers in East Africa and Central America? As the Kremlin's global network abruptly went glimmering, leaving behind a handful of stranded clients in Cuba, Yemen, and North Korea, three schools emerged to dominate American naval thought.

The "transitioners" saw a world minus the Soviets "as still quite dangerous" and insisted that the possession and where necessary exercise of sea power was an essential prerequisite to the transition into a more peaceful world. "Cold warriors" never quite believed that the Soviets had gone away. Russian (and Chinese) munitions technologies could still dangerously unbalance the world, while political and social preoccupations within the United States eroded American military power and technology to the vanishing point, leaving the nation and its friends helpless before the next inevitable "'global threat,' however remote that may seem today." Finally, the "Big Stick" school "look[ed] ahead to the next regional dustup." Its adherents foresaw a series of dangerous future conflicts, like the Gulf War, in a still destabilized and religiously and ethnically turbulent Third World. Although most navy leaders seemed to be "transitioners," others urged the "Big Stick." Whatever course the service took, all three visions shared a common assumption and theme: the world was still too dangerous a place to entertain thoughts of substantial national disarmament.[1]

As sailors were well aware, not everyone agreed. "Whether we admit it to ourselves or not, we are afraid," a scholar sympathetic to and well versed in naval affairs wrote in 1994. "The defense world we built for a Cold War is slipping away." The navy "*was* the nation in World War II, and that ideal remained throughout the Cold War. . . . The Navy was committed to the world because the United States was committed to the world. It was a 50-year-long global crusade." But with the collapse of the Soviet Union Americans became progressively less interested in what happened abroad. "It is getting harder to explain what we are doing in the world, and why the world still needs us so. It is becoming natural for us to compare 1991 to 1919, and to fear the worst for the Navy."[2] There was much absurdity in such breast-beating. The high-tech, intimately interrelated global communications world of the 1990s was about as far removed from 1919 as World War I was from the age of the Greek city-states. But the despair was real enough. Where were the world and the U.S. Navy going?

Members of the first Bush administration attempted to answer the question in a 1992 Defense Planning Guidance document that continued to focus national interest and emphasis on the Middle East. This was precisely the area in which a coherent international terrorist movement was growing, but the document's authors and sponsors remained fixated on Saddam Hussein and what they were convinced was his ongoing development of weapons of mass destruction. If the entire region was to be secure and the flow of critically important oil sustained, Saddam would have to go, and the only means seemed to be violent in nature. Paul Wolfowitz and his colleagues in the Pentagon proved blind to shifting regional realities, and their insistence on maintaining a high military presence in the gulf area at once wounded and inflamed Islamic sensibilities. In the event, the Defense Planning Guidance did little to clarify the navy's post–cold war role beyond justifying maintenance of at least one or two powerful carrier battle groups in the eastern Mediterranean and Persian Gulf, the latter far distant from the traditional maneuvering grounds of both the Sixth and Seventh Fleets.[3]

By the millennium, naval planners and strategists had begun moving toward a more realistic appreciation of the new and complex world created by the end of the cold war and the rise of Third World militancy. They were assisted by the many state-of-the-globe accounts that appeared about that time. One of the best and most influential was by freelance journalist Robert D. Kaplan, who made a powerful case that the pressure of steadily advancing overpopulation across Africa, the Mideast, and South Asia would constitute the main destabilizing element in early-twenty-first-century global politics. The crisis points would be the steamy, cramped, garbage-filled, disease-ridden slums and shantytowns of the cities that dotted an arc from West Africa through Anatolia and Caucasia to Pakistan and India. Although Kaplan did not dwell on the rising tide of organized transnational terrorism, he observed that the poverty and degradation found in these areas were the chief drivers of a new and fanatic religious and cultural particularism that was helping to shape our time.[4] The limited but effective application of sea power to support quick-strike operations in Panama, Grenada, Haiti, and Somalia in the waning years of the cold war and beyond seemed to confirm that "littoral" warfare would become the norm in Kaplan's emerging Africa–Middle East zone of instability during coming decades. Two striking naval successes in the late eighties and early nineties sharpened the perception.

When in 1986 a bomb detonated inside a Berlin disco killing two U.S. servicemen, American intelligence quickly traced the atrocity to Libya's Colonel Muammar-al-Qadhafi. President Reagan promptly ordered a retaliatory strike by long-range air force bombers flying down to the Mediterranean from England and close-in navy bombers from the carrier *America* lying off the Gulf of Sidra. Not only were the navy attacks more effective, the sailor-flyers also shot down several of Qaddafi's warplanes that foolishly came out to challenge the Americans. Seven years later President Clinton ordered a successful precision attack by twenty-three Tomahawk cruise missiles from warships in the Persian Gulf against Iraqi intelligence headquarters in central Baghdad in retaliation for hard evidence that Iraqi agents had planned to assassinate former president Bush when he visited Kuwait. According to one later authoritative U.S. government source, the aircraft assaults against Libya and the missile attacks against Iraq "symbolized for the military establishment effective use of military power for counterterrorism—limited retaliation with air power aimed at deterrence."[5] The coastal and riverine interdiction activities in Vietnam together with the first Gulf War might well prove a model for the kind of close-in Third World combat that the U.S. Navy and its sister services would have to wage in the coming century.

Under the lash of new realities, naval planners pondered further reforms of both organizational structures and weapon systems to successfully confront an emerging world characterized by "asymmetric threats" to U.S. national security interests worldwide. Their thinking was incorporated in "Forward . . . from the Sea" (U.S. Navy) and "Operational Maneuvers from the Sea" (Marine Corps).

In early 1999 a Marine Corps general summarized the gist of the two documents: "Expeditionary Warfare is taking on a major role in the United States national maritime strategy. . . . A requirement for a flexible, dynamic and dominant force in the [world's] littorals is steering the course of Expeditionary Warfare. Developments within the Surface Warfare community reflect the trend toward projecting power ashore and dominating the littorals, while not requiring host nation support."[6]

Yet a clear pattern of future warfare on and from the sea proved elusive. Was sea power to be employed primarily against amorphous, stateless, transnational terrorist groups? Against warring states? Or in situations of civil war? Or in some combination of two or all three situations? And how could effective power be brought to bear in each instance? The successive crises in the former Yugoslavia during the late nineties seemed to refute Kaplan's model of abject Third World poverty as the generative force behind impending global destabilization. The cluster of ethnic and religious groups—southern Slavs, Croats, Bosnians, Macedonians, Slovenes, Christians, Muslims—that Josip Broz Tito had bludgeoned back into nationhood after 1945 (Yugoslavia had first been formed as a consequence of the Versailles Treaty of 1919) had apparently fashioned a reasonably prosperous and stable regime under a nominal Communist banner. But the inexorable collapse of the country in the decade after Tito's death in 1980 culminated in brutal efforts by Belgrade and restive, violent Serbian minorities elsewhere in the former Communist state to create a greater Serbia out of large parts of the newly independent nations of Croatia and Bosnia-Herzegovina. The result was a civil war of incredible savagery. The "ethnic cleansing" of thousands of Bosnian Muslims by minority Serb elements in 1992 not only revolted the world when they were uncovered but also ignited complex waves of hatred, military aggression and counteraggression, and outright terror against helpless civilians throughout much of the former Yugoslavia. For a time Western governments were confounded. Surely, Europe had moved beyond such barbarities; clearly, it had not. Slowly cobbling together fragile agreements, statesmen and diplomats in the spring of 1995 imposed a no-fly zone over Bosnia. Air force F-16s provided most of the American contribution, but the Sixth Fleet made a dramatic statement of its own capabilities that demonstrated the enormous advances in search and rescue since Vietnam and the continued willingness of the American fighting man to go to the aid of comrades in peril.

On the night of June 2, air force captain Scott O'Grady was blown out of the skies over Bosnia by a Soviet-made antiaircraft missile. Momentarily stunned, O'Grady stayed with his ruined F-16 as it dropped like a stone through heavy cloud cover. At last the pilot ejected, but to comrades nearby it appeared that the aircraft had largely disintegrated with no survivor. Family members were notified by air force officers and chaplains that the young captain was missing and probably dead, while O'Grady spent the next six days and nights eluding Bosnian Serb forces looking for him. What doubtless saved O'Grady was the global positioning system. Once the downed flyer managed to contact determined but increasingly discouraged searchers above, they were able to almost instantly pinpoint his position. An air force rescue team could be readied and sent to O'Grady's assistance within four hours, but a forty-one-man TRAP (tactical recovery aircraft and personnel) team attached to the Twenty-fourth Marine Expeditionary Unit was aboard the amphibious-assault ship *Kearsarge* offshore in the Adriatic just moments away. Soon a rescue "package" composed of several Marine Corps F-18A strike fighters from a supercarrier together with Harrier jets, Cobra helicopter gunships, and several CH-53 Super Stallion heavy assault–rescue helicopters from *Kearsarge* were thundering across the Bosnian hills and valleys in steadily deteriorating weather to pluck O'Grady from under Serb noses.[7]

Later that summer when Bosnian Serbs refused to stop shelling the Croatian safe-haven city of Sarajevo or suspend offensive actions against other previously agreed-upon safe areas, NATO concluded in time-honored fashion that it was necessary once again to bomb fractious enemies to the peace table. It commenced an air offensive against rebel Serbian positions in Bosnia. The Sixth Fleet became an integral part of the response, ominously labeled Operation Deliberate Force. In late August and again in September the supercarrier *Theodore Roosevelt* launched several heavy air strikes against Bosnian Serb positions threatening the Sarajevo Safe Area. At one point during this sharp but violent exercise, the Aegis cruiser *Normandy* launched thirteen T-LAMs against Bosnian Serb air-defense "assets" in northwestern Bosnia. Within weeks, Bosnian, Croat, and Serbian foreign ministers (the latter representing the Bosnian Serbs) agreed to a cease-fire, and a fragile "permanent agreement" was reached on the political, ethnic, and religious futures of Croatia, Bosnia-Herzegovina, and Serbia at Dayton, Ohio, the following December. A UN peacekeeping force had been sent to Bosnia in the early nineties, and although it was ineffective, it was at least on the ground. The Dayton accords stipulated that a multinational military implementation force, the IFOR, would be sent to Bosnia-Herzegovina under NATO command, operating with a grant of authority from the United Nations.[8]

Less than four years later, however, the Serbian province of Kosovo erupted in civil war between Serbs and an Albanian minority that claimed to have been oppressed for years and demanded a sizable enclave of its own. No outside peace-keepers were present. President George H. W. Bush had warned Serbian president Slobodan Milošević as early as 1992 that the United States would use force if the Serbian Army tried to seize all of the province. When the Serbs appeared ready to do just that in the face of initial ethnic Albanian provocation and later Albanian willingness to negotiate, NATO launched a highly controversial aerial campaign against Serbian forces both in Kosovo and in Serbia itself. The Sixth Fleet was again called upon to provide vitally important strike support, and once more *Theodore Roosevelt* was on hand to provide the naval aviation component.

Following upon the brief air and missile campaign against Bosnian Serb elements four years before, Kosovo proved to be yet another critical transition in naval warfare. In many ways the 1999 campaign harkened back to the frustrating days of Vietnam and even Korea. Surface and air operations were again subordinate not only to U.S. Air Force planners but also to the demands of a NATO command structure far removed from the realities of combat. The pilots of the *"Teddy"* suffered as badly from political interference with targeting selection as had their fathers thirty years earlier in the skies above Southeast Asia. Indeed, NATO interference was perceived as so frustrating that at one point a U.S. Air Force general nearly quit in disgust.

But half a century of experience had taught admirals, pilots, marines, and sailors how complex Third World battlefields could be. Unlike Korea and even Vietnam the U.S. Navy now possessed promising new tools to prosecute relatively low-intensity wars of potential frustration. One such tool was the multimission warship—missile-laden cruisers and destroyers whose "offensive power projection capabilities" in the T-LAM system was "without precedent in the annals of naval warfare." Another was the dedicated, quick-response-mode amphibious-assault ship whose helicopters and fast landing craft could propel several thousand marines ashore within a few hours at most. If these weapons were to be employed to their maximum potential in congested, close-in coastal areas teeming with noncombatants and menaced by fast enemy attack boats, aircraft, minisubmarines, minefields, and other low-intensity warfare systems, it was essential to understand the nature and dimensions of an ever shifting littoral battlefield at any given moment. In Operation Allied Force off Kosovo, all elements from Sixth Fleet headquarters in Italy down to individual guided-missile cruisers and destroyers, the amphibious group and mine-countermeasures squadron, to the *Theodore Roosevelt* carrier battle group "were inexorably bound together by the connectivity of SIPRNET, a high-speed data network." Dispensing with cumbersome "hard-copy" message traffic, SIPRNET's computers provided local and regional naval commanders with "real-time situational aware-ness" of all elements on and adjacent to the battlefield. Thus, Tomahawk strike teams aboard the cruisers and destroyers could not only follow the progress of their own precision missile attack on enemy positions ashore but also obtain data from orbiting surveillance planes regarding the progress of other such strikes, while constantly "revis[ing]" the "waterspace management overlay" on their computers and status boards

> to reflect a transiting French submarine entering the Adriatic and an Ital-ian boat leaving. The Operations Officer is having a lengthy discussion with his Amphibious Squadron 2 counterpart regarding this morning's pending move of the U.S.S. *Gunston Hall* (LSD 44) to a position less than three miles from the Albanian coastline to facilitate transfer of the 26th Marine Expeditionary Unit personnel to complete surveying of a site for the construction of another... refugee camp.[9]

While surface commanders and sailors were learning to bind the complex activities of littoral warfare together through high-speed electronic communica-tions and coordination, at least one squadron aboard *Theodore Roosevelt* elabo-rated a whole new doctrine of finding and bombing comparatively small enemy forces hiding in mountainous terrain under often abominable weather conditions and protected by sophisticated shoulder-launched and occasionally emplaced surface-to-air missiles.

Historically for navy and marine pilots flying close air support, finding and killing enemy troops or destroying their armor had involved close coordination with friendly ground forces who provided coordinates covering both their po-sitions and those of the enemy. But Kosovo was a new type of political war. There were no friendly troops on the ground. The objective was to stop Serbian military operations solely through airpower. "Alpha Strikes"—raids against ma-jor enemy fixed installations like bridges, barracks, weapon and fuel-storage depots, airfields, and the like—were still required to stop Serb aggression, and *Theodore Roosevelt*'s airmen mounted a number of these. But three weeks into the bombing campaign it was clear to NATO planners that bombing such tra-ditional targets was not going to prevent individually operating companies and regiments of the Serbian Army in Kosovo from butchering scores if not hun-dreds of ethnic Albanians in the short term. But how could small armored and troop elements be found and either destroyed or terrorized into impotence? One man with the Black Aces F-14 squadron aboard the carrier thought he knew. Lieutenant Commander Brian B. Brurud, a thirty-eight-year-old Oklahoman, had recently trained with the marines in close air-support weapons and tactics, learning the importance of SCAR (strike-coordinated armed reconnaissance) missions whose essence was roaming the battlefield looking for enemy forces, then pouncing while protected from above by aircraft carrying high-speed radiation missiles (HARMs). The air force and navy both had flown SCAR raids in the Gulf War, but there the weather was ideal, the terrain tabletop flat with no place for enemy forces to hide, and SAMs nearly nonexistent. In Kosovo the weather was nearly as bad as it had been during the Korean winters nearly half a century before, the terrain was as hilly and mountainous, and SAMs, never encountered in Korea and often operated by former Soviet officers and noncoms, constituted a daunting barrier to low-level attacks.

In a series of highly stressful missions over a roughly four-week period, Brurud, his fellow pilots, and their radar-intercept officers worked out the numerous problems of locating, identifying, and destroying Serb military units from thousands of feet without gravely compromising civilian safety. Essentially, "Bru" and his colleagues coordinated their technology and tactics superbly to produce a new ground-attack doctrine. They blended previously impossible-to-obtain ground intelligence with their exotic "black box" technologies (LANTIRN— low-altitude navigation and targeting infrared for night, FLIR—forward-looking infrared radar—and TARPS—a tactical air-reconnaissance pod system) to produce an unprecedentedly detailed view of the battlefield, then cunningly employed the laser-guided weaponry finally in their arsenals in such a way that a bomb from one aircraft might ride the laser beam of another plane to target. NATO had initially dictated a minimum twenty thousand–foot ceiling for air raids against all enemy targets in Serbia and Kosovo. The Black Aces brought the attack floor down to ten to fifteen thousand feet, but the imaginative combination of infrared detection and laser-guided weaponry often brought them atop the enemy SAM sites before the defenders had any inkling they were there. A6-E Prowlers and the first-generation F-18 fighters rode above the raiders, their HARM missiles ready to strike and suppress SAM sites as soon as enemy radar was turned on.

Such tactics did not "win" the war in Kosovo. Air force fighter and bomber jets did as much or more to wear down Serb resistance by destroying the enemy infrastructure in northern Serbia around Belgrade, while the navy was doing the less glamorous work in southern Serbia and Kosovo. But the Black Aces raids did suggest a new and potentially devastating way of dealing effectively with small, difficult-to-detect enemy ground units operating in rough geography under poor weather conditions, even when protected by formidable defenses.

No one in 1999 could guess what the future of warfare would be. Organized terrorism remained on the periphery of international life and the post–cold war world seemed reasonably safe and stable. But the Black Aces had developed one more competence in high-technology warfare that the United States Navy could employ if and when necessary to project its power "from the sea."

Running a racecourse pattern in a secret position on the Ionian Sea, *Theodore Roosevelt,* together with one of the three British light carriers, launched almost daily attack sorties against targets in Serbia and Kosovo throughout NATO's controversial eleven-week aerial assault against the Serb government and military. One of the *Teddy*'s escorts, the new *Arleigh Burke*–class missile destroyer *Gonzales,* launched more than half a dozen T-LAMs against Serb targets. On the other side of the Balkan Peninsula, the Aegis missile cruiser *Philippine Sea* inaugurated the air campaign with several T-LAM shots of its own. After the first "bird" was shot off, launches became so routine that the ship did not even go to general quarters. While "about one-third of the crew began the deliberate preparations for the missile launch, the rest mostly turned over in their racks and fell back to sleep." The Twenty-Sixth Marine Expeditionary Unit (MEU) sailing nearby aboard *Kearsarge* became part of the first wave of NATO troops to enter Kosovo once Serb president Slobodan Milošević capitulated. The *Teddy*'s comparative handful of fliers seemed lost amid the many planes and pilots contributed by nearly all of NATO's nineteen-member countries, but they did their job admirably.[10]

The generally impressive performances of both the navy and the marines in Kosovo did not impress America's foremost naval analyst when he submitted his latest massive report on the ships and aircraft of the U.S. Fleet two years later. "The U.S. Navy is ill-prepared to enter the 21st century," Norman Polmar concluded. "The service is plagued by major personnel problems, too few ships for assigned missions, less-than-optimal aircraft, and, to some degree, a headquarters organization that is unable to develop a unified naval strategy." (So much for "Forward . . . from the Sea"!) The Marine Corps was in somewhat better shape, Polmar continued, but "is experiencing a decline in amphibious lift and is engaged in several expensive projects that will provide minimal enhancement of its combat capabilities," a clear reference to the costly and accident-prone Osprey tilt-rotor multipurpose aircraft. Long a confidant of leading naval figures, including several chiefs of naval operations, Polmar had at least implicitly lent a hand in shaping U.S. naval policy, and he intuitively grasped some changing realities. Ever since Vietnam with its hundreds of thousands of reluctant draftees, individual warriors had ceased being ciphers and had become personalized—soldiers, airmen, even sailors, with a human face and a vulnerable soul. Each warrior's death diminished a nation increasingly involved with all mankind. If possible, warriors must not fight because they must not die; they must not even be captured, and if they were, everything must be done to rescue them. When terrorists struck the marines in Beirut in 1983 President Reagan had promptly ordered a retaliatory strike against Syria that resulted in the loss of two carrier aircraft, the death of one pilot, and the capture of the other. A private citizen, the Reverend Jesse Jackson—known to Arab governments as both a friend of the Palestinians and a champion of Third World causes—promptly went to Damascus and, cutting out, overriding, or perhaps fulfilling his government's interests, negotiated the release of the navy lieutenant.[11] The incident was not lost on perceptive analysts like Polmar. Although the navy lost no planes in either Bosnia or Kosovo, employing costly manned warplanes from expensive carriers against an always elusive enemy in the post–cold war era could be dramatically counterproductive since downed pilots made superb bargaining chips for pitiless enemies. Comparatively inexpensive unmanned guided missiles, on the other hand, posed no such risk.

9/11 changed everything. Third World terrorism abruptly emerged as the new symbol of global discord and pandemonium. Within hours al Qaeda and its Taliban sponsor in Afghanistan created new mission responsibilities for the American military establishment and whatever allies it could entice to its side. Forgotten or dismissed—at least for the moment—were the divisive issues of race and gender. Isolated acts of terrorism over the past thirty years had suddenly coalesced into a global movement, so it was said, and U.S. national defense policy and strategy must resume that global cast first assumed in the earliest months and years of the cold war. Post-1989 neo-isolationism, which in many circles had seemed plausible as well as attractive, was no longer tenable. Six weeks after Operation Enduring Freedom officially began on October 7, 2001, an American military analyst wrote that the campaign in Afghanistan "has given the world a stark view of a new American doctrine to make war on the sources of terrorism in the world." The defeat of the Taliban and the destruction of its infrastructure have "sent an unambiguous warning far beyond the war theater to a number of nations that continue to provide bases and training to terrorist groups. The warning is: this could happen to you."[12]

The need to strike and destroy the Taliban as soon as possible permitted no leisurely buildup, as in the Gulf War nearly a decade before. U.S. military and civil strategists had to employ what forces they had or could quickly bring to bear in the region. There was no time for that elaborate strategizing that inevitably brought out barely concealed interservice rivalries and defined postaction arguments over which service and weapon systems had contributed most to victory. Navy carrier and amphibious battle groups were either in position in the northern Arabian Sea or nearby; they inevitably became among the first major strike forces employed.

The supercarrier *Carl Vinson* battle group from the Pacific Fleet was already in the Arabian Sea, while the Norfolk-based supercarrier *Enterprise* and its supporting ships had just exited the Strait of Hormuz, heading home after conducting combat patrols over southern Iraq all summer in heat that often reached 130 degrees on the flight deck. Word of the attacks on the World Trade Center reached the *Enterprise* task force along with orders to sail immediately to join *Carl Vinson.* Two weeks later the carrier's commanding officer strode into one of the ready rooms where a briefing was about to take place, set a cluster of baseball caps emblazoned with logos of the New York City Police and Fire Departments on a table, and told his pilots they would strike Afghanistan that night. The *Enterprise* battle group remained on station for little more than a week before being relieved by *Theodore Roosevelt.* Meanwhile, the Twenty-sixth MEU hastily wound up Operation Bright Star in Egypt and headed for the battle area aboard their amphibious-assault ship *Bataan* (a newer sister to *Kearsarge,* which had carried the MEU off Kosovo). *Bataan* arrived later in October to join the older *Peleliu,* which had reached the area shortly after 9/11 with the Fifteenth MEU. Like the carriers, the amphibious ships met halfway around the world from their respective home ports of Norfolk and San Diego.[13]

On the evening of October 7, as the first F-14 and F/A-18 strike fighters screamed off the decks of *Vinson* and *Enterprise,* fifty Tomahawk long-range cruise missiles shot out of their tubes aboard the guided-missile cruisers and destroyers escorting the big ships. Within moments the missiles were raining down on Taliban targets in southern Afghanistan. Several hours later the F-14s and F/A-18s arrived to deliver their strikes in an unrelenting campaign that went on without respite as the two carriers alternated day and night duties. This time the navy had the in-air refueling services (initially from hastily summoned British Royal Air Force tankers) and all the "smart" weapons required for a sustained, pinpoint air assault, including two thousand–pound joint direct-attack munitions (JDAMs) and thousand-pound laser-guided bombs that "virtually wiped out" in the first hours of the campaign "any significant threat" from the Taliban's handful of interceptor aircraft or radar-guided surface-to-air missiles. As in all wars, a fraction of these "precision" weapons "hit structures other than their intended targets," in the delicate words of military spokesmen, and as Taliban power crumbled that regime began positioning its forces in heavily populated civilian areas, including homes and mosques, in hopes of discouraging further U.S. strikes. Casualties among the innocent were bound to occur, and they did, probably at rates higher than the United States was willing to acknowledge.[14]

Within days the air force weighed in with its own units, as B-2 bombers flying out of Whiteman Air Base in Missouri flew halfway around the world, refueled at the Indian Ocean island base of Diego Garcia (British owned but American developed and a reasonably well-kept secret for many years), then flew up to Afghanistan to drop their loads before returning to Missouri. These were "the longest-range strikes ever made by manned aircraft . . . in a shuttle-bombing operation reminiscent of the 8th Air Force Missions that shuttled between England and the Soviet Union during World War II." The handful of B-2s were supplemented by aging B-52s that flew in to Diego Garcia from the States and mounted bombing campaigns from there. Although the air force effort was quite spectacular, it was also fearfully costly, and until the diplomats could negotiate base agreements with other central-Asian nations, naval aircraft supplemented with periodic Tomahawk missile assaults remained the quickest, cheapest means of employing crushing U.S. power against Taliban forces and infrastructure.[15] The pattern of the Gulf War had been reversed.

Doubtless, the most salient feature of the war from a naval standpoint was its location. Kabul, Qandahār, and the mountains of eastern Afghanistan were hundreds, not tens, of miles from the sea. Yet, confounding skeptics, the United States Navy was able to effectively project massive amounts of power ashore. The key lay in its small, versatile, but aging fleet of S-3 aircraft that came into the fleet in the 1970s primarily as antisubmarine-warfare platforms, though some planes were given limited ground-attack missions in Desert Storm. S-3As and -Bs were subsequently employed in an electronics intelligence role in the early and mid-1990s before many 3Bs were finally reconfigured as aerial tankers. Along with U.S. Air Force and Royal Air Force tankers they formed "the bucket brigade" that refueled the navy's short-range, carrier-based F/A-18s and F-14s, allowing the strike aircraft "to reach targets deep inside the Asian landmass." Because the navy either possessed or could draw upon this critically important capability, there was indeed no place on earth that terrorists could hide from the might of the world's single great sea power.[16]

The emerging global war on terrorism as first waged in Afghanistan not only restored the navy to an essential place in the American defense establishment but also "pressed" all America's armed forces "toward a world in which parochial differences, while not eliminated, were filed down dramatically." Afghanistan was a multifront war that demanded the best efforts of all four branches, and their respective chiefs claimed to have learned an "enduring lesson" from the first year "of this new campaign against terror." The American military was "no longer fighting single-front battles against a clearly defined enemy." Without "dropping the ball" in other areas of commitment—Kosovo, Bosnia, and South Korea, to name but three—the U.S. armed forces had "been everything from on borders to protecting airports and ports and bridges, and going forward with very competent and highly skilled soldiers to fight the war in Afghanistan." No single service could carry out any large mission responsibility on its own. Early-twenty-first-century warfare required "interoperable" responses. The navy offered its aging supercarrier *Kitty Hawk*—temporarily stripped of its air group—as "a huge, mobile base" for Afghani operations, "so Special Operations forces and Marine expeditionary troops" could "strike targets with speed and secrecy… when no land base [was] was available." The S-3 tanker planes proved too few and small to adequately constitute the "bucket brigade" fueling the carrier jets to and from their target areas. Bigger and more numerous air force tankers were critical in sustaining carrier air operations. And learning proper air-ground battle-field coordination at last, "Air Force ground spotters embedded in Army Special Forces units called in air strikes from carrier-based naval aircraft hours from their floating bases. The navy and Air Force are now working to develop a new electronic-jamming aircraft that both services can use."[17] The always jealous, often vicious early postwar debate over unification seemed to have at last been resolved in a creative blur of joint mission roles and responsibilities.

The pace of operations, as in every conflict from World War I through Vietnam, "was frenetic, stressful, and exciting." Most pilots flew at least one seven- to eight-hour mission per day over Afghanistan, sometimes two. "Crews preparing weapons could barely keep up, hustling to fill the bomb hangar, only to see it empty two hours later." The professionals loved it; this was meat and drink, what they had been trained for and lusted to do. No war since 1945 had given them a greater sense of moral justification, professional purpose, and personal satisfaction. "All we did was eat, sleep, brief and fly," one reported. Both pilots and sailors agreed that they "were able to handle the high tempo" of operations day after day, "though many confessed to feeling exhausted" once they left the battle area. " 'People just clicked into another mode,' " said one F-14 squadron commander. " 'We could have done more,' " if asked.[18]

The marines were as flexible as their colleagues aloft, coming into Afghanistan with army special forces and mountain and airborne divisions to send the Taliban and al Qaeda packing. The Fifteenth and Twenty-sixth Marine Expeditionary Units constituted "a versatile force . . . trained in special operations and ready to go 'any time, anyplace.'" Landing at Qandahār, the Fifteenth MEU carried out its objective of limiting enemy "movements in or out of their last remaining strongholds." Each MEU contained about twenty-two hundred marines and sailors and was designed "to give the U.S. military a way to put personnel with various specialties into a troubled region for extended periods of time—even when support bases are distant or non-existent." The marines "who spend six months in special forces training" brought with them from the sea light armored vehicles, a handful of small battle tanks, assault helicopters, and Harrier jets capable of vertical takeoffs and landings. Such a force proved perfectly suitable for conditions in southern Afghanistan.[19] Like the navy, the United States Marines in Afghanistan proved capable of projecting their power—their "beachhead"—far into the Asian landmass.

The reputation of the U.S. Navy and Marine Corps had not been so high in more than half a century. "To Iraq, Iran, Yemen, Somalia, Syria, Libya, Sudan . . . Yasir Arafat's Palestinian Authority," and all terrorist regimes, organizations, and supporters throughout the Third World, "the United States military has demonstrated as it did in the Persian Gulf war in 1991, the shattering effect of 500-pound bombs dropped on troop concentrations." If the first aerial assaults of Enduring Freedom were less than perfect, "once Special Forces spotters got on the ground" in Afghanistan, "American commanders showed how a large arsenal of precision guided weapons could lay the Taliban forces naked to the Navy's carrier-based bombers." Early in 2002 the navy's critical role in the anti-terrorist war was confirmed when the Pentagon approved a request by General Tommy Franks, the overall commander of Mideast operations, "to station two aircraft carriers and thousands of marines aboard ships in the northern Arabian Sea through March. . . . Navy officials expect that request could be renewed every three months." Rumblings began to be heard throughout the service—especially from those returning from the Arabian Sea—that the ancient dream of fifteen-carrier battle groups (which would necessitate at least a five hundred—if not six hundred—ship navy) must be fulfilled to ensure an adequate measure of national security.[20] Amid a declining national economy and in the burst of feverish patriotism unleashed by September 11, all of America's armed services might expect to obtain the well-educated and sophisticated manpower, if not the financial and material resources, required to ramp up to full readiness.

But as the Afghan war progressed, frustration grew along with civilian casualties. Total victory proved elusive. Defense secretary Donald Rumsfeld admitted as early as mid-November 2001, a month into the campaign, that al Qaeda leader Osama bin Ladin had probably "left the building" and that "the Taliban are still there . . . in the mountains . . . in the neighboring countries. . . . I think it would be a mistake to say that they've . . . gone and have disappeared."[21] As the obvious targets were destroyed, naval forces were reassigned to the more mundane and boring task of searching ships coming out of Pakistani ports in hopes of seizing at least a part of the terrorist leadership.

Had the effort been sufficient? Was it even relevant? Just a month into the campaign, serious critics were raising serious issues:

> With its caves, tunnels and urban hiding places, Afghanistan has proved to be an especially difficult battlefield. . . . The Bush administration initially hoped that it could destroy the Qaeda terrorists and topple the Taliban regime that protects them through a combination of day and night airstrikes, commando raids and support of anti-Taliban groups. . . . It hoped for large defections from the Taliban that have not occurred, and it underestimated the Taliban's resilience.[22]

A year later, bin Ladin remained at large, along with much of his and the Taliban's senior officials and military staffs. The terrorists had been driven underground, to be sure, but not thoroughly beaten.

All this raised fundamental questions of the role and relevance of U.S. military and naval forces in a terrorist world. On the one hand, the international community universally if reluctantly granted the United States supreme power. America at the beginning of the twenty-first century was not just the biggest kid on the block, nor just the only kid on the block, it apparently owned the block, militarily, economically, and, to a degree, culturally as well. The euphoria over the nation's world power position that led the Bush administration in mid-September 2002 to declare America's right to strike preemptively anywhere and anytime it felt its global security threatened paralleled the exuberant but fallacious thinking in the mid- and late 1990s that Wall Street could and would continue to shower investors with soaring returns year after year, decade after decade. The doctrines of unilateral right of preemptive strike and eternal military superiority, both dramatic departures from recent national practice, reflected a disturbing hubris that could readily lead to disasters such as those that occurred in Southeast Asia in the 1960s and early '70s and on a far smaller scale in Somalia twenty years later.[23]

Nonetheless, some in the United States, mainly academics and journalists, including Robert Kaplan and Paul Kennedy, a Yale professor "who 10 years ago was predicting America's ruin from imperial overreach," welcomed the new American empire. Kennedy gushed in a British publication that not even ancient Rome approached America's position astride the world. The great empires of the past—Rome included—all had competitors, even if, in Rome's heyday, the Chinese empire was on the other side of the Eurasian landmass, too far away to affect events. Today, no other military power on the planet remotely approaches the United States. Whereas in the nineteenth century the Royal Navy enjoyed superiority "only to the next two navies" (those of France and Russia), "right now all the other navies in the world combined could not dent American maritime supremacy." Moreover, the Americans continued to expand their ongoing technological revolution, incessantly developing new systems and applications to military and naval affairs in an ongoing effort that no other country or even group of countries can begin to approach. Defense "scholars" in the Pentagon and numerous "think tanks" continue to ponder the nation's future security needs years into the future and how best to develop and apply the people, resources, and systems to meet those needs.[24]

But to what end? Nine-eleven obscured a crucial fact: the post–cold war world basked in unprecedented peace. No great power coveted the lands or the trade of any other to the point of contemplating war; no single nation or bloc of nations threatened the general peace. There were, and remain, tensions aplenty: Beijing's insistence that Taiwan must, someday, be part of greater China; the ever simmering Indo-Pakistani relationship; the drive for possession of nuclear weapons by Iran and North Korea; and, of course, that swirling cauldron of hatreds: Israel-Palestine. Sub-Saharan Africa constitutes a politico-economic basket case all its own. Within this unstable context, a number of countries—undeterred by America's incredible lead in high-tech warfare—pursued sea power both for national security and as the best means of expressing and exerting local and regional influence.

Britain's exercise of world power was so prolonged and intense that the island people can never wholly escape its legacy. As the old imperial lands of the Middle East continued to churn and memory of the Falklands remained, the Royal Navy was able to convince Parliament of sufficient funding to maintain a small strategic-ballistic-missile submarine flotilla of four boats and a moderately sized surface fleet built around its three small "jump-jet" carriers. Early in the millennium, the Royal Navy decided to resume the historic power-projection role it had surrendered in the wake of the CVA-01 debacle nearly forty years before. As currently projected, two big fleet carriers will come into the fleet in 2012 and 2015, carrying names redolent of Britain's age of naval glory: *Queen*

Elizabeth and *Prince of Wales.* With various parts of each ship to be built in four yards, the big carriers will deploy, if all goes well, with ship's company of no more than six hundred, who will be almost completely dependent upon an electronic suite of unprecedented sophistication to carry out their work. As with every other postwar British carrier design, the new ships will have a novel feature, in this case two "island" structures rather than one. The forward tower will contain all the conning and navigation facilities, while the after tower will contain "flyco," the flight- and flight-deck-control spaces. Yet the ships share another salient feature with their predecessors: they are disappointing. For all their size (about fifty-five thousand tons), the vessels will carry only about forty to fifty aircraft, and their speed will be well below thirty knots, possibly as low as twenty-five. Reports in early 2006 cast some doubt on whether the vessels, "beset by political infighting and rising costs," will appear at all.[25]

The Royal Navy is, of course, a historic friend—at least since World War II. Those who claim to be farsighted observers see other navies as perhaps challenging U.S. global supremacy in one or another region of the world ocean. In early 2005 a study of the Indian Navy concluded that within five to seven years, "Delhi plans to control the Indian Ocean with two carrier battle groups backed by nuclear powered submarines . . . supported by long-range, shore-based naval aviation, with communications and targeting provided by a constellation of specialized Indian-made [space] satellites." According to a later source, one of the two carriers would be the ex-Soviet cruiser-carrier *Admiral Gorshkov.* The "prime mission of this force" in wartime would be to "quickly eliminate Pakistan's eight outdated destroyers and frigates, hunt down its seven conventional[ly powered] submarines, and blockade Karachi and Gwadar . . . cutting off imports of fuel, munitions, spare parts, and strategic goods." Later that year and on into 2006, a flurry of magazine articles speculated that the People's Republic of China with its booming economy and growing reliance on foreign energy reserves was certain to become a future enemy. These developments prompted a former U.S. vice chief of naval operations to declare with a bellicosity worthy of British imperialist forebears: "Nations that seek general or focused parity with the U.S. on economic, political, technological, or military terms will remain a strategic concern."[26]

One reason may be that the U.S. Navy's high-tech lead is capable of being penetrated by advanced foreign weaponry. In the early nineties rumors circulated throughout the West about the latest ultimate weapon at sea, the VA-111 "Shkval," or "Squall," rocket-powered torpedo, initially deployed by the USSR in 1977 after seventeen years of development. Shkval was apparently first semi-officially mentioned in a 1995 issue of *Jane's Intelligence Review.* According to that authoritative British journal, the solid-fuel rocket torpedo employed "redirected thrust ejected from its nose and skin" to create "a semi-vacuum bubble or 'supercavity'" around it, permitting the missile to travel through the water at an incredible 230 miles per hour, about five times as fast as the best Western weapon. Advanced surplus Russian submarines, like the ultraquiet, diesel-driven *Kilo* class, are capable of carrying a number of Shkvals and could thus sneak up on unwary U.S. aircraft carrier battle groups and let fly. Fortunately, the Shkvals possess a limited range of only seventy-five hundred yards. But even once detected within that range, *Kilo* submarines could devastate American naval forces, since their Shkvals would reach target long before American ordnance could hit the *Kilo*. Ominously, China began purchasing Shkvals from Russia in 1998 together with four *Kilo*s. Some intelligence analysts believed as early as 2003 that China "is building a navy capable of operating far from the Asian continent, armed with a combination of silent subs, supersonic nuclear tipped Stealth missiles, and the Shkval." (In the late summer of 2006, press reports indicated that Iran was test-firing a variation of this weapon, called "Hoot," together with a submarine-to-surface ballistic missile called "Thaqeb" during war games in the Persian Gulf.)[27] Steady Sino-Indian tensions over Tibet, Nepal, and other border areas, together with long-standing Chinese demands to incorporate Taiwan, could entice Beijing into a further substantial increase of its modest naval force.

But building an electronic-age naval fleet of even modest size, then maintaining and upgrading it for decades, can be a treasury-breaking enterprise. It demands, as we have seen, not only industrial competence of a high order in the construction phase but also sailors familiar and comfortable with the most advanced electronic systems and their use in the operational phase. By and large, the U.S. Navy has not sold or shared its advanced technologies. Ambitious young sea services have thus had to look elsewhere, and in most instances (the French Exocet missile being a major exception) the only readily available supplier has been the rusting Soviet fleet. The Indian, Chinese, and other world fleets have been forced to accept and adapt for use flawed Soviet designs, ships, and spare parts that will become increasingly scarce and worn out as the years progress. The state of play on the world ocean does not suggest that a serious challenge to U.S. sea power will materialize any time soon.

Submarines and aircraft carriers, for instance, are not only expensive to build but costly to run. Other than the United States, only two nations, France and the Soviet Union, have built fleet carriers over the past thirty years, and their records are not impressive, as the mournful tale of the *Charles de Gaulle* attests. The only nuclear-powered aircraft carrier in active service outside the U.S. fleet was launched in May 1994 with serious flaws already evident. At 850 feet, *de*

Gaulle could still carry only thirty-six fixed-wing aircraft, and its designed speed was twenty-seven to twenty-eight knots, barely sufficient, at top speed, to generate the flight-deck wind necessary for jet-aircraft operation. During the construction phase, builders experienced problems with the nuclear heat shield, then discovered that they not only had to widen the angled flight deck but also had to extend it some 14 feet because the initial design was discovered to be too short to land and launch the Grumman E-2C Hawkeye surveillance aircraft that were a key component of the aerial-defense system. The ship finally began sea trials in January 1999, which were still being conducted nearly two years later "when a large section of the port propeller was lost while steaming at high speed [25 knots] in the west Atlantic." The carrier limped home to Toulouse, where it languished for five months while a spare propeller from a smaller, older, decommissioned carrier was put on. When it returned to sea, *de Gaulle* could make only twenty-three knots. Nonetheless, the French Admiralty declared the vessel operational in December 2001, and it promptly sailed for the Indian Ocean and the allied fleet waging air war over Afghanistan. When the carrier returned to France, "new propellers were not fitted as expected during a four month refit in 2003 and this is likely rescheduled for the next docking period," whenever that would be. A far more serious problem was leaking radiation from the vessel's nuclear reactor. A press report in 1999 stated that several engineering officers aboard the carrier had been "irradiated."[28]

Advanced carrier operations are highly complex, having become, in the U.S. Navy, a blend of tradition and constant training. Since the appearance of their first true fleet carriers, *Lexington* and *Saratoga,* in 1927, American sailors and airmen have had nearly eighty years of continual, routine carrier operations in peace and war. The skills of flight- and hangar-deck crews, aircraft-maintenance and -repair personnel, and pilots have been honed to a high degree of competence. The Russians, on the other hand, engaged in limited flight operations from their only sporadically deployed cruiser-carriers for at most a dozen years. Very few flight operations appear to have been conducted from the two later sixty-five thousand–ton carriers *Varig* and *Admiral Kuznetsov.* Since the Russians never understood the absolute requirement for upkeep and repair—"preventive maintenance"—of their vessels, the ships swiftly fell into poor material condition. When the Soviet Union collapsed, the Red Fleet rapidly withered, rusted, aged. Yet this fleet provided the only inventory for fledgling sea powers like India and China to find the hardware necessary to transform maritime pretensions into instant credibility.

Both New Delhi and Beijing pondered buying Soviet big ships, like *Admiral Gorshkov*—the last of the four Soviet cruiser-carriers of the late seventies and eighties—and *Varig* and *Admiral Kuznetsov.* After some consideration, however, China and India wisely backed off. Where the Indian Navy will get the pair of carriers for a modern battle group is quite unclear. The only carrier the Indian Navy possesses, *Viraat,* is the old HMS *Hermes,* which was about ready for the breaker's yards when it participated in the Falklands war a quarter century ago. If India decides on indigenous construction, its builders will confront a ship type and size utterly foreign to them. Construction of a Chinese carrier or two has been debated desultorily in Beijing since the early nineties with no resolution as yet in sight. The notion waxes with each appearance of an American carrier battle group in the Taiwan Strait, then dies down shortly after its departure.

India also pondered buying several strategic-ballistic-missile submarines from Moscow, but apparently that purchase also fell through. China, on the other hand, began making modest submarine purchases from Moscow in the late sixties and during the following decade started to produce its own nuclear submarines under Soviet license. China then constructed several *Xia*-class SSBNs of its own, leading naval observers John Wilson Lewis and Xue Litai to conclude in 1994 that the People's Republic had achieved an "integrated sea-based nuclear deterrence." From that time to the millennium and beyond, the People's Liberation Army-Navy (PLAN) "successfully transformed its construction activities from building first-generation naval vessels and weapon systems to second-generation armaments," including cruise-missile-firing destroyers. Beijing also began purchase of advanced French electronic devices, most notably surveillance and fire-control radar, while building up its own capabilities in this area. In short, the People's Republic was roughly replicating early-twentieth-century Japan in acquiring, absorbing, and modifying Western (including Russian) technologies to suit its own needs. China could thus be expected to progressively show and flex its naval muscles in East Asian seas, much as it had done before the humiliation of the 1894–1895 Sino-Japanese War. Some observers feared that Beijing's interest stretched farther than that, past the Strait of Malacca and into the Indian Ocean.[29]

The fact remains, however, that these two numerically small regional navies rely almost wholly on Soviet naval architecture and technology for their most powerful sea-based weapons systems. Despite recent exaggerations by those looking around for the next-generation enemy to confront, Bernard D. Cole's 2001 assessment of the Chinese Navy holds true for India as well:

> China's strategic view, budgetary limitations, foreign relations, and domestic political situation all indicate that the PLAN will continue to be modernized as a regional rather than global navy. From Beijing's perspective, the

PLAN must be able to prevent any other Asian navy interfering with China's national security objectives (read Taiwan), and to at least give pause to U.S. maritime intervention (read Taiwan). A globally capable PLAN would have to be able to project power around the world from the Western Pacific to the Western Atlantic, clearly an ambition beyond China's goals for the twenty-first century.[30]

If serious competition for the seas is not something American citizens or sailors had to much worry about in the post–cold war era, terrorism certainly was. Yet when carefully considered after 9/11, *terrorism* proved a broad, infuriatingly elusive term that could mean many things. National security analyst James Bamford put the matter succinctly: was the United States to treat bin Ladin and those of his ilk as "superhuman" heads of a practical terrorist state without borders with whom we must "war" or, as Bamford clearly preferred, as merely thuggish "mass murderer[s]—a Timothy McVeigh–in–robes"?[31] Should the "War on Terrorism" be conducted by soldiers, sailors, and airmen or by Interpol and the world's most advanced national intelligence agencies?

Americans would soon discover that terrorism is essentially a state of mind, not a government, or a town, or even a well-developed—and thus vulnerable—network. It is grievance politics writ large and taken to the extreme. Although it may be paramilitary in its operations and organization, it is so radically decentralized as to be largely immune to classic military force. Like everyone else, the United States Navy at the beginning of the twenty-first century was far behind the learning curve regarding this phenomenon, as demonstrated by the fate of the destroyer *Cole*, severely damaged by terrorist attack while in the harbor at Aden. Looking back on 1945–1946 from the perspective of a quarter century, former secretary of state Dean Acheson recalled, "Only slowly did it dawn upon us that the whole world structure and order that we had inherited ... was gone" and that the struggle to replace it with a better or equal structure would be incredibly difficult.[32] In March 2003 the Bush administration took the final step toward global imperial power when it determined to replace the short-lived post–cold war international structure with one of its own devising. Abandoning allies who had been more or less steadfast through more than half a century of war and fragile peace, the United States, with Britain its only major supporter, invaded Iraq on what turned out to be not just flimsy but flagrantly erroneous pretexts, in order, it was said, to democratically reform the entire tension-filled, terror-drenched Middle East.

The second Gulf War (Gulf II) underscored the ambiguities inherent in America's military domination of the globe. On the one hand, the armed forces, having shed the cumbersome dogmas, strategies, and organization of the cold war era, proved up to any task on and above the Iraqi battlefields. Revolutionary technological advances since Desert Storm, however exhausting and demoralizing they might have been to those responsible for incorporating and employing them, had created a remarkable system of "network interoperability" between and among the armed services. But a "stripped down," "lean and mean military machine" fully capable of brushing aside Third World armed forces in the field proved incapable of transforming successful invasion into humane occupation. The occupation of Iraq may have tarnished irretrievably the reputation of the American military establishment in that part of the world Washington deemed most critical to national security.

Defense secretary Rumsfeld had come to office in 2001 dazzled and awed by his country's advanced technological prowess and determined "to speed-march the military into the information age." Only later would the dark side of this commitment become clear in terms of a grossly overextended and underfunded defense establishment. In the meantime industry, led by the Boeing Corporation, "scrambled" to meet his demands. By 2002 Boeing's "Battlefield Integration Center" in Anaheim, California, had elaborated the old C3I into an elaborate "C4IST" (command, control, computers and communications, intelligence, surveillance, and targeting). "The new gospel was 'transformation' and it meant a leaner fighting force that would be quicker to deploy, more agile in battle, capable of killing with greater accuracy from greater distances and more 'networked.'"

Command arrangements were now highly integrated, permitting rapid and flexible applications of force when and where needed by whichever service could best and most speedily accomplish the mission. Unlike Desert Storm, for example, senior-level navy fliers, well versed in the realities of electronic warfare, were integrated during Gulf II into the JFACC air-war command structure. As a consequence, "planning was very detailed and coordinated between the 5th Fleet and the 9th Air Force." Satellite positioning, surveillance, and communication data tied to high-speed computers together with real-time radar and targeting systems (including handheld laser "devices" with direct links to nearby command centers) permitted those at the highest levels of command to view the battlefield whole, in detail, and in real time. "Predator" unmanned aerial-surveillance vehicles supplemented and expanded the system. The progressive elaboration of "smart" weapons that "can be carried by almost all navy and Air Force fighters and bombers" ensured that combat would be conducted with an incredible accuracy of standoff firepower. On the desert tabletop and low rolling hills of Iraq, quickly moving armored ground units supported at every stage by "fast, extremely lethal and extremely flexible battlefield air power" swept aside even significant resistance without much pause or heavy casualties either to combatants or to civilians. Operation Enduring Freedom "was joint war fighting at the highest form of the art I've ever seen," enthused Fifth Fleet commander Timothy J. Keating. "There was understanding, friendship, familiarity and trust among all the services and special forces." Chief of Naval Operations Vernon Clark told Keating, "I would have anything at my disposal to present to" General Tommy Franks, the overall theater commander. "So there were five carrier strike groups, more than a dozen submarines, scores of surface ships, military sealift command ships, and amphibious task forces east [Persian Gulf] and west [Mediterranean], all of which deployed and arrived in theater ready, well before the war started. . . . If I had to characterize the planning and execution of this operation in one word," Keating concluded, "the word would be speed. I've been at this for decades, and I have never imagined the ability to do so many things so rapidly." Gulf II confirmed the United States Army, Navy, Air Force and Marines as the most integrated, powerful, and efficient military force in human history.[33]

From its inception, Gulf II was decidedly more favorable than its predecessor to America's sailors who played a distinct, essential, if interrelated role throughout the campaign. Before hostilities began, navy public information officers saw to it that the media were deeply "embedded" aboard the big carriers. Dramatic shots of jet fighter bombers whipping and screaming down broad, night-blackened flight decks in a blast of flame were readily available, as were thousands of sailors and airmen of both genders and many racial and ethnic groups to tell poignant stories of separation anxieties, commitment, loneliness, excitement, and boredom.

As with Gulf I, the opening moments of the second war belonged to the navy. In the early morning hours of March 20, 2003, forty Tomahawk land-attack cruise missiles roared away from their canisters aboard cruisers, destroyers, and submarines in the Persian Gulf and the Mediterranean and Red Seas. The orders to "spin up" the missiles, that is, assign specific targets to each, and send them on their way came so quickly and were carried out so rapidly that some off-duty crewmen aboard the cruiser *Cowpens* in the Red Sea realized they were at war only when awakened by the launch. Long moments later, guided precisely by the global positioning satellite system, the missiles crashed hundreds of miles away on target in the heart of Saddam Hussein's governing, military, and living complexes in downtown Baghdad. Half a century before, I was proudly told by a boot camp instructor that a battleship's guns could place a sixteen-inch shell in a sailor's white hat at twenty-three miles. Now, more powerful Tomahawk warheads are as precise at nearly fifty times the range. When the "Shock and Awe" air campaign got under way the next night, scores of F-14s and 18s together with EA-6 Prowlers from three carriers in the Gulf of Oman joined their air force colleagues over and near Baghdad, blasting away with their deadly cargoes of laser-guided bombs and JDAMs. Several dozen fighter bombers from *Theodore Roosevelt* steaming in the eastern Mediterranean pounded key airfields in western Iraq. Pilots over Baghdad that first full night of the air war saw skies filled with "masses of airplanes"; antiaircraft fire that "climbed up, stalled, then died away"; and explosions from Tomahawk missiles slamming into their targets that lit up entire cloud formations from beneath. The city glowed a lurid green through night goggles.[34]

Nonetheless, Shock and Awe failed to produce the quick knockout blow that navy and air force strategists confidently predicted and raised the specter of unacceptably high civilian casualties from occasionally errant ordnance. After a week of intense bombing and missile attack Saddam Hussein had not only survived "regime decapitation" but was still on the air, still directing his troops and stiffening civilian morale through television exhortations.[35]

Navy fighter bombers and Tomahawk missiles were thus redirected from strategic to tactical targets, supporting ground operations as marine and army units raced toward Baghdad. Not even a violent wind- and sandstorm over the gulf and most of Iraq could completely disrupt operations, as carrier pilots and cruise-missile guidance systems relied on the global positioning system for precise targeting. After several days of steady winds, dust, and sand, aircraft returning to their carriers had to be "talked down" to landings through a steady gusty gloom that left some pilots weak-kneed on landing. Approaching their flight decks at more than a hundred and fifty miles an hour, "The view from the cockpit was a wash of gauzy beige. No ocean, no ships, no horizon—nothing." Then, suddenly, "like a photographic image developing in a chemical bath, the faint outlines of the aircraft carrier's tower [island structure] . . . emerged on the right through the sandy fog" as the onrushing aircraft groped for the deck, then for the arresting gear. Come in too far to the right, and a plane would crash into fueled and armed aircraft awaiting taxiing for launch, killing pilots and flight-deck crew by the several hundreds. Come in too far to the left, and the Tomcat or Hornet would take out the entire landing-signal gang near the stern. Come in too low, and a plane would smash into the ship's stern. Remarkably, only one plane had to be "waved off" for another go-around, reflecting magnificent flying by increasingly weary aircrews who had been bombing around the clock for six days. As exhausted and shaken airmen taxied to their parking area or to an elevator that would whisk them down to the hangar, their planes left tracks through the powdery film that covered the flight deck.[36]

The storm did eventually force a slowdown, as navy (and air force) commanders feared the blowing dust and sand might clog engines and bring down attacking aircraft. Rising above the storm proved no solution because icing at fifteen thousand feet not only affected aircraft stability but also clogged turbines, "wreak-[ing] havoc on engines." The older carrier *Constellation* was the first of the big three flattops in or near the gulf to suspend flight operations. *Kitty Hawk* and *Abraham Lincoln* scrubbed fourteen strike missions because of weather, roughly 20 percent of the daily schedule. "We wouldn't even dream to fly today, if not for the war," one strike coordinator told the media pool aboard *Lincoln*.[37]

Over in the Mediterranean, the Sixth Fleet carriers *Harry S. Truman* and *Theodore Roosevelt* launched strike aircraft at a tempo matching that of their Seventh Fleet sisters in the gulf, while cruisers and destroyers let fly with several salvos of cruise missiles. The two carriers were so deficient in escorts, however, that they were forced to rely on the coast guard high-endurance cutter *Dallas* to provide escort and rescue services during flight operations. Although the coast guard had occasionally pulled plane-guard duty before, "it was a rarity for a cutter to be the only surface ship protecting two carriers." *Dallas* performed outstandingly, and when a storm suddenly swept over the fleet one night the cutter's masthead lights "lit the way home" for the carrier jets.[38]

Deteriorating weather did not deter continuing Tomahawk attacks. Apparently, onboard propulsion and guidance systems were sufficiently hardened against the elements to permit the vast majority of missiles to reach their targets. Eighteen days into the conflict, the navy had launched more than seven hundred Tomahawks; only seven had fallen short of target, for a rather astonishing 1 percent failure rate. "One Pentagon official said that with a weapon system as sophisticated as a precision-guided cruise missile, a failure rate of 5 percent would be considered 'very good.'" But very good was not good enough so far as the Turkish and Saudi governments were concerned. The great percentage of failed Tomahawks landed in their territories. Fortunately, the missile warheads were programmed to go active only within target range. But Ankara and Riyadh were not impressed and promptly closed down the missile "lanes" through their airspaces. U.S. cruiser and destroyer "shooters" in the Mediterranean and Red Seas were forced to suspend operations as they steamed hastily toward new launch positions in the gulf. Although Central Command insisted there would be no significant letup in the missile campaign against Iraq, some officials on the ground fretted that the narrow lanes through Kuwaiti airspace were insufficient to really blanket Iraqi targets. Whether one or more Tomahawks may subsequently have gone astray near their target areas and hit civilians in Baghdad or whether casualties were due to fatal debris from Iraqi antiaircraft fire has never been conclusively determined.

Meanwhile, ground forces, assisted every step of the way by U.S. Navy, Marine Corps, and Air Force tactical aviation, rolled relentlessly toward the Iraqi capital. "As in Afghanistan . . . the cooperative choreography of Army, Marines, air power and Special Operations—rivals who have in the past tended to get in one another's way—has at times been breathtaking. Technology . . . seems to have given commanders all over Iraq a more vivid picture of the battlefield than in any previous war."[39] As the army and marines tightened the noose around Baghdad, fighter bombers from all three services maintained a twenty-four-hour vigil over the city. There were, to be sure, the usual human errors—miscommunications, misunderstandings, mistargeting, and hair-trigger responses—that led to tragic results. But considering the enormous firepower that air and naval forces laid down, tragedy was minimal. The multiple frustrations and humiliation of Vietnam, of the failed attempt to rescue American diplomats in Iran in 1980, of the fumbling, bumbling efforts to oust Cuban paramilitary elements from Grenada three years later, even of Korea, were but dim memories of a finally unified and integrated American military refreshed by its own achievements.

Naval air was a major element in victory. Deploying independently or in pairs, "all-precision" F-14s and -18s flew roughly three-quarters of the strike sorties, achieving an astounding 93 percent accuracy per aircraft per mission, "a monumental shift from the mass force packages of Operation Desert Storm." In the dozen years since the first Gulf War, the navy's research, development, and acquisition communities had done a remarkable job of redesigning aircraft weapons and avionics systems to ensure delivery of precise combat power. "Almost 80% of the aircraft launched in Enduring Freedom combat sorties were unaware of exact target locations. But with their war-fighting tools they adapted quickly and used a full quiver of weapons that ranged from the Joint Direct Attack Munition [JDAM] to 20 mm cannon."[40]

Serious systemic problems remained, however. Splendid as the troops, fliers, and sailors were, how much could they be asked to give over a prolonged period? Behind Iraq loomed North Korea and, it was whispered, perhaps Syria and Iran as well. Would India and China be someday added to the list? In a time of expanding and potentially limitless global responsibilities, a leaner American military—however concentrated its force and firepower—required far more of each human and mechanical component than was perhaps possible. The probability that people would wear out and equipment wear down increased exponentially at a time when the U.S. government was committed to drastic decreases in taxes and spending.

The supercarrier *Abraham Lincoln* was in many ways the showboat of the coalition naval forces that initially operated in the Gulf of Oman before entering the Persian Gulf itself. The ship was coming off a routine six-month deployment in the area and had reached Perth in western Australia when it was suddenly recalled to duty. For the next three-plus months the carrier patrolled, then fought as war came. It served magnificently, but as the media corps who trooped aboard reported, the strain for some became nearly unbearable. Twenty-first-century sailors on America's big warships had available all sorts of resources denied earlier generations of seamen: e-mail, videocassettes, recreation rooms, ship-to-shore telephones in an emergency, comfortable curtained bunks with reading lamps instead of closely slung hammocks or "racks," and all sorts of religious and psychiatric specialists and resources. Those who steamed fourteen laborious months around the world with the Great White Fleet or who hauled ass with Halsey for months at a stretch during World War II, terrified daily by kamikazes and rewarded only with two warm beers in a few hours on a hot, crowded Pacific island beach, would surely have envied such luxuries. But they weren't enough for America's twenty-first-century seamen. The sailors and flyers of Gulf II came from a society whose security and affluence were beyond the wildest dreams of the young men of 1908 and 1944. At the same time, they bore social burdens and expectations that earlier generations would have found incredible. It all added up to a completely different world.

As *Lincoln* raced back to the gulf and began launching patrols again while diplomats at the UN argued about deadlines and inspectors, the crew assumed a protective mantle of numbness. "Life aboard this 1,092 foot–long carrier on 'Operation Southern Watch' is a curious mix of boredom and tension," a reporter cabled home. "No one thinks about war, and everyone thinks about it, all the time. It could happen. It could not happen. Everything could remain the same. Everything could change in an instant." Crewmen turned off CNN and began running movies on their CD players. "They say they're sick of it, sick of all the false promises" of a war that would at least bring resolution and a vague promise of termination and home. "'The less I know, the better,'" one petty officer remarked. Periodically, Captain Kendall Card addressed the crew over the intercom, reminding them that they were in the gulf for "a great purpose" and warning of attacks out of the blue, or the dark, whenever this or that dead-line was passed. But the sailors shrugged. So many deadlines had come and gone. One young aviator said that the joke was that March 17 would become March 31 would become April 13 and so on, ad infinitum, while the carrier continued to steam and launch aimlessly.

Every moment, twenty-four hours a day, *Lincoln* was awash in noise, move-ment, stress, and tension. Life and time seemed perpetually suspended. The ship had a clinical psychologist on board who described her job as "all about damage control. People get frustrated and angry and sad." Wisely, Lieutenant Rose Rice refused to lie to them "and try to tell them they should be happy to still be out here." The situation was rough, and all she could do was to "keep it from getting worse." Ironically, things were worse for new arrivals, flown out to Perth or perhaps even the gulf itself to replace those whose enlistments or duty duration had expired. The newcomers encountered rigid cliques and in-groups who told them they had no right to complain—"You haven't been stuck out here for eight months." The ship was hot and crowded. "Sleep's bad. Then there's the heartache . . . [Y]ou think, 'I don't know how this is going to end. But you can't vent because those who have been out here for so long are struggling with other issues,'" one of which (another irony) was electronic mail. Instant com-munication without voice or physical contact proved a double-edged sword. E-mail permitted arguments and disputes without resolution. Many an outraged sailor hit his "send" button then instantly regretted what he had done. Lieu-tenant Rice urged some to retreat to snail mail for the sake of family harmony. "I advise them to slow down, to write letters. Or write an e-mail, save it a day and if it is still what you want to say, then send it." Always, there was the unremitting mental and emotional stress of living every day with the same people in the same cramped areas. Of the fifty-six hundred–plus men and women aboard the carrier, perhaps five or six hundred at most worked at exciting, dan-gerous jobs in the Aviation and Operations Departments. The vast majority were responsible for maintaining small spaces and doing routine tasks belowdecks; many did not see sun, sky, or sea for weeks on end. The longer one stayed aboard, the more listless one became beyond the fulfillment of one's duty. "People are living in berthing areas with 50 to 60 people. In December (when the ship was steaming home) it was, 'Oh, I can put up with this person for one more month. Now there's no end date, and it's 'How much longer can I stand it?'" After eight or nine or ten months, "Four and a half acres is only so big. There's only so much area to get away from everyone, only so many times you want to eat with the same people."[41]

When war came at last, *Lincoln*'s pilots confronted the age-old problems of the warrior about to go into battle. A few had children they had never seen and wondered if they ever would see. All were aware that other children would be beneath their bombs, and could die hideously before they had ever lived. "War is a very, very ugly thing," *Lincoln*'s deputy air wing commander said. "This is not a solution to turn to." But the youngsters under his command flew off and did the jobs they were ordered to do.[42]

Over in the eastern Med, life and perspectives were remarkably similar aboard *Theodore Roosevelt*. Only a fraction of the massive carrier's huge enlisted complement had anything to do with the vessel's mission. One day of flight operations melded into another, and the line between peacetime practice and wartime missions remained blurred, producing a widespread sense of fatalism among the crew. Whereas pilots exulted in a sense of mission ("I always consider it a great privilege to be in combat for my country," one F-14 squadron commander said), a young petty officer told reporter Janine Zacharia that war with Iraq "really... doesn't concern me right now because we're here to do a job. That's what we signed up for, so whatever happens, happens. If we do go to war, it's fine. If we don't it's fine, too." The youngster was ambivalent about ousting Saddam. He supported the move "because we fight for our freedom." He opposed it "because it's taking me away from my family." Life was especially arduous for the young women aboard. A junior officer named Emily "had to choose her wedding dress on the Internet," while several hundred young mothers (the *Teddy* carried eight hundred female sailors, "more than any other ship in the U.S. Navy") fretted about children in the unaccustomed care of fathers.

More than half the crew had experienced Operation Enduring Freedom in Afghanistan when the ship spent an astounding 159 days at sea without a port call. "This time the carrier left" Norfolk "January 6, expecting to be at sea for a five-week exercise. Instead they were sent to the Mediterranean for an indefinite deployment," throwing everyone's life into "disarray." The last port call had been in Crete a month before, and here they were with no prospect of shore leave. The eastern Med had suddenly become a hostile place, as inflamed Arab opinion produced "a high level of anti-American sentiment." Even friendly Israel was now considered dangerous after a recent suicide bombing. "Beer was loaded on board in Crete—a bad sign. The U.S. Navy is one of the last 'dry' navies in the world; only if the ship spends 45 straight days at sea is each person on board entitled to two beers."[43]

Reporters confined themselves to the huge carriers where life was dramatic, human interest stories abounded, and amenities were comparatively plentiful.

But *Lincoln* and *Theodore Roosevelt* spearheaded carrier battle groups that included much smaller guided-missile cruisers and destroyers, whose "shooters" confronted the same ethical crises as carrier pilots and far greater tedium than was found aboard the big ships. On the "small boys" and the replenishment ships that supported the battle fleet, chances for a change in personal contacts, to say nothing of opportunities for privacy, were nil. One can imagine what life must have been like for the 350 to 400 men and women crowded aboard one of *Lincoln*'s or *Teddy*'s five escort ships with less than one-fifth the deck space. An officer aboard the missile cruiser *Anzio* reported that his ship spent eighty-three days at sea between port visits to Gibraltar and Jabal 'Ali in the United Arab Emirates.[44] Nonetheless, the missions were accomplished. Imperceptibly, America's sea warriors were developing the same rather grim and joyless but determined imperial cast of thought and professionalism that sustained their British cousins ashore and afloat across the world throughout several earlier centuries.

But no military force, however strong its competence and allegiance, can long sustain such a tempo. The steel-hulled ship is itself an anomaly, since it is constantly being corroded by sea and wind, while propulsion and other machinery are being continually stressed. A week after the commencement of Gulf II, the navy reported that fully 68 percent of its surface warships and 51 percent of the submarine force were away from their home ports—an exceptionally high number, nearing the ratios demanded in World War II. Fifty-four percent of the surface combatants and 36 percent of the submarines were "on deployment." For the carrier battle groups this meant either the Persian Gulf or the Sea of Japan, keeping an eye on North Korea. At least five carriers—nearly half the navy's flattop fleet—were operating around the clock.[45]

Should the future navy find itself in a more or less continuous cycle of patrol and combat, the need to replace even the stoutest, most efficient ships long before their designed age limits will become imperative. Shortly after the war, Vice Admiral Charles Moore Jr., deputy chief of naval operations for fleet readiness, reported that although it cost three billion dollars more each year to keep aging ships and aircraft operational, the budget for new construction was down 13 percent. By 2004 the navy clearly faced a crisis. A Pentagon report in August noted sharply increased engineering and manufacturing development costs for the navy's projected CVN-21 future supercarrier, even as the first five *Ticonderoga* Aegis–class cruisers along with initial units of the *Spruance*-class guided-missile destroyers (commissioned as recently as 1975–1977) were deemed too overstressed to remain in service. The cruiser *Valley Forge* had been in commission for just eighteen hard-driven years before it was mothballed. At the same time, the financially strapped Pentagon proposed only a four-ship new-construction program for the fiscal year, all of which were auxiliary vessels. Chief of naval operations Admiral Vernon Clark promised significant cost savings through "dramatic innovations" in automating various ships' systems, including unmanned engine rooms and "as needed" maintenance systems. Clark and others in the naval establishment emphasized that advanced automation had worked for years aboard merchant ships and that it only made sense to transfer such promising technologies to naval vessels.[46] But such thinking may prove fallacious. Warships are not merchant ships; naval operations, especially under combat conditions, are far more stressful, demanding labor-intensive manning not required aboard cargo ships or passenger liners. But under increasingly onerous budget constraints, the navy had little choice but to rather frantically search out whatever cost savings it could, whether they made operational sense or not. The result promised to be a progressive drawdown of U.S. naval power past the point of acceptability.

The stunning accuracy of America's weaponry during Gulf II negated much of the criticism that the navy had become too small, its firepower insufficient. No weapon system had improved more dramatically in precision and power than the Tomahawk land-attack cruise missile. By Gulf II every combatant from the twenty-seven *Ticonderoga*-class cruisers through the sixty-odd *Arleigh Burke*– and *Spruance*-class guided-missile destroyers (with a score more building or planned) to the fifty *Los Angeles*–class and three *Seawolf*-class submarines carried at least ten or more of these weapons possessed of a thousand-mile range and a building-busting capability. Each surface ship could be quickly configured to carry far more T-LAMs. Thus, the United States Navy could deploy several thousand of these lethal long-range weapons at comparatively short notice.

T-LAMs provided the navy—and the American taxpayer—with a spectacular multiplier effect, for at a stroke they changed the status of the 150-ship surface navy "from escorts to capital ships." For half a century after 1941, carrier air groups not only far outranged but exceeded any firepower that the mightiest surface ships could deliver. Inevitably, even battleships were reduced to the primary role of carrier escort, with shore bombardment rather tacked on as a secondary mission. The T-LAM changed everything. Conceived from the start as a nuclear-armed cruise missile, the Tomahawk transformed even the lowliest destroyer into an unimaginably powerful "shooter." Whereas in the twentieth century even the greatest navies might possess at most a score of capital ships, the United States Navy of the early twenty-first century suddenly possessed nearly ten times that number, including the dozen powerful supercarriers.[47]

The mix of missiles and manned aircraft thus seemed about right. No one could deny either the horrifying power of a coordinated T-LAM attack on enemy installations and troop concentrations or the priceless direct battlefield-support and rapid-response capabilities provided by naval and marine aviation as well as the air force. But for all its spectacular capabilities, the T-LAM remained a comparatively inflexible weapon system. So, argued critics, did the unmanned aerial vehicles (UAVs) that began trickling into the fleet in the early twenty-first century. "Remote robotic weapons," which is what the T-LAMs and UAVs essentially are, "will never replace the human's ability to adapt and respond to a fluid combat environment. . . . [T]hey will never completely replace the fighter pilot and manned aircraft."[48] Perhaps, but are the huge, manned aircraft–carrying ships cost-effective? Each of the big flattops deployed roughly thirty-six to forty-eight attack aircraft; the remainder of its air group played a support role. Moreover, carrier-based aircraft, no matter how ingeniously designed, remain notoriously short-range. The naval air war against the Taliban, however spectacular, relied on costly, cumbersome, time-consuming aerial refueling for success. The price of these ships had risen steadily from roughly two *billion* to six *billion* dollars over the twenty-eight years since the lead vessel, *Nimitz,* put to sea. These were design and construction costs alone and did not include operating costs, periodic dry docking and upgrades, and so on.

And the huge craft, crammed with thousands of mechanical and electronic machines, tend to age poorly if not attended to with the greatest, most meticulous care. In December 2001 the commanding officer of *John F. Kennedy* was relieved of command on the eve of the carrier's six-month deployment in the Mediterranean. "Thousands of needed repairs" had not been made, and the navy concluded that Captain Joyce had not properly assessed either his ship's material condition or crew training levels. Ten months later the skipper of *Kennedy*'s sister ship, *Kitty Hawk,* was "fired" because he "lost control of his crew—and his ship." Not surprisingly the two vessels were the oldest supercarriers in the fleet, and the commander of the Atlantic Fleet Naval Air Force admitted publicly that *Kennedy* had been "systematically underfunded for years." There was less excuse for *Kitty Hawk*'s abysmal state, since the carrier was homeported in Japan where lower labor costs made it "less vulnerable to the widespread maintenance funding shortfalls that became evident in much of the U.S. military in the late 1990's."[49]

In its drainage of funds from other promising or essential weapon systems, America's small carrier fleet had thus come to resemble Japan's superbattleships *Yamato* and *Musashi* of the early forties, which, however impressive as potential intimidators, proved so expensive as to skew the Imperial Fleet's balance and fatally impair its efficiency. Moreover, Pentagon estimates consistently posited the need for at least fifteen supercarriers to fulfill America's strategic commitments in Europe and the Mediterranean, the Persian Gulf and adjacent waters, and the western Pacific. In 2004 naval analyst Norman Polmar cited one example from 1999 in which the navy was forced to stretch its then eleven-unit carrier fleet so thinly to cover the Kosovo crisis that the resulting "shell game" left the strategically critical western Pacific region bereft of a carrier battle group for eighty-six days.[50]

One solution to the potentially crippling cost program was greater reliance on T-LAMs. Some navy men on the eve of the second Gulf War revived the notion of a small flotilla of barely manned, very high-tech (though slow-moving) arsenal ships, each equipped with several hundred or more T-LAMs plus other missiles for defense. But although missiles may be programmed to "loiter" around a battlefield, the rapidity and fluidity of current combat suggest a continued need for some sort of manned aircraft to respond in very near real time to erupting crises of a local or broader nature. The elaboration of speedy, effective, and powerful vertical- or short-takeoff and -landing (VSTOL) aircraft might provide an answer to the stupendous costs of a huge nuclear-powered aircraft carrier. "Jump jets" like the current AV-8B take up comparatively little deck space, nor do they require cumbersome steam-catapult and arresting-wire systems that add so much extra weight and machinery to a carrier while severely taxing its propulsion system during launch operations. The highly advanced F-35 VSTOL aircraft that will enter the fleet in increasing numbers after 2012 together with the promise of totally unmanned but human-directed UCAVs (unmanned combat aerial vehicles like the upgraded "Predator" reconnaissance drones) should allow for the construction of much smaller and operationally far less costly carriers roughly two-thirds the size and half the displacement and manning requirements of the *Nimitz*-class behemoths, yet with a roughly comparable air group and magazine capability. As late as 2004, however, the Pentagon seemed wedded to the huge, expensive, nuclear-powered "fleet" carrier.[51]

Gulf II demonstrated beyond question that the key to America's military and naval dominance in the world lay in the steady elaboration of advanced and, above all, integrated technologies. Ever more accurate intelligence was fed to the guidance systems of increasingly powerful weapons that delivered ordnance ever more precisely. But however spectacular, the weapons and their delivery systems were as inhuman as any German U-boat of 1917 and 1942 or any submarine-based ballistic missile of the nuclear age. With the T-LAM, JDAM, and similar ordnance the United States had at last reached the threshold of that long-predicted age of "push button warfare," in which "war will be fought in the absence of warriors."[52]

As early as Gulf I, American flyers and sailors were as awed by the standoff power of their weapons as they were by watching commercial television news accounts of the result. "There was a little time after we'd fired where we had such a rush," one sailor aboard the destroyer *Paul F. Foster* recalled. "We thought, 'God, what did we just do? We just launched cruise missiles. At people.' It was kinda scary." Another crew member got knots in his stomach. "I said to myself, 'I can't believe we're doing this!'" Soon enough, however, the missile launches became a familiar pattern of life at sea. "The first couple of times it was really a big deal, but after that it got almost routine to fire a Tomahawk missile. It was surprising how, basically, we started a war and then went back to life as normal." Pilots flying combat air patrols at fifteen to twenty thousand feet off the super-carrier *Ranger* were treated to a spectacular display as the Tomahawk launches far below looked like flares coming out of the launch ships. Soon after, the carrier's pilots went on their own strike missions over Iraq. Landing back aboard, they went to their informal chow hall, "ate a 'slider' (hot dog) and watched Bernard Shaw and Peter Arnett getting bombed in Baghdad." Crewmen and pilots alike aboard the big ship were enthralled when about thirty minutes after launch of a strike package, "Peter Arnett would be live from Baghdad saying, 'Holy shit! Look what's coming in!' And everyone back on the *Ranger* was watching and cheering."[53]

During Gulf II more than a decade later, standoff weaponry had advanced to the point that fliers seldom even glimpsed the targets they obliterated. Their bombs traveled as much as fifteen miles from release point to target. By that time they had banked their jet and raced twenty to thirty more miles from the target. "There is no screaming to hear, no explosion, no sound at all." This was also true of the strategic bombing campaigns of World War II, Korea, and Vietnam. But bomber streams over Germany and to a lesser extent in the early days over Japan and later Korea were subjected to vicious attacks by waves of defending fighters and often deadly accurate flak. They thus became an intimate part of the battles their bombing initiated. In the uncontested firebomb raids against Japan's cities, the B-29s flew in so low they could feel the heat and even smell the burning flesh of those they incinerated. Only B-52 pilots high over Vietnam where surface-to-air missiles seldom reached were as detached from the dreadful punishment they delivered as were the pilots of Gulf II.

Evidence is accumulating that growing reliance on "standoff" ordnance can only tarnish America's international image, especially since even the most sophisticated weaponry will occasionally go awry. When President Clinton ordered his 1998 retaliatory T-LAM attack on suspected al Qaeda headquarters in Afghanistan following the devastating car bombings of embassies in Africa, the action provoked "scalding criticism" at home and abroad as being both cowardly and excessive. What the world apparently did not know—though Islamabad did—was that one of the T-LAMs went astray and hit a Pakistani village, killing several people. President Clinton found Pakistani officials understanding when he called to apologize, but the editors of the influential newsmagazine *Economist* asked if the U.S. cruise missiles had not "created 10,000 new fanatics where there would have been none."

Push-button warfare generates fear, hatred, and contempt within those many societies and cultures that cling to traditional warrior norms of combat. Washington understood the potentially devastating consequences of "collateral damage" and according to the 9/11 Commission looked for other ways to get at al Qaeda following the 1998 missile attacks.[54] Gulf II, with its generous employment of T-LAMs, JDAMs, and other "smart" but occasionally errant weaponry, generated a disturbing reaction among the weaker members of the international community. Even as fighting raged in and around Baghdad, North Korea announced that it not only possessed one or more atomic bombs but was regenerating the nuclear weapon program that created them in the first place. Pyongyang insisted that Washington defer to its demands for a nonaggression pact on North Korean terms. Any effort to destroy or forestall the North Korean weapon program might well induce the unstable regime in Pyongyang to lash out at its enemies with suitcase weapons, sneak nuclear-missile attacks against South Korea or Japan, or other forms of open or clandestine assault. On the other hand, deference to the North Korean nuclear reality or appeasement of the regime would surely encourage Pyongyang to become the chief supplier of nuclear materials to terrorists eager to strike other deadly blows at the United States.

"The undigitalized human will is able to frustrate our most elaborate schemes and lofty policies," a prominent columnist wrote shortly after the second anniversary of 9/11. "What unleashed Shock and Awe and the most extravagant display of American military prowess ever" in the skies over Iraq "was a bunch of theologically deranged Arabs with box cutters. The Bush Administration thought it could use scientific superiority to impose its will on alien tribal cultures. But we're spending hundreds of billions subduing two backward countries," Iraq and Afghanistan, "without subduing them. After the president celebrated victory in our high tech war in Iraq, our enemies came back to rattle us with a diabolically ingenious low tech war" of truck bombs, ambushes, and sabotage of power and water lines.[55]

America's seamen, naval airmen, and marines were thus finding the twenty-first century as challenging as its predecessor, with new, often ill-defined, mission responsibilities well beyond imagining in the just concluded cold war era while burdened with an administration and a defense secretary whose defense budget had not been matched in folly since the time of Harry Truman and Louis Johnson. Six months after Gulf II the navy announced it was not only trimming the fleet but also "up to 10,000 sailors" from its ranks through "early outs, tougher re-enlistments, fewer recruits." "This is an effort that has been going on since before the war on terror," the chief of naval operations announced. The navy needed to "realize cost savings" while becoming more efficient, more capable. This newest edition of a new navy would be better through technology—through "human systems integration." Subordinates tasked with the nearly impossible goal of making vague policy statements work were not as cocksure as Admiral Vernon Clark. The disappearance of the Soviet Union as a major "technical competitor," one wrote, removed an essential "external driver" of U.S. military technology. "Internal technology goals" in the post–cold war era were subject to whim. "They change radically and quickly as political and military leaders come and go. Because of the mismatch between technology processes and technology objectives, the navy is not fielding new systems and new ideas any faster despite its best efforts. And slow or inconsistent development almost always drives up costs." In such an environment, cost cutting became an obsession. A press report early in 2004 stated that Vice Admiral Moore had admitted his service was "so short of money it's requiring pilots to fly simulators rather than real jets to practice carrier landings." A year later the Congressional Research Service concluded, "Since February 2003, if not earlier, there has been no current, officially approved, unambiguous plan for the future size and structure of the Navy." An impending Quadrennial Defense Review conducted by Rumsfeld's experts and analysts assumed "baseline defense budgets . . . to be flat for the foreseeable future" with the expectation that "the capital-intensive Navy and Air Force" would suffer significant program reductions whose savings would be "redirected toward the Army, Marine Corps and Special Operations Forces."[56]

Spare and uncertain budget policies disrupted not only technological development but daily lives as well. During and after Gulf II, all the armed services were forced to rely increasingly on reservists whose prolonged service time often led to drastically reduced incomes, destroyed careers, and ruined marriages.

A thirty-nine-year-old flyer with Strike Fighter Squadron 201 claimed to have suffered a 60 percent decline in pay from what he was making as a commercial airline pilot. A twenty-three-year-old marine reserve lance corporal employed as a rape counselor had to ask his wife to stop working and take care of their two-year-old daughter when he was called up. "We almost separated," he told a newsman. "She was real stressed out." Days after he returned from the Middle East, a fifty-year-old reserve maintenance officer who had deployed to the gulf with Strike Fighter Squadron 201 lost his executive-level job with a major U.S. corporation. "It was a matter of business timing," he later explained. "I wasn't there at a crucial time. I'm pretty disheartened."[57]

In November 2003 word raced through the fleet of deep, painful cuts in ways of life. A headline in *Navy Times,* a normally sober and authoritative journal, screamed: "DoD wants to close up to 38 commissaries, Cut your pay, Give away your stateside schools." The latter proposal generated the most outrage. Many service-run elementary, middle, and high schools on military and naval bases throughout the nation were superior, often markedly so, to their civilian counterparts. This was particularly true in large areas across the South and in urban areas of the North. Enlisted pay rates in America's armed forces have never approached the civil sector. Only a handful of perquisites, including free medical and dental care, sharply reduced prices at on-base commissaries, occasional on-base housing (or stipends for off-base living), and efficient service-run schools, were sufficient to attract and hold the kind of talented people the services, and especially the navy, desperately required. Now Rumsfeld and his bean counters seemed ready to cut or destroy even these modest benefits for those charged with homeland security and national defense at a time when pay levels in the civil sector remained consistently higher.[58]

One solution to these myriad problems was simply to designate a future enemy and build a fleet and a strategy around impending conflict with him. The early-twentieth-century "War Plan Orange" against Japan—and Japan's own strategic planning and assumptions—more than hinted at self-fulfilling prophecy. A century later, some armchair strategists began proposing an inevitable future conflict with China over Taiwan, global trade, and possibly other issues. The intellectually fertile if not always reliable Robert Kaplan proposed, "in essence, three separate navies": a traditional blue-water sea-air fleet "as a platform for offshore bombing (to support operations likes the ones in Iraq and Afghanistan); one designed for littoral Special Operations combat (against terrorist groups based in and around Indonesia, Malaysia, and the southern Philippines, for example); and one designed to enhance our stealth capabilities (for

patrolling the Chinese mainland and the Taiwan Strait, among other regions)."
The navy's construction of small, stealth "littoral combat ships" together with
the maintenance of a traditional blue-water fleet (albeit at a nearly historic low
level) suggest that Kaplan's theorizing springs as much or more from interviews
with carrier- and surface-combat admirals frustrated with the glacial pace of
brown-water warfare as from his own speculations. As one of them remarked,
"The Navy needs to spend less time in that salty little mud puddle" that is the
Persian Gulf "and more time in the [western Pacific Ocean] pond."[59]

The Bush administration's 2006 Quadrennial Review muddied the strategic
waters still further. On the one hand, it proclaims that "joint maritime forces,
including the Coast Guard, will conduct highly distributed operations with a
networked fleet that is more capable of projecting power in the 'brown and
green waters' of coastal areas." Such "distributed operations" would require special operations forces, or SOFs. There was nary a mention of the navy's only
new blue-water "capital" ship, the DD (X) advanced destroyer. Indeed, chief of
naval operations Admiral Mike Mullen admonished his sailors to "think . . . more
SOF-like." On the other hand, the review also emphasizes the need to "retain
the Pentagon's world-beating dominance in more conventional warfare" in order
to counter the growing power of China. "Of all the major and emerging powers," the report continues, "China has the greatest potential to compete militarily with the United States." For the past decade, "Chinese military modernization has accelerated . . . in response to central leadership demands to develop
military options against Taiwan scenarios." The fact that the current Beijing
regime has actively coveted the island from the beginning and has doubtless
developed countless "military options" and "Taiwan scenarios" down the years
without doing anything about it seems to have escaped the current administration's strategic team whose grasp of even recent history is fragile and tenuous
at best.[60]

In November 2005 Mullen floated yet another strategic concept, a "1,000
Ship" international navy "for worldwide maritime cooperation." All the world's
fleets, large and small, would join in a gigantic, ongoing effort to police the
seven seas so that they not become either the transportation route or the arena
for international terrorism. Reactions from other fleets were generally positive.
After all, the U.S. Navy had been conducting operations with allied fleets under
and beyond the NATO umbrella since the earliest days of the postwar era, and
the notion of a thousand-ship international naval force was a logical extension
of the irresistible movement toward globalization. The Royal Navy's Admiral

Sir Alan West replied that "ensuring the security of our [international] trade routes is as much a problem now as it was many years ago. . . . Today the security and economic prosperity of our nations is utterly dependent on ensuring that freedom of the seas is maintained and this will continue to be the case as the pace of globalization continues. We simply cannot afford to have disruptions to shipping or increased costs of shipping as the result of threats of attack." Others, however tentatively, pointed out "problems and challenges" that would have to be addressed and met. How willing would the United States be to share its advanced communication and munition technologies with the rest of the world? Would true "interoperability" require a generosity so great that the United States would lose much if not all of its enormous edge?[61] And where in this new age of globalization and decentralized international terror was the need for more ninety thousand–ton supercarriers and their costly planes and escorts?

The U.S. Navy is no stranger to crises in finance and technology, or cacophonies of competing strategic visions. America's sailors came to dominate the world ocean and its littorals in the twentieth century precisely by responding courageously and creatively to challenges posed as much by parsimonious, unimaginative Congresses and administrations as by a series of maritime crises in both Europe and the Pacific. In this they followed in the footsteps of their British cousins—those Tommy Adkinses and Jack Tars and their "solid bottomed ladies, with solid bottom loyalties" whom journalist Theodore White encountered in 1938 on a Butterfield and Swire steamship sailing between Shanghai and Hong Kong. "They added to the sightseer's ineradicable affection for the British," White wrote, "which persisted long after [I] recognized, years later, that the British had lost their greatness when they came to despise such simple ladies, whose men had made Britain great."[62] Twenty-first-century American seamen, and their ladies, are no longer simple folk, but their solid-bottomed loyalties are as often exploited, not so much by a contemptuous and uncaring ruling class as by a country—and a national administration—that insists on a global empire for liberty and wealth without pain to any except those with their boots literally on the ground or on deck who must shape and defend it. Riven and fractured as it has been—and may yet be again—by cultural, racial, and gender conflicts, chronically strapped if not starved of adequate funding, burdened by mission responsibilities that stretch people and resources to the limit, wholly uncertain of its future, the United States Navy, like its sister services, continues to rely on a patriotism and self-discipline that the civilian world simply cannot match, indeed can scarcely conceive. A frequently hypercritical press and people would do well to acknowledge the achievements of a service that over the past hundred years and more has accepted and tried to carry out every dubious mission, every questionable assignment, every dirty detail assigned to it with loyalty, fidelity, and, in the end, no little honor. In more than a century of tension and conflict all too often defined by blood, blunder, and betrayal, that is an impressive legacy.

Abbreviations

CWIHPB	*Cold War International History Project Bulletin*
FRUS	*Foreign Relations of the United States,* U.S. Department of State
HSTL	Harry S. Truman Library, Independence, Missouri
NIP	*U.S. Naval Institute Proceedings*

Chapter 1. Grand Strategy

1. Unless otherwise noted, the following quotes regarding enlisted opinion in the United States Navy at the end of World War II are from Guy Richards, "What the Sailors Say about the Navy."

2. A perfect example of the strange combination of sternness and flippancy that usually characterized relations between ranks and rates in the United States Navy occurred one evening during the war aboard the presidential yacht. Admiral King walked onto the quarterdeck, saluted, turned to the young sailor standing there, and handed him a package, saying: "Son, keep this for me till I go ashore." The youngster said, "Aye-aye, sir," then perhaps roguishly added: "Your wish is my command, Admiral!" The old man turned his cold, steel-gray eyes on the boy and said softly, "You're goddam right it is!" J. Bryan III, *Aircraft Carrier,* 106–7.

3. Paul Fussell, *Wartime: Understanding and Behavior in the Second World War,* 79–95.

4. Richards, "What the Sailors Say," 41.

5. Eric J. Grove, *From* Vanguard *to Trident: British Naval Policy since World War II,* 3.

6. James Cable, *Britain's Naval Future,* 18.

7. Stalin and Molotov are quoted in Woodford McClellan, "Molotov Remembers," *CWIHPB,* no. 1 (spring 1992): 17–18.

8. Michael A. Palmer, *Origins of the Maritime Strategy,* 6; Arnold J. Rogow, *James Forrestal: A Study of Personality, Politics, and Policy,* 105–6, 133–34; Walter Millis and E. S. Duffield, eds., *The Forrestal Diaries,* 14, 42; Arthur H. Vandenberg Jr. and Joe Alex Morris, *The Private Papers of Senator Vandenberg,* 169.

9. Palmer, *Maritime Strategy,* 3–4.

10. Ibid., 12–13.

11. Vandenberg and Morris, *Papers of Vandenberg,* 246–51.

12. Soviet wartime and postwar espionage is the subject of Robert Louis Benson and Michael Warner, eds., *Venona: Soviet Espionage and the American Response, 1939–1957,* xviii–xxii (quote on p. xx). Development of the Eighth Fleet as an Atlantic-Mediterranean crisis-response tool is in Palmer, *Maritime Strategy,* 21–22, which includes Mitscher's reply to Burke's query.

13. Palmer, *Maritime Strategy,* 14–15.

14. Soviet pressure on Iran, Turkey, and elsewhere is briefly summarized in Lisle A. Rose, *After Yalta: America and the Origins of the Cold War,* 163–73 (newspaper quotes are on p. 171). An excellent overall summary of the *Missouri* mission is in Robert W. Love, *A History of the U.S. Navy, 1775–1991,* 2:281–84. The origins of the mission can be found in Millis and Duffield, *The Forrestal Diaries,* 141, 144–45; and Palmer, *Maritime Strategy,* 22. The *Missouri* mission is transcribed and edited from the *Dictionary of American Naval Fighting Ships* by Larry Jewell for the Internet site http://www.hazegray .org. The *Fargo* mission is transcribed from the dictionary for that site by Michael Hansen. They are found at http://www.hazegrey.org/danfs/battlesh/bb63_and_/cruisers/ c1106. *The Dictionary of American Naval Fighting Ships* was originally published by the U.S. Government Printing Office in nine volumes between 1959 and 1991. Information on the *Providence* visit to Cairo is in the official U.S. Navy Bureau of Personnel monthly *All Hands,* no. 353 (July 1946): 2, found at http://www.news.navy.mil/media/ allhands. The impact of a powerful naval presence can be seen in the cover picture of *Fargo* lying just off Venice in August 1947 in *U.S. Navy Cruiser Sailors Association Journal* 12:2 (spring 2003). Tito's threat was recalled by Tom Anderson in "Mail Call," ibid., 12:3 (summer 2003): 47.

15. The origins and development of the Joint Chiefs' recommendation of July 27, 1946, is in James F. Schnabel, *The History of the Joint Chiefs of Staff: The Joint Chiefs of Staff and National Policy,* 103–8. A complete text of the report, further amplified by presidential counselors Clark Clifford and George M. Elsey, is in Arthur Krock, *Memoirs: Sixty Years on the Firing Line,* 389–456. The *Franklin D. Roosevelt* mission is transcribed and edited from the *Dictionary of American Fighting Ships* by Michael Hansen and is found in http://www.hazegrey.org/danfs/carriers/cvb42.

16. Palmer, *Maritime Strategy,* 21.

17. Cunningham's remark to Sherman is in ibid., 22; Millis's observation is in Millis and Duffield, *The Forrestal Diaries,* 141; Alvin J. Cottrell and Wynfred Joshua, "The United States—Soviet Strategic Balance in the Mediterranean," 90–91; Jonathan Trumbull Howe, *Multicrises: Sea Power and Global Politics in the Missile Age,* 3–28; John R. Davis, "'Med' Replenishment—Suda Bay, Crete, 1947," *U.S. Navy Cruiser Sailors Association Journal* 13:1 (winter 2004): 47; Love, *History of the U.S. Navy,* 2:284–85; Kenneth J. Hagan, *This People's Navy: The Making of American Sea Power,* 336–37; Michele Cosentino, "A Legacy Presence," *NIP* 126:3 (March 2000): 50–51.

18. Francis McMurtrie, ed., *Jane's Fighting Ships, 1949–50,* vi, 105–10, 126–10, 148–50a, 173–85, 210–15.

19. Edward J. Marolda, "The U.S. Navy and the 'Loss of China,' 1945–1950," reprinted online at http://www.marshallfoundation.org/pdf/18marolda, 1–3 (quotes on p. 3).

20. Ibid., 3–7.

21. Ibid., 6.

22. NSC 48/2, which folds in the tentative Far East security conclusions of the Joint Chiefs of Staff contained in NSC 37/7, is printed in *FRUS, 1949,* vol. 7, pt. 2, 1215–20. See especially paragraph g(2), 1219–20. Two excellent discussions of U.S. naval operations in the Far East in the 1950s are Arthur W. Radford, "Our Navy in the Far East"; and Franc Shor and W. E. Garrett, "Good Will Ambassadors of the U.S. Navy Win Friends in the Far East."

23. NSC 48/2, paragraph g(2), 1219.

24. John F. Lehman Jr., *On Seas of Glory: Heroic Men, Great Ships, and Epic Battles of the American Navy,* 300.

25. Stuart Symington, oral history interview, May 29, 1981, 29, 42, Symington Papers, HSTL.

26. Quoted in undated memorandum titled "The Hazards of Merger," pt. 2, pp. 8–9, appended to "Memorandum for the President" by James H. Foskett, January 14, 1947, in "President Truman's Fight to Unify the Armed Services," box 17B, folder 13, Harry S. Truman Papers: Student Research File, HSTL.

27. Quoted in ibid., 9.

28. Quoted in "The Hazards of Merger." A slightly different and greatly toned-down version of the speech that is identified as having been given at an Armed Forces Staff College dinner in early 1947 is printed in Stephen Howarth, *To Shining Sea: A History of the United States Navy, 1775–1991,* 477. It is entirely possible that the zealous Armstrong could have given the speech twice and that he was inebriated when he addressed the forum.

29. See, for example, V. I. Achkasov and N. B. Pavlovich, *Soviet Naval Operations in the Great Patriotic War, 1941–1945.* From the outset of the cold war, Soviet authorities mounted countless disinformation campaigns designed to convince their Western opponents of Russian military and naval prowess. One of the earliest efforts appeared in *Jane's Fighting Ships, 1949–50.* Under the heading "New Construction" (271) in the Soviet section of the authoritative British naval annual, editors Francis E. McMurtrie and Raymond V. B. Blackman state that the Russian fleet had either deployed or was about to deploy two 860-foot, 35,000-ton battleships mounting not only six 16-inch guns, but also radio-controlled, long-range rockets. The artist depicted the vessels as possessing long, sleek hulls with clipper bows, flowing superstructures, and a single fat but rakish funnel. One or both ships had either been laid down in Leningrad in 1939 or Archangel Oblast three years later and obviously owed their revolutionary rocket

armament to the work of captured Nazi scientists. The vessels never again appeared in *Jane's* or any other reputable naval publication.

30. James A. Field Jr., *History of U.S. Naval Operations in Korea,* 26. The quote and statistics on the relative size of the Red and Western armies in the late forties are from Norman Friedman, *The Fifty-Year War: Conflict and Strategy in the Cold War,* 62.

31. Jonathan D. Spence, *The Search for Modern China,* 511. An excellent account of the *London-Amethyst* incident is in Iain Ballantyne, *Warships of the Royal Navy: H.M.S. London,* 140–53.

32. Harry S. Truman, "Our Armed Forces MUST Be Unified," *Colliers,* August 26, 1944, 62, copy in "President Truman's Fight," box 17A, folder 4, Truman Papers, HSTL.

33. Kenneth W. Hechler to Clark M. Clifford, with enclosure, December 8, 1953, in ibid., folder 8; "Memorandum to the President" from Secretary of the Navy James Forrestal, with enclosure, December 1, 1945, ibid., folder 1.

34. Undated memorandum (probably late 1945 or early 1946) titled "Restatement of the Navy's Views with Regard to Reorganization," "President Truman's Fight," box 17B, folder 14, Truman Papers, HSTL.

35. Unless otherwise cited, the following discussion of postwar unification is based primarily on three splendid, detailed studies: Jeffrey G. Barlow, *Revolt of the Admirals: The Fight for Naval Aviation, 1945–1950;* Paolo E. Coletta, *The United States Navy and Defense Unification, 1947–1953;* and Kenneth W. Condit, *The History of the Joint Chiefs of Staff: The Joint Chiefs of Staff and National Policy.* Other works that touch on the subject less intensively but often with equal incisiveness include George W. Baer, *One Hundred Years of Sea Power: The U.S. Navy, 1890–1990,* 276–313; Clay Blair, *The Forgotten War: America in Korea, 1950–1953,* 4–23; Hagan, *This People's Navy,* 335–40; Howarth, *To Shining Sea,* 476–81, 485–86; Rogow, *James Forrestal,* 210–34, 285–304; Harry S. Truman, *Memoirs,* 2:63–71; and Clark G. Reynolds's especially careful account, "Cherokee Jocko Fights the Cold War."

36. Captain Arleigh Burke to Congressman W. Sterling Cole, June 6, 1947, in "Pre-CNO Files," box 5, folder 16, Arleigh Burke Papers, Naval Historical Branch, Washington Navy Yard, Washington, D.C.

37. A prime expression of early postwar naval policy is contained in a memorandum for Admiral William H. P. Blandy signed by Captain P. A. Edwards dated September 1, 1947, for Blandy's use "in the preparation of your lecture at the Army Command and General Staff College, Fort Leavenworth" on the subject "Future Trends in Naval Warfare" in ibid., folder 18. See also the memorandum from Burke to Admiral Towers, August 14, 1947, regarding the interest of the General Board of the navy in all aspects of atomic defense organization (ibid., folder 17) and the undated memorandum (sometime in January 1948) "Subject: Naval Operating Forces—Examination of," in ibid., folder 18.

38. The initial draft of Burke's memorandum titled "Tentative Outline on Serial no. 315: The Functions of the Navy in Support of a National War Effort," dated March 4, 1948, is in ibid., folder 18. The final report is summarized and assessed in David

Alan Rosenberg, "Arleigh Albert Burke," in *The Chiefs of Naval Operations,* edited by Robert William Love Jr., 270–71. Burke continued to make this point in an internal memorandum in June 1948: "There will be so many demands made upon the Navy for immediate operations in widely separated parts of the world that fulfillment of all demands may well be beyond the capacity of the *United States* Navy" (Palmer, *Maritime Strategy,* 59).

39. Richard G. Hewlett and Frederick Duncan, *Nuclear Navy, 1946–1962,* 3.

40. Palmer, *Maritime Strategy,* 27.

41. Ibid.

42. Sherman's January 1947 presentation to Truman and other key officials is summarized and partially quoted in ibid., 29–30. Nimitz is quoted in Condit, *Joint Chiefs of Staff,* 169.

43. W. H. P. Blandy, "Report on Bikini," *All Hands* 355 (September 1946): 2–9 (quotes on p. 6); Frank A. Weighs, "Bombs Usher in New Era," ibid., 354 (August 1946): 2–7 (quotes on p. 4).

44. The eyewitness account of the shock and awe of the Bikini underwater test is in Weighs, "Bombs Usher in New Era," 2. Blandy's comments and conclusions are in "Report on Bikini," 8–9.

45. David E. Lilienthal, *The Journals of David E. Lilienthal,* 230, 454.

46. The following discussion of the origins of the supercarrier concept is derived from Norman Friedman, *U.S. Aircraft Carriers: An Illustrated Design History,* 14, 21, 231–233, 247 (quotes on p. 231).

47. Barlow, *Revolt of the Admirals,* 137.

48. Reynolds, "Cherokee Jocko," 18–19.

49. Memorandum, "The Role of the Carrier in Warfare, Prepared by Dr. H. M. Dater, Aviation History Unit, Op-50D-1," appended to "Memorandum for Mr. [John] Sullivan," February 12, 1948, in box 10, folder "Aircraft Carriers, Documents Pertaining to U.S.S. *United States,*" Sullivan Papers, HSTL. The quotations are on pp. i and 2 of the memorandum.

50. Ibid.

51. J. S. Thach, "A New Look at Air Power," undated manuscript in "Subject File, 1942–1976," box 11, folder "National Military Establishment, 1948–1949," Sullivan Papers, HSTL (quotes on pp. 4, 6).

52. Bob Lawson, "Lest We Forget: VC-5 'The Savage Sons,'" *NIP* 121:2 (February 1996): 94.

53. A copy of the memorandum "Imbalance within the Naval Establishment" is in RG 200, box 7, "Personal-Official File, 1942–Fiscal Year 1951," folder "Navy Dept–Navy Correspondence (Memorandum and Reports)," George J. Richards (army comptroller) Papers, HSTL (quote on p. 1). Truman is quoted in Margaret Truman, *Harry S. Truman,* 445.

54. David Alan Rosenberg, "American Atomic Strategy and the Hydrogen Bomb Decision," 64.

55. Baer, *One Hundred Years,* 279, 284–92.

56. Robert H. Ferrell, *Harry Truman: A Life,* 352–53.

57. Rosenberg, "American Atomic Strategy," 68. The statistics on the U.S. nuclear arsenal are from Ronald Schaffer, *Wings of Judgement: American Bombing in World War II,* 191.

58. Condit, *Joint Chiefs of Staff,* 18–19, 133 (Clay quote). Robert Ferrell maintains that the air force's new Strategic Air Command (SAC) was incapable of bombing accuracy "until the time of the Korean War," presumably as a result of the loss of expertise due to massive demobilization in 1945–1946 (*Harry Truman: A Life,* 353).

59. "Memorandum for [presidential speech writer] Judge [Samuel] Rosenman," December 18, 1945, in "President Truman's Fight," box 17A, folder 5, Truman Papers, HSTL; "Memorandum for Commander Clifford from George M. Elsey," November 29, 1945, folder 8, ibid.

60. The complex, protracted, and intensely bureaucratic struggle between the American armed forces for a favorable share of mission responsibilities (and thus the lion's share of the dwindling defense budget) is ably set forth in Condit, *Joint Chiefs of Staff,* 167–89. See also Barlow, *Revolt of the Admirals,* 137–41; and Friedman, *Fifty-Year War,* 124.

61. Draft letter dated February 14, 1949, to be signed by the chief of naval operations to Congressman Robert L. Coffey Jr., "Pre-CNO Files," box 6, folder 21, Burke Papers, Naval Historical Center. The air force change of heart is noted in Friedman, *Fifty-Year War,* 124.

62. Thomas B. Buell, *Naval Leadership in Korea: The First Six Months,* 7.

63. Barlow, *Revolt of the Admirals,* 208.

64. "The Strategic Bombing Myth," box 12, Subject File, 1942–1976, folder "National Military Establishment, 1948–49, 5 of 5," Sullivan Papers, HSTL (quote on p. 41).

65. Barlow, *Revolt of the Admirals,* 209–45. Perhaps it was fortunate that the tests never took place, for navy jet controllers often experienced difficulties in vectoring the fast new aircraft into a proper intercept mode. Donald D. Engen, *Wings and Warriors: My Life as a Naval Aviator,* 98.

66. The incident is related in Buell, *Naval Leadership,* 6; the exercise involving the carrier *Franklin D. Roosevelt* is discussed in Reynolds, "Cherokee Jocko," 21.

67. Whether Truman knew, approved, or ordered the firings is a matter of some debate. Admiral Robert Dennison, then a captain in the Pentagon, was told by Matthews to monitor Denfeld's speech to Congress and became convinced that Truman did not directly fire or order the firings of Denfeld and the others. The guilty parties were the infuriated Johnson and, above all, Matthews. Dennison also claims that Denfeld's firm, if unanticipated, defense of Radford served as a lightning rod that kept Radford himself from being sacked. Robert L. Dennison, oral history interview, 199–203.

68. Daniel V. Gallery, "Don't Let Them Cripple the Navy," 36–37; Gallery, "If This Be Treason." Capture of the U-505 in 1944 and its subsequent fate are dramatically

recounted in William T. Y'Blood, *Hunter-Killer: U.S. Escort Carriers in the Battle of the Atlantic,* 196–212.

69. Postwar discontent within navy ranks and the culminating embarrassment of the Thimble Shoals incident are recounted in John A. Butler, *Strike Able-Peter: The Stranding and Salvage of the U.S.S.* Missouri. See esp. pp. 18–19.

70. Dwight D. Eisenhower, *The White House Years: A Personal Account,* 1:445.

71. Dean Acheson, *Present at the Creation: My Years in the State Department,* 454, 486–97, is the most authoritative insider's account of the development of the new national security policy contained in NSC 68. The document as submitted to Truman on April 7, 1950, is printed in *FRUS, 1950,* 1:234–92 (quotes on pp. 279, 287–88, 292).

72. Dean C. Allard, "An Era of Transition," in *In Peace and War: Interpretations of American Naval History, 1775–1978,* edited by Kenneth J. Hagan, 295–96; James C. Fahey, *The Ships and Aircraft of the U.S. Fleet,* 7:14–15.

73. Palmer, *Maritime Strategy,* 63–66 (map on pp. 64–65).

Chapter 2. Going MAD: The Nuclearization of Sea Power

1. Michael T. Eisenberg, *Shield of the Republic: The United States Navy in an Era of Cold War and Violent Peace, 1945–1962,* 337.

2. E. T. Wooldridge, ed., *Into the Jet Age: Conflict and Change in Naval Aviation, 1945–1975,* xviii–xix.

3. Eisenhower is quoted in Robert H. Ferrell, ed., *The Diary of James C. Hagerty: Eisenhower in Mid-Course, 1954–1955,* 134, 140–41.

4. Eisenhower summarized his "New Look" policy and the navy's response in *White House Years,* 1:449–53.

5. Friedman, *U.S. Aircraft Carriers,* 263.

6. Norman Friedman, *Seapower as Strategy: Navies and National Interests,* 200.

7. Despite the implication of some scholars that the three *Midways* carried atomic bombs in their magazines during the earliest deployments to the Mediterranean in the late forties, the consensus is that the American fleet did not possess a nuclear-delivery capability before midcentury. Experts disagree on the precise date when the *Midway*-class carriers were first assigned a nuclear-strike role. Norman Friedman suggests 1953; Norman Polmar states that it was 1951. Hagan, *This People's Navy,* 337; Friedman, *U.S. Aircraft Carriers,* 248; Polmar, *The Naval Institute Guide to the Soviet Navy: Third Edition,* 2n.

8. Eisenhower's conversation with Hagerty is in *FRUS, 1955–1957,* 2:408–9.

9. Arleigh Burke, oral history interview, 1–2, in "Series of Interviews on the Subject of POLARIS," Oral History Department, U.S. Naval Institute, Annapolis, Maryland. Hereafter cited as Burke, oral history interview, in Polaris Missile Interviews.

10. William F. Raborn, oral history interview, 17, in ibid. Hereafter cited as Raborn, oral history interview, in Polaris Missile Interviews.

11. An excellent brief discussion of the Regulus program and operations is Nick T. Spark, "Battle Stations Missile!" *Midway's* launch of a V-2 and *Randolph's* successful shot of a Regulus nearly nine years later are noted in Michael Hanson, s.vv. "Midway, CVB-41," "Randolph, CV 15," in *Dictionary of American Naval Fighting Ships* (http://www.hazegrey.org/danfs/carriers/cvb41 and cv15.htm). Regulus operations from *Grayback* in 1959 are illustrated in Shor and Garrett, "Good Will Ambassadors," 296–97, which also includes the caption quotes. Arleigh A. Burke, "The Future of the Navy," is an authoritative sketch by the CNO of navy missile development to that time. The quotation on difficulties in integrating missile systems is in Thomas B. Buell, "When the Birds Didn't Fly," *NIP* 125:1 (January 1999): 77.

12. Thomas H. Moorer, oral history interview, 306–8; Fahey, *Ships and Aircraft,* 7:32.

13. Rosenberg, "Arleigh Albert Burke," in *Chiefs of Naval Operations,* edited by Love, 270–72. A brief but authoritative survey of the U.S. Navy's dramatic surge into nuclear and guided-missile warfare between 1955 and 1961 is Karl Lautenschläger, "Technology and the Evolution of Naval Warfare." Information on the origins of the T-LAM system are in R. O. Holbrook, comment on "Battle Stations Missile!" See also Fahey, *Ships and Aircraft,* 8:4–5, 41; and Norman Polmar, *The Naval Institute Guide to the Ships and Aircraft of the U.S. Fleet,* 13th ed., 438.

14. Burke, "Future of the Navy;" Thomas S. Gates, "Naval Supremacy Vital to Our National Security," 114–16; Fahey, *Ships and Aircraft,* 7:32.

15. Burke, oral history interview, 4–7. For Burke's earlier contacts with the Johns Hopkins Applied Physics Lab, see "Pre-CNO Files," box 5, folder 17, Burke Papers, Naval Historical Center.

16. Charles Elliott, oral history interview, 316; Kent L. Lee, oral history interview, 366–67; Elmo Zumwalt, oral history interview, 233; Alfred G. Ward, oral history interview, 248–49.

17. Norman Polmar and Thomas B. Allen, *Rickover,* 20–21, 27–32, 50–59.

18. In early 1950, Rickover went up to Portsmouth, New Hampshire, intending to award the Navy Yard there a contract for the first two nuclear submarines. But the admiral in charge balked. He already had in hand contracts to build the navy's latest diesel-powered submarines and did not like Rickover's insistence that "the shipyard personnel assigned to the nuclear submarine project report directly to him" as well as through normal channels. "Without hesitation Rickover reached across the desk of the shipyard commander" and placed a call to his contact at the Electric Boat Company in Groton, Connecticut. "Robinson immediately informed Rickover that his yard would be able to construct both of the planned nuclear submarines." Electric Boat continued to build all the navy's "nukes" for some years thereafter, and General Dynamics/Electric Boat remains a prime contractor to this day. Ibid., 117–47 (the incident with Portsmouth Navy Yard is on p. 147). See also Hewlett and Duncan, *Nuclear Navy, 1946–1962,* 88.

19. Thomas R. Weschler, oral history interview, 313; A. G. Ward, oral history interview, 248–49.

20. Weschler, oral history interview, 315.

21. Robert E. Kuenne, *The Polaris Missile Strike: A General Economic Systems Analysis,* 53–54.

22. D. Douglas Dalgleish and Larry Schweikart, *Trident,* 6.

23. Burke, oral history interview, 8, 10, 11, 19.

24. Norman Polmar, *The Death of the U.S.S.* Thresher, 124–25, 132–33; Charles Loughlin, oral history interview, 298.

25. I. J. Galantin, *Submarine Admiral: From Battleships to Ballistic Missiles,* 312–14; A. G. Ward, oral history interview, 246.

26. Dagleish and Schweikart, *Trident,* 7; Rosenberg, "Arleigh Albert Burke," in *Chiefs of Naval Operations,* edited by Love, 277–79 (quote on p. 279). See also Hagan, *This People's Navy,* 351.

27. W. F. Raborn, "The Polaris Submarine." The admiral subsequently reiterated and somewhat elaborated on this address in his oral history interview in the "Series of Interviews on the Subject of POLARIS." See Raborn, oral history interview, in Polaris Missile Interviews.

28. Friedman, *Seapower as Strategy,* 107.

29. Dennison, oral history interview, 321–23.

30. Cable, *Britain's Naval Future,* 2.

31. Hanson W. Baldwin, "The New Navy: A Reporter's Notebook," 26–27, 85.

32. Gates, "Naval Supremacy," 116.

33. Dennison, oral history interview, 325–27. Information on the precise number of sea-based nuclear ballistic missiles deployed by the USSR, United States, and, on a far lesser scale, Britain, France, and China near the end of the cold war is in Richard Fieldhouse and Shunji Taoka, *Superpowers at Sea: An Assessment of the Naval Arms Race,* 89–99 (charts).

Chapter 3. "Grey Diplomats": The Sixth and Seventh Fleets in the 1950s

1. See, for example, the alphabetized operational histories of *Midway, Coral Sea, Franklin D. Roosevelt, Tarawa,* and *Philippine Sea* in relevant volumes of *Dictionary of American Fighting Ships.*

2. "Guardian of the Mediterranean: The U.S. Sixth Fleet," *Newsweek,* October 8, 1951, 42.

3. Untitled memorandum in "Personal-Official File, 1942–Fiscal Year 1951," box 7, folder "Navy Dept–Navy Correspondence (Memoranda and Reports)," Richards Papers, HSTL.

4. "Britain Relies on U.S. Navy: An Interview with Admiral Richard L. Conolly."

5. "Guardian of the Mediterranean," 42, 44.

6. "National Intelligence Estimate" (NIE) 25, "Probable Soviet Courses of Action to Mid-1952," August 2, 1951; NSC 114/1 "Status and Timing of Current U.S. Programs for National Security," August 8, 1951, in *FRUS, 1951,* 1:120–57 (quotes on pp. 121, 130, 132, 149).

7. The prospect of a hydrogen bomb that appeared at the end of the 1940s caused thinking about atomic warfare to become rather muddled. Some in Washington concluded that atomic bombs would soon be reduced to the status of conventional weaponry—extravagant to be sure, but in the end indecisive in a war certain to involve the use of thermonuclear weapons. Others recoiled from even imagining nuclear or thermonuclear warfare and revived the notion that World War III could and might well be waged with conventional weaponry over a prolonged period. This had been the position of many in the navy throughout the prolonged fight over armed forces unification and roles and missions between 1945 and 1949. See Lisle A. Rose, *The Cold War Comes to Main Street,* 86–89; and Brian McMahon to Harry Truman, *FRUS, 1949,* 1: 588–95.

8. *FRUS, 1951,* 4:773–813. See especially the acting secretary of state to the embassy in Spain, 803.

9. Friedman, *U.S. Aircraft Carriers,* 292–95; "Britain Relies on U.S. Navy," 37; "Armed Forces: The H-Bomb Navy," *Time,* December 13, 1954, 15.

10. Acheson, *Present at the Creation,* 515–16, 721–28; Eisenhower, *White House Years,* 2:22.

11. Fouad Ajami, *The Dream Palace of the Arabs: A Generation's Odyssey;* Vera Micheles Dean, *The Nature of the Non-Western World;* "Risk and Riddle: Our Action and Nasser," *Newsweek,* July 28, 1958, 16–17.

12. David Schoenbaum, *The United States and the State of Israel,* 102–3; Eisenhower, *White House Years,* 2:265.

13. A. J. Barker, *Suez: The Seven-Day War,* 86, 90, 97; John S. Pallot, "Suez Remembered," 5.

14. Harold M. Marten, "Cat Brown's Kittens Have Claws," 84; Barker, *Suez,* 91, 97–98; Hugh Thomas, *The Suez Affair,* 141; Eisenhower, *White House Years,* 2:72–92; "The Suez Crisis: An Affair to Remember," *Economist* 380:8488 (July 29, 2006): 23–25. Anglo-French bitterness over Suez has not materially abated over the past half century and has yielded some dubious claims. In September 2003, an author named Tom Cooper published an Internet article for the "ACIG" (the Air Combat Information Group [http://www.acig.org]), which identifies itself as "a multinational project dedicated to research about air wars and air forces since 1945." Titled "Middle East Data Base—Suez Crisis, 1956," the unpaginated article claims, among other things, that "USN Furies" "penetrated the defense perimeter around British carriers on two occasions" during the course of air operations against Egypt, "forcing a scramble." Moreover, "the local USN commanders [unnamed] demanded even a permission to strike the British and the French, so bad were mutual U.S.-British relations at the time." Finally, Cooper asserts that on November 4, while Anglo-French carrier strikes were taking place against Luxor, "the USN's Coral Sea carrier battle group sailed through the center of the Royal Navy Task Force launching [its] own aircraft. As in a miracle, there were no collisions." Needless to say, no responsible seaman—American, British, or even, in the worst stages of the cold war, Soviet—would have risked such havoc. And

Suez, no matter how badly it strained Anglo-American relations, did not call for such a potentially catastrophic response from the Sixth Fleet. Nor is there any record or hint that Cat Brown, the ONLY "USN commander" on the spot, requested permission to attack the Anglo-French task force. Clearly, Mr. Cooper and the ACIG are victims of the fudged data that Commander Pallot had warned us about.

15. Eisenhower's message to Congress is in *Public Papers of the President: Dwight D. Eisenhower, 1957,* 6–16.

16. Charles R. Brown, "The Best Job in the Whole Navy," 143.

17. Marten, "Cat Brown's Kittens," 81–82; "Mission of a Navy Cruiser," *All Hands* (July 1958): 498, 8; the quote on going "toe to toe . . . with the Russkies," is, of course, from the prestrike pep talk given to his B-52 crew by Major Kong in the motion picture *Dr. Strangelove; or, How I Stopped Worrying and Learned to Love the Bomb.*

18. Marten, "Cat Brown's Kittens," 82. In the fifties the navy made a sincere effort to acquaint its recruits with their responsibilities as uniformed ambassadors of the United States. My boot-camp company 112 at Great Lakes in the summer of 1954 heard several lectures on unacceptable behavior in foreign ports, and the consequences. Particular emphasis was laid on a recent incident in which drunken sailors in (pre-Castro) Havana climbed and defaced a national statue. Everyone was court-martialed.

19. Ajami, *Dream Palace,* 11–12; "The King Didn't Flinch," *Newsweek,* July 28, 1958, 20; Eisenhower, *White House Years,* 2:265.

20. Eisenhower, *White House Years,* 2:264–65; *FRUS, 1958–1960,* 11:1–23. Quote is from telegram from the embassy in Lebanon to the Department of State, April 18, 1958, 23.

21. "Memorandum of a Conversation between the President and the Secretary of State, Washington, May 2, 1958"; "Memorandum of a Conversation, White House, May 13, 1958," *FRUS, 1958–1960,* 11:27–28 (quote) and 45–48 (quotes on pp. 46, 48, 48n); Eisenhower, *White House Years,* 2:266.

22. Eisenhower, *White House Years,* 2:267–69; Howe, *Multicrises,* 266; *FRUS, 1958–1960,* 11:101–9; "Telegram from the Chief of Naval Operations to the Commander in Chief, United States Naval Forces, Eastern Atlantic and Mediterranean, June 17, 1958," ibid., 144–45.

23. Congressional Quarterly, *The Middle East,* 205.

24. Eisenhower, *White House Years,* 2:270–73; Arleigh Burke to James Holloway, June 14, 1958, *FRUS, 1958–1960,* 11:231.

25. "On Scene: Lebanon," *Newsweek,* July 28, 1958, 17; embassy in Lebanon to the Department of State, July 15, 1958, *FRUS, 1958–1960,* 11:240–41.

26. Embassy in Lebanon to the Department of State, July 15, 1958, *FRUS, 1958–1960,* 11:247.

27. Embassy in Lebanon to the Department of State, July 16, 1958; "Memorandum of a Telephone Conversation between the Secretary of State in Washington and the Ambassador in Lebanon, July 16, 1958," ibid., 254–56 (quotes on p. 254); "On Scene: Lebanon," 17–18.

28. "On Scene: Lebanon," 18.

29. Raymond V. B. Blackman, ed., *Jane's Fighting Ships, 1958–59,* vii, 275–300, 331–434.

30. "Risk and Riddle," 16; *Newsweek* covers, July 28, August 4, 1958; embassy in the Soviet Union to the Department of State, July 16, 1958; "Editorial Notes 218, 287," embassy in Jordan to the Department of State, September 9, 1958, *FRUS, 1958–1960,* 11:257, 372, 510–11; 557; Howe, *Multicrises,* 24. Information from Soviet archives on the proposed Eisenhower letter is reprinted in Timothy Naftali, "Word for Word/Khrushchev Unplugged: From the Middle East to Cuba, the Fine Art of Political Bluster," *New York Times,* September 14, 2003, sec. 4, p. 7.

31. "Armed Forces: Restrained Power," *Time,* August 4, 1958, 10; "Risk and Riddle," 18; embassy in Lebanon to the Department of State, August 27, 1958, *FRUS, 1958–1960,* 11:529–31 (quote on p. 530).

32. "Risk and Riddle," 16–17; Bernard Lewis, *What Went Wrong? The Clash between Islam and Modernity in the Middle East,* 159; "In the Name of Islam: A Survey of Islam and the West," *Economist* 368:8341 (September 13–19, 2003): special section, 3.

33. The possibility of a Chinese Communist assault on Taiwan just prior to the Korean War is considered in Rose, *Cold War,* 178. Clandestine CIA-sponsored Nationalist Chinese raids on the southeast China coast during the Korean War are recounted with remarkable candor by one of the sponsors in Frank Holober, *Raiders of the China Coast: CIA Covert Operations during the Korean War.*

34. The June 16, 1954, Eisenhower-Dulles conversation is in *FRUS, 1952–1954,* 14:472–74. Robert Accinelli, *Crisis and Commitment: United States Policy toward Taiwan, 1950–1955,* provides an overview of emerging tensions in the Taiwan Strait in 1953–1954.

35. Dana Priest, *The Mission: Waging War and Keeping Peace with America's Military,* 61–77.

36. Robert Ginsburgh, "Interview with Admiral F. B. Stump, Commander in Chief, Pacific," *U.S. News and World Report,* August 27, 1954, 24–26.

37. Accinelli, *Crisis and Commitment,* 174, 179.

38. Robert P. Martin, "The Seventh Fleet—Ready to Fight for Formosa"; Paul Lashmar, *Spy Flights of the Cold War,* 217.

39. Martin, "Seventh Fleet," 35; Franc Shor, "Pacific Fleet: Force for Peace," 316.

40. Yeh's comments came in a meeting with Dulles and others at the State Department on January 19. See "Memorandum of Conversation," in *FRUS, 1955–1957,* 2:41.

41. Robert P. Martin, "Eyewitness Account—Mighty Seventh Fleet Presides over Another Pull-Out." See also "First A-bomb Navy: Set for Action Off Formosa."

42. Harriet Dashiell Schwar, "Taiwan Straits Crises," in *East Asia and the United States: An Encyclopedia of Relations since 1789,* edited by James I. Matray, 2:602–3.

43. Martin, "Seventh Fleet," 35.

44. Ibid., 37.

45. The following account of *Tingey's* patrol—and of its sister destroyer and the downed Chinese Nationalist pilot—is based on William L. Worden, "Cold War in the Formosa Strait," 27, 115–16, 118.

46. Eisenhower and Dulles are quoted in Howe, *Multicrises,* 166n. Dulles drafted his own memorandum of the conversation he had with Senator George (in *FRUS, 1955–1957,* 2:337). Because of their determination to defend the offshore islands with nuclear weapons if need be, leading administration officials reacted sharply when others uttered statements clearly designed to fan the flames of war. Ike's angry explosion at Mick Carney who had stated that Communist forces could seize Jinmen in a week and the Mazus within the month was very much in that vein. The president insisted that although the "Chinese Reds are fanatical Communists," he was determined to maintain a formal peace with them. See ibid., 408–9.

47. Captain John Herrick's interpretation of his own command's weakness that led to the "Tonkin Gulf Incident" is quoted in William Manchester, *The Glory and the Dream: A Narrative History of America, 1932–1972,* 1246. The other defining crisis that led to massive American intervention in Vietnam was, of course, the VC rocket attack on the Bien Hua air base the following February.

48. George T. Kittredge, "Ships Leave Yokosuka for Gigantic Atomic-Age Amphibious Operation," reprinted in *U.S. Navy Cruiser Sailors Association Journal* 12:2 (spring 2003): 25.

49. Burke is quoted in Howe, *Multicrises,* 164.

50. Walter Robertson to Everett Drumright, April 29, 1958; Vice Admiral Roland M. Smoot to CinCPac Admiral Felix Stump, August 4, 1958; "Editorial Note," *FRUS, 1958–1960,* 19:19, 39, 42–43; Howe, *Multicrises,* 184; Eisenhower, *White House Years,* 2:292.

51. "Minutes: Conversation between Mao Zedong and Ambassador Yudin, 22 July 1958," *CWIHPB,* no. 6–7, 155; Vladislav M. Zubok, "The Mao-Khrushchev Conversations, 31 July–3 August 1958 and 2 October 1959," ibid., no. 12–13, 244–45.

52. Zubok, "Mao-Khrushchev Conversations," 246.

53. Wu Lenxi, "Memoir: Inside Story of the Decision Making during the Shelling of Jinmen," in "Mao Zedong's Handling of the Taiwan Straits Crisis of 1958: Chinese Collections and Documents," by Li Xiaobing et al., *CWIHPB,* no. 6–7, 208–9; "Memorandum from the Assistant Secretary of State for Far Eastern Affairs (Robertson) to Secretary of State Dulles," August 8, 1958, *FRUS 1958–1960,* 19:44.

54. Eisenhower, *White House Years,* 2:295; "Summary of Meeting at White House on Taiwan Straits Situation," August 25, 1958, *FRUS, 1958–1960,* 19:73–74; "White House Press Release, Newport, Rhode Island," September 4, 1958, ibid., 135.

55. Howe, *Multicrises,* 206, 217, 218. Eisenhower agreed to transfer the USS *Essex* and four destroyers from the Mediterranean to the Far East via the Suez Canal as early as the White House meeting on August 25, but he ordered no press announcement at the time (*FRUS, 1958–1960,* 19:73–74).

56. *FRUS, 1958–1960,* 19:131, 136–38.

57. Zubok, "Mao-Khrushchev Conversations," 246–47.

58. Robert S. Elegant, "Our Fleet Draws the Line," *Newsweek,* September 15, 1958, 47; "Report by the Commander, U.S. Taiwan Defense Command to the Commander in Chief, Pacific," undated, *FRUS, 1958–1960,* 19:502–3.

59. Zubok, "Mao-Khrushchev Conversations," 247.

60. Peng's messages are summarized in *FRUS, 1958–1960,* 19:329n, 451n.

Chapter 4. The A-frame Factor and Other Frustrations: Korea and Vietnam

1. Burke, oral history interview, 1:185.

2. Buell, *Naval Leadership,* 14–15.

3. The three standard accounts of U.S. naval operations in Korea are Walter Karig, Malcolm W. Cagle, and Frank A. Mason, *Battle Report: The War in Korea,* which covers the period only to the defeat of UN forces in North Korea and their evacuation at the end of 1950. Malcolm W. Cagle and Frank A. Manson, *The Sea War in Korea,* and Field, *History of Naval Operations,* cover the navy's role throughout the conflict. An excellent summary is in Eisenberg, *Shield of the Republic,* 177–284. Richard P. Hallion, *The Naval Air War in Korea,* provides a short general survey of its subject, as does Richard C. Knott, *Attack from the Sky: Naval Air Operations in the Korean War.* A good survey of carrier operations in the Korean War is in Andrew Faltum, *The* Essex *Aircraft Carriers,* 119–30. James A. Michener's novel *The Bridges at Toko-Ri* and especially the 1954 motion picture offer gritty looks at the rigor and terror of day-to-day carrier operations off Korea. The essays by retired admirals Gerald Miller, John S. Thach, and Captain Gerald G. O'Rourke in *Into the Jet Age,* edited by Wooldridge, 150–207, emphasize the frequent frustrations and sense of inconclusiveness that characterized the entire naval air campaign. Conrad C. Crane's *American Airpower Strategy in Korea, 1950–1953* focuses almost exclusively on air force operations, strategy, and tactics but does briefly consider the strengths and weaknesses of joint air force–navy cooperation in both tactical and strategic operations throughout the war.

4. Burke, oral history interview, 1:177–79; Knott, *Attack from the Sky,* 11–12.

5. Buell, *Naval Leadership,* 18–30 (quote on p. 24).

6. An excellent account of the Inchon operation is Robert Debs Heinl Jr., *Victory at High Tide: The Inchon-Seoul Campaign.* The Clark mission is recounted in Eugene Franklin Clark, *The Secrets of Inchon: The Untold Story of the Most Daring Covert Mission of the Korean War.* Burke, oral history interview, 1:188–91, is an eyewitness account from the perspective of MacArthur's headquarters. Moscow's and Beijing's alertness to the possibility of an amphibious assault against Inchon and North Korean unwillingness to listen are in Rose, *Cold War,* 224.

7. Buell, *Naval Leadership,* 36–47 (quotes on pp. 39, 40–41); Burke, oral history interview, 1:192, 223.

8. When President Johnson queried Defense officials about the wisdom of committing large numbers of troops in the summer of 1965, Chief of Naval Operations David McDonald said, "More troops are needed to turn the tide. Otherwise we'll lose slowly." When Johnson pressed him further with respect to future troop commitments, McDonald added: "I believe that sooner or later we'll force the enemy to the conference table," but "we can't win an all out war" (Clark Clifford, *Counsel to the President: A Memoir*, 413).

9. David Rees, *Korea: The Limited War*, 366–69.

10. Zumwalt, oral history interview, 218, 219, 221.

11. Robert F. Dorr and Warren Thompson, *Korean Air War*, 143.

12. Willie M. Martin, "One of the 'Train Busters,'" in *I Remember Korea: Veterans Tell Their Stories of the Korean War, 1950–1953*, edited by Linda Grandfield, 36.

13. Unless otherwise cited, I have relied on the following sources in describing coastal and riverine operations in Vietnam: Love, *History of the U.S. Navy*, 2:537–61, 569–72 (his description of the PBRs is on p. 539); Lehman, *On Seas of Glory*, 324–35; R. L. Shreadley, "The Naval War in Vietnam, 1950–1970," *NIP* 97:819 (May 1971): 185–208; Victor Croizat, *The Brown Water Navy: The River and Coastal War in Indo-China and Vietnam, 1948–1972*, 113–39 (quotes on pp. 113, 114, 118, 119, 128); and Thomas J. Cutler, *Brown Water, Black Berets: Coastal and Riverine Warfare in Vietnam*. Vietcong tactics and the American preference for helicopter assaults in Vietnam are discussed by a battlefield reporter in Kuno Knoebl, *Victor Charlie: The Face of War in Vietnam*, 200–213. The young officer on "junk patrol" is quoted in Glenn Munson, ed., *Letters from Vietnam*, 45. The recollections of riverine veteran Wynn Goldsmith are from Goldsmith, *Papa Bravo Romeo: U.S. Navy Patrol Boats at War in Vietnam*. See especially pp. vii–viii, 47, 74–77, 115–16, 119, 137–69, 179–81. Crowe's experiences are recounted in William J. Crowe Jr., *The Line of Fire: From Washington to the Gulf, the Politics and Battles of the New Military*, 78–79, 81, 83.

14. Front page, Mobile Riverine Force Association Web site (http://www.mrfa.org).

15. Douglas Daniels, "Tiny Fleet, Big Job," *Naval History* 19:4 (August 2005): 50–54 (quotes on pp. 50, 51, 52).

16. U.S. Department of the Navy, Chief of Information, *The Navy in Vietnam*, 5–7. A copy of this official document has been posted by the Mobile Riverine Force Association at http://www.mrfa.org. Many materials on this site, however, are of a private, not official, nature, and the association urges researches to contact it before citation.

17. Ibid., 9.

18. Croizat, *Brown Water Navy*, 122.

19. Ibid., 124–28, 132 (quotes on pp. 128, 132).

20. Goldsmith, *Papa Bravo Romeo*, vii.

21. Douglas Brinkley, *Tour of Duty: John Kerry and the Vietnam War*, 77–335; John E. O'Neill and Jerome Corsi, *Unfit for Command: Swift Boat Veterans Speak Out against John Kerry*.

22. The following account of Boatswain Williams's exploits is based on Lehman, *On Seas of Glory,* 330–35; and Thomas J. Cutler, "Lest We Forget: John Elliot Williams," *NIP* 129:9 (September 2003): 11.

23. Goldsmith, *Papa Bravo Romeo,* 115–16.

24. Paul A. Yost, "Swift Boats: Hard Day on the Bo De," *NIP* (October 2004): 66–69. Perhaps characteristically, swift boat commanders who were not present during the operation condemn Yost for his overall critical "tone" and especially his slandering of the senior mission officer who later became a prominent critic of Kerry during the 2004 election. Yost is also charged with misidentifying the river on which the operation took place. Robert B. Shirley, response to "Swift Boats: Hard Day on the Bo De," *NIP* 130:11 (November 2004): 15–16.

25. In the summer and autumn of 1952, carrier jets struck key industrial targets in upper North Korea. In the largest navy raid of the war in September, 142 aircraft from three carriers destroyed the Aoji oil refinery and hit other objectives at Munsan and Chongjin. "These were in an area less than five miles from Manchuria and less than eleven miles from the USSR, and the raids caught enemy fighters and flak defense completely by surprise" (Crane, *American Airpower Strategy,* 123–24, 129–30). Burke, oral history interview, 1:177. In Vietnam, naval aircraft saw limited action in phase 4 of Operation Rolling Thunder (October 1966 to May 1967) when the air campaign at last shifted focus "to industrial targets and power generating plants" in North Vietnam. Navy fighter bombers played a more significant role five years later in the first of two Linebacker operations dedicated to halting the North's first open and significant effort to invade, defeat, and occupy the South. But naval air's chief targets were confined to bridges, railroad rolling stock, trucks, and so on. When President Nixon and Secretary of State Henry Kissinger decided to go after the heart of North Vietnam's limited industrial complex during Linebacker II in December 1972, they relied on the air force's Strategic Air Command B-52 bombers, though naval aircraft did mine some subsidiary North Vietnamese rivers. See John Darrell Sherwood, *Afterburner: Naval Aviators and the Vietnam War,* 12–13, 262–87.

26. In fact, Tarrant was based on Admiral John Parry.

27. Michener, *The Bridges at Toko-Ri,* 27. Stockdale is quoted in Zalin Grant, *Over the Beach: The Air War in Vietnam,* 21.

28. Rees, *Korea: The Limited War,* 375.

29. Stephen Budiansky, *Air Power: The Men, Machines, and Ideas That Revolutionized War from Kitty Hawk to Gulf II,* 370, 382.

30. Burke, oral history interview, 1:201–2.

31. Budiansky, *Air Power,* 376–77; Frank Uhlig Jr., *How Navies Fight: The U.S. Navy and Its Allies,* 303–4; Radford, "Our Navy," 547.

32. See Gerald E. Miller, "Korea—the Carrier War," in *Into the Jet Age,* edited by Wooldridge, 162.

33. Rees, *Korea: The Limited War,* 378.

34. Sherwood, *Afterburner,* 39–41.

35. Grant, *Over the Beach,* 108–10; Robert S. McNamara and Brian Van De Mark, *In Retrospect: The Tragedy and Lessons of Vietnam,* 283–85.

36. Matthew B. Ridgway, *The Korean War,* 238.

37. Quoted in Michael Barone, *Our Country: The Shaping of America from Roosevelt to Reagan,* 398; and John B. Nichols and Barrett Tillman, *On Yankee Station: The Naval Air War over Vietnam,* 16.

38. The incident is recounted in Kent L. Lee, "The *Enterprise* in WestPac," in *Into the Jet Age,* edited by Wooldridge, 240–41; Friedman, *Seapower as Strategy,* 53.

39. As one veteran explained, although "you couldn't play around too much in the northern area [of North Vietnam] around Hanoi and Haiphong," pilots flying armed reconnaissance missions "down in the southern reaches below about latitude 20 could do about anything [they] wanted within reason" (James D. Ramage, oral history interview, 288).

40. Admiral Thomas B. Hayward, interview by author, Seattle, May 2, 2002.

41. In congressional testimony in the summer of 1967, McNamara admitted that the objectives of the air war were not to defeat the enemy but to increase the cost of Hanoi's continued infiltration of men and supplies to the South, to raise South Vietnamese morale, and to make clear to North Vietnam's leaders that so long as they continued the war in the South, "they would pay a price in the North." Grant, *Over the Beach,* 27; McNamara and Van De Mark, *In Retrospect,* 286.

42. Grant, *Over the Beach,* 27; Richard P. Hallion, *Storm over Iraq: Air Power and the Gulf War,* 19; Scott McGaugh, Midway *Magic,* 113–14, 149–50; Hayward, interview by author, May 2, 2002.

43. Grant, *Over the Beach,* 28.

44. Ibid., 42; John J. Hyland, "You Only Go Around Once," in *Into the Jet Age,* edited by Wooldridge, 226–27.

45. Ramage, oral history interview, 290–92.

46. John J. Hyland, oral history interview, 357–59.

47. Ibid.

48. Admiral Johnson's obsession with maintaining navy independence in the Vietnamese air war and his admonition to Hyland to stay out of the clutches of MACV is recounted in Hyland, "You Only Go Around Once," in *Into the Jet Age,* edited by Wooldridge, 225. The other quotes are from Grant, *Over the Beach,* 110–11.

49. Frank Harvey, *Air War—Vietnam,* 167; Grant, *Over the Beach,* 46.

50. The following account is based on Franklin Metzner, "I Fly the Night Skies over Korea," 26–27, 48.

51. James Michener, "The Forgotten Heroes of Korea," 19–21, 124, 126, 128 (quote on p. 128).

52. Rees, *Korea: The Limited War,* 364–84.

53. Bill Mauldin, *Bill Mauldin in Korea,* 149–51. The air force crisis is ably set forth in Crane, *American Airpower Strategy,* 97–105.

54. Michener, "Forgotten Heroes," 128.

55. James Michener, "All for One: A Story from Korea," 1–2.

56. Grant, *Over the Beach,* 151–54; McGaugh, Midway *Magic,* 147, discusses North Vietnamese exploitation of the survival beacons. John B. Nichols and Barrett Tillman skim over the issue of search and rescue (SAR) in their all too brief and much too sketchy account of the naval air war over Vietnam. Their anecdotal and impressionistic account suggests that SAR activities flagged seriously after 1966, though there was one spectacular exception in 1968 involving a downed pilot off the carrier *Ticonderoga.* Nichols and Tillman, *On Yankee Station,* 117–22.

57. McGaugh, Midway *Magic,* 136–37.

58. Grant, *Over the Beach,* 77. John Nichols nonetheless stoutly maintains that "morale held" during the final phases of Rolling Thunder. The flyers of Task Force 77 were no "less interested in doing the job." It was only after the cessation of aerial assaults against the North and the return to tedious, endless interdiction missions against the Ho Chi Minh Trail in Laos and the western border of South Vietnam, "designed to cover the American withdrawal from South Vietnam," that "a new sense of awareness" grew among flight crews that "the politicians didn't quite know what to do with us, so we'd have to look out for ourselves." Nichols and Tillman, *On Yankee Station,* 37. The comment regarding the air war against the Ho Chi Minh Trail is from Sherwood, *Afterburner,* 15.

59. William P. Lawrence, "Vietnam—the Final Chapter," in *Into the Jet Age,* edited by Wooldridge, 260, 263.

60. Dorr and Thompson, *Korean Air War,* 129, 157; Harvey, *Air War—Vietnam,* 6.

61. Dorr and Thompson, *Korean Air War,* 178–79.

62. Wyman is quoted in Grant, *Over the Beach,* 60–61; the *Shangri-La* incident is recounted in Sherwood, *Afterburner,* 23; Harvey, *Air War—Vietnam,* 1.

63. McGaugh, Midway *Magic,* 120.

64. Ibid., 121.

65. Sherwood, *Afterburner,* 23, 57; Gregory L. Vistica, *Fall from Glory: The Men Who Sank the U.S. Navy,* 239.

66. Crane, *American Airpower Strategy,* 44–45, 156 (caption); Engen, *Wings and Warriors,* 121–22.

67. Crane, *American Airpower Strategy,* 73.

68. A. G. Ward, oral history interview, 113.

69. Edward L. Beach Jr., *The United States Navy: 200 Years,* 493.

70. A. G. Ward, oral history interview, 253–54.

71. Sherwood, *Afterburner,* 47, 53, 55.

72. Nichols and Tillman, *On Yankee Station,* 33.

73. Lee, "The *Enterprise* in WestPac"; Lawrence, "Vietnam—the Final Chapter," both in *Into the Jet Age,* edited by Wooldridge, 252–53, 261–62, 264, 266.

74. Leonard F. Guttridge, *Mutiny: A History of Naval Insurrection,* 255–56; Grant, *Over the Beach,* 90; McGaugh, Midway *Magic,* 133.

75. McGaugh, Midway *Magic,* 133.

76. Paul Johnson, *Modern Times: The World from the Twenties to the Eighties,* 637–38.

77. Sherwood, *Afterburner,* 263, 288.

78. Ibid., 289–91; Nichols and Tillman, *On Yankee Station,* 136, 159–61.

Chapter 5. Crisis and Consequence: Cuba, 1962

1. Karen Armstrong, *Holy War: The Crusades and Their Impact on Today's World,* xvi.

2. See Peter Wyden, *Bay of Pigs: The Untold Story.*

3. "Mongoose" can be traced in some detail in U.S. Senate, *Alleged Assassination Plots Involving Foreign Leaders: An Interim Report of the Select Committee to Study Governmental Operations with Respect to Intelligence Activities,* 67–178; and *FRUS, 1961–1963,* vol. 10. What the Soviets knew and did not know is discussed in James G. Hershberg, "More New Evidence on the Cuban Missile Crisis: More Documents from the Russian Archives," *CWIHPB,* no. 8–9 (winter 1996–1997), 271–72.

4. Love, *History of the U.S. Navy,* 2:445. Information on the *Komar*-class missile boats is from Raymond V. B. Blackman, ed., *Jane's Fighting Ships, 1962–63,* 422–23.

5. R. Malinovsky and M. Zakharov, "Memorandum on Deployment of Soviet Forces to Cuba, 24 May 1962," in "New Evidence on the Cuban Missile Crisis: Khrushchev, Nuclear Weapons, and the Cuban Missile Crisis," by Raymond L. Garthoff, *CWIHPB,* no. 11 (winter 1998), 254–56; Dennison, oral history interview, 405–13; Curtis A. Utz, *Cordon of Steel: The U.S. Navy and the Cuban Missile Crisis,* 20.

6. Blackman, *Jane's Fighting Ships, 1962–63,* 400–425; John M. Young, *When the Russians Blinked: The U.S. Maritime Response to the Cuban Missile Crisis,* 104–5.

7. Love, *History of the U.S. Navy,* 2:447.

8. The documents in question are reprinted in Mary S. McAuliffe, ed., *CIA Documents on the Cuban Missile Crisis, 1962,* 71, 91–92. For State Department skepticism, see Dean Rusk and Richard Rusk, *As I Saw It,* 229. The early presence of Soviet nuclear warheads in Cuba is from Peter A. Huchthausen's well-researched *October Fury,* 26.

9. "Memorandum from Secretary of Defense McNamara to President Kennedy," October 4, 1962, *FRUS, 1961–1963,* 11:10–11.

10. "Minutes of the 506th Meeting of the National Security Council," October 21, 1962, in ibid., 146–47; George W. Anderson, "The Cuban Missile Crisis," in *Into the Jet Age,* edited by Wooldridge, 211, 213–14. See also Dennison, oral history interview, 416–21.

11. A. G. Ward, oral history interview, 193; Dennison, oral history interview, 425.

12. Dennison, oral history interview, 424; Young, *When the Russians Blinked,* 78–79; Utz, *Cordon of Steel,* 22–29.

13. Anderson, "The Cuban Missile Crisis," in *Into the Jet Age,* edited by Wooldridge, 212.

14. Huchthausen, *October Fury,* 18–20, 46, 47, 63.

15. Malinovsky and Zakharov, "Memorandum on Deployment," in "New Evidence," by Garthoff, 255; M. Zakharov and S. P. Ivanov to N. S. Khrushchev, September 14, 1962, in "More New Evidence," by Hershberg, 278.

16. Garthoff, "New Evidence," 251.

17. Huchthausen, *October Fury,* 78.

18. Robert F. Kennedy, *Thirteen Days: A Memoir of the Cuban Missile Crisis,* 60–61; Dennison, oral history interview, 429.

19. For disagreements on dates and places of intercept, see Huchthausen, *October Fury,* 146–54; and Love, *History of the U.S. Navy,* 2:459–60. Roger Hilsman, *To Move a Nation: The Politics of Foreign Policy in the Administration of John F. Kennedy,* 215, together with Huchthausen, *October Fury,* contain the fullest account of the angry Anderson-McNamara exchange. Rear Admiral Norvell G. Ward was on duty that night and witnessed the incident. He recalled for an interviewer McNamara's insistence on placing individual ships along the quarantine line and what he characterized as Anderson's restrained response (oral history interview, 423–24). Admiral Alfred Ward's comments are in his oral history interview, 194. Dennison's recollections are in his oral history interview, 423.

20. See the pertinent cables and memoranda in Hershberg, "More New Evidence," 327–37.

21. A. G. Ward, oral history interview, 197–98.

22. Huchthausen, who was on *Blandy's* bridge that day, dramatically re-creates the incident in *October Fury,* 192–219.

23. Garthoff, "New Evidence"; Vladislav M. Zubok, "Dismayed by the Actions of the Soviet Union: Mikoyan's Talks with Fidel Castro and the Cuban Leadership, November 1962," *CWIHPB,* no. 5 (spring 1995), 96; *Charleston News and Courier,* quoted by Admiral Alfred G. Ward in his oral history interview, 210.

24. Dennison, oral history interview, 437; Rusk and Rusk, *As I Saw It,* 243.

Chapter 6. Red Fleet Rising

1. Vladimir V. Stefanovsky, "Their System Still Needs Victims," *NIP* 118:8 (August 1992): 64; Sergie Gorshkov, "Navies in War and Peace," *NIP* 100:9 (September 1974): 60–61. Gorshkov's perspective was, not unnaturally, fixed upon the Nazi-Soviet conflict on the eastern front between 1941 and 1945. The Battle of the Atlantic was at best marginal to this titanic struggle, Gorshkov argued, and the Pacific naval war even more so.

2. Christopher Andrew and Vasili Mitrokhin, *The Sword and the Shield: The Mitrokhin Archive and the Secret History of the KGB,* 556; Andrew Cockburn, *The Threat: Inside the Soviet Military Machine,* 441–59; Vistica, *Fall from Glory,* 55.

3. Gary E. Weir and Walter J. Boyne, *Rising Tide: The Untold Story of the Russian Submarines That Fought the Cold War,* 33–73, 103–13, 137–39; Peter A. Huchthausen, *K-19, the Widowmaker: The Secret Story of the Soviet Nuclear Submarine.*

4. Stefanovsky, "Their System," 64.

5. Ibid.; Peter A. Huchthausen, Igor Kurdin, and R. Alan White, *Hostile Waters;* Weir and Boyne, *Rising Tide,* 143–53.

6. A fact successfully obscured for decades by the hysteria in the late 1950s over an ostensible literacy "gap" between Russian and American children summed up in the memorable phrase, "Why Johnnie Can't Read—and Ivan Can!" One is forced to conclude that the hysteria may well have been the product of one of the Kremlin's more successful disinformation programs.

7. A fact to which anyone could attest who traveled twenty miles beyond Moscow, as I did in November 1986.

8. Stefanovsky, "Their System," 65–68.

9. Hedrick Smith, *The Russians,* 405.

10. Guttridge, *Mutiny,* 290–94; Cockburn, *Threat,* 434–38.

11. Stefanovsky, "Their System," 64; Huchthausen, Kurdin, and White, *Hostile Waters,* 11, 71–73; Polmar, *Guide to the Soviet Navy: Third Edition,* 53–54; Ronald H. Spector, *At War at Sea: Sailors and Naval Warfare in the Twentieth Century,* 380, 381.

12. S. A. Tyushkevich, *The Soviet Armed Forces: A History of Their Organizational Development, a Soviet View,* 399, 423–34.

13. Peter Truscott, *Kursk: Russia's Lost Pride,* 26.

14. Thomas A. Brooks, "Soviet Weaknesses Are U.S. Strengths," *NIP* 118:8 (August 1992): 68; Weir and Boyne, *Rising Tide,* 258.

15. Donald W. Mitchell, *A History of Russian and Soviet Sea Power,* 458–59, 464.

16. Friedman, *Fifty-Year War,* 13.

17. Richard A. Russell, *Project Hula: Secret Soviet-American Cooperation in the War against Japan,* 3 (quote); Robert Waring Herrick, *Soviet Naval Strategy: Fifty Years of Theory and Practice,* 45.

18. Tobias R. Philbin III, *The Lure of Neptune: German-Soviet Naval Collaboration and Ambitions, 1919–1941,* 24–25; Ernest McNeill Eller, *The Soviet Sea Challenge,* 86; Herrick, *Soviet Naval Strategy,* 31–32.

19. Cockburn, *Threat,* 399; Friedman, *Fifty-Year War,* 11; Robert Waring Herrick, *Soviet Naval Theory and Policy: Gorshkov's Inheritance,* 141.

20. Herrick, *Soviet Naval Theory and Policy,* 143, 233–53 (quotes on pp. 143, 239, 240, 249).

21. Ibid., 243, 251.

22. Thomas Brooks, "The Soviet Navy in 1989: A U.S. View," *NIP* 116:5 (May 1990): 235–36; Weir and Boyne, *Rising Tide,* 288; Huchthausen, *October Fury,* 5, 12–14, 58.

23. Cable, *Britain's Naval Future,* 2; Raymond V. B. Blackman, ed., *Jane's Fighting Ships, 1960–61,* vii.

24. Blackman, *Jane's Fighting Ships, 1960–61,* v.

25. Gorshkov, "Navies in War and Peace"; Blackman, *Jane's Fighting Ships, 1970–71,* 571.

26. The quotes are from Arnold M. Kuzmack, "Where Does the Navy Go from Here?" and Barry M. Blechman, "The Evolution of the Soviet Navy," in *Sea Power in the 1970's,* edited by George H. Quester, 55, 70. See also John T. Hayward, "The Case for a Modernized U.S. Navy," in ibid., 4–5; and Cottrell and Joshua, "Strategic Balance," 92.

27. Gorshkov is quoted in Hayward, "Case for a Modernized U.S. Navy," in *Sea Power in the 1970's,* edited by Quester, 4. Soviet naval activities are recounted in Blechman, "Evolution of the Soviet Navy," in ibid., 80–81; and D. Mitchell, *Russian and Soviet Sea Power,* 545; and fully summarized in Brian Larson, "Soviet Naval Responses to Crises," in *The Soviet Navy: Strengths and Liabilities,* edited by Bruce W. Watson and Susan M. Watson, 256–63.

28. Cottrell and Joshua, "Strategic Balance," 85, 97; James L. Holloway, "The Navy and Its Third Century," 3–4.

29. Polmar, *Guide to the Soviet Navy: Third Edition,* 68–74, 85–88.

30. Blackman, *Jane's Fighting Ships, 1970–71,* 571–75, 589–97; Hayward, "Case for a Modernized Navy," in *Sea Power in the 1970's,* edited by Quester, 5; MORFLOT Yearly Calendar, 1987, unpaginated (copy in my possession); U.S. Department of Defense, *Soviet Military Power, 1985,* 105.

31. A. Jay Cristol, *The* Liberty *Incident: The 1967 Israeli Attack on the U.S. Navy Spy Ship,* 3.

32. David F. Winkler, *Cold War at Sea: High-Seas Confrontation between the United States and the Soviet Union.*

33. Andrei A. Kokoshin, *Soviet Strategic Thought, 1917–91,* 230–31; Polmar, *Guide to the Soviet Navy: Third Edition,* 38, 76.

34. U.S. Department of Defense, *Soviet Military Power, 1985,* 120.

35. A. G. Ward, oral history interview, 167, 256; Bobby Ray Inman quoted in James Bamford, *The Puzzle Palace: A Report on America's Most Secret Agency,* 112–113; Baer, *One Hundred Years,* 399.

36. Blackman, *Jane's Fighting Ships, 1970–71,* 82; Polmar, *Guide to the Soviet Navy: Third Edition,* 74 (caption).

37. David Fairhall, *Russian Sea Power,* 265.

38. Limited documentation on the First and Second UN Conferences on the Law of the Sea is in *FRUS, 1958–1960,* 2:649–708, 765–826. Documentation on the third UN conference has not yet been compiled. A superb overview of the Law of the Sea process down to the midseventies is John Norton Moore, "U.S. Position on the Law of the Sea Reviewed," *Department of State Bulletin* 70:816 (April 15, 1974): 397–402.

39. Blackman, *Jane's Fighting Ships, 1970–71,* 84; Raymond L. Garthoff, *Détente and Confrontation: American-Soviet Relations from Nixon to Reagan,* 300n.

40. Zumwalt, oral history interview, 414.

41. Friedman, *Seapower as Strategy,* 201. In the eyes of many, Zumwalt's liberal proposals on race relations compounded his felonies on sea power, a matter taken up in Chapter 8.

42. Huchthausen, Kurdin, and White, *Hostile Waters,* 42–77; Sherry Sontag and Christopher Drew with Annette Drew, *Blind Man's Bluff: The Untold Story of America's Submarine Espionage,* 25–45, 121–157.

43. D. Mitchell, *Russian and Soviet Sea Power,* 542; Lyle J. Goldstein and Yuri M. Zhukov, "Superpower Showdown in the Mediterranean, 1973," 33.

44. Vojtech Mastny, "Was 1968 a Strategic Watershed of the Cold War?" 176.

45. Henry Kissinger, *Crisis: The Anatomy of Two Major Foreign Policy Crises,* 28.

46. Ibid., 11–12, 33; William B. Quandt, *Peace Process: American Diplomacy and the Arab-Israeli Conflict since 1967,* 149.

47. Kissinger, *Crisis,* 28, 31, 50, 71. An excellent account of the naval aspects of the 1973 war is Edward N. Luttwak and Robert G. Weinland, "Superpower Naval Diplomacy in the October 1973 Arab-Israeli War: A Case Study," 57–90. See also Uhlig, *How Navies Fight,* 352–62; and Elmo R. Zumwalt Jr., *On Watch: A Memoir,* 432–49 (quote on p. 432).

48. Goldstein and Zhukov, "Superpower Showdown," 33.

49. Ibid.; Kissinger, *Crisis,* 145; Avner Cohen, "The Last Nuclear Moment," *New York Times,* October 6, 2003.

50. Kissinger, *Crisis,* 148, 169.

51. Luttwak and Weinland, "Superpower Naval Diplomacy," 81; Goldstein and Zhukov, "Superpower Showdown," 33.

52. Sontag and Drew with Drew, *Blind Man's Bluff,* 172–73.

53. Kissinger, *Crisis,* 194, 202–3, 212–21, 261–62; Marvin Kalb and Bernard Kalb, *Kissinger,* 541.

54. Kissinger, *Crisis,* 194, 266.

55. Quandt, *Peace Process,* 173; Kissinger, *Crisis,* 343, 344 (quotes).

56. Goldstein and Zhukov, "Superpower Showdown," 34.

57. Scott D. Sagan and Jeremi Suri have argued persuasively that the October 1973 nuclear alert should be seen "as consistent with a pattern, rather than an aberration in the diplomacy of Nixon" and Kissinger, a pattern established precisely four years earlier when Nixon secretly ordered a nuclear alert as a signal to the Kremlin—and China—that the United States was losing patience with the Vietnam debacle and might react accordingly. Sagan and Suri, "The Madman Nuclear Alert: Secrecy Signaling and Safety in October 1969," *International Security* (spring 2003), reprinted online by MIT Press Journals at http://www.mitpress.mit.edu/journal (quote on pp. 3–4).

58. Zumwalt, *On Watch: A Memoir,* 437, 447.

59. Goldstein and Zhukov, "Superpower Showdown," 34–35.

60. Luttwak and Weinland, "Superpower Naval Diplomacy," 90.

61. Kokoshin, *Soviet Strategic Thought,* 239.

62. Blackman and McMurtrie, eds., *Jane's Fighting Ships, 1961–62,* 73–284.

63. Blackman, *Jane's Fighting Ships, 1969–70,* 95–101, 115–18, 163–71, 282–85, 298–99.

64. John E. Moore, ed., *Jane's Fighting Ships, 1981–82,* 131–32.

65. Norman Polmar, *The Naval Institute Guide to the Soviet Navy: Fifth Edition,* 135.

66. U.S. Department of Defense, *Soviet Military Power, 1985;* Garthoff, *Détente and Confrontation,* 648–49.

67. Sontag and Drew with Drew, *Blind Man's Bluff,* 248–50; Lehman, *On Seas of Glory,* 320.

Chapter 7. Reversals of Fortune

1. Hayward, interview by author, May 2, 2002.

2. Ibid.

3. John B. Hattendorf, "The Evolution of the Maritime Strategy, 1977 to 1987," 1.

4. John B. Hattendorf, *The Evolution of the U.S. Navy's Maritime Strategy, 1977–1986,* 6–12 (quote on p. 8).

5. Hayward, telephone interview by author, March 18, 2006.

6. Hattendorf, "Evolution of the Maritime Strategy," 14.

7. The U.S. Navy's newfound confidence and aggressiveness disturbed some of its NATO allies, most notably Norway, one of whose spokesmen noted uneasily in 1988 that his country "is likely to view with concern an American forward maritime strategy which would go beyond surveillance and aim at keeping the Soviet SSBN force at risk through *peacetime trailing....* A forward maritime strategy which involves *permanent naval presence* in the Norwegian Sea would similarly seem to break with the pattern of mutual restraint which has been observed hitherto and which made the naval competition in the Norwegian Sea systematically different from that in the Mediterranean" (Johan Jørgem Holst, "The Security Pattern in Northern Europe: A Norwegian View," in *Britain and NATO's Northern Flank,* edited by Geoffrey Till, 45; emphasis in original).

8. John J. Mearsheimer, "A Strategic Misstep: The Maritime Strategy and Deterrence in Europe," 47–69 (quotes on pp. 47, 48, 49, 58).

9. Ibid., 59; Polmar, *Guide to the Soviet Navy: Third Edition,* 37; Central Intelligence Agency, *National Intelligence Estimate NIE 11–15–82/D: Soviet Naval Strategy and Programs throughout the 1990s,* 5. The title page of this document carries the (undated) notation: "Approved for Release, CIA Historical-Review Program." I am grateful to Professor David Alan Rosenberg who provided me with a copy of this document before it was reprinted in full in Hattendorf, *Navy's Maritime Strategy,* 101–84, and is printed in part in Hattendorf, *Naval History and Maritime Strategy: Collected Essays,* 208–9.

10. See, for example, Tyushkevich, *Soviet Armed Forces;* Kokoshin, *Soviet Strategic Thought;* and Gorshkov's own thoughts scattered through the eleven articles he wrote for the Soviet publication *Morskoi Sbornik* in 1972. They were subsequently reprinted in the West as Gorshkov, "Navies in War and Peace," *NIP* (January–November 1974).

11. Polmar, *Guide to the Soviet Navy: Third Edition,* 67–70; Sontag and Drew with Drew, *Blind Man's Bluff,* 245.

12. Lehman, *On Seas of Glory,* 320.

13. James D. Watkins, "The Maritime Strategy," *NIP* (May 1986): 4–15.

14. Friedman, *Seapower as Strategy*, 202–3.

15. Bradley Peniston, *Around the World with the U.S. Navy: A Reporter's Travels*, 78. Aegis was complemented by the Phoenix fleet defense missile specifically designed to counter Soviet bomber aircraft and their long-range "standoff" weapon systems. Phoenix itself was so big and sophisticated that its deployment was restricted to the equally advanced F-14 fighter aircraft that flew only from supercarrier flight decks. See Norman Polmar, *The Naval Institute Guide to the Ships and Aircraft of the U.S. Fleet*, 17th ed., 509.

16. Polmar, *Ships and Aircraft*, 13th ed., 447; James Zike, "Missiles Answer Sea Strike, Sea Shield Questions," 18–19.

17. An excellent discussion of the emergence, nature, and selling of the six hundred–ship navy concept during the Reagan years is Frederick H. Hartman, *Naval Renaissance: The U.S. Navy in the 1980s.*

18. Lehman, *On Seas of Glory*, 363.

19. Robert Strausz-Hupé, "World in Revolution," 33.

20. "Desert 1" is recounted and condemned in Howarth, *To Shining Sea*, 535; and Hallion, *Storm over Iraq*, 84–88 (quote on p. 87).

21. Hayward, telephone interview by author, April 10, 2006; The National Commission on Terrorist Attacks upon the United States, *The 9/11 Commission Report: Final Report of the National Commission on Terrorist Attacks upon the United States, Authorized Edition*, 96.

22. Cable, *Britain's Naval Future*, 19.

23. Theodore Ropp, *War in the Modern World*, 401–2.

24. Raymond V. B. Blackman, ed., *Jane's Fighting Ships, 1958–59*, v, 12, 13–17 (quote on p. v); Blackman, *Jane's Fighting Ships, 1960–61*, 7–13; Cable, *Britain's Naval Future*, 19.

25. Howe, *Multicrises*, 24, 84, 268.

26. Friedman, *U.S. Aircraft Carriers*, 263. An American admiral who observed closely the Royal Navy's limited carrier operations in Korea recalled that "British [naval] aircraft at that time had severe operating restrictions.... [T]hey could only stay in the air about an hour and fifteen minutes. They couldn't go very far and they didn't have much in the way of IFF [identification, friend or foe] equipment, so they couldn't be under positive control of the radar direction net.... We handled the British carrier by assigning an isolated section on the western end of the bombline. Everybody else stayed out of that area. We let them run that any way they wanted—picking their targets and so forth. This was somewhat frustrating to the British. I remember the young flight [control] commander in Seoul would give me a hard time every once in awhile, about letting them get into the war. I pointed out that if they could get some modern equipment, we could be more aggressive in what we assigned them" (Miller, "Korea—the Carrier War," in *Into the Jet Age*, edited by Wooldridge, 163).

27. Grove, *From* Vanguard *to Trident*, 267–77.

28. Ibid., 281; Grove, "The Royal Navy, 1945–90," in *Technology and Naval Combat in the Twentieth Century and Beyond*, edited by Phillips Payson O'Brien, 185–99; John F. Lehman Jr., *Command of the Seas*, 270; Blackman, *Jane's Fighting Ships, 1970–71*, 84.

29. John E. Moore, ed., *Jane's Fighting Ships, 1978–79*, 131.

30. Lehman, *Command of the Seas*, 271.

31. The best and most comprehensive study of the Falklands war, though unwarrantedly complimentary to the British in general and the Royal Navy in particular, is Max Hastings and Simon Jenkins, *The Battle for the Falklands*. A good brief account that inexplicably fails to mention or analyze British naval weaknesses is Uhlig, *How Navies Fight*, 363–74. An even better account that mentions such weaknesses without dwelling upon them is Grove, *From* Vanguard *to* Trident, 358–81. A solid account of the Falklands air campaign is Jeffrey Ethell and Alfred Price, *Air War: South Atlantic*. See also Sandy Woodward with Patrick Robinson, *One Hundred Days: The Memoirs of the Falklands Battle Group Commander*. Pertinent criticisms of the Royal Navy in the South Atlantic including a long and learned disquisition on the limited utility of small, vertical- or short-takeoff and -landing aircraft carriers are in Lehman, *Command of the Seas*, 271–82. Cable, *Britain's Naval Future*, xii–xvii, is a bracing criticism of the Thatcher government and the Ministry of Defence for regarding "the Soviet Union as the only enemy and the Central Front as the only theater" of operations, thus failing to acknowledge the possibility of "the contingency of limited war" in distant seas (xiii–xiv). For the slow redevelopment of British and French amphibious-warfare capabilities in the nineties, discussed at the end of the summary of the Falklands war, see Larrie Ferreiro, "Designing and Buying Warships: France, Great Britain, and the United States," *NIP* (March 1997): 57.

32. Grove, *From* Vanguard *to* Trident, 381; Cable, *Britain's Naval Future*, xii, xiii. Information of force percentages is from an internal U.S. Department of the Navy assessment, *Lessons of the Falklands: Summary Report, February 1983*, 25. The document was provided to me by Professor David Alan Rosenberg.

33. Woodward with Robinson, *One Hundred Days*, 5.

34. Grove, *From* Vanguard *to* Trident, 369.

35. For a counterview, see Edgar O'Ballance, "The Falklands," in *Assault from the Sea: Essays on the History of Amphibious Warfare*, edited by Merrill L. Bartlett, 428–36, originally published as "The San Carlos Landing," *Marine Corps Gazette* (October 1982). O'Ballance emphasizes that Argentina's invasion came "out of the blue," and rightly praises the British for their rapid response. Despite their many technological and tactical shortcomings that led to needless loss of ships and men, the amphibious assault and subsequent campaign are praised by O'Ballance as "a textbook operation, with a little luck thrown in, conducted with an 8,000 mile logistic line across the ocean" (436).

36. Grove, *From* Vanguard *to* Trident, 380–81. Hayward, interview by author, May 2, 2002. See also U.S. Department of the Navy, *Lessons of the Falklands*, 31–32.

37. Peter Nailor, "The Development of the Royal Navy since 1945"; and Peter Stafford, "The Current Position of the Royal Navy," in *The Future of British Sea Power,* edited by Geoffrey Till (quotes on pp. 23, 36).

38. Norman Friedman, *Desert Victory: The War for Kuwait,* 318.

39. Lieutenant General John J. Yeosock comment in Walter E. Boomer, John J. Yeosock, Stanley R. Arthur, and Charles A. Horner, "What We Should Have Done Differently," pt. 2 in *In the Wake of the Storm: Gulf War Commanders Discuss Desert Storm,* edited by John F. Votaw, 18–19.

40. Comments of Generals Horner, Rhame, and Boomer and of Admiral Arthur in ibid., 20, 22, 26, 32, 36. The U.S. Navy's weakness in countermine warfare (the result of chronic neglect throughout the postwar era), the near-fatal mining of *Princeton* and *Tripoli,* and Iraq's fortuitous "ineptitude in mine laying" are discussed in Edward J. Marolda and Robert J. Schneller Jr., *Shield and Sword: The United States Navy and the Persian Gulf War,* 261–68. See also Crowe, *Line of Fire,* 326–27.

41. Hallion, *Storm over Iraq,* 135, 137.

42. Norman Schwarzkopf, "A Tribute to the Navy–Marine Corps Team," *NIP* (August 1991): 44. See also James A. Winnefeld, Preston Niblack, and Dana J. Johnson, *A League of Airmen: U.S. Air Power in the Gulf War,* 265, 267. An authoritative discussion of the origins of "maritime prepositioning" forces that lay in the navy's inherent distrust of any joint ad hoc regional planning or commands is in Marolda and Schneller, *Shield and Sword,* 16–18.

43. Jeffrey Record, *Hollow Victory: A Contrary View of the Gulf War,* 116.

44. Winnefeld, Niblack, and Johnson, *League of Airmen,* 267–71 (quote on p. 267).

45. Dennison, oral history interview, 263–64, 289–94, 399–400; Vistica, *Fall from Glory,* 176–78.

46. Winnefeld, Niblack, and Johnson, *League of Airmen,* 264.

47. Edward C. Mann III, *Thunder and Lightning: Desert Storm and the Air Power Debates,* 188.

48. Hayward, interview by author, May 2, 2002. On the initial use of "smart" weaponry in Vietnam as early as 1970, see Sherwood, *Afterburner,* 46.

49. Marolda and Schneller, *Shield and Sword,* 369–70.

50. Ibid. The authors emphasize the comparative age and weakness of frontline naval aircraft in the Gulf War, especially the A-7 and A-6 attack planes. The FA-18 proved to be a very short-range aircraft suitable at best for battlefield interdiction missions but not for deep-strike penetration. Also, naval aircrews "had not been well trained" for strategic or tactical bombing missions. See pp. 370–72.

51. "Mine Warfare: Desert Storm and After," http://www.exwar.org/Htm/ 8000PopP2, 1; "The Royal Navy and the Gulf," http://www.btinternet.com/~warship/ Feature/gulf.htm, 2–3; "U.S. Navy in Desert Shield/Desert Storm," http://www.history .navy.mil/wars/destorm/ds5.htm, 5; Marolda and Schneller, *Shield and Sword,* 47–432.

Chapter 8. Rocks and Shoals

1. Bernard C. Nalty, *Long Passage to Korea: Black Sailors and the Integration of the U.S. Navy,* 17–24 (quote on p. 17); Richard Polenberg, *War and Society: The United States, 1941–1945,* 124–25.

2. Zumwalt, *On Watch: A Memoir,* 236.

3. Ibid., 168–78 (quote on p. 178).

4. Robert F. Dunn, "The Spirit of *Saratoga,*" 19–20; Robert Timberg, *The Nightingale's Song,* 59.

5. Guttridge, *Mutiny,* 258.

6. Sherwood, *Afterburner,* 262–91. The most complete accounts of the *Kitty Hawk* and *Constellation* incidents are in Guttridge, *Mutiny,* 261–80; Zumwalt, *On Watch: A Memoir,* 217–35; and the hastily drafted but nonetheless factually detailed U.S. Congress, House Committee on Armed Services, *Report by the Special Subcommittee on Disciplinary Problems in the U.S. Navy,* 1–24, found at U.S. Department of the Navy, Naval Historical Center, http://www.history.navy.mil/library/special/racial-incidents.htm.

7. H. R. Haldeman, *The Haldeman Diaries: Inside the Nixon White House,* 649.

8. The classic indictment of the navy that Ronald Reagan and John Lehman built and that led directly to Tailhook is Vistica, *Fall from Glory;* see pp. 258–69, 273–80, 289–91, 310, 341–42.

9. Daniel F. Harrington, "That '70s Military Is Back?" *NIP* (April 2000): 112.

10. The best extant account of Tailhook remains W. Hays Parks, "Tailhook: What Happened, Why & What's to Be Learned," *NIP* (September 1994): 89–103 ("mother" quote on p. 93). Lieutenant Coughlin is quoted in Bob Woodward, *Shadow: Five Presidents and the Legacy of Watergate,* 196.

11. Michael Sullivan, executive producer, *Navy Blues.* Garrett's abrupt dismissal and his wife's comment are in Woodward, *Shadow,* 196.

12. Richard Rayner, "The Warrior Besieged," *New York Times Magazine,* June 22, 1997, 26–27; Jean T. Palmer, "WAVES," and Sue S. Dauser, "Navy Nurses," in *Battle Stations! Your Navy in Action,* by Admirals of the U.S. Navy, 130; letters of Sergeant Bob Bowie and Private William J. Robinson reprinted in *The Best from "YANK," the Army Weekly,* 422–23.

13. Rayner, "The Warrior Besieged," 26.

14. James Jones, *WW II: A Chronicle of Soldiering,* 25.

15. The following account of the Cubi Point "zoo" during the Vietnam years is from Nichols and Tillman, *On Yankee Station,* 46–47.

16. James Webb, "Women Can't Fight," 145, 147, 275.

17. Paul E. Roush, "A Tangled Webb," *NIP* (August 1997): 42–45.

18. "Women in Combat: The Movie . . . ," *Washington Post,* August 30, 1997. Fred Ikle and Edward N. Luttwack are quoted in Rayner, "The Warrior Besieged," 27, 29.

19. Harrington, "That '70s Military Is Back?" 112. Problems aboard *Theodore Roose-*

velt are recounted in Robert K. Wilcox, *Black Aces High: The Story of a Modern Fighter Squadron at War,* 191.

20. For comments and quotes on the Lister issue and related matters, see "Gender and the Civil-Military Gap," *NIP* (March 2000): 10–14. For the most recent exchange of views on the *Vincennes* incident, see "Human-Centric Warfare," *NIP* (March 2000): 26, 28.

21. Evan Thomas and Gregory L. Vistica, "At War in the Ranks."

Chapter 9. Navy Imperial

1. Thomas P. M. Barnett and Henry H. Gaffney, "It's Going to Be a Bumpy Ride," *NIP* (January 1993): 23–26.

2. Michael Vlahos, "The Navy and the Nation," *NIP* (May 1994): 56–63 (quotes on pp. 56, 61).

3. An excellent summary of the 1992 defense document and the thinking behind it is in James Mann, *Rise of the Vulcans: The History of Bush's War Cabinet,* 209–15. See also Bryan Burrough et al., "The Path to War," 232.

4. Robert D. Kaplan, *The Ends of the Earth: From Togo to Turkmenistan, from Iran to Cambodia—a Journey to the Frontiers of Anarchy,* esp. pp. 116–18.

5. The National Commission on Terrorist Attacks upon the United States, *9/11 Commission Report,* 97–98.

6. Dennis T. Krupp, "Expeditionary Warfare: Conquering the Littorals," *Surface Warfare* (January–February 1999): 11. See also Mike Mulleny, "Surface Warfare: Into the Millennium," *Surface Warfare* (January–February 1999): 2–9.

7. See Scott O'Grady and Jeff Coplon, *Return with Honor.*

8. Information on the origins and course of the Bosnian crisis, including the Sixth Fleet's contribution to its resolution, may be found in the following sources: "Report of the Secretary of the Navy," undated, http://www.dod.mil/execsec/adr96/navy-report .html; "Task Force Eagle—SFOR XIII: History of BiH," http://www.tfeagle.army.mil/ TFE/bosnia_history.htm; and "Navy News Service: Bosnia Operations, 30 August, 6, 13 September 1995," http://www.chinfo.navy.mil/navpalib/bosnia/adrift/adriat05,06,07.html.

9. Richard L. Wright and Teri Sanford, "Present at the Creation: Operation Allied Force, a Prototype for 21st Century War in the Littoral," *Surface Warfare* (January–February 2000): 10–11.

10. Wilcox, *Black Aces High,* 11–265, provides an outstanding account of the development of the new ground-attack doctrine by the Black Aces squadron. Further information on Operation Allied Force in Kosovo during the spring of 1999 can be found at three Internet sources: "The Untold Story of the Strikes," http://www.cnn.com/ specials/1998/10/kosovo; "The Story of the NATO Strikes," http://news.bbc.co.uk/ hi/english/static/kosovo-fact-files/default.stm; and "U.S. Navy—Operation Allied Force,"

http://www.chinfo.navy.mil/navpalib/news/kosovo/alliedforce.html. The *Philippine Sea*'s missile launch is recounted in Peniston, *Around the World,* 94–96.

11. Polmar, *Ships and Aircraft,* 17th ed., 1; Hagan, *This People's Navy,* 385; Barone, *Our Country,* 638.

12. Patrick E. Tyler, "Direction of Global War on Terror Raises Unsettling Questions," http://www.nytimes.com, November 21, 2001.

13. James Dao, "War Mutes Critics of Costly Carrier Groups," *New York Times,* November 11, 2001; Richard R. Burgess, "U.S. Strikes Terrorist, Taliban Sites: Sea Services Mobilize for Long War"; M. E. Sprengelmeyer, "Special Marine Unit Is Highly Versatile," *Seattle Post-Intelligencer,* November 27, 2000.

14. Burgess, "U.S. Strikes Terrorist, Taliban Sites"; Richard R. Burgess, "Air Strikes Hit Afghan Front Lines," 25.

15. Burgess, "U.S. Strikes Terrorist, Taliban Sites."

16. Burgess, "Air Strikes Hit Afghan Front Lines"; Polmar, *Ships and Aircraft,* 17th ed., 411–12.

17. Thom Shanker and Eric Schmitt, "Service Chiefs Say Afghan Battle Will Help Military Get Smarter, Stronger and Faster," http://www.nytimes.com, September 10, 2002.

18. See Dao, "War Mutes Critics."

19. The distinct capabilities of the marine expeditionary units are discussed in Sprengelmeyer, "Special Marine Unit." See also Steven Lee Meyers and James Dao, "The Marines' 21st-Century Beachhead Is Far Inland," http://www.nytimes.com, December 22, 2001.

20. Meyers and Dao, "Marines' 21st-Century Beachhead"; Tyler, "Direction of Global War"; Eric Schmitt and James Dao, "U.S. Is Building Up Its Military Bases in Afghan Region," http://www.nytimes.com, January 9, 2002.

21. William M. Arkin, "Osama Has Left the Building," http://www.washingtonpost.com, November 18, 2001."

22. Michael R. Gordon, "A Month in a Difficult Battlefield: Assessing U.S. War Strategy," http://www.nytimes.com, November 8, 2001.

23. Summaries and comments on the Bush administration's new "National Security Strategy of the United States," released to Congress and the public on September 20, 2002, may be found in David E. Sanger, "Bush Outlines Doctrine of Striking Foes First," http://www.nytimes.com, September 20, 2002; and Randall Mikkelsen, "Bush Outlines Strategy of Preemptive Strikes," http://www.washingtonpost.com, September 20, 2002.

24. Emily Eakin, "Let American 'Empire' Rule, Enthusiasts Say," *Seattle Times-Post Intelligencer,* March 31, 2002; Bill Keller, "How to Fight the Next War," *New York Times Magazine,* March 10, 2002, 32–37, 48, 59, 68, 72.

25. Information has been gleaned from the British Royal Navy Web site, http://www.royal-navy.mod.uk, and from http://www.naval-technology.com. See also A. S. C. Wilson, "Whither the Flattops?" *NIP* (March 2006): 68–71.

26. Eric S. Margolis, "India Rules the Waves," *NIP* (March 2005): 67; Eric Wertheim, "World Navies in Review," *NIP* (March 2006): 57 (caption); John B. Nathman and Clay Harris, "Shaping the Future," *NIP* (January 2006): 19.

27. Truscott, *Kursk: Russia's Lost Pride*, 119–21; Ali Akbar Dareini, "Iran Tests Submarine-to-Surface Missile," www.washingtonpost.com, August 27, 2006; Norman Polmar, "Atomic Fish," *NIP* (August 2006): 31.

28. Basic, if circumspect, information on *Charles de Gaulle* can be found in Stephen Saunders, ed., *Jane's Fighting Ships, 2001–02*, 218; *2002–03*, 220 (quote); and *2004–05*, 226 (quote). See also *"Charles de Gaulle,"* in http://www.romanchess.com/DeGaulle and Wise News communiqué, January 23, 1999, and "French Nuclear Aircraft [Carrier] Problems" at http://www.antenna.ne/wise/505.

29. John Wilson Lewis and Xue Litai, *China's Strategic Seapower: The Politics of Force Modernization in the Nuclear Age*, 224 (quote in chart), 236–37; Srikanth Kondapalli, *China's Naval Power*, 77–112; K. R. Singh, *Navies of South Asia*, 373–410.

30. Bernard D. Cole, *The Great Wall at Sea: China's Navy Enters the Twenty-first Century*, 187.

31. James Bamford, "Strategic Thinking," *Washington Post*, September 8, 2002.

32. Acheson, *Present at the Creation*, 922.

33. Among the flood of articles that appeared before, during, and immediately after Gulf II about America's astounding new war-making capabilities, the following proved most helpful: "Military Revolutions: Warfare Meets the Age of Information Technology," *Economist* 364:8282 (July 20–26, 2002): 7–9; Bill Keller, "Rumsfeld and the Generals," http://www.nytimes.com, April 5, 2003; Stephen Budiansky, "Air War: Striking in Ways We Haven't Seen," http://www.washingtonpost.com, April 6, 2003; and Gregg Easterbrook, "American Power Moves beyond the Mere Super," *New York Times*, April 27, 2003. The best after-action assessment is Milan Vego, "Learning from Victory," *NIP* (August 2003): 32–36. Admiral Keating's views were set forth in a Pentagon interview on May 8, 2003, with Fred Schultz and Fred Rainbow of the U.S. Naval Institute and published under the title "This Was a Different War," *NIP* (June 2003): 30–33.

34. M. L. Lyke, "The Day of Reckoning Arrives—at Last—for *Lincoln*'s Crew," *Seattle Post-Intelligencer*, March 22, 2003; Michael Brown, Grant Johnson, and Gerry Gilmore, "Tomahawks Fly for Iraqi Freedom," *Surface Warfare* (summer 2003): 10–11.

35. Eric Schmitt, "Top General Concedes Aerial Bombardment Did Not Fully Meet Goal," http://www.nytimes.com, March 26, 2003; Jonathan Weisman, "Pentagon Says Some Missiles Strayed," http://www.washingtonpost.com, March 30, 2003.

36. Eric Schmitt, "Top General Warns of Heavy Air Strikes to Come," http://www.nytimes.com, March 25, 2003; M. L. Lyke, "Change of Role for Air Crews," *Seattle Post-Intelligencer*, March 25, 2003; Lyndsey Layton, "A Harrowing Homecoming in a Sandy Fog on the Sea," http://www.washingtonpost.com, March 27, 2003.

37. Layton, "Harrowing Homecoming"; M. L. Lyke, "Flying through Desert Storms," *Seattle Post-Intelligencer*, March 27, 2003.

38. David Brown, "Aquidneck Probes Iraqi Shipwrecks for Arms, Spies."

39. Keller, "Rumsfeld and the Generals."

40. David L. Parsons, "Naval Aircraft and Weapon Developments," *NIP* (May 2003): 120.

41. M. L. Lyke, "Medical Team Braces for Worst That War Can Bring—on Board with Ship's Clinical Psychologist Rose Rice," *Seattle Post-Intelligencer,* March 17, 2003.

42. M. L. Lyke, "Many Aboard USS *Lincoln* Geared Up, Aviators Pensive," *Seattle Post-Intelligencer,* March 20, 2003.

43. Janine Zacharia, "Mediterranean Sea Dispatch: Smooth Sailing."

44. Michael P. Donnelly, "U.S.S. *Anzio* 2003 Mediterranean/Persian Gulf Deployment."

45. United States Navy Fact File "as of March 26, 2003," http://www.chinfo.navy.mil/navpalib/news.

46. David Wood, "Is U.S. Military Reaching Its Limits, or Is Nation's Will?" *Seattle Times,* March 14, 2004; "Washington Report: DoD—Costs Up, Delays Mount for Naval Weapons Programs," 8; Margaret Roth, "Ship System Innovations Will Have Lasting Impact on Navy's Future," 18–19.

47. Norman Friedman, "The Transformation of the U.S. Navy," in *Technology and Naval Combat,* edited by O'Brien, 238–47 (quote on p. 238).

48. Nathan Brasher, "Unmanned Aerial Vehicles and the Future of Air Combat," *NIP* 131:7 (July 2005): 37.

49. William H. McMichael, "Skipper Fired: Japan-Based Carrier Commander Sacked after Liberty Incidents," *Navy Times,* September 16, 2002, 8.

50. Polmar, *Ships and Aircraft,* 17th ed., 3 (quote), 652 (cost figure).

51. John Byron, "A New Navy for a New World," *NIP* 129:3 (March 2003): 86–88; Hunter Keeter, "New Carrier Island Is at Heart of Higher Sortie Rates for CVN 21," 23–24.

52. Christopher Coker, *Waging War without Warriors? The Changing Culture of Military Conflict,* 194, 195.

53. Barry McWilliams, *This Ain't Hell . . . but You Can See It from Here: A Gulf War Sketchbook,* 57, 67.

54. The National Commission on Terrorist Attacks upon the United States, *9/11 Commission Report,* 118, 134–35.

55. Maureen Dowd, "Gunsmoke and Mirrors," *New York Times,* September 14, 2003.

56. David Brown and Mark D. Faram, "Shrinking the Force," *Navy Times,* September 15, 2003, 1, 8; David H. Lewis, "Naval Technology Development Must Change," *NIP* 129:10 (September 2003): 2; Moore's admission reported in Wood, "Reaching Its Limits?"; Norman Polmar, "Submarines under Attack," *NIP* 131:6 (June 2005): 88; Jason Sherman, "Getting It Right," 14.

57. Rick Maze, "Total Force Crossroads," *Navy Times,* September 15, 2003, 14–16.

58. Karen Jowers, "'An Act of Betrayal,'" *Navy Times,* November 3, 2003, 14–16.

59. Robert D. Kaplan, "How We Would Fight China," 58, 64.

60. Bradley Peniston, "The QDR: Where Are the Blue Water Ships?" *NIP* 132:3 (March 2006): 17–18; Dafina Linzer, "The NSC's Sesame Street Generation," *Washington Post*, March 12, 2006.

61. "The Commanders Respond," *NIP* 132:3 (March 2006): 34–51. West is quoted on p. 51; see also the comments of Rear Admiral Nils Wang, Royal Danish Navy, pp. 37–38.

62. Theodore H. White, *In Search of History: A Personal Adventure*, 90.

SELECTED BIBLIOGRAPHY

THE FOLLOWING BIBLIOGRAPHY is highly selective, listing only those works that immediately and directly influenced my thinking on the course of early-twentieth-century sea power in the context of international politics and economic, social, and technological development. Citations of the numerous articles from the *U.S. Naval Institute Proceedings* have been excluded for space reasons. Sufficient citations may be found in the appropriate endnotes.

Manuscript Collections

Harry S. Truman Library, Independence, Missouri

Clark Clifford Papers
George M. Elsey Papers
Dan A. Kimball Papers
Francis P. Matthews Papers
George J. Richards Papers
John Sullivan Papers
Stuart Symington Papers
Harry S. Truman Papers: Student Research File
James E. Webb Papers

National Archives, Washington, D.C.

Record Group 218: Records of the Joint Chiefs of Staff

Naval Historical Center, Washington Navy Yard, Washington, D.C.

Arleigh A. Burke Papers, "Pre-CNO File"

Interviews, Oral History Collection, U.S. Naval Institute, Annapolis, Maryland

George W. Anderson
Arleigh Burke
Robert L. Dennison
Daniel V. Gallery
Thomas F. Gates
John Hyland
Stephen Jurika Jr.
Kent Lee
Charles Loughlin
Thomas Moorer
Robert B. Pirie
Polaris Missile Interviews
William F. Raborn
James D. Ramage
Joseph J. Rochefort
Alfred G. Ward
Norville G. Ward
Thomas Weschler
Elmo Zumwalt

Personal Interview

Admiral Thomas B. Hayward, Seattle, Wash., May 2, 2002, March 16, April 10, 2006.

Government Documents

Central Intelligence Agency. *National Intelligence-Estimate NIE 11-15-82/D: Soviet Naval Strategy and Programs throughout the 1990s.* Washington, D.C.: Director of Central Intelligence, 1983.

U.S. Congress. House Committee on Armed Services. *Report by the Special Subcommitee on Disciplinary Problems in the U.S. Navy.* 92nd Cong., 2d sess., January 2, 1973. Available online at the U.S. Department of the Navy, Naval Historical Center: http://www.history.navy.mil/library/special/racial-incidents.htm.

U.S. Department of Defense. *Soviet Military Power, 1985.* Washington, D.C.: U.S. Government Printing Office, n.d.

———. *Soviet Military Power, 1999.* Washington, D.C.: U.S. Government Printing Office, n.d.

U.S. Department of the Navy. *Lessons of the Falklands: Summary Report, February 1983.* Washington, D.C.: U.S. Government Printing Office, n.d.

———. Chief of Information. *The Navy in Vietnam.* Washington, D.C.: U.S. Government Printing Office, 1968.

U.S. Department of State. *Foreign Relations of the United States, 1949.* Vol. 1, *National Security Affairs: Foreign Economic Policy.* Vol. 7, part 2, *The Far East and Australasia.* Washington, D.C.: U.S. Government Printing Office, 1976.

———. *Foreign Relations of the United States, 1950.* Vol. 1, *National Security Affairs: Foreign Economic Policy.* Washington, D.C.: U.S. Government Printing Office, 1977.

———. *Foreign Relations of the United States, 1951.* Vol. 1, *National Security Affairs: Foreign Economic Policy.* Vol. 4, *Europe: Political and Economic Relations.* Washington, D.C.: U.S. Government Printing Office, 1980, 1985.

———. *Foreign Relations of the United States, 1952–1954.* Vol. 14, *China and Japan.* Washington, D.C.: U.S. Government Printing Office, 1985.

———. *Foreign Relations of the United States, 1955–1957.* Vol. 2, *China.* Vol. 12, *Near East: Multilateral Relations—Iran, Iraq.* Washington, D.C.: U.S. Government Printing Office, 1992.

———. *Foreign Relations of the United States, 1958–1960.* Vol. 2, *General: United Nations.* Vol. 11, *Lebanon and Jordan.* Vol. 19, *China.* Washington, D.C.: U.S. Government Printing Office, 1991, 1992, 1996.

———. *Foreign Relations of the United States, 1961–1963.* Vol. 10, *Cuba, 1961–1962.* Vol. 11, *Cuban Missile Crisis and Aftermath.* Washington, D.C.: U.S. Government Printing Office, 1997.

———. *Foreign Relations of the United States, 1964–1968.* Vol. 19, *Arab-Israeli Crisis and War, 1967.* Washington, D.C.: U.S. Government Printing Office, 2004.

U.S. Senate. *Alleged Assassination Plots Involving Foreign Leaders: An Interim Report of the Select Committee to Study Governmental Operations with Respect to Intelligence Activities.* 94th Cong., 1st sess., Report 94–465. Washington, D.C.: U.S. Government Printing Office, 1975.

Other Sources

Accinelli, Robert. *Crisis and Commitment: United States Policy toward Taiwan, 1950–1955.* Chapel Hill: University of North Carolina Press, 1996.

Acheson, Dean. *Present at the Creation: My Years in the State Department.* New York: Signet Books, 1969.

Achkasov, V. I., and N. B. Pavlovich. *Soviet Naval Operations in the Great*

Patriotic War, 1941–1945. Translated by U.S. Naval Intelligence Command Translation Project. Annapolis: Naval Institute Press, 1981.

Admirals of the U.S. Navy. *Battle Stations! Your Navy in Action.* New York: William H. Wise, 1946.

Ajami, Fouad. *The Dream Palace of the Arabs: A Generation's Odyssey.* New York: Vintage Books, 1998.

Alford, Jonathan, ed. *Sea Power and Influence: Old Issues and New Challenges.* Osmun, Sweden: Gower and Allenheld, 1980.

Allen, Thomas B. "Return to the Battle of Midway: Ghosts and Survivors." *National Geographic* 195:4 (April 1999): 81–103.

Anderson, Orvil A. "Air Warfare and Morality." *Air University Quarterly Review* 3:3 (winter 1949).

Andrew, Christopher, and Mitrokhin, Vasili. *The Sword and the Shield: The Mitrokhin Archive and the History of the KGB.* New York: Basic Books, 1999.

Armstrong, Karen. *Holy War: The Crusades and Their Impact on Today's World.* New York: Anchor Books, 2001.

Baer, George W. *One Hundred Years of Sea Power: The U.S. Navy, 1890–1990.* Stanford: Stanford University Press, 1994.

———. "U.S. Naval Strategy, 1890–1945." *Naval War College Review* 44:1 (winter 1991): 6–31.

Baldwin, Hanson W. "The New Navy: A Reporter's Notebook." *New York Times Magazine,* October 13, 1957, 26–27, 85.

Ballantyne, Iain. *Warships of the Royal Navy: HMS* London. Barnsley, South Yorkshire: Leo Cooper, 2003.

Bamford, James. *Body of Secrets: Anatomy of the Ultra-Secret National Security Agency.* New York: Doubleday, 2001.

———. *The Puzzle Palace: A Report on America's Most Secret Agency.* New York: Penguin Books, 1985.

Barker, A. J. *Suez: The Seven-Day War.* London: Faber and Faber, 1964.

Barlow, Jeffrey C. *Revolt of the Admirals: The Fight for Naval Aviation, 1945–1950.* Washington, D.C.: U.S. Department of the Navy, Naval Historical Center, 1994.

Barone, Michael. *Our Country: The Shaping of America from Roosevelt to Reagan.* New York: Free Press, 1990.

Bartlett, Merrill L., ed. *Assault from the Sea: Essays on the History of Amphibious Warfare.* Annapolis: Naval Institute Press, 1983.

Beach, Edward L., Jr. *The United States Navy: 200 Years.* New York: Henry Holt, 1986.

Benson, Robert Louis, and Michael Warner, eds. *Venona: Soviet Espionage and the American Response, 1939–1957.* Washington, D.C.: National Security Agency, Central Intelligence Agency, 1996.

The Best from "YANK," the Army Weekly. Washington, D.C.: Council on Books in Wartime, 1945.

Blair, Clay. *The Forgotten War: America in Korea, 1950–1953.* New York: Times Books, 1987.

Boot, Max. "A Century of Small Wars Shows They Can Be Won." *New York Times,* July 6, 2003.

Brinkley, Douglas. *Tour of Duty: John Kerry and the Vietnam War.* New York: Harper Collins, 2004.

"Britain Relies on U.S. Navy: An Interview with Admiral Richard L. Conolly." *U.S. News and World Report,* July 1, 1949, 34–37.

Bronner, Michael. "The Recruiters' War." *Vanity Fair* 541 (September 2005): 303–18.

Brown, Charles R. "The Best Job in the Whole Navy." *Life* 41:24 (December 10, 1956): 143–48.

Brown, David. "Aquidneck Probes Iraqi Shipwrecks for Arms, Spies." *Seapower* 46:7 (August 2003): 27–28.

Browning, David. *The Seafire: The Spitfire That Went to Sea.* 1973. Reprint, Annapolis: Naval Institute Press, 1989.

Bryan, J., III. *Aircraft Carrier.* New York: Ballantine Books, 1954.

Budiansky, Stephen. *Air Power: The Men, Machines, and Ideas That Revolutionized War from Kitty Hawk to Gulf II.* New York: Viking Press, 2004.

Buell, Thomas B. *Naval Leadership in Korea: The First Six Months.* Washington, D.C.: U.S. Department of the Navy, Naval Historical Center, 2002.

Burgess, Richard R. "Air Strikes Hit Afghan Front Lines." *Seapower* 44:12 (December 2001): 25.

———. "U.S. Strikes Terrorist, Taliban Sites: Sea Services Mobilize for Long War." *Seapower* 44:11 (November 2001): 23.

Burke, Arleigh A. "The Future of the Navy." *Vital Speeches of the Day* 23:1 (October 15, 1956): 110–12.

Burrough, Bryan, Evgenia Peretz, David Rose, and David Wise. "The Path to War." *Vanity Fair* 525 (May 2004): 228–44, 281–94.

Butler, John A. *Strike Able-Peter: The Stranding and Salvage of the U.S.S. Missouri.* Annapolis: Naval Institute Press, 1995.

Byrd, Richard E. "Our Navy Explores Antarctica." *National Geographic* 92:4 (October 1947): 429–522.

Cable, James. *Britain's Naval Future*. London: Macmillan Press, 1983.

Cagle, Malcolm W., and Frank A. Manson. *The Sea War in Korea*. Annapolis: Naval Institute Press, 1957.

Clark, Eugene Franklin. *The Secrets of Inchon: The Untold Story of the Most Daring Covert Mission of the Korean War*. New York: Putnam's, 2002.

Clifford, Clark. *Counsel to the President: A Memoir*. New York: Random House, 1991.

Cockburn, Andrew. *The Threat: Inside the Soviet Military Machine*. New York: Vintage Books, 1984.

Coker, Christopher. *Waging War without Warriors? The Changing Culture of Military Conflict*. Boulder: Lynne Rienner Publishers, 2002.

Cole, Bernard D. *The Great Wall at Sea: China's Navy Enters the Twenty-first Century*. Annapolis: Naval Institute Press, 2001.

Coletta, Paola E. *The United States Navy and Defense Unification, 1947–1953*. Newark: University of Delaware Press, 1981.

Condit, Kenneth W. *The History of the Joint Chiefs of Staff: The Joint Chiefs of Staff and National Policy*. Vol. 2, *1947–1949*. Wilmington, Del.: Michael Glazier, 1979.

Congressional Quarterly. *The Middle East*. 5th ed. Washington, D.C.: Congressional Quarterly, 1981.

Cottrell, Alvin J., and Wynfred Joshua. "The United States–Soviet Strategic Balance in the Mediterranean." In *R.U.S.I. and Brassey's Defence Yearbook, 1974*. London: Brassey's Naval and Shipping Annual, 1974.

Crane, Conrad C. *American Airpower Strategy in Korea, 1950–1953*. Lawrence: University Press of Kansas, 2000.

Cristol, A. Jay. *The* Liberty *Incident: The 1967 Israeli Attack on the U.S. Navy Spy Ship*. Washington, D.C.: Brassey's, 2002.

Croizat, Victor. *The Brown Water Navy: The River and Coastal War in Indo-China and Vietnam, 1948–1972*. Poole, U.K.: Blandford Press, 1984.

Crowe, William J., Jr. *The Line of Fire: From Washington to the Gulf, the Politics and Battles of the New Military*. New York: Simon and Schuster, 1993.

Cutler, Thomas J. *Brown Water, Black Berets: Coastal and Riverine Warfare in Vietnam*. Annapolis: Naval Institute Press, 1988.

Dalgleish, D. Douglas, and Schweikart, Larry. *Trident*. Carbondale: Southern Illinois University Press, 1984.

Daniels, Douglas. "Tiny Fleet, Big Job." *Naval History* 19:4 (August 2005): 50–54.

Davis, John R. "'Med' Replenishment—Suda Bay, Crete, 1947." *U.S. Navy Cruiser Sailors Association Journal* 13:1 (winter 2004): 47.

Dean, Vera Micheles. *The Nature of the Non-Western World.* 1957. Reprint, New York: New American Library, 1965.

Dehio, Ludwig. *The Precarious Balance: Four Centuries of the European Power Struggle.* Translated by Charles Fullman. 1948. Reprint, New York: Vintage Books, 1962.

Dictionary of American Fighting Ships. 8 vols. Washington, D.C.: U.S. Department of the Navy, Naval Historical Center, 1959–1981.

Donnelly, Michael P. "U.S.S. *Anzio* 2003 Mediterranean/Persian Gulf Deployment." *U.S. Navy Cruiser Sailors Association* journal 13:1 (winter 2004): 43.

Dorr, Robert F., and Warren Thompson. *Korean Air War.* St. Paul: Motorbooks International, 2003.

Dunn, Robert F. "The Spirit of *Saratoga.*" *Naval History* 11:6 (December 1997): 19–20.

Eisenberg, Michael T. *Shield of the Republic: The United States Navy in an Era of Cold War and Violent Peace, 1945–1962.* New York: St. Martin's Press, 1993.

Eisenhower, Dwight D. *The White House Years: A Personal Account.* 2 vols. Vol. 1, *Mandate for Change.* Vol. 2, *Waging Peace.* Garden City, N.Y.: Doubleday, 1963, 1965.

Eller, Ernest McNeill. *The Soviet Sea Challenge.* New York: Cowles, 1971.

Engen, Donald D. *Wings and Warriors: My Life as a Naval Aviator.* Washington, D.C.: Smithsonian Institution Press, 1997.

Ethell, Jeffrey, and Alfred Price. *Air War: South Atlantic.* New York: Macmillan, 1983.

Fahey, James C., ed. *The Ships and Aircraft of the U.S. Fleet.* Vols. 6–8. Annapolis: Naval Institute Press, 1994–1996.

Fairhall, David. *Russian Sea Power.* Boston: Gambit, 1971.

Faltum, Andrew. *The* Essex *Aircraft Carriers.* Baltimore: Nautical and Aviation Publishing Company of America, 1996.

Ferguson, Niall. *Empire: The Rise and Demise of the British World Order and the Lessons for Global Power.* New York: Basic Books, 2002.

Ferrell, Robert H., ed. *The Diary of James C. Hagerty: Eisenhower in Mid-Course, 1954–1955.* Bloomington: Indiana University Press, 1983.

———. *Harry S. Truman: A Life.* Columbia: University of Missouri Press, 1994.

Field, James A., Jr. *History of U.S. Naval Operations in Korea.* Washington, D.C.: U.S. Government Printing Office, 1962.

Fieldhouse, Richard, and Shunji Taoka. *Superpowers at Sea: An Assessment of the Naval Arms Race.* Oxford: Oxford University Press, 1989.

"First A-bomb Navy: Set for Action Off Formosa." *U.S. News and World Report,* February 4, 1955, 23.

Flynn, Ramsey. *Cry from the Deep: The Submarine Disaster That Riveted the World and Put the New Russia to the Ultimate Test.* New York: HarperCollins, 2004.

Friedman, Norman. *Desert Victory: The War for Kuwait.* Annapolis: Naval Institute Press, 1991.

————. *The Fifty-Year War: Conflict and Strategy in the Cold War.* Annapolis: Naval Institute Press, 2000.

————. *Seapower as Strategy: Navies and National Interests.* Annapolis: Naval Institute Press, 2001.

————. *U.S. Aircraft Carriers: An Illustrated Design History.* Annapolis: Naval Institute Press, 1983.

Fussell, Paul. *Wartime: Understanding and Behavior in the Second World War.* New York: Oxford University Press, 1989.

Galantin, I. J. *Submarine Admiral: From Battleships to Ballistic Missiles.* Urbana: University of Illinois Press, 1995.

Gallery, Daniel V. "Don't Let Them Cripple the Navy." *Saturday Evening Post* 222:18 (October 29, 1949): 36–37, 44, 46, 48.

————. "If This Be Treason." *Colliers* 125:3 (January 21, 1950): 15–16, 45.

Garthoff, Raymond L. *Détente and Confrontation: American-Soviet Relations from Nixon to Reagan.* Washington, D.C.: Brookings Institution, 1985.

Gates, Thomas S. "Naval Supremacy Vital to Our National Security." *Vital Speeches of the Day* 23:4 (October 29, 1956): 114–16.

Georgetown University, Center for Strategic Studies. *Soviet Sea Power.* Washington, D.C.: Georgetown University, Center for Strategic Studies, 1969.

Ginsburgh, Robert. "Interview with Admiral F. B. Stump, Commander in Chief, Pacific." *U.S. News and World Report,* August 27, 1954, 24–26.

Goldsmith, Wynn. *Papa Bravo Romeo: U.S. Navy Patrol Boats at War in Vietnam.* New York: Ballantine Books, 2001.

Goldstein, Lyle J., and Yuri M. Zhukov, "Superpower Showdown in the Mediterranean, 1973." *Seapower* 46:10 (October 2003): 32–35.

Graebner, Norman A. *An Uncertain Tradition: American Secretaries of State in the Twentieth Century.* New York: McGraw-Hill, 1961.

Grandfield, Linda, ed. *I Remember Korea: Veterans Tell Their Stories of the Korean War, 1950–1953.* New York: Clarion Books, 2003.

Grant, Zalin. *Over the Beach: The Air War in Vietnam.* New York: Pocket Books, 1988.

Gregory, William H. *The Defense Procurement Mess: A Twentieth Century Fund Essay.* Lexington, Mass.: D. C. Heath, 1989.

Grossnick, Roy A., et al. *United States Naval Aviation, 1910–1995.* Washington, D.C.: U.S. Department of the Navy, Naval Historical Center, 1997.

Grove, Eric J. *From* Vanguard *to Trident: British Naval Policy since World War II.* Annapolis: Naval Institute Press, 1987.

Guttridge, Leonard F. *Mutiny: A History of Naval Insurrection.* Annapolis: Naval Institute Press, 1992.

Hagan, Kenneth J. "On (the Gulf) War." *Naval History* 13:2 (March–April 1999).

———. *This People's Navy: The Making of American Sea Power.* New York: Free Press, 1991.

———, ed. *In Peace and War: Interpretations of American Naval History, 1775–1978.* Westport, Conn.: Greenwood Press, 1978.

Haldeman, H. R. *The Haldeman Diaries: Inside the Nixon White House.* New York: Berkley Books, 1995.

Hallion, Richard P. *The Naval Air War in Korea.* Baltimore: Nautical and Aviation Publishing Company of America, 1986.

———. *Storm over Iraq: Air Power and the Gulf War.* Washington, D.C.: Smithsonian Institution Press, 1992.

Hanson, Victor Davis. *Carnage and Culture: Landmark Battles in the Rise of Western Culture.* New York: Anchor Books, 2002.

Hartman, Frederick H. *Naval Rennaissance: The U.S. Navy in the 1980s.* Annapolis: Naval Institute Press, 1990.

Harvey, Frank. *Air War—Vietnam.* New York: Bantam Books, 1967.

Hastings, Max, and Simon Jenkins. *The Battle for the Falklands.* New York: W. W. Norton, 1983.

Hattendorf, John B. *Doing Naval History: Essays toward Improvement.* Newport, R.I.: Naval War College Press, 1995.

———. "The Evolution of the Maritime Strategy, 1977 to 1987." *Naval War College Review* 41:3 (summer 1988): 8–27.

———. *The Evolution of the U.S. Navy's Maritime Strategy, 1977–1986.* Naval War College Newport Papers, no. 19. Newport, R.I.: Naval War College Press, 2004.

———. *Naval History and Maritime Strategy: Collected Essays.* Malabar, Fla.: Krieger Publishing, 2000.

Heinl, Robert Debs, Jr. *Victory at High Tide: The Inchon-Seoul Campaign.* Philadelphia: Lippincott, 1968.

Herrick, Robert Waring. *Soviet Naval Strategy: Fifty Years of Theory and Practice.* Annapolis: Naval Institute Press, 1968.

————. *Soviet Naval Theory and Policy: Gorshkov's Inheritance.* Annapolis: Naval Institute Press, 1988.

Hewlett, Richard G., and Francis Duncan, *Nuclear Navy, 1946–1962.* Chicago: University of Chicago Press, 1974.

Hilsman, Roger. *To Move a Nation: The Politics of Foreign Policy in the Administration of John F. Kennedy.* New York: Dell, 1967.

Holbrook, R. O. Comment on "Battle Stations Missile!" by Nick T. Spark. *Naval History* 17:5 (October 2003): 7, 10.

Holloway, James L. "The Navy and Its Third Century." In *Science and the Future Navy: A Symposium in Celebration of the Thirtieth Anniversary of the Office of Naval Research.* Washington, D.C.: National Academy of Sciences, 1977.

Holober, Frank. *Raiders of the China Coast: CIA Covert Operations during the Korean War.* Annapolis: Naval Institute Press, 1999.

Howarth, Stephen. *To Shining Sea: A History of the United States Navy, 1775–1991.* New York: Random House, 1991.

Howe, Jonathan Trumbull. *Multicrises: Sea Power and Global Politics in the Missile Age.* Cambridge: MIT Press, 1971.

Huchthausen, Peter A. *October Fury.* Hoboken, N.J.: John Wiley and Sons, 2002.

————. *K-19, the Widowmaker: The Secret Story of the Soviet Nuclear Submarine.* Washington, D.C.: National Geographic, 2002.

Huchthausen, Peter A., Igor Kurdin, and R. Alan White. *Hostile Waters.* New York: St. Martin's Press, 1997.

Hugill, Peter J. *World Trade since 1431: Geography, Technology, and Capitalism.* Baltimore: Johns Hopkins University Press, 1993.

Hyatt, A. M. J., ed. *Dreadnought to Polaris: Maritime Strategy since Mahan.* Papers from the Conference on Strategic Studies at the University of Western Ontario, March 1972. Annapolis: Naval Institute Press, 1973.

Johnson, Paul. *Modern Times: The World from the Twenties to the Eighties.* New York: Harper Colophon, 1985.

Jones, James. *WW II: A Chronicle of Soldiering.* New York: Ballantine Books, 1975.

Kalb, Marvin, and Bernard Kalb. *Kissinger.* New York: Dell, 1975.

Kaplan, Robert D. *The Ends of the Earth: From Togo to Turkmenistan, from Iran to Cambodia—a Journey to the Frontiers of Anarchy.* New York: Vintage Books, 1996.

———. "How We Would Fight China." *Atlantic* 295:5 (June 2005): 49–64.

Karig, Walter, Malcolm W. Cagle, and Frank A. Manson. *Battle Report: The War in Korea.* New York: Rinehart, 1952.

Keeter, Hunter. "New Carrier Island Is at Heart of Higher Sortie Rates for CVN 21." *Seapower* 46:6 (June 2003): 23–24.

Kennan, George F. *American Diplomacy, 1900–1950.* New York: Mentor Books, 1952.

———. *Russia and the West under Lenin and Stalin.* New York: Mentor Books, 1961.

Kennedy, Paul M. *The Rise and Fall of the Great Powers: Economic Change and Military Conflict from 1500 to 2000.* New York: Random House, 1987.

Kennedy, Robert F. *Thirteen Days: A Memoir of the Cuban Missile Crisis.* New York: W. W. Norton, 1969.

King, Edward L. "How the Army Destroyed Itself." *Saturday Review,* May 6, 1972.

Kissinger, Henry. *Crisis: The Anatomy of Two Major Foreign Policy Crises.* New York: Simon and Schuster, 2003.

Kittredge, George T. "Ships Leave Yokosuka for Gigantic Atomic-Age Amphibious Operation." *Seahawk* (Yokosuka Naval Base newspaper), February 11, 1956, reprinted in *U.S. Navy Cruiser Sailors Association* journal 12:2 (spring 2003): 25.

Knoebl, Kuno. *Victor Charlie: The Face of War in Vietnam.* Translated by Abe Farbstein. New York: Frederick A. Praeger, 1967.

Knott, Richard C. *Attack from the Sky: Naval Air Operations in the Korean War.* Washington, D.C.: U.S. Department of the Navy, Naval Historical Center, 2004.

Kokoshin, Andrei A. *Soviet Strategic Thought, 1917–91.* Cambridge: MIT Press, 1998.

Kondapalli, Srikanth. *China's Naval Power.* New Delhi: Knowledge World in association with Institute for Defence Studies and Analyses, 2001.

Krock, Arthur. *Memoirs: Sixty Years on the Firing Line.* New York: Popular Library, 1968.

Kuenne, Robert E. *The Polaris Missile Strike: A General Economic Systems Analysis.* Columbus: Ohio State University Press, 1966.

Lacey, Robert. *The Kingdom: Arabia and the House of Sa'ud*. New York: Avons Books, 1981.

Lashmar, Paul. *Spy Flights of the Cold War*. Annapolis: Naval Institute Press, 1996.

Lautenschläger, Karl. "Technology and the Evolution of Naval Warfare." *International Security* 8:2 (fall 1983): 206–12.

Lehman, John F., Jr. *Command of the Seas*. New York: Scribner, 1988.

———. *On Seas of Glory: Heroic Men, Great Ships, and the Epic Battles of the American Navy*. New York: Free Press, 2001.

Lewis, Bernard. *What Went Wrong? The Clash between Islam and Modernity in the Middle East*. New York: Perennial Books, 2002.

Lewis, John Wilson, and Xue Litai. *China's Strategic Seapower: The Politics of Force Modernization in the Nuclear Age*. Stanford: Stanford University Press, 1994.

Lilienthal, David E. *The Journals of David E. Lilienthal*. 7 vols. Vol. 2, *The Atomic Energy Years, 1945–1960*. New York: Harper and Row, 1964–1983.

Lippmann, Walter. *The Cold War: A Study in U.S. Foreign Policy*. New York: Harper and Row, 1947.

Love, Robert William, Jr. *History of the U.S. Navy, 1775–1991*. 2 vols. Harrisburg, Pa.: Stackpole Books, 1992.

———, ed. *The Chiefs of Naval Operations*. Annapolis: Naval Institute Press, 1980.

Luttwak, Edward N. *The Pentagon and the Art of War*. New York: Simon and Schuster, 1985.

Luttwak, Edward N., and Robert G. Weinland. "Superpower Naval Diplomacy in the October 1973 Arab-Israeli War: A Case Study." In *Sea Power in the Mediterranean: Political Unity and Military Constraints*. The Washington Papers, vol. 6, no. 61. Beverly Hills: Sage Publications, 1979.

Manchester, William. *The Glory and the Dream: A Narrative History of America, 1932–1972*. Boston: Little, Brown, 1974.

Mann, Edward C., III. *Thunder and Lightning: Desert Storm and the Air Power Debates*. Maxwell Air Force Base, Ala.: Air University Press, 1995.

Mann, James. *Rise of the Vulcans: A History of Bush's War Cabinet*. New York: Viking, 2004.

Marolda, Edward J. "The U.S. Navy and the 'Loss of China,' 1945–1950." In *George C. Marshall's Mediation Mission to China, December 1945–January 1947*, edited by Larry I. Bland, 409–20. Lexington, Va.: George C. Marshall Foundation, 1998.

Marolda, Edward J., and Robert J. Schneller Jr. *Shield and Sword: The United*

States Navy and the Persian Gulf War. Washington, D.C.: U.S. Department of the Navy, Naval Historical Center, 1998.

Marten, Harold M. "Cat Brown's Kittens Have Claws." *Saturday Evening Post* 229:35 (March 2, 1957): 32–33, 81–84.

Martin, Robert P. "Eyewitness Account—Mighty Seventh Fleet Presides over Another Pull-Out." *U.S. News and World Report,* February 18, 1955, 44–46.

———. "The Seventh Fleet—Ready to Fight for Formosa." *U.S. News and World Report,* October 1, 1954, 35–38.

Masterson, Danel M., ed. *Naval History: The Sixth Symposium of the U.S. Naval Academy.* Wilmington, Del.: Scholarly Resources, 1987.

Mastny, Vojtech. "Was 1968 a Strategic Watershed of the Cold War?" *Diplomatic History* 29:1 (January 2005): 149–79.

Matray, James I., ed. *East Asia and the United States: An Encyclopedia of Relations since 1789.* 2 vols. Westport, Conn.: Greenwood Press, 2002.

Mauldin, Bill. *Bill Mauldin in Korea.* New York: W. W. Norton, 1952.

McAuliffe, Mary S., ed. *CIA Documents on the Cuban Missile Crisis, 1962.* Washington, D.C.: Central Intelligence Agency History Staff, 1992.

McCarthy, LaDonne. "The First Day of the Rest of Their Lives: The Survival of an A-6 Crew." *Hook* 19:1 (spring 1991).

McGaugh, Scott. Midway *Magic.* New York: CDS, 2004.

McNamara, Robert S., and Brian Van De Mark. *In Retrospect: The Tragedy and Lessons of Vietnam.* New York: Vintage Books, 1996.

McNeill, William H. *The Rise of the West: A History of the Human Community.* New York: Mentor Books, 1965.

McWilliams, Barry. *This Ain't Hell . . . but You Can See It from Here: A Gulf War Sketchbook.* Novato, Calif.: Presidio Press, 1992.

Mearsheimer, John J. "A Strategic Misstep: The Maritime Strategy and Deterrence in Europe." *International Security* 11:2 (fall 1986): 47–101.

Metzner, Franklin. "I Fly the Night Skies over Korea." *Saturday Evening Post* 225:26 (December 27, 1952): 26–27, 48.

Michener, James A. "All for One: A Story from Korea." *Reader's Digest* 61:363 (July 1952): 1–2.

———. *The Bridges at Toko-Ri.* New York: Bantam Books, 1955.

———. "The Forgotten Heroes of Korea." *Saturday Evening Post* 224:45 (May 10, 1952): 19–21, 124–28.

Miller, David, and Chris Miller. *Modern Naval Combat.* New York: Crescent Books, 1986.

Millet, Allen R. *Semper Fidelis: The History of the United States Marine Corps.* New York: Macmillan, 1980.

Millis, Walter, and E. S. Duffield, eds. *The Forrestal Diaries.* New York: Viking Press, 1951.

Mintz, John. "Navy Developing Revolutionary Radio-Control Ships." *Seattle Post-Intelligencer,* June 23, 1996.

Mitchell, Donald W. *A History of Russian and Soviet Sea Power.* New York: Macmillan, 1974.

Mitchell, William. *Winged Defense: The Development and Possibilties of Modern Air Power—Economic and Military.* New York: G. P. Putnam's Sons, 1925.

Modelski, George, and William R. Thompson. *Seapower in Global Politics, 1494–1993.* Seattle: University of Washington Press, 1988.

Moore, John Norton. "U.S. Position on the Law of the Sea Reviewed." *Department of State Bulletin* 70:816 (April 15, 1974): 397–402.

Munson, Glenn, ed. *Letters from Vietnam.* New York: Parallax, 1966.

Nalty, Bernard C. *Long Passage to Korea: Black Sailors and the Integration of the U.S. Navy.* Washington, D.C.: U.S. Department of the Navy, Naval Historical Center, 2003.

The National Commission on Terrorist Attacks upon the United States. *The 9/11 Commission Report: Final Report of the National Commission on Terrorist Attacks upon the United States, Authorized Edition.* New York: W. W. Norton, 2004.

Nichols, John B., and Barrett Tillman. *On Yankee Station: The Naval Air War over Vietnam.* Annapolis: Naval Institute Press, 1987.

Nimitz, Chester W. "Your Navy as Peace Insurance." *National Geographic* 89:6 (June 1946): 681–720.

O'Brien, Phillips Payson. *Technology and Naval Combat in the Twentieth Century and Beyond.* London: Frank Cass, 2001.

O'Grady, Scott, and Jeff Coplon. *Return with Honor.* New York: Doubleday, 1995.

O'Neill, John E., and Jerome Corsi. *Unfit for Command: Swift Boat Veterans Speak Out against John Kerry.* Washington, D.C.: Regnery, 2003.

Pallot, John S. "Suez Remembered." *Seapower* 47:5 (May 2004): 5.

Palmer, Michael A. *Origins of the Maritime Strategy: American Naval Strategy in the First Postwar Decade.* Washington, D.C.: U.S. Department of the Navy, Naval Historical Center, 1988.

Parrish, Thomas. *The Submarine: A History.* New York: Viking, 2004.

Peniston, Bradley. *Around the World with the U.S. Navy: A Reporter's Travels.* Annapolis: Naval Institute Press, 1999.

Philbin, Tobias R., III. *The Lure of Neptune: German-Soviet Naval Collaboration and Ambitions, 1919–1941*. Columbia: University of South Carolina Press, 1994.

Polenberg, Richard. *War and Society: The United States, 1941–1945*. Philadelphia: J. B. Lippincott, 1972.

Polmar, Norman. *The Death of the U.S.S. Thresher*. Guilford, Conn.: Lyons Press, 2001.

————. *The Naval Institute Guide to the Ships and Aircraft of the U.S. Fleet*. 13th ed. Annapolis: Naval Institute Press, 1984.

————. *The Naval Institute Guide to the Ships and Aircraft of the U.S. Fleet*. 17th ed. Annapolis: Naval Institute Press, 2001.

————. *The Naval Institute Guide to the Soviet Navy: Third Edition*. Annapolis: Naval Institute Press, 1983.

————. *The Naval Institute Guide to the Soviet Navy: Fifth Edition*. Annapolis: Naval Institute Press, 1991.

Polmar, Norman, and Thomas B. Allen. *Rickover*. New York: Simon and Schuster, 1982.

Potter, E. B., ed. *Seapower: A Naval History*. Englewood Cliffs, N.J.: Prentice Hall, 1960.

President's Air Policy Commission. *Survival in the Air Age: A Report by the President's Air Policy Commission*. Washington, D.C.: Superintendent of Documents, 1948.

"Preview of the War We Do Not Want." *Colliers,* October 27, 1951.

Priest, Dana. *The Mission: Waging War and Keeping Peace with America's Military*. New York: W. W. Norton, 2003.

Public Papers of the Presidents of the United States: Dwight D. Eisenhower. Washington, D.C.: U.S. Government Printing Office, 1958.

Public Papers of the Presidents of the United States: Harry S. Truman. Washington, D.C.: U.S. Government Printing Office, 1961.

Purnell, Sonia. "Forces' Equipment Old, Late, or Faulty." *Independent,* February 13, 2000.

Quandt, William B. *Peace Process: American Diplomacy and the Arab-Israeli Conflict since 1967*. Washington, D.C.: Brookings Institution, 1993.

Quester, George H., ed. *Sea Power in the 1970s*. New York: Dunellen, 1975.

Raborn, W. F. "The Polaris Submarine." *Vital Speeches of the Day* 24:14 (May 1, 1958): 428–31.

Radford, Arthur W. "Our Navy in the Far East." *National Geographic* 104:4 (October 1953): 337–78.

Ranf, Bryan, and Geoffrey Till, eds. *The Sea in Soviet Strategy*. London: Macmillan, 1983.

Record, Jeffrey. *Hollow Victory: A Contrary View of the Gulf War*. Washington, D.C.: Brassey's, 1993.

Rees, David. *Korea: The Limited War*. Baltimore: Penguin Books, 1964.

Reynolds, Clark G. "Cherokee Jocko Fights the Cold War." *Naval History* 19:3 (June 2005): 18–22.

Richards, Guy. "What the Sailors Say about the Navy." *Life*, November 5, 1945, 41.

Ridgway, Matthew B. *The Korean War*. New York: Popular Library, 1967.

Roberts, J. Baylor. "Our Navy in the Far East." *National Geographic* 104:4 (October 1953): 537–77.

Rogow, Arnold. *James Forrestal: A Study of Personality, Politics, and Policy*. New York: Macmillan, 1963.

Ropp, Theodore. *War in the Modern World*. New York: Collier Books, 1962.

Rose, Lisle A. *After Yalta: America and the Origins of the Cold War*. New York: Scribner's, 1973.

———. *The Cold War Comes to Main Street: America in 1950*. Lawrence: University Press of Kansas, 1999.

Rosenberg, David Alan. "American Atomic Strategy and the Hydrogen Bomb Decision." *Journal of American History* 66:1 (June 1979): 62–87.

Roth, Margaret. "Ship System Innovations Will Have Lasting Impact on Navy's Future." *Seapower* 47:10 (October 2004): 18–19.

Royal United Services Institute for Defence Studies. *Brassey's Defence Yearbook, 1974*. London: Brassey's Naval and Shipping Annual, 1974.

Rusk, Dean, and Richard Rusk. *As I Saw It*. New York: Penguin Books, 1990.

Russell, Richard A. *Project Hula: Secret Soviet-American Cooperation in the War against Japan*. Washington, D.C.: U.S. Department of the Navy, Naval Historical Center, 1997.

Sagan, Scott D., and Jeremi Suri. "The Madman Nuclear Alert: Secrecy, Signaling, and Safety in October 1969." *International Security* 27:4 (spring 2003). Available online at http://mitpress.mit.edu/journal.

Schaffer, Ronald. *Wings of Judgement: American Bombing in World War II*. New York: Oxford University Press, 1985.

Schnabel, James F. *The History of the Joint Chiefs of Staff: The Joint Chiefs of Staff and National Policy*. Vol. 1, *1945–1947*. Washington, D.C.: Office of the Chairman of the Joint Chiefs of Staff, 1996.

Schoenbaum, David. *The United States and the State of Israel.* New York: Oxford University Press, 1993.

Schwoebel, Richard L. *Explosion Aboard the* Iowa. Annapolis: Naval Institute Press, 1999.

Scott, Harriet Fast, and William F. Scott. *The Armed Forces of the U.S.S.R.* Boulder: Westview Press, 1981.

Sherman, Jason. "Getting It Right." *Seapower* 48:6 (June 2005): 14.

Sherwood, John Darrell. *Afterburner: Naval Aviators and the Vietnam War.* New York: New York University Press, 2004.

Shor, Franc. "Pacific Fleet: Force for Peace." *National Geographic* 116:3 (September 1959): 283–335.

Shor, Franc, and W. E. Garrett. "Good Will Ambassadors of the U.S. Navy Win Friends in the Far East." *National Geographic* 116:3 (September 1959): 283–335.

Simonsen, S. G. "Russia's Northern Fleet in Heavy Seas." *Slavic Military Studies* 9:4 (December 1996): 713–29.

Singh, K. R. *Navies of South Asia.* New Delhi: Institute for Defence Studies and Analyses, 2002.

Smith, Hedrick. *The Russians.* Rev. ed. New York: Ballantine Books, 1976.

Sontag, Sherry, and Christopher Drew with Annette Drew. *Blind Man's Bluff: The Untold Story of American Submarine Espionage.* New York: Public Affairs Press, 1998.

Sorenson, Theodore H. *Kennedy.* New York: Bantam Books, 1966.

Spark, Nick T. "Battle Stations Missile!" *Naval History* 17:4 (August 2003): 24–27.

Spector, Ronald H. *At War at Sea: Sailors and Naval Warfare in the Twentieth Century.* New York: Viking, 2001.

Spence, Jonathan D. *The Search for Modern China.* New York: W. W. Norton, 1990.

Strausz-Hupé, Robert. "World in Revolution." *Saturday Evening Post* (August 15, 1959): 33, 64, 66–68.

Sullivan, Michael, executive producer. *Navy Blues.* Public Broadcasting System Frontline Series. Boston: WGBH Television, 1997.

Thomas, Evan, and Gregory L. Vistica. "At War in the Ranks." *Newsweek,* August 11, 1997, 32–33.

Thomas, Hugh. *The Suez Affair.* London: Weidenfeld and Nicolson, 1966.

Till, Geoffrey, ed. *Britain and NATO's Northern Flank.* London: Macmillan, 1988.

————. *The Future of British Sea Power*. London: Macmillan, 1984.

Timberg, Robert. *The Nightingale's Song*. New York: Simon and Schuster, 1995.

Truman, Harry S. *Memoirs*. 2 vols. New York: Time, 1955–1956. Reprint, New York: Signet Books, 1965.

Truman, Margaret. *Harry S. Truman*. New York: Pocket Books, 1974.

Truscott, Peter. *Kursk: Russia's Lost Pride*. London: Simon and Schuster U.K. Pocket Books, 2003.

Tyushkevich, S. A. *The Soviet Armed Forces: A History of Their Organizational Development, a Soviet View*. Moscow: n.p., 1978. Translated by the CIS Multilingual Section, Translation Bureau, Secretary of State Department, Ottawa, Canada. Published under the Auspices of the United States Air Force.

Uhlig, Frank, Jr. *How Navies Fight: The U.S. Navy and Its Allies*. Annapolis: Naval Institute Press, 1994.

Utz, Curtis A. *Cordon of Steel: The U.S. Navy and the Cuban Missile Crisis*. Washington, D.C.: U.S. Department of the Navy, Naval Historical Center, 1993.

Vandenberg, Arthur H., Jr., and Joe Alex Morris. *The Private Papers of Senator Vandenberg*. Cambridge, Mass.: Houghton Mifflin, 1952.

Van Tol, Jan M. "Military Innovation and Carrier Aviation: An Analysis." *Joint Force Quarterly* (autumn–winter 1997–1998): 97–109.

Vistica, Gregory L. *Fall from Glory: The Men Who Sank the U.S. Navy*. New York: Simon and Schuster Touchstone Books, 1996.

Volkogonov, Dmitri. *Autopsy for an Empire: The Seven Leaders Who Built the Soviet Regime*. Translated by Harold Shukman. New York: Free Press, 1998.

Votaw, John F., ed. *In the Wake of the Storm: Gulf War Commanders Discuss Desert Storm*. Cantigny Military History Series. Wheaton, Ill.: Catigny First Division Foundation, 2000.

"Washington Report: DoD—Costs Up, Delays Mount for Naval Weapons Programs." *Seapower* 47:10 (October 2004): 8.

Watson, Bruce W., and Susan M. Watson, eds. *The Soviet Navy: Strengths and Liabilities*. Boulder: Westview Press, 1986.

Webb, James. "Women Can't Fight." *Washingtonian* 15:2 (November 1979): 144–48, 273–75, 278, 280, 282.

Weir, Gary E., and Walter J. Boyne. *Rising Tide: The Untold Story of the Russian Submarines That Fought the Cold War*. New York: Basic Books, 2003.

White, Theodore H. *In Search of History: A Personal Adventure*. New York: Warner Books, 1978.

Wilcox, Robert K. *Black Aces High: The Story of a Modern Fighter Squadron at War*. New York: Thomas Dunne, St. Martin's Press, 2002.

Williams, William Appleman. *America in Vietnam: A Documentary History.* Garden City, N.Y.: Doubleday Anchor Books, 1985.

Winkler, David F. *Cold War at Sea: High-Seas Confrontation between the United States and the Soviet Union.* Annapolis: Naval Institute Press, 2000.

Winnefeld, James A., Preston Niblack, and Dana J. Johnson. *A League of Airmen: U.S. Air Power in the Gulf War.* Santa Monica, Calif.: Rand, 1994.

Woodward, Bob. *Shadow: Five Presidents and the Legacy of Watergate.* New York: Touchstone Books, 2000.

Woodward, Sandy, with Patrick Robinson. *One Hundred Days: The Memoirs of the Falklands Battle Group Commander.* London: Harper Collins, 1992.

Wooldridge, E. T., ed. *Into the Jet Age: Conflict and Change in Naval Aviation, 1945–1975.* Annapolis: Naval Institute Press, 1995.

Worden, William L. "Cold War in the Formosa Strait." *Saturday Evening Post* 227:46 (May 14, 1955): 27, 115–16, 118.

Wyden, Peter. *Bay of Pigs: The Untold Story.* New York: Simon and Schuster, 1980.

Y'Blood, William T. *Hunter-Killer: U.S. Escort Carriers in the Battle of the Atlantic.* New York: Bantam Books, 1992.

Young, John M. *When the Russians Blinked: The U.S. Maritime Response to the Cuban Missile Crisis.* Washington, D.C.: U.S. Marine Corps History and Museums Division, 1990.

Zacharia, Janine. "Mediterranean Sea Dispatch: Smooth Sailing." *New Republic* 228:4603 (April 7, 2003): 10–11.

Zike, James. "Missiles Answer Sea Strike, Sea Shield Questions." *Surface Warfare* 28:4 (summer 2003): 16–21.

Zumwalt, Elmo R., Jr. *On Watch: A Memoir.* New York: New York Times Book Company, 1976.

INDEX

Note: Numbers in italics refer to illustrations

ABOUT THE AUTHOR

LISLE A. ROSE is the author of eight previous books, including *The Ship That Held the Line: U.S.S.* Hornet *and the First Half of the Pacific War* and *The Cold War Comes to Main Street: America in 1950.* He served in the U.S. Navy from 1954 to 1957 and in the U.S. Department of State's Bureau of Oceans and International Environmental and Scientific Affairs from 1978 to 1989. He lives in Edmonds, Washington.